THE ALAMANNI AND ROME 213–496
(CARACALLA TO CLOVIS)

The Alamanni and Rome 213–496 (Caracalla to Clovis)

JOHN F. DRINKWATER

OXFORD
UNIVERSITY PRESS

OXFORD

UNIVERSITY PRESS

Great Clarendon Street, Oxford OX2 6DP

Oxford University Press is a department of the University of Oxford.
It furthers the University's objective of excellence in research, scholarship,
and education by publishing worldwide in

Oxford New York

Auckland Cape Town Dar es Salaam Hong Kong Karachi
Kuala Lumpur Madrid Melbourne Mexico City Nairobi
New Delhi Shanghai Taipei Toronto

With offices in

Argentina Austria Brazil Chile Czech Republic France Greece
Guatemala Hungary Italy Japan South Korea Poland Portugal
Singapore Switzerland Thailand Turkey Ukraine Vietnam

Oxford is a registered trade mark of Oxford University Press
in the UK and in certain other countries

Published in the United States
by Oxford University Press Inc., New York

A catalogue record for this title is available from the British Library

Library of Congress Cataloging in Publication Data
Data available

Typeset by SPI Publisher Services, Pondicherry, India

Printed in Great Britain
on acid-free paper by
Biddles Ltd., King's Lynn, Norfolk

ISBN 978–0–19–929568–5

10 9 8 7 6 5 4 3 2 1

To Gillian
Without whom, nothing

Preface

This is a book that I never planned to write. It sprang unexpectedly from work on Later Roman Gaul. While attempting to analyse the interaction between the Empire and Germanic newcomers, I realized that I knew little about the identity, organization and activities of the Alamanni, and turned aside to see what I could find out about them. An exercise that I envisaged would take only a few days stretched into years as I encountered the mass of recent work on Alamanni in particular and *Germani* in general.

I was willing to devote time to this because it was a job that needed doing, and because it allowed me to develop thinking on the relationship between Rome and the Rhine-*Germani* that I had only sketched out elsewhere. This is to be found in papers for Sam Lieu's colloquium in honour of John Matthews and Ian Wood's conference on Gregory of Tours, held in Oxford in 1992 and 1994 respectively. The ideas developed here, on the reliability of Ammianus Marcellinus and on Roman dealings with Franks and Alamanni, formed the basis of further papers, at Ralph Mathisen and Hagith Sivan's 'Shifting Frontiers' conference in Lawrence, Kansas, in 1995, and at Jan Willem Drijver and David Hunt's 'Ammianus' conference at Durham in 1997. I am greatly obliged to the organizers of these events for inviting me to speak, and to Martin Heinzelmann for publishing what amounted to an extension of my Lawrence paper in *Francia* in 1997.

I was able to collect my first thoughts on the Alamanni and Rome in a paper for the Nottingham Classics Research Workshop, published in the *Festschrift* to Carl Deroux in 2003. Again, I must thank organizer and editor, Caroline Vout and Pol Defosse respectively, for giving me this opportunity.

In looking back over the writing of this book, I am struck by how much it may have been affected by current events. It is a truism that history is a product of its age: no historian can ever produce the 'right' answer about events in the distant past. All that he can do is interpret these as conscientiously as possible, while acknowledging the contemporary influences that are likely to have shaped his thinking. In proposing that we should look at the Alamanni and Rome in the context of 'the power of nightmares, the politics of fear' (p. 12), I guess I have been influenced first by the apparent sham of the threat of the Warsaw Pact and then, after 1997, by the growing acceptance in British politics and public life of 'spin'.

A number of scholars very kindly provided me with published material that I would otherwise have overlooked or found very difficult to obtain: Profs. A. R. Birley, B. Bleckmann, R. Bratož; Dr M. Carroll; Prof. H. Castritius; Dr H. Elton; Prof. F. J. Guzmán Armario; Drs J. Haberstroh, G. Halsall, A. Kreuz; Profs. H. Leppin, J. H. W. G. Liebeschuetz, D. Miller, R. Rollinger; Dr I. Runde; and Prof. C. Schäfer.

Valuable advice on practical military matters was given to me by my friend and neighbour, Col. R. G. Holdsworth T.D., R.E. (ret'd).

I am immensely grateful to Maureen Carroll, Angela Kreuz and Wolf Liebeschuetz for reading and commenting on part or whole of earlier drafts, as I am to the two anonymous readers of the Clarendon Press (who subsequently allowed themselves to be identified as Hugh Elton and Ralph Mathisen) for their identification of toe-clenching errors and omissions, and their suggestions as to how I might improve the readability of the work. None is, of course, responsible for how I have used their proposals.

The book is one fruit of a strange form of study-leave imposed on me by chronic illness. The condition also gave me the inclination and opportunity to renew contact with two former teachers, Ron Higginbottom and Ian Kane, whose inspiration I acknowledge here. However, there have been bad times, through which I have, as always, been carried by the absolutely unselfish and unstinting support of my wife, Gillian, to whom this book is dedicated.

JFD
Nottingham, 2005

Acknowledgements

I would like to thank the following for permission to reproduce published material: Archäologisches Landesmuseum Baden-Württemberg (Figs 6, 7, 15, 26); *Journal of Roman Archaeology*, Portsmouth RI (Fig. 12); Prof. A. Pabst, University of Erlangen (Figs 23, 24); Prof. C. Schäfer, University of Hamburg (Fig. 24); Prof. H. Steuer, University of Freiburg-im-Breisgau (Figs 13, 14); Jan Thorbecke Verlag, Ostfildern (Fig. 9).

Contents

Figures

Introduction

Alamannic warriors figure significantly in later Roman history.[1] In 365, the emperor Valentinian I refused to go to the help of his brother against the usurper, Procopius, on the grounds that he was needed in the west to face major attacks by the Alamanni. According to Ammianus Marcellinus, he kept saying that, while Procopius was only the enemy of himself and Valens, the Alamanni were the enemies of the entire Roman world.[2] According to tradition, in 496 or 497 the Frankish king Clovis, whose destiny it was to assume the mantle of Rome in western Europe, first openly rejected the gods of his forefathers and appealed to Christ at a crucial point in the defeat of Alamanni at the great battle of Zülpich.[3] The impact of the Alamanni still rings in the modern French and Spanish for Germany: *Allemagne, Alemania.* However, though they have received some attention in modern studies, there is still relatively little available on them in English, and what there is does not fully reflect the results of recent work on their origins and development.[4] Two distinct lines of research have come together to change our thinking on the Alamanni.

[1] Geuenich (1997a: 20–1) explains why he prefers 'Alemanni' and 'Alemannic' to 'Alamanni' and 'Alamannic'. His arguments are sound, but concern German orthography. Here, I keep to common English usage.

[2] Ammianus Marcellinus [henceforth 'AM'] 26.5.13. Cf. below 267, 273–4.

[3] Gregory of Tours, *Dec. Lib. Hist.* 2.30. Cf. below 332.

[4] The pioneering work of Okamura has not been followed up (see his complaints, 1984: viii). More recently see, for example, Matthews (1989), Todd (1992) and Hummer (1998). What I say here about the lack of English publications on Alamannic research echoes the remarks of Creighton and Wilson (1999: 9) in respect of Romano-German studies in general, though this problem has been eased by the appearance of Carroll (2001).

The first, historical, was stimulated by Wenskus' *Stammesbildung und Verfassung*.[5] It seeks to understand the nature of the Germanic peoples who eventually took over the western Empire. Its practitioners reject nineteenth and early-twentieth-century interpretation of Germanic groupings as discrete 'tribes' or 'peoples', the ancient creators and hereditary transmitters of eternal and heroic folk values and institutions, moving into the Empire from the heart of Europe. Rather, they see them as the consequence of a continuing process by which a wide variety of communities continually dissolved and re-formed to create new aggregations of peoples: the process of 'ethnogenesis'.[6] Ethnogenesis has generated controversy, becoming part of a much wider debate with important contemporary political resonances, over 'ethnicity'.[7] I will touch on aspects of this below. For the moment, however, it is sufficient to say that in dealing with the Alamanni, ethnogenesis is a useful concept. In particular, it frees us from notions of mass migration.

[5] Wenskus (1961). See also Pohl (2000: 103), (2002a: 17), (2002b: 223–5).

[6] Seminally, Wolfram (1979); most recently concerning the western *Germani*, Pohl (2002a: 18–20). For discussion and acceptance of the views of Wenskus and Pohl in this respect, see, e.g. Keller (1998: 584–9); Steuer (1998: 272, 283). As far as anglophone scholarship is concerned, ethnogenesis has provoked a mixed reaction. Heather rejects it (1991: 317–30), but cf. his qualification in 1998 (107); Amory (1997) accepts it (see 34–5 for a useful summary), but significantly modifies—in his words, 'complicates'—it (13). This he does by stressing the importance of existing local and institutional allegiances within the Empire. These allegiances became the building blocks of shifting political identities, as late Roman leaders adapted their definitions of insiders and outsiders—Amory's 'ideologies'—to meet differing circumstances. All this involved no racial or even loosely 'ethnic' affiliations: there was no—not even 'non-tribal'—movement of barbarians over the frontier and so no 'Roman/barbarian' divide. Rather (e.g. 26–32), following Whittaker (1994), Amory sees what happened as the result of the expansion of the 'frontier zone', the newly powerful inhabitants of which were cast as Germanic 'peoples' by the educated classes of the centre. Amory is persuasive, but I do not follow him here because I believe that there was new 'Germanic' settlement (despite Amory's criticism of the term as linguistic, not cultural or ethnic (xv, 33), we have to call these people something) east of the upper Rhine and north of the upper Danube, and because I have doubts about the validity of the 'frontier zone' (see below 35–40, 349, 354).

[7] See, e.g. Graves-Brown, Jones, and Gamble (ed.) (1996); the very useful survey offered by Geary (1999); and, most recently, the fiercely hostile assessments of the work of Wenskus and his pupils in Gillett (ed.) (2002a). The basic problem is, as Amory (1997: 15) observes, the inevitable association of ethnicity with race, and racism: its 'insidious sub-text'.

The second line of research is the result of fresh energy and confidence on the part of archaeologists working in south-west Germany. The discovery of new sites and new forms of site, and reconsideration of older finds, have prompted revision of many aspects of the Alamannic settlement of former imperial territory west of the Rhine and north of the upper Danube.[8] Important catalysts in promoting such studies and encouraging both sets of practitioners to seek common ground have been the discovery of a major inscription in Augsburg in 1992, and conferences and exhibitions on both Franks and Alamanni held to celebrate the 1500th anniversary of Zülpich.[9]

The aim of this book is to review this work and to present my own ideas on the relationship between the Alamanni and imperial Rome. It is not intended as a survey of the Alamanni from the Roman into the medieval period. Most of the current debate on the Alamanni and Rome is being conducted among a small group of early-medieval historians and prehistoric archaeologists.[10] These, in their readiness to accept the Roman historical background as a datum, run the risk of missing current shifts in opinion in this field, for example, concerning the reliability of Ammianus Marcellinus' *Res Gestae*.[11] Conversely, historians of the Late Empire are ignoring what their medieval and archaeological colleagues have to tell them about the Alamanni. I must, however, concede that this book would have been impossible to write if I had not been able to draw upon a number of recent syntheses by specialists in both areas. The most useful were: Geuenich's general history; Lorenz's study of the mid-fourth-century campaigns; the catalogue of the great Alamannic exhibition of 1997/98; and Geuenich's edition of the proceedings of the Zülpich conference of 1996 (published in 1998).[12] Also handy was Pohl's

---

[8] Keller (1993: 85).

[9] Steuer (1998: 270–1); Pohl (2000: 108). The actual date and circumstances of Clovis' conversion, and so of the significance of the battle of Zülpich, remain hotly debated: see Wood (1994: 43–8); Geuenich (1997a: 78–84). Cf. below 335.

[10] The medieval character of such studies is explicit in the title of Wenskus (1961). For the prehistoric character of the archaeological tradition see Haberstroh (2000a: 11), with Brather (2002: 149).

[11] For excessive trust in Ammianus see, e.g. Geuenich (1997a: 32–5, 42, 53). Cf. below 177–8.

[12] Geuenich (1997a); Lorenz, S. (1997); *Alamannen* (1997); Geuenich (ed.) (1998).

summary of modern work on the Alamanni.[13] What follows must still be regarded as provisional, since much modern thinking about the Alamanni remains uncertain, including basic issues of methodology and even terminology.[14]

An immediate problem is, indeed, simply what to call them. The derivation and meaning of *Alamanni* will receive attention later.[15] Here, it is necessary only to recall that all our literary information concerning the Alamanni comes from Greco-Roman writers.[16] This includes their name: we do not know what they called themselves. In these circumstances, the historian might well expect help from archaeology. One might hope, for example, for the identification of a discrete and coherent new Germanic community within the area that the Romans knew as Alamannia which might serve to justify their, and our, labelling all its inhabitants 'Alamanni'. However, this is not available. Settlement remains are poor.[17] This forces dependence upon funerary archaeology, but there is a remarkable shortage of early Germanic graves in the region. We have a small number of high-status inhumations, but the vast majority of corpses must have been disposed of in ways which currently elude archaeological detection.[18] In addition to the problem of finding early Alamannic graves, there is that of how much historical information can be won from the study of archaeological material.[19] Much depends on what can be deduced from the classification, dating and mapping of standard grave-goods. Traditionally, such exercises have been used to show when and how

[13] Pohl (2000: 101–7).

[14] See, e.g. Fingerlin (1997b: 125), especially in respect of problems relating to the dating of archaeological material. A serious technical problem has been, until recently at least, the confusion of late-Iron Age and early-Germanic ceramics: Fingerlin (1990: 102); Bücker (1999: 19, 25–160, 217). See also below, 5, on the interpretation of distribution-maps; and the judicious remarks of Keller (1993: 87–8) on the difficulty of synthesis and on the historian's obligation to undertake it.

[15] See below 63–9.

[16] Steuer (1998: 278).

[17] Cf. Bücker et al. (1997: 311–12), mainly concerning the Merovingian period, but noting similar problems in dealing with earlier times—in particular, the tendency of simple, wooden-built houses and settlements regularly to shift position within a 'home-area'.

[18] Fingerlin (1990: 117, 121), (1993: 72); Schach-Dörges (1997: 85–6, 95) and Keller (1998: 594–5), together estimating that we have only around 80 reliable burial sites, comprising about 200 graves, for the period from the third to the fifth century.

[19] Keller (1998: 588); Steuer (1998: 271–3).

peoples migrated from their homelands, but argument has long raged as to the scientific validity of distribution-maps. These can illustrate the activities of modern researchers quite as much as those of ancient communities.[20] Furthermore, even if there is enough material to produce valid distribution-maps showing the existence of various 'culture-groups', such groups do not necessarily indicate distinct ethnicities nor do they give any hint of the political loyalties of the communities who deposited the objects concerned.[21] (Political loyalties might be wider, being shared with other, culturally distinct groups, or narrower, causing conflict within the same cultural group, or a mixture of both.) These waters were muddied by the readiness of the pioneers of culture-group studies to permit their findings to be used to support late-nineteenth/early-twentieth-century European nationalisms: in particular, Gustaf Kossinna, whose name many now regard as anathema.[22] For this reason, some contemporary scholars prefer to talk of no more than 'zones of circulation' of goods or 'long distance contacts' between peoples, social and commercial as well as migratory.[23] Others believe that archaeology has no role in the writing of ethnic history.[24] It has recently been proposed that a more statistical approach to grave-assemblages might yet yield reliable information on ethnic identity and political affiliation; but all remains very problematical.[25] One has to accept that the Alamanni are archaeologically invisible: it is currently impossible to detect even historically attested sub-groups of the Alamanni (Bucinobantes,

[20] Schach-Dörges (1997: 81); Pohl (1998a: 643); Steuer (1998: esp. 271–4, 289–301).

[21] Roth (1998: 630); Steuer (1998: 279, 289, 314). Cf. Amory (1997: 16): 'It is not easy to determine subjective ethnic identity from objectively visible culture.'

[22] Pohl (2000: 47–9); Curta (2002a: 202–3, cf. 211–13, later Soviet exploitation of this methodology). Curiously, Graves-Brown, Jones, and Gamble (ed.) (1996) contains many references to Kossinna and his school, but none to Wenskus.

[23] Steuer (1998: 287, 307): 'Verkehrsräumen', 'Fernbeziehungen'. Cf. below 46.

[24] Brather (2002: 150, 170, 174); Fehr (2002: 200). Cf. the critique of Brather by Schmauder (2003: 292–8).

[25] See, e.g. Keller (1998: 588 and n. 19) on the potential of 'Bestattungssitte', though as markers of socio-political change, not ethnicity; Siegmund (1998: 558–9, 560–1, 567–70) proposing that the study of burial customs enables us to distinguish between Frankish and Alamannic areas of settlement in the period *c.*450–520/23, and now (2000) extending the period covered to *c.*670, and taking into account Saxons and Thuringians. On Siegmund, see Drinkwater (2001); Brather (2002: 153–5). On the issue in general, see (relatively positively) Schmauder (2003: esp. 298).

Lentienses etc.) in the record.[26] It is no wonder that some archae-ologists are reluctant to attach any literary-based name, in particular 'Suebian', 'Gothic', 'Frankish' or 'Alamannic', to artefacts, the areas in which they are found, or the people who might have produced or used them, favouring instead the bland but safer 'Germanic'.[27] It may appear, therefore, that in respect of the Alamanni, history and archaeology are on divergent paths.

In such a situation, a firm decision has to be taken to prevent paralysis. One must work from the better to the less well-known, which returns us to the literary sources. Even though his account presents problems, our most detailed informant is Ammianus Marcellinus. He tells us that by the middle years of the fourth century the Romans accepted that all the land over the Rhine and the Danube which had formerly been part of the provinces of Upper Germany and Raetia, and even a section of Raetia south of the Danube to Lake Constance, was now in the hands of people they called Alamanni.[28] This is entirely consistent with later sources which tell us that Clovis decisively defeated the Alamanni and that much of their territory was eventually integrated into the Frankish Empire as 'Alamannia'.[29] Ammianus' testimony is also consistent with earlier texts, from around the end of the third century, which indicate that Alamanni had taken over Roman territory beyond the Danube and the Rhine a generation or so before.[30] It also fits archaeological findings, both negative (the disappearance of Latin inscriptions from and the large-scale supply of imperial coinage to this area) and positive (late-Roman military building along the Rhine and upper Danube as a

[26] Fingerlin (1993: 60). Cf. below 96, 122, 126. Behind this problem is the surprising uniformity of Germanic archaeology, with few if any artefacts that may be reliably assigned to a specific population mentioned in the literary sources: cf. Siegmund (2000: 301–2).

[27] See, e.g. Steuer (1998: 275); Bücker (1999: 16), explicitly preferring 'Germanic' to 'Alamannic'; and Trumm (2002: 17). Kulikowski (2002: 69, n. 2) goes even further, preferring 'barbarian' to 'Germanic'.

[28] Cf. Martin (1997b: 163); Steuer (1998: 275–6).

[29] Geuenich (1997a: 78–108).

[30] *Pan. Lat.* 4 (8) [Galletier].10.2 (297): Raetia was lost under Gallienus; *Laterculus Veronensis: Nomina provinciarum omnium* 14 [Riese (1892: VIII.79)] (*c.*300): a list of transrhenish *civitates* supposedly lost to the barbarians during the reign of Gallienus. See also Drinkwater (1987: 82, 86–7); Nuber (1993: 101), (1998: 373).

new frontier was created to the rear of the old).[31] All this provides a basic working framework. Change was afoot in the region; amplification will follow, but to get this book started it seems acceptable to call the people who brought it about the Alamanni.

Anticipating material that will be presented later, I should explain how I see these Alamanni, which returns us to the issue of ethnicity. Ethnicity is very difficult to tie down because its basic vocabulary, in both ancient and modern European languages (*ethnos*, *gens*, *natio*, 'people', 'tribe', 'Volk', 'Sippe', 'Stamm' etc.), is hard to control. It is difficult to define each term precisely, and still more difficult to relate them all to each other, and this can lead to endless misunderstanding and qualification.[32] It is little wonder that Amory cut through the Gordian knot by beginning his study of the Ostrogoths with his own definition of ethnicity.[33] I follow his lead. Here, I take an ancient people or folk to be an established community, aware of its identity and of something of a common history. Its identity is formed by how it characterizes itself and how it is seen by outsiders. It is not racially 'pure' or exclusive, but it has a strong tradition of endogamy—there has to be some sort of biological link—and, as it develops, it may be inclined to trace its foundation to a mythical ancestor. It need not be politically united: one has only to think of the endless wars between the ancient Greeks, despite their acceptance of each other as fellow 'Hellenes'. However, as it develops it may exhibit the potential to come together under strong leadership. Such periods of unity are important because they may become permanent or, if only temporary, they give a people the moral strength to survive conquest by outsiders.

The earliest, third-century, Alamanni were not an *ethnos*, a *gens*, a people, or a 'Volk'. As long-distance raiders, they arrived in modern south-west Germany randomly, not by tribal migration. The name Alamanni, though it had Germanic roots, won general currency as a Roman designation, identifying barbarians coming from and settling over the Rhine and Danube. Ethnogenesis, the process that eventually made these disparate incomers a people, began in the fourth century. Then, forming static communities settled close to the

[31] Nuber (1993: 102); Mackensen (1999: esp. 201).
[32] Cf. Wolfram (1998: 608–9).
[33] Amory (1997: xiv).

Empire and under the influence of Rome, they began to see themselves collectively as Alamanni. However, they never acted together.
In this lack of cohesion they resemble the neighbouring Franks,
concerning whom we possess an important piece of evidence for
the emergence of ethnic identity in a period of political fragmenta-
tion. This is a personal inscription from Hungary which declares, 'A
Frankish citizen, I fought as a Roman soldier'.[34] Franks did not
cooperate militarily and politically until they produced strong leaders in the later fifth century. The first signs of Alamannic unity
appeared only in the face of the emerging Frankish threat.

A remaining complication is that very often the rhythm of English
makes it awkward not to write 'the Alamanni', so I do. However, when the
definite article might erroneously suggest the deployment of a cohesion
and force which these people never possessed, I employ bare 'Alamanni'.

A major line of argument in this study of the Alamanni and Rome is
the political and military inferiority of the former to the latter. Again
anticipating future discussion, I feel I should alert the reader to the
main points of my interpretation of the Germanic 'threat'. It is
important not to judge Germanic history from the popular view of
what happened under the Late Empire: of a prolonged mass movement
of barbarian peoples who conquered the Roman west. This creates
deceptive images of, say, a rising flood that eventually broke through
the dyke of imperial defences or, in Miller's rightly critical words, of
'a Europe full of restless tribes constantly itching to be somewhere
else, preferably at someone else's expense and with as much attendant
violence as possible'.[35] There were disruptive and destructive movements of barbarian people and armies in the late fourth and fifth
centuries. However, it is now realized that, say, Goths and Vandals
were extremely complex in their composition and aims (in particular,
that 'people', the raw material of ethnogenesis, are not the same as
'peoples', its product), and that elsewhere the process of domination
of Roman soil was much slower and even more convoluted.

Such was the case on the Rhine and upper Danube, where Rome first
confronted *Germani*. In the first to the early third centuries this area was
not subject to growing barbarian 'pressure'. And during the mid-third

---

[34] *CIL* 3.3576 (*ILS* 2814): *Francus ego cives, Romanus miles in armis...*
[35] Miller (1996: 160).

to the fifth centuries it was not the target of massive migrations. Instead, what we see are occasional disturbances by communities on the border (sanctioned by and usually cooperative with the Empire), and unpredictable attacks by long-distance raiders from the interior.

It would be perverse to deny that such trouble was highly unpleasant for those caught up in it. For imperial soldiers and civilians alike, life along the border and its hinterland could be made dangerous and wretched by Germanic warriors intent on plunder and glory. These needed to be policed and, from time to time, brought to heel with punitive expeditions, often led by emperors. Roman rulers were entitled to believe that there was a real threat, the countering of which was a genuine service to their subjects. On the other hand, this threat was always tactical, never strategic. What it amounted to was chronic banditry, of the type that Britain faced on the North-West Frontier of India in the nineteenth and early twentieth centuries.[36] Like the Pathans and the Raj, the *Germani* posed no danger to the existence of the Roman Empire or its military and political dominance of the region. Thus 'policing' expeditions, to be turned into, or even mounted as, major campaigns, were aimed at increasing imperial prestige.

The essential question is: what would have happened if there had been no Roman Empire, or if the Empire had not insisted on a frontier on the Rhine? As Germanic raiding led to settlement in Alamannia so, no doubt, earlier raiding would have led to settlement west of the Rhine. There was much to entice *Germani* to lands open to Mediterranean culture. However, this would not have led to their complete conquest of the west: their population was too low. The default position was the emergence of Germanic communities along both sides of the Rhine and the upper Danube.[37] Instructive here, albeit undoubtedly somewhat exaggerated, are the comments of Julian the Apostate and Ammianus Marcellinus on the extent of the short-lived Germanic expansion over the Rhine in 355–7.[38] What they describe—a zone *c.*55 km (33 statute miles) wide—would have given these *Germani* an area comparable in size and location to historical Germanophone settlement west of the river, in the Netherlands,

[36] Elton (1993), a paper that has greatly shaped my thinking. For barbarian raiders as 'bandits' on the middle Danube under Commodus, see Grünewald (2004: 21–2).

[37] Cf. Pohl (2000: 13).

[38] Julian, *Ep. ad Ath.* 279A–B; AM 16.11.8.

Belgium, Luxembourg, western Germany, Lorraine, Alsace and Switzerland.[39] This process was arrested by Caesar's conquest and, down to the fifth century, by continuing Roman control of the Rhine frontier.

All dates are AD, and all English translations of Greek and Latin texts are taken from Loeb editions, unless otherwise indicated.

Finally, while 'upper' Rhine (lower case) signifies the general southern course of this river, from Lake Constance to around Mainz, 'Upper' Rhine (upper case) is used much more precisely, following German hydrological usage, of the stretch between Basel and Bingen. Likewise, 'High' Rhine denotes the river between Lake Constance and Basel; 'Middle' Rhine from Bingen to Bonn; and 'Lower' Rhine from Bonn to the sea[40] (Fig. 1).

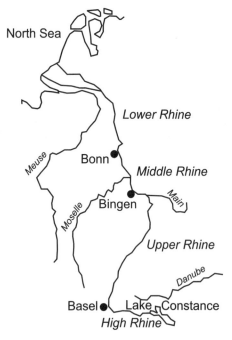

Fig. 1   The Rhine: High, Upper, Middle, and Lower regions.

39 Cf. Heinen (1985: 324).
40 For these definitions, see Höckmann (1986: 385–9).

1

Prelude

As indicated, a major argument in this work is the inferiority of Alamanni to Rome. Later Roman emperors habitually exploited *Germani* for their own political ends. To a large degree, the very structure of the western Empire in the fourth century was supported by the careful fostering of the illusion of a 'Germanic threat'.[1] If this is to convince, it must be shown that Roman superiority and exploitation were a feature of imperial life in other regions and periods. A comprehensive investigation would be a massive undertaking. Here, I confine myself to events on the Rhine from the first century BC to the third century AD, up to Rome's first contact with Alamanni. However, significant aspects of Roman superiority and exploitation have been identified from an eastern perspective in the Early Empire by Isaac. These include emperors' political dependence on the army, which forced them to lead their troops in glorious foreign campaigns; the very personal criteria on which they decided to go to war; and even the idea of frontier troubles as an excuse for conflict.[2] Guzmán Armario's study of Roman perceptions of barbarians of every hue, from Caesar to Ammianus Marcellinus, demonstrates the role of 'the frontier' in legitimizing not only emperors but also the imperial aristocracy.[3] And, in his survey of the northern frontier in the Late Empire, Burns argues that the 'barbarian threat' was a Roman construct, an essential element in creating and maintaining

---

[1] Esp. below 359–62.

[2] Isaac (1992: 372–418, esp. 379–83, 387, 389), on Septimius Severus' decision to conquer Britain for entirely non-military reasons: 'It was, in other words, a war of choice initiated by the emperor, who used frontier troubles as an excuse' (392–3).

[3] Guzmán Armario (2002: e.g. 167, 285, 539–42).

the image of Rome's manifest destiny and in justifying the continued existence of the two pillars of imperial rule, emperor and army.[4] All these points will recur in what follows.

Hugh Elton recently asked, 'What was the function of the army on the frontier?' Answering himself, he declared, 'Its main priority was to keep barbarians out of the Empire.'[5] With regard to the Rhine/upper Danube frontier from the first to the third century, I take a different view. Here, the western *Germani* posed no real threat. Instead, they were used to generate what have become known in the modern geopolitical context as 'the power of nightmares, the politics of fear'.

Contemporaries saw the great incursion into the west by Cimbri and Teutones at the end of the second century BC as a 'Celtic', not a Germanic, phenomenon. Rome's dealings with 'the *Germani*' start, as with so many things, with Julius Caesar. He is usually credited with the very invention of the term: having come across the word *Germani* in a way which remains unknown to us, he used it to identify a distinct, non-Celtic, population, made up of various tribes (*gentes*) living for the most part east of the Rhine.[6] Caesar cited *Germani* to justify his protracted intervention in Gaul (58–50 BC), which led to the Roman conquest of the country. In his 'Gallic War', he describes how the Celtic Helvetii, living in the area of modern Switzerland, attempted to move westwards into Gaul, in part to escape Germanic pressure from over the Rhine. Their migration enabled Caesar to claim that Rome's possessions in the south and her Celtic allies in the north needed protection from the disruption that would result from such movement and from the likely occupation of an abandoned Helvetian homeland by *Germani*.[7] Caesar was drawn further into the affairs of northern Gallic communities when these asked him for help against specific *Germani* in the shape of the war-leader Ariovistus and his followers. Invited in as mercenaries, these now seemed set on

---

[4] Burns (2003: e.g. 30, 153, 176, 292); cf. Drinkwater (2004).

[5] Elton (1996b: 59), though qualifying himself to some extent at 111, where he concedes that some frontier dwellers might never have seen a barbarian raid.

[6] e.g. Caesar, *BG* 4.1.3 (Suebi). For this and what follows see, e.g. Baatz (1975: 47–8); Drinkwater (1983a: 12–16); Pohl (2000: 12–13, 51–3, 89–90). For all the sources, see Goetz and Welwei (1995: 1.275–361); here, I cite only the most significant or representative passages in Caesar's 'Gallic War'.

[7] Caesar, *BG* 1.28.4.

taking over the whole of Gaul.[8] Since 59 BC, and thanks to Caesar, Ariovistus had been recognized as 'king' and 'friend' of the Roman Republic. However, Caesar, projecting his force as renascent 'Germanic' Cimbri and Teutones,[9] now made him out to be a deadly threat, and broke him in battle.[10] Caesar's subsequent destruction of various small 'Germanic' communities west of the Rhine and his spectacular construction and demolition of two bridges used to launch punitive expeditions against transrhenish *Germani* in 55 and 53 BC served to underline his designation of the river as the boundary between the civilized and the Germanic worlds. The proximity of alien and hostile *Germani*[11] then served to justify the permanent presence of the Roman army in Gaul, and of the taxation of Gaul to pay for the security it provided. As Tacitus made the Roman general Cerialis declare to Gallic communities in AD 70:

We have occupied the banks of the Rhine not to protect Italy but to prevent a second Ariovistus from gaining the throne of Gaul...Although often provoked by you, the only use we have made of our rights of victors has been to impose on you the necessary costs of maintaining peace; for you cannot secure tranquillity among nations without armies, nor maintain armies without pay, nor provide pay without taxes...For, if the Romans are driven out...what will follow except universal war among all peoples?[12]

We must be careful as to how far we accept Caesar's story. Rome would anyway have intervened in the affairs of northern Gaul. Ariovistus became 'Friend of the Roman People' as a result of a Gallic war scare, and this is likely to have returned. Sooner or later the Empire would have extended its sphere of influence to the Rhine. What Caesar did was to accelerate the process, to 'protect' Italy against 'new' Cimbri and Teutones.[13] In other words, along with *Germani*, Caesar also invented the Germanic threat. The *Germani* were, as it turned out, a real phenomenon; but what was the validity of their threat? Caesar's activities in Gaul gave him the military and financial power to take a leading role in Roman politics, and

[8] Caesar, *BG* 1.31.4–11.
[9] e.g. Caesar, *BG* 1.33.3–4, 40.5.
[10] Caesar, *BG* 1.53.1–4.
[11] e.g. Caesar, *BG* 4.4.
[12] Tacitus, *Historiae* 4.73–4. Cf. below 41–2.
[13] e.g. Caesar, *BG* 5.29.1, 55.1; 6.2.1–2.

eventually to dominate the state. He was playing a long game, and the explanations of his actions which he proposes in his 'Gallic War' must be taken with a pinch of salt. What really happened?

Overall, we can identify two developments: the beginning of the inevitable involvement of Germanic war-leaders in the affairs of western communities; and the temporary (until *c*.AD 450) disruption of such involvement by Rome's establishment of a political frontier. In Ariovistus and his followers we can see the 'natural' course of Gallo-Germanic history. Germanic raiding into Gaul made Gallic communities aware of Germanic military strength and encouraged them to cooperate with leading *Germani* for their own protection. Allowed to proceed, such a process encouraged the spread of Germanic influence and even the acquisition of territory by *Germani* in eastern Gaul, but it did not threaten full-scale conquest of the country: there were simply too few *Germani* available (Caesar's many thousands must be inflated).[14] We are dealing with raiding-parties, not peoples on the move.[15] (The women present in Ariovistus' baggage train should be seen as high-status dependants of leaders, not as mothers and daughters of migrating families.[16])

There was no rising Germanic tide that threatened civilization. Rather, *Germani* were soon recruited into Roman armies;[17] and in the two devastating rounds of Roman civil war (49–45 BC; 44–31 BC) that followed Caesar's withdrawal from Gaul and then his assassination, we hear of no serious trouble with *Germani*. As the Roman Empire was consolidated north of the Alps by Caesar's heir, Octavian (from 27 BC called Augustus), there developed a new pattern: of routine border policing occasionally interrupted by major action for imperial ends. The question is whether such ends were defensive or aggressive.

In the civil-war period, Gaul was used as a holding-ground for the armies of the various contestants.[18] Octavian took over the country

[14] e.g. Caesar, *BG* 1.31.5. Henige (1998).

[15] Cf. Nicolay (2003: 359), citing the work of Hiddinck, that *Germani* fought for booty and glory, not territory.

[16] Caesar, *BG* 1.51.3; cf. below 49.

[17] e.g. Caesar, *BG* 7.13.1, 7.65.4.

[18] Drinkwater (1983a: 120).

in 40 BC. From this date to 16 BC we see the first round of active imperial policing on the Rhine, involving Agrippa (38 BC), C. Carrinas and Nonius Gallus (30–29 BC), M. Vinicius (25 BC), and Agrippa again (21 BC). These took action against Germanic raiding, the hiring of Germanic mercenaries by communities west of the Rhine, Germanic action against Roman traders, and generally showed the imperial flag.[19] In 16 BC, however, we have apparent confirmation of the continuing existence of the Germanic threat. Sugambri, Usipetes and Tencteri crucified a number of Romans in their own territories, then crossed the Rhine and plundered eastern Gaul. They fell on the army of M. Lollius, commander-in-chief in the region, and captured the standard of the Fifth legion. The incident forced Augustus to travel to Gaul, where he remained for three years.[20] It is not surprising that this 'Lollian disaster' (*Lolliana clades*)[21] has been seen as the immediate stimulus for the subsequent concentration of Roman forces on the Rhine and, from 12 BC, a great push into Free Germany.[22] This is unconvincing. Dio tells us that, in 16 BC, agreement was soon reached with the *Germani*; and Suetonius comments that what happened to Lollius was more shameful than damaging.[23] We are again in the presence of high-level raiding, not invasion. Probably, as was to happen in the mid-fourth century,[24] Roman complacency led to events getting out of hand, with relatively minor casualties (Lollius himself survived) but great Roman embarrassment.[25] More likely is that, having arrived in Gaul, Augustus took stock of the situation in the west and only then determined on expansion into Germania. The time was ripe. Spain and Gaul were now for the most part subdued. On the upper Rhine and upper Danube all that remained was the subjugation of the Alpine areas, achieved by the campaigns of Drusus and Tiberius, Augustus' stepsons, in 16–15 BC.[26] The transportation infrastructure that enabled men and *matériel* to be brought easily from the Empire's

---

[19] Dio 48.49.3; 51.20.5, 21.5–6; 53.26.4; 54.11.1–2.

[20] Velleius Paterculus 2.97.1; Dio 54.20.4–5.

[21] Tacitus, *Annales* 1.10.3.

[22] e.g. Drinkwater (1983a: 122); Wolters (as cited by Gechter (2003: 146)).

[23] Dio 54.20.6; Suetonius, *Augustus* 23.1.

[24] See below 255, 260 (Libino), 267, 276–7 (Charietto).

[25] Cf. Gechter (2003: 146).

[26] Drinkwater (1983a: 122, 125); Goetz and Welwei (1995: 2.16, n.29).

Mediterranean core to the military zone on the Rhine was complete.[27] Drusus began the transrhenish campaign in 12 BC, nominally in response to further attacks by Sugambri, Tencteri and others. He pursued it until his accidental death in 9 BC, after which it was continued by his older brother, Tiberius. As a result, by 7 BC direct Roman military and political power had been extended to the Elbe[28] (Fig. 2).

There have been many suggestions as to what motivated Augustus to undertake such costly warfare, ranging from long-term strategic planning via ambitions of world empire to ad hoc reaction to the developing military situation in Germania. All acknowledge the concomitant acquisition of military glory by the reigning ruler and his possible successors.[29] However, other, internal, factors need to be taken into account. First is the advisability of moving troops from Gaul to allow the country to develop without constant disruption by the military.[30] Second is the need to justify the continued mainten-ance of large forces in the west—allegedly to protect the provinces, but also to support the structure of political power that Augustus had created in Rome.[31] The latter returns us to the notion of the 'Germanic threat' as an essential element in the justification of the actions of Roman emperors and of the mechanisms of imperial rule.[32] What has to be recognized is the high degree of Roman aggression that was involved in initiating and pursuing major con-flict. Habitual raiding by Germanic border communities was used to excuse all-out war, and Germanic attempts to make peace were swept aside.[33] There was much destruction and loss of life. The severe disruption to living-conditions in Germania is demonstrated in the migration of Marcomanni to Bohemia, and the subsequent settle-ment (ironically, by Rome) of Hermunduri on part of their former territory.[34] There was a threat on the Rhine frontier from 16 BC, but it was Roman, not Germanic.

[27] Gechter (2003: 147).
[28] Livy, *Perioch.* 142; Velleius Paterculus 2.97.2–4; Dio 54.32.1–3, 33.1–4, 36.3; 55.1.2–2.1.
[29] Cf. Florus 2.30.21; Suetonius, *Claudius* 14 (on desire for glory of Augustus and Drusus). For the debate see Pohl (2000: 14, 94–5), noticing the work of Mommsen, Wells, Timpe, Christ and Whittaker.
[30] Drinkwater (1983a: 123).
[31] Burns (2003: 18–19, 30, 141, 152–3, 175–6), with Drinkwater (2004).
[32] Cf. Burns (2003: 30, 153, 176, 292).
[33] See Dio 55.6.1–3.
[34] Velleius Paterculus 108; Dio 55.10a.1–2; Schnurbein (2000: 51). Cf. below 39.

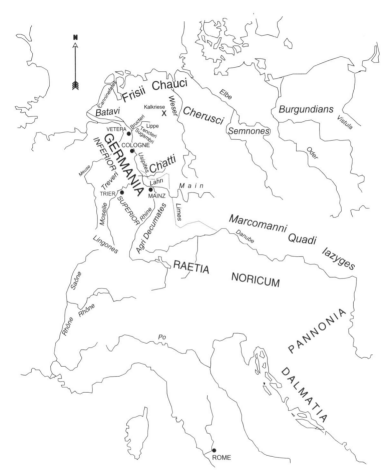

Fig. 2 The north-western provinces, first–second centuries.

The turn of the first centuries BC and AD saw further pacification of the conquered territories by Domitius Ahenobarbus and M. Vinicius—more police work.[35] However, one cannot help but suspect that this was undertaken with an eye to enhancing the military reputation of the generals concerned, particularly Ahenobarbus, who had married into the imperial family. The same may be said of Tiberius' second phase of major campaigning in Germania in 4–5.[36] This followed a prolonged period of tension between Tiberius and Augustus, which had ended with the latter making the former his heir presumptive. Tiberius' great deeds in 4–5 would have served to confirm his fitness for his position. Indeed, it appears that this campaigning was in preparation for new expansion: Tiberius' subjugation of the Marcomanni, under king Maroboduus. This war, in Wells' words 'another act of shameless aggression',[37] began in 6 but was soon abandoned following serious uprisings in Pannonia and Dalmatia.[38]

In 9 came the 'Varian disaster' (*Variana clades*),[39] in which forces under the rebel Cheruscan, Arminius, destroyed the entire army of the Roman governor of Germany, P. Quinctilius Varus.[40] The massacre seems the classic demonstration of innate Germanic aggression, but this is not the case. What happened was more the result of Roman incompetence. Integration was proceeding (Arminius himself was an officer in the Roman army), but Varus pushed change too far, too fast.[41] German reaction was against the invader, not the Empire. Some have even suggested that Arminius' revolt began as a military mutiny, not a nationalistic rebellion, and was thus even less of a challenge to the imperial structure. It seems likely that Arminius 'the Liberator of Germany' was a Tacitean construct, in criticism of the principate. Arminius did not lead a united Germania: he was opposed by important pro-Roman Germanic leaders, including his own brother.[42] Crucial for this study is that, though the spectre of

---

[35] Dio 55.10a.3; Tacitus, *Annales* 4.44.2. Wells (1972: 158–9).
[36] Velleius Paterculus 2.104–6; Dio 55.13.2.
[37] Wells (1972: 161).
[38] Velleius Paterculus 2.108, 110.
[39] Tacitus, *Annales* 1.10.3.
[40] Velleius Paterculus 2.117; Dio 56.18.1–21.
[41] Drinkwater (1983a: 23–4).
[42] Tacitus, *Annales* 2.88.3; 1.55, 2.9. Goetz and Welwei (1995: 2.3) and Pohl (2000: 96), both citing Timpe.

returning Cimbri and Teutones again made an appearance, as far as we know Arminius made no attempt to cross the Rhine, a decision that was more important for Roman security than emergency measures to secure the line of the river.[43]

Roman reprisal raiding was undertaken in 10–11, involving Tiberius and then his nephew and adopted son, Germanicus.[44] These, though no doubt bloodthirsty, did not penetrate far beyond the Rhine.[45] A major change came in 14 when Tiberius, now emperor, allowed Germanicus to avenge Varus in force. Continuing Germanic disunity (including rifts in Arminius' own family) meant that there was no real threat to justify major campaigning.[46] It was probably against Tiberius' better judgement and may have been in accordance with the intentions of the recently dead Augustus.[47] However, there were now additional reasons for attacking *Germani*. The change of ruler had unsettled Roman armies in Pannonia (under Tiberius' son, Drusus II) and the Germanies (under Germanicus). In Lower Germany there had even been talk of Germanicus' taking the throne. Once order had been restored, it was prudent for Germanicus to give his men the opportunity to work off their frustrations and to redeem themselves after their recent sedition.[48] The fighting, from 14 to 17, was characterized by the worst excesses of Roman militarism. Arminius suffered personal loss and strategic defeat, but was neither killed nor captured. Germanicus' most memorable achievement was his visit to the site of Varus' defeat, and his dutiful interment of the bones of the Roman dead. As the cost in men and resources mounted, Tiberius withdrew him, gave him a triumph, and packed him off to the east, where he died just over two years later.[49]

The destruction that resulted from Germanicus' expeditions must have been massive. The economic, social and political instability that resulted was demonstrated in a significant increase in internecine

---

[43] Velleius Paterculus 2.120; Dio 56.22.2a–b (melodramatically attributing Arminius' 'failure' to the resistance of a single Roman stronghold), 32.1. Pohl (2000: 14).
[44] Velleius Paterculus 2.120; Suetonius, *Tiberius* 18.
[45] Dio 56.25.2.
[46] Pohl (2000: 95).
[47] Drinkwater (1983a: 26).
[48] Tacitus, *Annales* 1.3.6, 49.5–6; Dio 57.6.1. Pohl (2000: 15).
[49] For the details, see Tacitus, *Annales* 1.51, 54–5, 57, 61–70; 2.5, 8–19, 25–7, 41.

warfare, in particular between Arminius and Maroboduus. What Tacitus characterizes as 'traditional' strife had been raised to new heights through contact with the Empire, and it is significant that both sides now used Roman battle techniques. Rome could look on with satisfaction as her 'enemies' destroyed themselves.[50] As Pohl has remarked, Tacitus records more fighting between *Germani* and *Germani* than between *Germani* and Romans.[51]

It is worth asking why Rome did not try to exploit such weakness, and why it took over 150 years for the Empire to recommence full-scale campaigning in Germania under Marcus Aurelius. A rational explanation is that Augustan and Tiberian experience had revealed the difficulties of fighting in a land which, by imperial standards, was massively under-developed and so unable to support large armies in the field.[52] This may be correct, but it is by no means certain. We cannot say what might have happened but for the Varian disaster. During the first stages of its occupation of land east of the Rhine, the Empire had taken great pains (shown, above all, in the provision of urban buildings and facilities at Waldgirmes, on the Lahn, and perhaps elsewhere between the Rhine and the Weser[53]) to stimulate economic and social growth, and not without some success.[54] In rational terms, perhaps more likely is that emperors realized that it was cheaper to control Germanic communities through diplomacy than by direct intervention.[55] However, in line with 'the power of nightmares and the politics of fear', instinct may have proved more powerful than reason. The Varian disaster had caused a loss of nerve; and Germania could serve imperial political interests more easily as a source of external danger and, as required, military glory than as the location of a new province.

Thus followed a period of relative tranquillity. The Frisian revolt of 28, which resulted in major Roman casualties, was an internal affair, caused by imperial mismanagement of taxation.[56] Later in Tiberius'

---

[50] For all this see Tacitus, *Annales* 2.44.2, 45.3, 46.5, 62–3, 68. Pohl (2000: 15).

[51] Pohl (2000: 16).

[52] Groenman-van Waateringe (1979). Cf. Drinkwater (1983a: 23); Whittaker (1994: 87). Most recently, Heather (2005: 57–8).

[53] Schnurbein (2003: 98–105 (Waldgirmes), 96–7 (Haltern), 97–8 (Anreppen)).

[54] Cf. below 39 (on the stimulation of the local economy).

[55] Erdrich (2000a: 194–5).

[56] Tacitus, *Annales* 4.72–4.

reign, further imperial laxness appears to have encouraged habitual raiding over the upper Rhine.[57] Large-scale renewal of Roman aggression threatened in the late 30s. Tiberius died in 37 and was succeeded by Gaius, who showed an interest in Germania. The details of Gaius' notorious Germanic 'campaign' of 40 are very difficult to establish from our hostile sources, Suetonius and Dio. Contrary to what they claim, the emperor must have journeyed to the Rhine on more than a whim.[58] Gaius needed military success, and it would have suited him to distance himself from political troubles in Rome. As a descendant of Julius Caesar, the grandson of Drusus I and the son of Germanicus, it was fitting for him to carry Roman arms over the Rhine on a grand scale.[59] That, in the event, there was little more than small-scale fighting, may have resulted from panic caused by the supposed conspiracy of Cn. Cornelius Lentulus Gaeticulus in Upper Germany. This cut across Gaius' preparations, prompting him to leave Italy in haste and making him nervous of unpredictable long-distance undertakings.[60] The western *Germani* continued to be left for the most part in peace.

More border control characterized the reigns of Gaius' successors, Claudius (41–54) and Nero (54–68). (The former confined his campaigning to Britain; the latter, to his cost, took no interest in military affairs.) In 41, Gabinius Secundus, commander of Lower Germany, fought against Chauci, was victorious, but perhaps exaggerated the significance of his achievements. In the same year, Sulpicius Galba, the future emperor, then commanding Upper Germany, overcame Chatti.[61] In 47, the Cherusci asked for a king since—a further sign of disruptive Roman influence on Germanic society—civil war had destroyed their nobility. Claudius returned to them the sole surviving member of their royal house, Arminius' nephew, then resident in Rome.[62] In 48, temporary Roman administrative weakness allowed Chauci to practise piracy along the coasts of Gaul. This was ended by

[57] Suetonius, *Galba* 6.3, 8.1.
[58] Suetonius, *Gaius* 43–5, 47; Dio 59.21.1–3. Barrett (1989: 125, 129).
[59] *Contra* Barrett (1989: 129).
[60] Drinkwater (1983a: 35–6); Barrett (1989: 103–12); Goetz and Welwei (1995: 2.144, n. 21).
[61] Suetonius, *Claudius* 24.3; Dio 60.8.7. Goetz and Welwei (1995), 2.151 n. 35.
[62] Tacitus, *Annales* 11.16–17.

the general Corbulo, who also finally settled the still simmering Frisian unrest.[63] Nothing reflects a general Germanic 'threat'. Indeed, to prevent Roman reprisals from unsettling neighbouring Germanic tribes, Claudius ordered Corbulo back from over the Lower Rhine.[64] In 50, Chattian raiders attacked Upper Germany and caused panic. However, laden down with booty, they were easily destroyed as they returned. The Chatti as a whole refused to be drawn into the conflict and, fearful of Roman intervention, meekly capitulated.[65] In the period 56–8 we hear of Roman border commanders eschewing war and turning their troops to useful civil works.[66] As a result, in 58, Frisians were emboldened to settle in the restricted military zone along the right bank of the Lower Rhine. The imperial authorities intervened, and the Frisian leaders were sent to Nero in Rome to petition for permission to remain. They caused a famous incident at the Theatre of Pompey, in which they proclaimed their loyalty to the Empire, but their request was refused, and force had to be used to evict the settlers. The same land was then occupied by Ampsivarii. Their case was put by an Ampsivarian who could claim years of service to Rome, but this too was rejected. The Ampsivarii prepared for war, calling on Bructeri, Tencteri and others, but a show of Roman military force frightened off the potential allies and the Ampsivarii drifted eastwards as refugees.[67] (Nero's handling of the Ampsivarii brings to mind Constantius II's treatment of the Alamanni in 357. Similarly, the great battle between Hermunduri and Chatti, over salt sources in the summer of 58, was a precursor of tension between Alamanni and Burgundians in the later third and fourth centuries.[68])

In 69–70, high drama returned with the 'Batavian uprising'. In 68, a short civil war had led to the death of Nero and to the accession of Galba. Throughout 69, more protracted civil war resulted in Vespasian becoming sole emperor. Most parts of the Empire were drawn into the conflict. In summer, there began serious fighting on

[63] Tacitus, *Annales* 11.18–19.
[64] Tacitus, *Annales* 11.19.6–20.1.
[65] Tacitus, *Annales* 12.27.3–28.
[66] Tacitus, *Annales* 13.53.
[67] Tacitus, *Annales* 13.54–6.
[68] Tacitus, *Annales* 13.57.1–3. Below 109–10, 190.

the Rhine, instigated by a Batavian prince and senior officer in the Roman army, Julius Civilis. Civilis eventually found powerful allies among the Gallic aristocracy in the Treverans, Julius Classicus and Julius Tutor (also high-ranking officers), and the Lingonian, Julius Sabinus. Their activities prolonged the fighting in the west late into 70. What happened can be examined in fairly close detail because Tacitus' account of the 'Batavian revolt' provides us with our most detailed narrative of Romano-German dealings between Caesar's earlier writing and Ammianus Marcellinus' later contribution.

Tacitus portrays outright nationalistic rebellion by *Germani* and Gauls. Supporters of Vespasian believed that Civilis was following their orders to stage a mock Germanic uprising in order to tie down the forces of Vitellius, Vespasian's imperial opponent.[69] However, according to Tacitus, Civilis already aimed at being the liberator of the Batavians and of all Germany. In persuading his Gallic allies to strive for the liberation of Gaul, and to set up a free 'Gallic Empire', to which defeated imperial troops swore allegiance, he was simply preparing his future prey: once Rome was defeated, Gaul would suffer Germanic aggression.[70] But characteristic Gallic division led to the speedy collapse of the Gallic Empire; and Civilis was hunted down by Vespasian's general, Petillius Cerealis.

It has long been customary to accept Tacitus' account of a brief but sincere demonstration of Germanic and Gallic nationalism.[71] However, in recent years there have been significant attempts to qualify his interpretation. In what follows I depend mainly, though not exclusively, on Urban for my interpretation of Civilis, and on Heinen for that of the 'Gallic Empire'.[72] Tacitus takes pains to depict Civilis and his followers from the start as outsiders, *Germani*, intent on overthrowing the Roman Empire. This will not do. By 69, Julius Civilis had long been a loyal servant of the Empire, but had suffered grave personal injustice at the hands of recent regimes. His community was now the target of rapacious military recruitment in the name of Vespasian's opponent, Vitellius; and Batavian regiments already serving in the Vitellian army had their own legitimate grievances. From

---

[69] Tacitus, *Historiae* 4.13.1: *tumultus Germanici specie*.
[70] Tacitus, *Historiae* 4.61.
[71] e.g. Syme (1958: 1.172–3); cf. Drinkwater (1983a: 45–7).
[72] Urban (1985); Heinen (1985: 72–81). On the debate see Pohl (2000: 17–18, 96–7).

his perspective, as from that of Vespasian's backers, he had every right to be involved in the process of establishing another, better, emperor. Thus Civilis, like thousands of others, was drawn as an insider into the civil war. In order to create the impression of Germanic insurrection, he appears to have incited raiding by Canninefates and Frisians. When this did not work, he called out his own Batavi.[73] (No doubt in all such cases, as Constantius II was to do with the Alamanni, he promised the leaders of the peoples concerned that Vespasian would treat their activities as those of allies.[74]) The stratagem succeeded. Embroiled in fighting on the Lower Rhine, and increasingly suspicious of the pro-Vespasianic sympathies of their own senior officers, in 69 the Roman armies on the Rhine were in no position to engage in the battle for Italy.

Change came with the defeat of the main Vitellian army in Italy in October 69, the death of Vitellius in December, and the Vespasianic party's subsequent consolidation of its control over Rome and most of the Empire. Civilis now confronted the problem of his own success. In tying down Roman troops, he had humiliated Roman arms. The Roman imperial establishment was not yet ready to accept the right of provincials to have a voice in central politics, especially if they based their claim to such a voice on local power. In 68, the Romanized Gallic aristocrat, Julius Vindex, had been destroyed for daring to use native levies against Nero.[75] Tacitus has the garrison of Vetera declare in 69 that 'it was not for a Batavian turncoat to sit in judgement on matters Roman'.[76] From early 70, Civilis must have begun to fear that a victorious Vespasianic party might disown him. This explains why he did not demobilize his troops and why, as Tacitus terms it, he 'began a second war' alongside the leaders of the 'Gallic Empire'.[77] The point of no return was reached following the successful termination of Civilis' second siege of Vetera, with the massacre of the surviving members of its garrison by his transrhenish Germanic allies.[78] Civilis' use of such *Germani*, to

---

[73] Tacitus, *Historiae* 4.15–16, 21.

[74] Below 202, 218.

[75] Drinkwater (1983a: 40–3).

[76] Tacitus, *Historiae* 4.21: *perfuga Batavus arbitrium rerum Romanarum ne ageret.*

[77] Tacitus, *Historiae* 4.54.

[78] Tacitus, *Historiae* 4.60.

which Tacitus makes constant critical reference, did not make him a nationalistic leader. The recruitment of *Germani* in emergencies was standard military procedure: there were *Germani*, alongside Batavians, in Vitellius' army;[79] and Vespasian's supporters enlisted the aid of Suebi at the second battle of Bedriacum.[80] The difficulty was to keep these people in check; and at Vetera they ran out of control.

Like Julius Civilis, Julius Classicus, Julius Tutor and Julius Sabinus should be seen not as nationalistic rebels but as Roman provincial noblemen whose position depended on the maintenance of the imperial hierarchy. They were supporters of Vitellius who, following the death of that emperor, resolved to retain control of the Rhine army in the hope that the Vitellian party might yet produce a successful challenger to Vespasian. So Classicus and Tutor initiated the rebellion by this army against Vespasian early in 70. The oath of loyalty to a 'Gallic Empire' which they supposedly imposed on Roman troops was in fact one to a Roman Empire which, for the moment, was lacking a legitimate emperor. Civilis and Classicus and his associates were from opposite sides of the imperial political fence, and to start with operated entirely independently of each other. However, the fact that Vespasianic forces were heading to crush all opposition made both parties de facto allies: both were looking for a new emperor to whom they could pledge their loyalty. This explains Tacitus' report that, just before the battle of Trier, Classicus and Civilis offered the throne to Cerealis.[81] But the Gauls, like Civilis, ran into the brick wall of Roman political prejudice. The breaking of their power base at the battle of Trier made all the rebels into exactly what Roman prejudice wanted to see them as. Civilis now had to depend on Germanic recruits; and the Gauls ended up as refugees with this Germanic renegade.[82]

The reports that have come down to us of these disturbances, principally that of Tacitus, but also a summary assessment by Josephus,[83] were influenced by traditional prejudice and by a pro-Vespasianic interpretation of events. The war on the Rhine had been

---

[79] Tacitus, *Historiae* 2.17.
[80] Tacitus, *Historiae* 3.5, 22.
[81] Tacitus, *Historiae* 4.75.
[82] Tacitus, *Historiae* 5.14, 16, 19.
[83] Josephus, *Bell. Iud.* 7.42 (75–81).

highly damaging to Roman military pride. It was dangerous for the new dynasty to be seen as having been responsible for it. It was therefore much better to explain Civilis' activities as stemming from barbarian nationalism rather than from imperial politicking. Tacitus' attractive circumstantial detail, such as the first secret assembly of the Batavians in a native shrine, Civilis' growing a long red beard, or 'Germanic' ambitions to annihilate Cologne, should be regarded with suspicion.[84] It is clear that in 69–70 there was no major 'Germanic' assault on the Roman Empire: generally, trans-Rhine *Germani* did not take civil war as an invitation to begin extensive raiding. There were incidents away from the main centres of action, for example by the Chatti, Usipetes (Tacitus' 'Usipi') and Mattiaci in their attack on Mainz,[85] but they were localized and easily dealt with. Major conflict was, in Tacitus' terms, 'civil', not 'external'.[86]

Civilis, Classicus, Tutor and the rest may be seen as victims of their age. By mid-70, what they lacked to give their activities legitimacy and coherence was an emperor. Two hundred years later they could simply have put up one of their own number. In the later Empire, though it was still impossible for a man of Germanic stock to become emperor, respectable provincials might act as figureheads. We see Civilis stumbling in this direction in his alliance with Gauls. As far as these Gauls are concerned, Classicus did not have the courage of his convictions when he chose to become *imperator*, 'commander-in-chief', but not *Augustus*, 'emperor'.[87] Julius Sabinus, however, sensed what was necessary in his later-derided claim to be a 'Caesar', descended from the great Julius Caesar.[88]

Vespasian (69–79) was succeeded by his sons Titus (79–81) and Domitian (81–96). We know nothing of Romano-Germanic dealings under the first two of these, but from 82 Domitian waged war in person on the Chatti.[89] This was a return to aggression for imperial

---

[84] Tacitus, *Historiae* 4.14–15, 61, 63–4.

[85] Tacitus, *Historiae* 4.37.

[86] Tacitus, *Historiae* 4.22, on the Roman and Germanic standards of Civilis' forces at the first siege of Vetera: *mixta belli civilis externique facies*. Cf. Goetz and Welwei (1995: 2.170, n.74).

[87] Cf. Heinen (1985: 76).

[88] Tacitus, *Historiae* 4.55, 67.

[89] Drinkwater (1983a: 59); Jones (1992: 128–31).

ends. Unlike his father and his elder brother, Domitian had no military reputation. He needed a successful war to generate a triumph; Germanic raiding would always provide a *casus belli*; and the Chatti obliged. All our main sources are hostile to Domitian, but there is probably some truth in Suetonius' remark that Domitian's campaign against the Chatti was by choice, not necessity.[90] From 84, attention was diverted from the Rhine and upper Danube by a major war in Dacia. In 89, however, there was trouble in Upper Germany, involving the governor, L. Antonius Saturninus. As Jones says, 'This was a military revolt, nothing more.'[91] It was quickly suppressed, with Domitian journeying to the Rhine to take charge in person. However, significant for this study is the report that Saturninus called on the Chatti for help, and that they were prevented from crossing into the Empire only in the nick of time.[92] The invocation of the 'Germanic threat', of the shades of Cimbri and Teutones, to malign a political enemy had become part of the repertoire of imperial invective. In the event, the 'real' Chatti appear to have quickly mended fences with the Empire.[93]

Then, for about 70 years, the western *Germani* more or less disappear from the historical picture. There must have been customary raiding, prompting routine Roman reprisals, and we have odd hints of colonial police work under Domitian and, perhaps, his successor, Nerva (96–98),[94] but no more. It appears that a waning of imperial interest, with emperors no longer feeling the need to attack *Germani*, resulted in the ending of imperial visits to the Rhine/ upper Danube frontier, and so the disappearance of references to events in this region in our sources. The perception of a 'Germanic threat' diminished; and the underlying absence of danger from this quarter (coupled, perhaps, with a desire to reduce the potential political power of troop concentrations[95]) was reflected in a major

[90] Suetonius, *Domitianus* 6.1: *sponte in Chattos.*
[91] Jones (1992: 147).
[92] Suetonius, *Domitianus* 6.2; Plutarch, *Aemilius Paullus* 25.5. Goetz and Welwei (1995: 2.271, n. 55).
[93] Jones (1992: 150).
[94] Pliny, *Epistulae* 2.7.2; cf. Goetz and Welwei (1995: 2.270–1, n. 50). Dio 67.5.1; cf. Goetz and Welwei (1995: 2.272, n. 56). Pliny, *Panegyricus* 14.2 (cf. 9.2); cf. Goetz and Welwei (1995: 2.274–5, n. 64).
[95] Cf. Syme (1999: 89).

reduction in the Rhine garrison. Over 30 years, the number of legions stationed there was cut from six to four.[96]

Peace, or lack of major activity, persisted under Trajan (98–117), Hadrian (117–38) and Antoninus Pius (138–61). It ended under Marcus Aurelius (161–80). Again, we hear of border warfare on the Rhine and upper Danube with, in 161 and 162, raiding by Chatti and, in 170–5, by Chatti and Chauci.[97] However, the greatest conflicts of the period were the Marcomannic Wars. This is the name given to the wars fought by the emperor Marcus Aurelius along the Danubian frontier in the period 168–80. The reconstruction of the sequence of these events and their precise chronology is contentious.[98] In what follows, I rely on A. R. Birley.[99]

On succeeding Antoninus Pius, Marcus Aurelius took as his co-emperor his step-brother, Lucius Verus. Almost immediately there was trouble in the east, and Lucius led a successful Parthian war from 162–6. Even before this war was over, Marcus was preparing a new campaign on the Danube. This began in 168, but was interrupted by the death of Lucius early in 169. It recommenced in 170, when a major Roman operation provoked barbarian incursions deep into the Empire: Quadi and Marcomanni reached northern Italy and Costoboci attacked Eleusis. Marcus and his generals acted swiftly to drive out the invaders, and then attacked them on their home territory. From 171–5 there was fighting against Marcomanni, Quadi and, further east, Iazyges, in which the Romans did well. However, this had to be given up on news of rebellion in the east, led by Avidius Cassius. After Cassius' defeat, Marcus returned to the Danube in 178, accompanied by his son and heir, Commodus. He repeated his earlier success. The period 179–80 saw the defeat of the Quadi, the submission of the Iazyges and the wearing down of the Marcomanni. Final victory seemed in sight; but early in 180 Marcus fell ill and died. Commodus made peace with the barbarians and ended the fighting.

The traditional interpretation of the Marcomannic Wars is heavily influenced by our sources' positive assessment of Marcus Aurelius,

---

[96] Drinkwater (1983a: 60, 62).
[97] *Historia Augusta, V. Marci* 8.7–8; *V. Didii Iuliani* 1.6–8. Drinkwater (1983a: 76).
[98] Garzetti (1974: 484).
[99] Birley (1987: 140–210, 249–55).

and by our knowledge of what was to happen to the Roman Empire from the third century. In short, Marcus is seen as the first Roman emperor to face the rising tide of Germanic migration, and the one who strengthened imperial defences just enough to hold it back for another couple of generations.[100] Much stress is laid on the attack on Italy of 170: the first by foreigners since the Cimbri in 102 BC, and a harbinger of the Iuthungian and Alamannic attacks of 260,[101] and of Alaric's sack of Rome, the very embodiment of the 'Germanic threat', in 410.[102] However, it is possible to paint a different picture. A principled man set on doing his public duty can be just as dangerous to ordinary people as a self-seeking rogue.

Marcus came to power relatively old (he was born in 121), and with no military experience. Indeed, as Birley observes, it is likely that until 168 he had never left Italy.[103] He delegated the eastern war to the younger Lucius, and Lucius did well. Had he been an ordinary Roman emperor, Marcus would have felt obliged to emulate his colleague's success; but Marcus was more than that. Apart from his own personal standing, he will have been conscious of the demands of duty: to undertake himself what he asked of subordinates; and, above all, to do right by the Empire over which he ruled.[104] There is also his state of mind. His private memorandum book, now known as his 'Meditations', shows that he was now absorbed with issues of mortality, and by the conviction that his own death was at hand.[105] Such reflections are likely to have been stimulated by chronic illness and more recent incidents such as the arrival of the plague and the deaths of Lucius and his own young son in 169. In such a state, he may have seen war not just as a means of demonstrating his abilities as leader but also as a test, an act of self-sacrifice, through which he might expiate whatever it was that was causing Heaven to inflict such suffering on his Empire. This would explain the attention that was given, once hostilities had begun, to various 'miracles' which showed the return of divine favour.[106] It is

---

[100] Garzetti (1974: 506).
[101] Below 52, 70–2.
[102] Cf. Birley (1987: 249).
[103] Birley (1987: 156).
[104] Cf. Birley (1987: 214, 216); Lendon (1997: 115–16).
[105] Cf. Birley (1987: 185, 214, 218–20).
[106] Cf. Garzetti (1974: 493); Birley (1987: 252–3).

no surprise, therefore, that Marcus was preparing a Germanic war even before the end of the Parthian war. There is no need to suppose that this war was a response to a major new threat. Germanic raiding was a feature of frontier life.[107] It could never have been difficult for any Roman ruler looking for a war to find a justification for action in one of these incursions. But in 170 things went badly wrong, and instead of Romans attacking barbarians, barbarians attacked the Empire.[108]

The basic cause of this trouble has usually been sought in the beginnings of the 'Völkerwanderungszeit': the 'Period of Migration'. As Goths moved from Jutland to the Black Sea, they pressured peoples to their south and west, who in turn pressured peoples on the borders of the Roman Empire, taking them, as Birley puts it, to 'breaking point' and forcing them to cross the imperial border.[109] Local factors have also been taken into account in explaining the final push of Marcomanni, Quadi, etc. into the Empire, such as rising population, caused by the more sedentary life created by their being held at the imperial frontier.[110] However, the domino effect remains the major explanation: for a spell, the Empire was swamped by the rising Germanic tide. However, what happened was short-term raiding, not invasion and conquest.[111] The supposed discovery of female warriors among the barbarian dead in northern Italy should be treated as sensationalism, not good history, and should not lead us to conclude that whole peoples were on the march in a search for land.[112] The Empire's 'enemies' at this time consisted of communities which had long lived close to it in relative harmony. If their young men did turn to what amounted to intense banditry in this period, the cause may have been much more close to hand than pressure from the interior. Given the close relationship between the Danube communities and the Roman army, the mass movement of troops to

[107] e.g. below 121, 207.

[108] Again, chronology of this is much disputed: see, e.g. Garzetti (1974: 486, 490) gives AD 167, possibly 169; Birley (1987: 250–2) gives AD 170.

[109] Garzetti (1974: 483–4); Birley (1987: 148 (quotation), 155, 253–5). Cf. the criticisms of Burns (2003: 235).

[110] Birley (1987: 148–9).

[111] Garzetti (1974: 486).

[112] Thus, *contra* Birley (1987: 169). Cf. Zonaras 12.23: the discovery of women's corpses among Persian dead in 260.

the east to fight the Parthian war and their return infected with disease could well have spelled social and economic disaster.[113] Raiding was an alternative means of survival, and would have been made easier by the depletion of the frontier garrisons. But, in the mid-160s, raiding drew imperial attention and resulted in a build-up of imperial forces clearly intent on aggression. No wonder that some Quadi and Marcomanni panicked and attacked first. And no wonder that Roman forces, expecting relatively easy victory, were surprised and let them through. The invasions of Italy and Greece should never have happened. But the basic weakness of the Empire's Germanic enemies is shown in how quickly Rome was able to restore the situation, and take the offensive. Again, Rome was the aggressor here: Marcus Aurelius was set on annexing new territories.[114]

The first phase of the Marcomannic Wars, from 168–75, was therefore not fought by an Empire on the defensive. The decisive incident was the 'invasion' of Italy—humiliating in itself and raising memories of the Cimbri, and even of Brennus. The second phase, from 178–80, followed exactly the same pattern, as Marcus, obstinately fulfilling his duty, returned to finish what had been interrupted by revolt. Now, however, there was an additional, more conventional, factor in play. The young (he was born in 161) Commodus' formal acceptance as heir had been accelerated to meet the challenge of Avidius Cassius, and as part of this process he needed to be accepted by the army. The second phase, like the first, was characterized by Roman aggression and military superiority.[115] Birley describes the conflict as 'a grim and sordid necessity'; but it was necessary only because Marcus regarded it as such. There appear to have been numerous opportunities for a negotiated peace, but these he chose to ignore.[116] Again as in 16 BC, there was a 'threat' on the Danube in the 170s but it was Roman, not Germanic.

Following Commodus' departure from the northern frontier, there was peace with the *Germani* for several decades. Even prolonged Roman political instability and civil war, prompted by the assassin-

---

[113] Burns (2003: 229–35); cf. below 49, n. 36.
[114] Birley (1987: 142, 163, 183, 207, 209, 253); Isaac (1992: 390–1).
[115] See Birley (1987: 207–9).
[116] See, e.g. Birley (1987: 155–6, 169–70).

ation of Commodus at the end of 192 and leading to the accession of
Septimius Severus (193–211), did not provoke significant raiding. In
213, Severus' successor, his son, Caracalla (211–17), made contact
with 'Alamanni' on the middle Main, which is when the following
chapter begins.

The preceding account of Roman dealings with western *Germani* is
based on the literary sources. It can be supplemented from archaeological research. The course of the Augustan and Tiberian campaigns
can be reconstructed through the study of right-bank forts and
marching-camps, etc.[117] However, these were temporary and, with
the exception of certain sites (in particular, that of Waldgirmes), will
not be considered further here. More important is what came later—
above all the development of the security line across the re-entrant
angle of the upper Rhine and upper Danube, now termed the 'Upper
German/Raetian *limes*'.[118]

Although imperial troops withdrew to the left bank of the Rhine
after the Varus disaster, it is unlikely that they abandoned the right
bank for any length of time. As early as Tiberius, a permanent Roman
bridgehead was established in Chattian territory at Hofheim, opposite Mainz; and the Roman military presence in this region appears to
have been strengthened under Gaius.[119] Under Claudius, this area
saw the opening of a silver mine near Wiesbaden, beginning imperial
exploitation of transrhenish resources that continued into the
fourth century.[120] The main advance, however, came under the
Flavians. Vespasian moved into the area north of the lower Main,
the Wetterau, and into the Neckar valley, and drove a road from the
Rhine to the Danube. In the course of his conflict with the Chatti,
Domitian built a set of defended roads in the Wetterau. He consolidated Roman presence on the Neckar, and threw open the land

---

[117] The classic study remains Wells (1972).

[118] Cf. below 50. I recognize the great problems involved in using *limes* as a
synonym for defended frontier line (see Isaac (1992: 408–9)) but, like other equally
questionable terms (such as 'Romanization'), it is too useful a piece of historical
shorthand to give up.

[119] Drinkwater (1983a: 36); Barrett (1989: 131). Schnurbein (2003: 104) suggests
the re-establishment of a Roman presence in the area before the death of Augustus.

[120] Tacitus, *Annales* 11.20.4: *in agro Mattiaci*. Cf. below 133.

between the Rhine and the Neckar, the *Agri Decumates*, to colonists from Gaul.[121] By 100, the protection of Roman territory south of the Main was centred on the Neckar and the Swabian Alp.

This remained the case until Antoninus Pius, when major change came with the projection of the Upper German border *c.*30 km to the east, its integration with the Raetian border, and the combined frontier being delineated by a palisade. This line, from Miltenberg-Ost, via Lorch, to the Danube near Eining, was given its final shape with the addition of a rampart and ditch backing onto the palisade in Upper Germany, and the replacement of the palisade with a stone wall in Raetia[122] (Fig. 2). The Upper German/Raetian *limes* was now in existence. Its most significant aspect is its vulnerability. Laid along two intersecting straight lines, it totally disregarded tactical topography, and appears to have been created more for show than for use. It could have offered little direct resistance to a large force of determined attackers.[123] As a military installation it could meet, at best, in Luttwak's terms, 'low intensity' threats posed by 'transborder infiltrations and peripheral incursions', that is raiding, banditry.[124] In short, it appears to reflect a lack of danger from the *Germani* whom it faced.

How does such an assessment of the Upper German/Raetian *limes* square with what we can say about these *Germani*? Roman military activity may be reconstructed from both texts and artefacts. Germanic settlement is accessible only through archaeology, and early Germanic archaeology is, as ever, very difficult.[125] However, it has long been thought that, although there was a strip of Germanic settlements along the right bank of the Lower Rhine, their main concentrations lay much further in the interior.[126] Of special significance for Alamannic studies is the fact that surprisingly few such settlements have been found skirting the Upper German/Raetian *limes*. To explain this, it has been suggested that the Romans simply

---

[121] Drinkwater (1983a: 57–60); below 126.
[122] For further details see Baatz (1975: 16, 58–62); Drinkwater (1983a: 60–3); Carroll (2001: 38–9).
[123] Cf. Isaac (1992: 414); Whittaker (1994: 84); Witschel (1999: 204).
[124] Luttwak (1976: 66); cf. Baatz (1975: 44); Drinkwater (1983a: 64). For low-level raiding as banditry, see Elton (1996a: 62).
[125] See Schnurbein (2000: 51–3); cf. above 4, and below 112.
[126] e.g. Baatz (1975: 49–50 and Fig. 29) (=Whittaker (1994: 89 and Fig. 22)).

appropriated all the best land in the region.[127] Thanks to recent research, we are now in a position to check both the general settlement pattern and the thinking it has generated.

A stretch of early Germanic settlement along the northern bank of the middle Lahn has recently been subjected to close scrutiny[128] (Fig. 3). Like the neighbouring Wetterau,[129] this region appears to have been subject to continuous settlement from the Celtic Late Iron Age into the Germanic period. It was not inferior land. Indeed, it has been suggested that finds of local non-Roman coinages at major Roman sites (in particular, Waldgirmes) built in the region under Augustus indicate the presence of relatively sophisticated Germanic

Fig. 3   The Lahn and Wetterau regions [after Abegg-Wigg, Walter, and Biegert (2000: 57 Fig. 1)].

---

[127] Whittaker (1994: 89).

[128] For this, and the bulk of what follows, see A. Wigg (1997) and Abegg-Wigg, Walter, and Biegert (2000). For a useful English summary of the work, see A. Wigg (1999).

[129] Lindenthal and Rupp (2000); Scholz (1997); Stobbe (2000).

communities that had adopted important aspects of Celtic economic and social behaviour.[130] The earliest Germanic presence was short-lived—disappearing early in the first century AD after the Varus disaster, along with the Roman garrisons. Users of Germanic 'Rhine–Weser'-style artefacts returned at the end of the same century, that is at the same time as the development of the Wetterau *limes*. The key archaeological sites are at Naunheim, Wettenberg and Lahnau. Ceramic remains indicate that their inhabitants imported goods from the Empire, whose border lay, at its closest point, just 15 km (9 statute miles) to the south.

However, the middle Lahn remains one of only three known areas of Germanic settlement on the northern half of the Upper German/Raetian *limes* (the *c.*300-km (180-mile) stretch between Rheinbrohl and Jagsthausen).[131] Of the rest, the two nearest to the study area lie 20 km (12 statute miles) to the north-west and 40 km (24 statute miles) to the north-east respectively. In other words, the most recent archaeological work appears to confirm sparsity of Germanic settlement close to the *limes*. Next to be noted is that importation of Roman-style artefacts took around 50 years, deep into the second century, to become significant. And, even then, the proportion of such artefacts found on the Lahn sites is small, with little metal and glass and relatively small amounts of pottery. There is no sign of 'technology transfer', that is styles and methods of production of Roman artefact forms being taken up by *Germani*. Further, analysis of Roman and indigenous wares suggests that though *Germani* may have imported some exotic foodstuffs, they made no fundamental changes to the content, preparation and presentation of their meals. This is confirmed by study of the animal and plant remains, which indicates direct continuation of Late Iron Age agricultural patterns—quite different from the neighbouring Wetterau where, for example, cattle gave way to pigs as Romanized settlers from Gaul further developed the land.[132] Finally, despite their proximity to the Empire, there is no indication that the middle-Lahn *Germani* were part of the imperial monetary economy.

---

[130] Wigg (2003). For reconstruction of the evolution of Wigg's 'Germanic' coinage from Celtic models, and its destruction by Drusus' campaigns, see Heinrichs (2003).

[131] Abegg-Wigg et al. (2000: 56).

[132] Stobbe (2000: 216).

Similar mixed results have come from study of the middle Main, centred on the prehistoric settlement of Gaukönigshofen, south of Würzburg[133] (Fig. 4). Again we see continuity of settlement from the Celtic Late Iron Age into the early Germanic period, with the first Germanic settlement being contemporary with Augustan expansion into Germania, and close contact between these earliest *Germani* and the Roman army. Again, too, there was a break at the beginning of the first century, followed in the mid-second century by the arrival of Rhine–Weser artefact-users at the same time as the final advancing of the *limes* line. The same period also saw Germanic settlement on the Tauber.[134] Roman products—represented by ceramics—were imported from Upper Germany and Raetia, though more from the former than the latter. Roman influence has been detected in the possible use of coins in trade, and in local house-building techniques.[135] There is also a case for believing that local *Germani* introduced Roman cattle/oxen as draught animals. And this is one of the areas where, in the third century, there was production of Roman-style wheel-thrown pottery ('the Haarhausen–Eßleben experiments').[136] On the other hand, the imported pottery was restricted to certain main lines and, oddly, in the light of the later strategic importance of the river, appears to have come by land, from the *limes* line, via Osterburken or Jagsthausen, not by water, up the Main.[137] Again there is little sign of such influence on the preparation and serving of food and drink (everyday and as part of rituals). And the pottery experiment was exceptional and short-lived, probably because it was dependent on Roman captives.[138] Further afield across Franconia, Germanic sites of the period of the Early and High Roman Empire generally show no long-term adoption of Celto-Roman agricultural methods. Even at Gaukönigshofen, the introduction of Roman stock produced no permanent improvement in local breeds.[139]

---

[133] See, generally, for what follows Steidl (1997), (2000).
[134] Frank (1997); Steidl (2000: 107, Fig. 9).
[135] Coins: Steidl (1997: 76). Cf. below 135, for the continuation of coin use into the fourth century. House-building: Steidl (2000: 104–5).
[136] Below 92.
[137] Steidl (2000: 106); cf. below 99, 113–15, 131–2, 190.
[138] Steidl (2000: 106, 109). Below 92–3.
[139] Benecke (2000: 253).

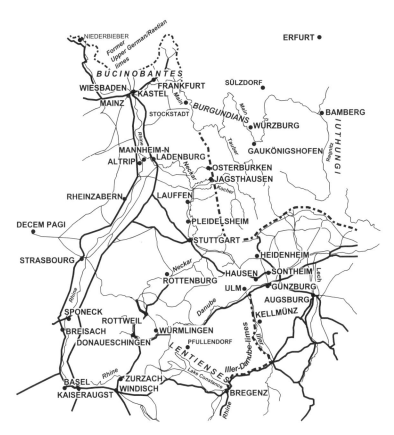

Fig. 4   Alamannia.

As Kreuz says, we must be careful in how we judge this. What we have is not so much a 'primitive' as a different sort of society, in which the preservation of social traditions was more important than possible gains through economic risk. The experimentation with wheel-thrown ceramics, and even the heavier draught animals, may have been the work of a reforming elite group or groups that enjoyed only short-lived predominance.[140]

It is odd that the more distant Main-*Germani* appear to have had more to do with the Empire than the Lahn-*Germani*. Similar unpredictability has been noted in Thuringia, in a study of the settlement at Sülzdorf. Roman artefacts have been found throughout Thuringia, and faunal studies suggest Roman influence on animal breeding, in particular of cattle, horse and dog.[141] In Sülzdorf, however, artefacts and influence are lacking. To explain this, the excavator proposes local conservatism.[142] In a sense, therefore, Sülzdorf may be seen as the non-Romanizing exception that proves the Romanizing rule. Again, however, the long-term impact of Roman influence on the quality of animal stock generally in Thuringia has been questioned.[143]

What conclusions may be drawn from this review of Germanic archaeology? First, as in the case of the Alamanni, there is no clear correlation between the historical and archaeological evidence. For example, without the literary sources we would have no inkling of the existence of the Chatti. Secondly, however, we can see the power that Rome had to disrupt Germanic society, already visible in the historical sources. Across Franconia there appears to have been a major break in settlement, from the first into the second century AD. This has also been observed recently along the High Rhine, between Basel and Lake Constance.[144] Only when Rome settled down could the Empire's Germanic neighbours find some peace. But, thirdly, there is now no doubt that *Germani* were attracted to Roman military sites. This occurs very early, at the time of the Augustan campaigns, and may also account for the settlements in the Lahn valley and on the middle Main. The phenomenon of barbarians 'setting up house on

---

[140] Cf. Kreuz (2000: esp. 238–9).
[141] Teichner (2000: 86–7).
[142] Teichner (2000: 87–8).
[143] Benecke (2000: 253); cf. Teichner (2000: 87, n.42).
[144] Trumm (2002: 212).

the doorstep of their supposed enemy' has also been noticed on the Danube.[145] It is reminiscent of Alamannic behaviour in the late third and fourth centuries; and, as in the case of the Alamannic settlements, we must suppose that the Rhine–Weser communities existed only under Roman licence and, perhaps, even encouragement.[146]

This notion of fluctuation in population is not without its difficulties. At the likely site of the *clades Variana*, at Kalkriese, the presence of Germanic warriors can be deduced only from Roman military remains. Similarly, without the help of Roman imports, it is very difficult to identify and date Germanic settlements, therefore the absence of imperial goods may create a false impression of demographic voids. It has been remarked, for example, that relatively high levels of Germanic pottery in the Augustan fort at Waldgirmes suggest a significant population in the Lahn valley, which would accord with the occurrence of native coinage in the area; but we do not know the sites at which these pots were produced. Likewise, pollen data in the Lahn valley and the Wetterau have been interpreted as indicating that both areas continued to be worked at more or less the same level of intensity from the Celtic through to the Germanic and Roman periods, suggesting no marked variations in population. Archaeologists may in the end detect technical flaws in the palynology or discover a highly peripatetic form of local agriculture which allowed a small population to spread cultivated pollens over a wide area, but for the moment there is certainly a discrepancy between the historical and archaeological, and the palynological evidence.[147]

It is, therefore, undeniable that, in Whittaker's phrase, the area around the Upper German/Raetian *limes* became a 'zone of interaction' as *Germani* were drawn to the frontier and appreciated the material benefits of imperial life. One is tempted, like Whittaker, to cite Cassius Dio's description of the natives' adaptation to the Roman world in the Augustan province of Germania prior to Varus: 'they were becoming different without realizing it'.[148] On the other hand, it

---

[145] Burns (2003: 231).

[146] Below 82, 89. A. Wigg (1997: 63), (1999: 49).

[147] Stobbe (2000: 217); Abegg-Wigg et al. (2000: 56); Lindenthal and Rupp (2000: 74); Schnurbein (2003: 103–4). There is no sign of the general surge in the 'Germanic-dominated' population of Europe proposed by Heather (2005: 86–7).

[148] Dio 56.18.3. Whittaker (1994: 130).

is important not to exaggerate the scale of the phenomenon. Dio's *Germani* were in the throes of full provincialization, stimulated by the facilities prepared for them at sites such as Waldgirmes.[149] With this abandoned, the process of acculturation became uneven and unspectacular. Above all, it appears to have produced no significant polarization of political and military power, reflected in, say, the concentration of high levels of imported artefacts at particular sites. In other words, against Whittaker, in this region at least we can see no rise of a sophisticated barbarian elite, willing to pursue its interests in the Empire peaceably or, if necessary, by force.[150]

Certainly, whatever was to follow in the later Empire, there is no sign here of the emergence of a new and dynamic composite culture, a 'Mischzivilisation', spanning the nominal frontier line and absorbing barbarians and Romans alike.[151] Recent research has emphasized the lack of cultural movement in the opposite direction, that is the lack of impact of Germanic ways on imperial border life, and this despite the fact that, along with Gauls, Rome appears to have settled some *Germani* in the *Agri Decumates*.[152] Although they have their problems, name-studies have failed to reveal any significant number of Rhine–Weser *Germani* in Heddernheim.[153] Likewise, Böhme-Schönberger has noted the absence of Germanic influence on Roman dress in the western border areas under the Early Empire.[154] Where we can glimpse acculturation in action, *Germani* go imperial. It was not until the fifth century that provincial Romans went Germanic, following the Frankish domination of Gaul. Until then, the stronger culture predominated.[155] The exception might seem to

---

[149] Schnurbein (2003: 104); above 20.

[150] Whittaker (1994: 127, 215–22); cf. Burns (2003: 231–2).

[151] On 'Mischzivilisation', see further below 348–57. Elsewhere from the first to the third centuries, in the northern Netherlands, Lower Saxony and Schleswig-Holstein, the Empire seems to have exercised a surprising ability to control the flow of its manufactured products to *Germani*, strictly according to its own military and political needs: Erdrich (2000a: 195–6), (2000b: 228–9), (2001: 79–135, 139–43, 146–50 (English summary)). The inhibition of a free market in such goods can only have hampered material acculturation.

[152] The 'Neckar Suebi': Heiligmann (1997: 58).

[153] Scholz (1997).

[154] Böhme-Schönberger (1997).

[155] Böhme-Schönberger (1997: 9–10), cf. Halsall (2000: 180): 'So, at least until about 400, if the cultural frontier zone was deepening, it was spreading from northern Gaul into *Germania Libera* and not *vice versa*.'

be military equipment: the Roman army always adopted the best weapons of its opponents. Even here, however, one of the best known cases of Roman borrowing, that of the *spatha*, is less straightforward than it seems, since the long-sword appears to have mixed—Germanic, but also Celtic and eastern—origins.[156]

Overall, therefore, there is no clear archaeological evidence for a high degree of direct Germanic pressure on the upper Rhine and upper Danube frontier from the first to the early third centuries AD. As far as can be seen, there were few Germanic settlements directly on the *limes*, and not many in its vicinity. Even if this is unreliable, and there were many more *Germani* in the area, we have to conclude from the absence of Roman artefacts that most of them can have had little contact with the Empire or its products. As the excavators say of the Lahn *Germani*, though neighbours, they were 'distant neighbours'.[157]

Without direct pressure on the Empire, where was danger likely to come from? There might, as in the case of the Marcomannic Wars, have been short-term difficulties with immediately adjacent, nominally friendly communities. In the longer term, the most likely threat was long-distance raiding—chronic but relatively infrequent and certainly manageable until it ran out of control in the third century.[158] If, as has been suggested from finds of brooches,[159] distant *Germani* could, from the first century, travel west to the Upper German/Raetian frontier to find service in the Roman army, they could do the same in war-bands. But the *limes* system was well able to cope with this level of aggression.[160]

If there was no pressing Germanic threat, why did early Roman emperors make so much of the Rhine frontier? Here, we return to the political symbiosis which is the main theme of this chapter. Fundamentally, the Germanic threat on the Rhine was played up by Roman emperors because it suited them to do so. Imperial campaigns occurred because the princes involved found them useful in acquiring or enhancing a military reputation (Tiberius, Domitian), steadying

---

[156] Gechter (1997: esp. 14); cf. below 341–2.

[157] Abegg-Wigg et al. (2000: 63): 'entfernte Nachbarn'.

[158] Witschel (1999: 205); cf. below 49.

[159] Böhme-Schönberger (1997: 9).

[160] Cf. Creighton and Wilson (1999: 25): the proximity of numerous villas to the *limes* in, say, Taunus or Raetia, as a sign of 'just how peaceful conditions must have been on the frontier for decades'.

their armies in uncertain political or military situations (Germanicus), and providing them with a reason to go to or remain in the west when, for political reasons, it suited them to be there (Gaius). Furthermore, imperial exploitation of neighbouring barbarians was essential in justifying the very position of the *princeps*, as Republican warlord became legitimate emperor. Emperors needed to foster the support of the army because, in the last resort, their power depended on its obedience. One of the best ways of obtaining such support was to lead their troops successfully against foreign foes, winning them and themselves honour, glory and booty and, as far as the wider political nation was concerned, reinforcing Roman beliefs in Rome's divinely ordained mission of world domination.[161] Germania was an abundant source of such foes. In addition, since the institution of a large standing army was relatively new in the Empire, expensive and, as emperors began to find to their cost, potentially dangerous as a breeding ground for disaffection, the army and its maintenance had to be justified and its potential political threat reduced. All this could be achieved by laying stress on outlying enemies, against whom the troops were projected as the Empire's sole defence, and to counter whom units could be distributed along the frontier, supported by local populations and at a safe (or, at least, safer) distance from the imperial centre and from each other. Tacitus hinted at this deceit when he claimed that the task of the Rhine army was as much to watch Gauls as *Germani*, but this was not even half the story. The vast majority of Gauls were, very soon, loyal Roman subjects and taxpayers; and, as Syme says, 'no enemy was likely to come from the Black Forest'.[162] There was no real threat either way: from the start Roman forces were stationed on the frontier not to counter a major 'barbarian menace', external or internal, but out of imperial political needs.[163]

---

[161] e.g. Burns (2003: 10–12, 93, 209, 272–4, 283); Isaac (1992: 379–83).

[162] Tacitus, *Annales* 4.5.1: *commune in Germanos Gallosque subsidium.* Syme (1999: 87).

[163] Below 360–1; cf. Guzmán Armario (2002: 122). Burns (2003: 18–19, 30, 141, 152–3, 175–6).

2

Arrival

Tacitus described a great arc of tribes, from modern Württemberg to the Vistula, which he classified as 'Suebi'. The 'oldest and noblest' of these were the Semnones, whom Tacitus appears to have located on the middle Elbe.[1] It used to be thought that the Alamanni were an old Suebian tribe under a new name, or a new but distinctly Suebian tribal confederation that, from around 200, pressed ever harder against the Rhine/Danube *limes* and then, at a specific date (traditionally 259/60), broke through and settled in part of Upper Germany and Raetia.[2] The first sign of this pressure was taken to be Caracalla's Germanic campaign of 213, which took him over the frontier from Raetia and into conflict with fierce people described in Cassius Dio's contemporary 'Roman History' as *Albannoi*, *Alambannoi*, or *Kennoi*. Dio's account is apparently confirmed by Aurelius Victor who, writing in the middle years of the fourth century, explicitly describes Caracalla's victories over Alamanni near the river Main.[3] However, simple invasion was questioned by Wenskus as part of his discussion of ethnogenesis, and the current *communis opinio* is that there was no third-century Suebian 'Völkerwanderung'—no 'migration'—and no sudden and decisive 'Landnahme'—no 'occupation'. Rather, it is now generally believed, the Alamanni came into being only after various Germanic groups found

---

[1] Tacitus, *Germania* 38–45, esp. 39.1.
[2] For a summary of such thinking, see Geuenich (1997a: 11–15, 22); Pohl (2000: 29).
[3] Dio 77(78).13.4–6, 14.1–2, 15.2 [Loeb]; *CIL* 6.2086 (*ILS* 451); *Quellen* 1, 9–11; Aurelius Victor, *Caesares* 21.2: *Alamannos . . . prope Moenum amnem devicit.* Cf. below 141–2.

themselves living permanently on former imperial territory.[4] Here occurred what might be termed 'ethnogenesis *sur place*' as the new-comers interacted with each other, and with Rome.[5]

An important element in the evolution of this hypothesis was that Greco-Roman usage of 'Alamanni' and 'Alamannia' did not begin until the late third century, being marked by the appearance of 'Alamanni' in a Latin panegyric of 289.[6] On this view, references to Caracalla's Alamanni in Cassius Dio are later interpolations or glosses; and Aurelius Victor projected the present upon the past.[7] This interpretation has recently been challenged by Bleckmann, who demonstrates the special pleading needed to sustain it and shows that there is no reason to doubt that Caracalla fought people whom he knew as Alamanni beyond the Danube in 213.[8] I would add that by 289 the word 'Alamanni' must have been sufficiently long in circula-tion for the cultivated Gallic orator who delivered the panegyric to Maximian to deploy it without fear of being accused of neologism. (After all, he goes out of his way to avoid the term 'Bagaudae'.[9])

The reinstatement of the earlier occurrence of Alamanni is important for the history of the name.[10] It is, however, less significant for the understanding of what happened in the third century. It does not compel a return to 'migration' and 'occupation'. Acceptance of the '289 argument' allowed historians to see the evidence in a

[4] Wenskus (1961), 499–500, 506–7, citing Bauer and Dannenbauer. The notion of their ethnogenesis in Alamannia was propounded independently by Springer, Castritius and Okamura: cf. Castritius (1998: 353 and n. 14, referring also to Kerler). I first encountered it in Okamura's meticulous doctoral dissertation (1984). The implications of his ideas were pursued by Nuber (1990), (1993), (1997). See also, more recently, Keller (1993: 83–6, 89–91); Geuenich (1997a: 11–12, 17), (1997b: 73, 76–7); Schach-Dörges (1997: 98); Nuber (1998: 378–9); Steuer (1998: 280–1).

[5] Keller (1993: 91, 96–7); Nuber (1993: 103); Geuenich (1997a: 16–17), (1997b: 74, 76); Martin (1997a: 119); Schach-Dörges (1997: 79, 85); Steuer (1997a: 149); (1998: 275–6, 278, 281, 315, 317); Castritius (1998: 357); Wolfram (1998: 613). A modern version of the traditional view has, however, been proposed by Strobel (1996: 131–5), (1998: 86–7), (1999: 16–21); cf. below nn. 94, 101.

[6] *Pan. Lat.* 2(10) [Galletier].5.1; cf. below 180.

[7] Okamura (1984: e.g. 86, 90–1, 116–17); Keller (1993: 90); Nuber (1993: 102 and n.27); Geuenich (1997a: 18–19). Cf. Castritius (1998: 353 and n.14); Steuer (1998: 274–5); Pohl (2000: 103).

[8] Bleckmann (2002).

[9] Drinkwater (1989: 193).

[10] Below 63.

different light. Whatever the original meaning of the term 'Alamanni' and the manner in which it became attached to a certain set of people, the lesson of fourth-century history and archaeology is that there was no invasion by a single, fully fledged people or consciously related association of tribes.[11] Roman writers clearly had very little idea as to who the Alamanni were and where they came from and nor, apparently, had the Alamanni themselves. Unlike Goths, Lombards and Franks, they do not appear to have possessed ancient stories tracing their ancestry back to a mythical past.[12] The absence of any royal or aristocratic 'Traditionskern'—'core of tradition'—distances Alamannic studies from current debate concerning the validity of the concept of ethnogenesis which is concerned most of all with whether each of these other peoples possessed its own such 'core'.[13] An attempt has been made to locate an ancient religious tradition at the heart of Alamannic identity, but it relies too much on cultural continuity in rapidly changing circumstances.[14] Alamannic ethnogenesis *sur place* can now stand on its own feet. South-west Germany was taken over gradually by a number of small and scattered groups which slowly became 'the Alamanni'. During the third century, 'Alamanni' was a description of type, not nationality: a generic, not an ethnic.[15]

This makes the identification of the Alamannic place of origin much less of an issue than used to be the case in Germanic scholarship.[16] However, scholars seem to agree that the models of Alamannic jewellery and ceramics and burial places originated in the lands on and to the east of the Elbe, from Mecklenburg to Bohemia. These types of artefacts and structures, termed 'Elbgermanic', spread into an area which may be roughly described as an inverted triangle, with its base on the Elbe and its apex in the

[11] Thus *contra* Bleckmann (2002: 146, 150, 168 ('Grossstamm', 'Volk', 'Gruppe/ Stamm mit eigener Identität')). Below 86, 124–6.

[12] Steuer (1998: 276–7).

[13] e.g. Amory (1997: 36–8). More recently Bowlus (2002: 245–6); Fewster (2002: 140); Goffart (2002: 21–3, 30–7); Kulikowski (2002: 72–4); Murray (2002: 46, 64–5); Pohl (2002b: 222, and see 228–32 for a summary and defence of the 'more diffuse', post-Wenskus, conception of the 'Traditionskern').

[14] Below 125.

[15] Cf. below 62 and, esp., 67.

[16] Cf. Steuer (1997a: 150), (1998: 278, 283, 287, 317).

Rhine–Danube re-entrant[17] (Fig. 5). Assuming that such an expansion in some way reflects movement of people,[18] it has to be conceded that the new approach locates the ancestors of the Alamanni firmly in the western section of Tacitus' 'Suebia'. Thus, as some critics have waspishly observed of ethnogenesis as a whole, the new version does not appear significantly different from the old.[19] However, it does not presuppose massive tribal migration or even a uniform ethnic or political background for the people concerned. Further, it allows for cultural, economic and political influences to circulate west to east, as well as east to west, within the triangle.[20]

Some awareness of the arrival of people from Suebia may explain why, in the works of some late-fourth/early-fifth-century poets, *Germani* who in the terms of this study are clearly Alamanni are occasionally termed 'Suebi'.[21] It is unlikely that the writers concerned possessed a deep understanding of contemporary developments within the Elbgermanic triangle. Much more probable is that they repeated the traditional ethnography of their education, that is the Tacitean model, 'confirmed' by later experience.[22] This also gave them a word—disyllabic *Suebi*—better suited to the complexities of Latin metre than trisyllabic *Alamanni*.[23] But 'Suebi' was a very imprecise term. For practical reasons Romans needed to come to grips with Elbe-*Germani* in or by the Rhine–Danube re-entrant. They needed to categorize the area and the people it contained, and for this purpose fell upon 'Alamannia' and 'Alamanni'.[24] The emphasis must

---

[17] Fingerlin (1993: 60); Nuber (1993: 103); Martin (1997a: 119); Schach-Dörges (1997: 79, 81–95); Steuer (1997a: 149, 151–2, 154), (1998: 291–301 and Fig. 2, 314, 316); Bücker (1999: 216); Haberstroh (2000b: 227).

[18] As Steuer (1998: 301).

[19] Tacitus, *Germania* 38–45; cf. Pohl (2000: 21–2). Goffart (2002: 31).

[20] As I understand it, this is the main force of Steuer's insistence (e.g. (1998: 295, 297, 306, 311) on 'Verkehrsräumen' and 'Verkehrszonen'—the spontaneous emergence of a number of areas of production and circulation (of artefacts, customs and fashions), linked by established regional lines of communication ('Verkehrsbahnen')). See also Brather (2002: 161–2).

[21] Ausonius 13.3.7, 4.3; 17.1.2; 20.2.29 [Green]; Claudian, *In Eutrop.* 1.394; *De Cons. Stil.* 1.190.

[22] Below 60.

[23] Green (1991: 535); Heinen (1995: 82). Bleckmann (2002: 157 n. 46).

[24] Lorenz, S. (1997: 18) and, esp., below 68–9.

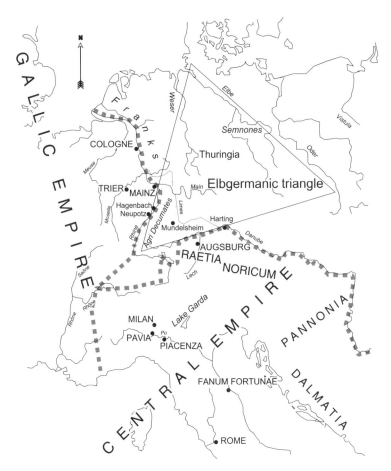

Fig. 5 The north-western provinces, third century.

have been on area not ethnicity. Elbe-*Germani* who drifted westwards
into Alamannia became Alamanni; Alamanni who drifted eastwards into Suebia became Suebi.[25] There were occasions, however,
on which 'Suebi' and its derivations appear to have been used delib-
erately. One example of this may be Ammianus Marcellinus' citation
of reports of Suebic raids on Raetia to explain Constantius II's
departure from Rome in 357.[26] The most important are descriptions
of the barbarian incursion of the early fifth century, made up of
Vandals, Alans and Suebi, and the re-naming of Alamanni and
Alamannia as 'Suebi' and 'Suebia' (so English 'Swabians' and
'Swabia') from the sixth century.[27] This probably reflects contact
with people from wider Elbgermanic communities living beyond
Alamannia proper. Constantius II moved far to the east of the
Alamanni;[28] and the Suebi of 406/7 appear to have come from the
Danube region.[29] The name change seems to have been generated by
political disturbance after 450.[30] Again, for most purposes we are safe
in referring to the people under examination here as Alamanni.

There is some debate as to whether, during the third century,
incoming groups that would cohere to form 'the' Alamanni were
just war-parties, consisting mainly of young males, or larger units,
with warriors and accompanying non-belligerent dependants.
Though there are very early female and infant burials in Alamannia,
war-parties seem the more likely on commonsense grounds.[31] In the
absence of a large migrating tribe, it is more plausible for an exposed
Roman frontier area to have attracted bands of raiders.

We may envisage these as operating independently of settled communities throughout the Elbgermanic triangle and plundering far
and wide, but, to begin with, returning home with their loot.[32] In
some cases 'home' would not have been far. We now know of likely
Elbgermanic settlement in the Upper Main–Regnitz regions (around

---

[25] Cf. below 124–5.
[26] AM 16.10.20.
[27] Below 321–4; Keller (1993: 91).
[28] Below 227, 242.
[29] Pohl (2002a: 73); Castritius (2005: 202–3); and below 324.
[30] Below 335.
[31] Presence of dependants: Schach-Dörges (1997: 81, 87, 96, 98, 100); raiding-
bands, not migrants: Wenskus (1961: 507) and Steuer (1998: 280, 288). Cf. below 83.
[32] Keller (1993: 97); Geuenich (1997a: 18, 24–5); Pohl (2000: 105–6).

Bamberg) from the later second century[33] (Fig. 4). In support of this
model, one may cite Tacitus' description of the Germanic *comitatus/*
retinue: the attachment of young warriors to the service of established 'chiefs' (*principes*) which encouraged warfare.[34] In addition,
there is now archaeological evidence for an increase in internecine
warfare in Free Germany during the third century in the shape of
votive deposits of military equipment found in southern Scandinavia
and along the southern coast of the Baltic. These have been interpreted as resulting from an expansion of activity by Germanic war-
bands, detached from their home tribes and directed by capable
leaders who were able to arm themselves and their followers with
good-quality weapons, made locally or, as in the case of swords, even
imported from the Roman Empire. It has been calculated that such
bands were capable of striking over fairly great distances, from *c.*400
to 800 km (250–500 statute miles). Their average complement has
been estimated at about 600, giving them significant but, relative to
the Roman Empire, far from overwhelming military power.[35] We do
not know the cause of this increase in warfare. Overpopulation has
been proposed, but only as a guess; and the relatively slow pace of
Alamannic settlement does not suggest land hunger as a major
motivating force.[36] The very early Alamannic graves are, as usual,
rare and high-status. They could have been dug to contain the
remains of the immediate family of the high-ranking individuals
who assembled and led the warrior-bands: the only people allowed
to have their wives and children travel with them.[37]

[33] Haberstroh (2000a: 128); (2000b: 227). Cf. below 80.

[34] Tacitus, *Germania* 13–14.

[35] Steuer (1997a: 149–50); (1998: 284–5, 314–17); Müller-Wille (1999: 41–63);
cf. Carroll (2001: 137). See also below 331, 334, for a band of 900 operating in the
mid-fifth century.

[36] Steuer (1998: 289). Pohl (2000: 25–7, 100–1), (2002: 154) apparently following
Wenskus (1961: 506), suggests disturbance by population movement—specifically,
Gothic migration—to the east, which strikes me as somewhat old-fashioned
(cf. above 30), or internal social stress. As Witschel (1999: 214) asks, if population
pressure was the cause, why did it take so long for the Alamanni to settle? See also
Schmauder (2002: 201) and below 83.

[37] Cf. below 89, 141, with Steuer (1998: 282), the settlement process which began
*c.*300 was initiated by 'kings', with families and dependants. Cf. Amory (1997: 41): a
mobile army cannot be 'a stable endogamous breeding group'.

If there was no decisive Alamannic invasion over the Upper German/Raetian *limes* and no single conquest of Roman territory in 259/60, then what happened? Instead of being the target of strategic assaults the Rhine–Danube frontier was probably, from around 200, subjected to an increase in habitual raiding by Germanic warbands.[38] These may have been capable of making alliances, but such agreements would have been temporary.[39] At first the Roman Empire may have suffered only in passing from unrest in Free Germany; we should not underestimate the damaging effect of changing conditions on Germanic communities.[40] However, a flaccid imperial response may have encouraged raiders to aim directly south-westwards, at the *limes*.[41]

The fact that Caracalla commenced his campaign of 213 from Raetia suggests that the first significant raids were into this province, uncomfortably close to Italy. However, we should be cautious in assessing their severity. The expedition allowed Caracalla to escape a difficult political situation in Rome, was brief, and probably did not involve massive forces.[42] In short, it was very much in the tradition of imperial exploitation. If the emperor headed directly northwards, he would have reached the middle Main which, at its closest point, is only 70 km (*c*.40 statute miles) as the crow flies from the Raetian *limes*.[43] Here, he would have been near to the Upper Main–Regnitz area where there is evidence of Elbgermanic settlement from the later second century, and therefore a region where he could have encountered roving Elbgermanic war-bands and other, more friendly, 'Rhine–Weser' *Germani* whom he tried to use against them. A route down the Tauber is likely, though one down the Regnitz itself is not impossible.[44] In such circumstances Dio's story of fearless 'Kennic', that is Alamannic, women, who preferred death to Roman slavery, may have derived from the behaviour of privileged

[38] Date: Schach-Dörges (1997: 81).

[39] Keller (1993: 97); Steuer (1998: 275, 281, 283, 285).

[40] For the decline of coastal *terp* settlements in Holland and North Germany see De Koning (2003).

[41] Cf. Pohl (1998a: 641); Steuer (1998: 284); Witschel (1999: 205).

[42] Okamura (1984: 10–11, 24–31).

[43] Cf. Bleckmann (2002: 161 and n. 60).

[44] Okamura (1984: 130); cf. Ellmers (1997: 5) on the likely river routes from Weißenburg, on the Raetian *limes*, north to the Main at Bamberg; and below 67–8.

dependants of warrior–leaders whose existence I have proposed above.[45] It is unclear precisely how Caracalla fared. Dio has him running into difficulties and having to buy off his opponents; Aurelius Victor makes him successful. His subsequent withdrawal into 'Germany'[46] indicates that he returned via the *Agri Decumates*, perhaps down the Main.

The significance of an east–west route into imperial territory became clear half a generation later.[47] The sources suggest that Germanic attacks from this direction became serious in the early 230s, causing Severus Alexander to move to Mainz, and then engaging the attention of his successor, the usurper Maximinus. Scholars have used literary, archaeological and, especially, numismatic evidence to propose further waves of trouble in the 240s and early 250s.[48] However, only the first of these (of 242) is securely attested; the seriousness of what happened in the early-to-mid-230s should not be exaggerated.[49] Again, we are in the presence of scattered raiders—some calling themselves Alamanni, others probably under different names—not organized invaders.[50]

Though the *limes* held against such marauders, its continued viability was under threat from events elsewhere in the Empire. First came a resurgence of Persian aggression under the Sassanid dynasty, and then heavy raiding by Eastgermanic Goths and their associates over the lower Danube and around the Black Sea. This double danger, which emerged in the late 240s, taxed Rome's military strength and revealed all the weaknesses of a political system in which an emperor had to show himself a capable general or face deposition.[51] It was this last which produced the real bane of the age, chronic civil war, which consumed resources, encouraged further external raiding and

[45] Dio 77(78).14.2. For 'Kennoi' as a corruption of 'Alamannoi', with nothing remaining of the original word but the double-n, see Bleckmann (2002: 148). Above 49.

[46] Dio 77(78).14.2: *es tēn Germanian*.

[47] On the strategic importance of the Main see also below 99, 113, 131–2, 190.

[48] Roeren (1960: 215–17).

[49] Drinkwater (2005: 29).

[50] Okamura (1984: 190–3, 202–3, 217–18, 219–24, 227, 229); cf. Strobel (1998: 83–4). Nuber (1990: 52), (1997: 60–1), (1998: 370–1) proposes a more traditional interpretation.

[51] Above 41–2.

overloaded the taxation system.[52] On the Rhine and Danube, troops were withdrawn for service elsewhere and not replaced.[53] In 253 the western army was further weakened by Valerian I's removal of forces to support his usurpation and then his Persian war. Valerian's co-ruler and successor, his son Gallienus, also removed troops to fight further down the Danube.[54] Despite Gallienus' move to the west around 257,[55] chronic Germanic raids appear to have unsettled the civil population east of the Rhine and north of the Danube. There are signs of civilians moving into forts and, perhaps, of the upper classes deserting the region entirely.[56] There is no direct evidence for a regular structure of local government in the region after 254.

On the other hand, we cannot take this date as that of the end of Roman rule there. The latest known military inscription of Upper Germany is from 249, well before any likely date for withdrawal from the *limes*, as is that from Raetia north of the Danube, from 254.[57] Abandonment came later, and was sudden; prior to this a full Roman presence was maintained or, at least, projected. There is no sign in the archaeological record of, say, a phased evacuation of forts. On the contrary, what we see in the reduction of bath buildings, the partial walling of gates and the reduction in size of buildings and of complete forts in the 230s and 240s are indications of efforts to maintain the system as a whole.[58]

The decision to abandon the Upper German/Raetian *limes* was made by Postumus, who in 260 successfully rebelled against Gallienus and assumed control of most of the western Empire. His usurpation followed a burst of Germanic raiding over the Rhine. Franks are reported to have reached Spain and even Africa, and Alamanni to have entered the central Swiss plateau, the Auvergne and even Italy.[59] But these troubles resulted from civil war precipitated by the

[52] On this see generally Drinkwater (2005).

[53] On all this see Nuber (1990: 52, 59–63), (1997: 61), (1998: 373); Strobel (1998: 84); Witschel (1999: 203, 209–10); Drinkwater (2005: 35, 37, 60).

[54] Nuber (1997: 62), (1998: 373).

[55] Drinkwater (1987: 21–2).

[56] Nuber (1997: 64–5); cf. below 127.

[57] Nuber (1990: 57–8), (1997: 66), (1998: 372). Ladenburg: *CIL* 13.9103; Heidelberg: *CIL* 13.9111; Jagsthausen: *CIL* 13.6562; Hausen ob Lontal: *CIL* 3.5933.

[58] Nuber (1990: 61–3), (1993: 101–2), (1997: 66–7), (1998: 373–4); Witschel (1999: 206–10).

[59] Drinkwater (1987: 23–4).

ignominious capture of Valerian by the Persians in the east: the problem was Roman weakness not Germanic strength. In Upper Germany and Raetia, civil war resulted in an impractical frontier between Postumus' 'Gallic' and Gallienus' 'Central' (both terms are modern) Empires that was consequently abandoned.[60] It did not fall to Germanic attack.[61] It is now accepted that internal conflict following Postumus' usurpation and not wholesale invasion caused the coin series at the *limes* fort of Saalburg to end with issues of this date, and led to a general interruption in the supply of imperial money to the region.[62] Further evidence of destruction in Roman frontier-forts in the region around 260 is rare. That which we have, such as at Niederbieber, may likewise be interpreted as the consequences of internecine Roman fighting. This also suggests that after such fighting came systematic clearing of certain sites and the re-use of their materials.[63]

Interest in events around 260 was recently stimulated by the discovery of a new inscription. This was found in August 1992 in Augsburg, as Augusta Vindelicum, capital of the Roman province of Raetia. It is cut into the front of a substantial limestone altar (from the bottom of its plinth, over 1.5 metres in height), with sculpted side-panels depicting (left) Victoria triumphing over a fettered barbarian and (right) armed Mars. It commemorates a victory won by the equestrian governor of the province, M. Simplicinius Genialis, over Semnones and Iouthungi [*sic*]. Through their success, Genialis and his mixed force, consisting of troops from Raetia and one or both of the provinces of Germany, and men raised locally, either as conscripts or members of a militia (*populares*—the sense is obscure[64]), liberated 'several thousand' Italians captured by the barbarians. The battle took place on 24 and 25 April and the altar was dedicated by Genialis, nominally in fulfilment of vows undertaken by himself and his army, on 11 September of the same year. There is a consular date for this year but it is irregular, naming the rebel Postumus and one Honoratianus. Both these and Genialis later suffered *damnatio memoriae*, that is their names and titles were

[60] Below 70.
[61] Okamura (1984: 248–61); cf. Jehne (1996: 203 and n.119).
[62] Stribrny (1989: 374–5, 400).
[63] Sommer (1999: 190 and n.62); Strobel (1999: 13–14).
[64] Strobel (1998: 87).

carefully chiselled out in the Roman period.[65] The Augsburg inscription is important for casting new light on the early 260s and on the activities of Iuthungi, later associated with the Alamanni, of whom it is now our earliest direct record (about 10 years before that of our previous earliest reference to them, also as 'Iouthungi', in Dexippus[66]).

We know that Postumus held several consulships while emperor of the west, and that he had consular status in the year of his usurpation, 260. It is now commonly accepted that this first consulship was extraordinary, deriving probably from Postumus' irregular assumption of the office following his usurpation.[67] He took his second consulship in 261. The fact that on the Augsburg inscription his consulship is followed by no iterations (II, III etc.) has caused commentators to conclude that this was his first, and therefore that the altar was set up in 260.[68] Since it is likely that Postumus did not usurp until the middle months of 260, after the capture of Valerian by the Persians, Genialis' victory will have been won when he was still loyal to Valerian and Gallienus.[69] Before their defeat, the Iuthungi had raided into Italy. Bakker and Jehne have proposed that their incursion took place in 259. Laden with booty and captives, they overwintered south of the Alps but were defeated on their way home the following spring.[70] Bakker and Jehne have further argued that if Iuthungi were able to invade Italy in 259, Gallienus must have been busy elsewhere. They propose that the usurpations of Ingenuus and Regalianus in the Balkans occurred not, as was usually thought, after the capture of Valerian, but from mid-259 into early 260. Jehne suggests that Gallienus went to deal with these and that, in his absence, there were two attacks on Italy. Iuthungi struck through

[65] Bakker (1993); Jehne (1996); König (1997); Strobel (1998).

[66] Dexippus, *Scythica*, F6 (F. Jacoby, *Die Fragmente der griechischen Historiker* 2A, no. 100, p. 457).

[67] Strobel (1998: 86); Watson (1999: 36, 220).

[68] e.g. Bakker (1993: 378); Jehne (1996: 187); Strobel (1998: 46).

[69] Drinkwater (1987: 23–4) (mid-260). Jehne (1996: 201) has Genialis loyal to Valerian's successors, Gallienus and Saloninus, in late April 260. However, I find it difficult to believe that Valerian was captured and the news of this event reached the west as early as late April 260, especially since, as Bakker (1993: 379) and Jehne (1996: 195 and n. 62, 201, 205) both state, Valerian was not captured by Shapur I before the late spring or early summer of this year.

[70] Bakker (1993: 377); Jehne (1996: 187–8).

Raetia and over the central Alps and penetrated perhaps as far as Rome; Alamanni came over the Upper Rhine and via eastern and southern Gaul into the upper Po valley.[71] (At the same time, Franks attacked over the Lower Rhine and penetrated Gaul and Spain.) Gallienus returned too late to deal with the Iuthungi (already crushed by Genialis), but scored a famous victory over the Alamanni at Milan. It was then that he received news of disaster in the east.[72]

Valerian's capture, and Gallienus' failure to avenge it or deal with its consequences, prompted the revolt of Postumus. From the Augsburg inscription we know, for the first time, that the usurper was recognized by the provincial administration in Raetia, and the 260 dating of the inscription would indicate that this recognition followed very quickly upon his proclamation. However, as Jehne has pointed out, the Augsburg inscription does not show that Postumus controlled Raetia, only that Genialis wanted him to; and at a later date, in 268, when Aureolus offered him northern Italy, Postumus showed himself unwilling to defend the indefensible. Unadopted, Raetia could have been recovered by Gallienus as early as 261, after his victory in the Balkans over Macrianus II.[73]

The preceding is based upon acceptance of the dating of the Augsburg inscription to 260. However, the advancing of the rebellions of Ingenuus and Regalianus to 259 is uncomfortable; and there is something odd about the 'monument' as a whole. Though quite large, it is not grand. It is a re-used block with a plain rear face, and its side-panels are hardly great works of art. It is possible that it was produced by more than one craftsman.[74] As König has observed, it is a mystery why, if the battle took place in April under Valerian and Gallienus, it took over four months for such an indifferent piece to be hurriedly commissioned in September under Postumus.[75] An alternative interpretation is possible which accommodates the inscription within both the traditional chronology and my understanding of the 'barbarian menace'.[76] I suspect that the monument offers an insight

---

[71] For further discussion of these attacks see below 70–1.
[72] Bakker (1993: 383–4); Jehne (1996: 189–92, 196–201).
[73] Jehne (1996: 203); cf. Strobel (1998: 88), (1999: 15): in 262.
[74] König (1997: 343), from Bakker (1993: 374–5, 385–6).
[75] König (1997: 348).
[76] Both Bakker (1993: 383) and Jehne (1996) seem to me to be too traditional in this respect, i.e. in accepting massive invading armies. Cf. below 179, 359.

into the political machinations of its day, and so return to Genialis'
intentions.[77] It is interesting that Genialis details the forces under his
command in April, and advertises that these were still at his disposal
in September: the altar was dedicated by him 'with the same army'
(*cum eodem exercitu*). This suggests that he saw himself as a significant participant in conflict between Gallienus and Postumus. By
giving Raetia and its army to Postumus he secured the usurper's
route into Italy and greatly increased his chance of success against
Gallienus. Once Postumus was emperor in Rome, Genialis might
expect generous reward. Such ambition is better suited to the year or
so following Valerian's capture, when Gallienus' failure to avenge this
disgrace or control the unrest that it occasioned seriously damaged
his reputation. The absence of iteration in Postumus' consulship has
to be set in the context of the irregular epigraphy of the period.
Because of this, the reconstruction of the consular *fasti* of the Gallic
Empire is generally very difficult and there is a case for dating the
consulships of the inscription and Genialis' defeat of the Iuthungi
later than 260, to 261 or 262.[78] I propose 261.

Thus the revolts on the Danube and barbarian incursions into Italy
and Gaul took place as previously thought, from mid-260. Postumus
then revolted and seemed likely to march on Rome. But he did not
do this immediately, which gave Genialis his first opportunity to fish
in troubled waters. Aware of the trouble in Gaul but for the moment
determined not to join in, he realized that a successful usurpation by
Postumus would seriously compromise maintenance of the Upper
German/Raetian *limes*. He therefore stripped it of its Raetian garrisons, and of such Upper German troops (*Germaniciani*) as he had
access to and who were willing to follow his orders (there are signs
that the army of Upper Germany was initially hostile to Postumus),
forming a composite force in which old unit names would have disappeared.[79] This was the first stage in considered Roman withdrawal

[77] Cf. Bakker (1993: 380), noting the delay, and having Genialis set up the altar to
demonstrate his loyalty to Postumus.

[78] See Jehne's citation of my argument, expressed in correspondence (1996: 187
and n.9). A later dating has also been independently proposed by Frei-Stolba and Lieb
(*AE* (1993) 1231: 354) and König (1997: 346–8, 352–3); cf. Watson (1999: 220).

[79] i.e. *contra* Nuber (1993: 102); cf. Jehne (1996: 204). Bakker (1993: 377, 383–4)
notes that Genialis did not record, and must therefore not have had access to, Leg. III
Italica of Regensburg, presumably earlier removed by Gallienus. Upper German
hostility: Okamura (1996: 15). Names: Witschel (1999: 212–13).

from the old frontier. Genialis reinforced his extraordinary command by calling up civilians (*populares*) and, in spring 261, defeated
the Iuthungi. These had entered Italy in 260, and had evaded Gallienus when he returned from the Danube and defeated the Alamanni
at Milan, wintering in the Alps. The victory was won in the name of
Gallienus. However, in late summer 261, with Gallienus' reputation
still deteriorating, Genialis turned kingmaker and declared for Postumus, calculating that this would encourage the usurper to move on
Italy. The Augsburg altar was hastily commissioned to advertise
Genialis' new loyalty. However, Postumus had by now established a
policy of remaining in the west. Genialis was left high and dry, and
fell to Gallienus in 261. Postumus' refusal to take responsibility for
Raetia was the second and final stage in the abandonment of the
Upper German/Raetian *limes* and its dependent territories west of
the Rhine and north of the Danube, driven by Roman military and
political strategy, not Alamannic pressure.[80]

As important for this study is the inscription's association
of Semnones and Iuthungi. The Semnones figure prominently in
Tacitus' description of the Suebi. We last hear of them late in the
second century, in passing, in an epitome of Cassius Dio's account of
Marcus Aurelius' dealings with the Quadi.[81] The Iuthungi appear
intermittently in third and fourth-century texts as enemies of the
Empire, alongside the Alamanni.[82] They disappear from view in
the middle years of the fifth century, following defeat at the hands
of the western Roman general, Aëtius. The crucial question is precisely who or what the Iuthungi were. Historians continue to accept
them as a 'tribe' or *gens*.[83] This practice derives from the ancient
ethnographical tradition, according to which a group-name was
taken to signify the existence of a people.[84] In the case of the Iuthungi,
it seems justified by the passage from Dexippus containing the earliest
literary reference to them. This (as it has come down to us, an isolated

---

[80] Cf. Jehne (1996: 204); Strobel (1998: 89).
[81] Dio 71.20.2.
[82] e.g. AM 17.6.1. For this, and what follows, see generally Castritius (1998: 354–5 and refs).
[83] e.g. Bakker (1993: 376); Jehne (1996: 190); König (1997: 349 citing Schmidt); Geuenich (1997a: 40); Strobel (1999: 17–18).
[84] Cf. Castritius (1998: 351).

passage: fragment 6) describes their conflict with Aurelian (270–5) and appears to record their own assertion of ethnic identity.

Aurelian, hunting down 'Iuthungian Goths' who had been making trouble for the Empire, confronted the survivors on the Danube. Their envoys attempted to talk their way out of trouble. Early in their address, they informed Aurelian that it was with only a very small part of their number that, at an unspecified date, they had attacked the cities on the Danube and occupied almost all of Italy.[85] They had fielded 40,000 cavalry, not 'mixed' or 'second-rate', but made up, as the phrase *Iouthoungōn katharōs* is often translated, of 'pure Iuthungi', skilled in mounted warfare.[86] This apparently very sharp distinction between pure Iuthungi and mixed others has been taken as the Iuthungian spokesmen's considered distancing of themselves from Agathias' 'mixed and heterogeneous' Alamanni.[87] On this basis, it has been proposed that the Iuthungi had managed to preserve 'their tribal identity more than other German groups'.[88] The impression of the Iuthungi as a 'tribe' appears to have been confirmed by the Augsburg inscription, which refers to Genealis' victory as being over 'barbarians of the tribe of the Semnones or Iouthungi' (*barbaros gentis Semnonum sive Iouthungorum*).

Discussion has tended to concentrate on the nature of the link between (ancient) Semnones and (new) Iuthungi: on the precise meaning of the conjunction *sive*/'or'. König treats *sive* as *sive potius*, translated 'oder vielmehr'/'or rather'.[89] He sees it as a statement by Genialis that the defeated barbarians consisted of both Semnones and Iuthungi, but that the latter were in the majority. Castritius observes that, if König were right, Genialis' inscription would have read *barbaros gentium* (plural) not *barbaros gentis* (singular).[90] It is probably better, with Bakker, Castritius and others, to treat *sive* as disjunctive and translate it as 'oder'/'beziehungsweise'/'that is to say'.[91]

[85] For further discussion of this issue, see below 74.

[86] F. Jacoby, *Die Fragmente der griechischen Historiker* 2A, no. 100, fr. 6.4: *kai toutōn ou migadōn oude asthenōn alla Iouthoungōn katharōs, hōn polus eph'hippomachiai logos*. Cf. Geuenich (1997a: 41: 'ein reines Volk').

[87] Below 63.

[88] Okamura (1984: 286). Cf. Wenskus (1961: 509); Geuenich (1997a: 41): a 'selbstbewußte(r) Volkstamm'.

[89] König (1997: 350).

[90] Castritius (1998: 364).

[91] Bakker (1993: 376); Castritius (1998: 351). Cf. Geuenich (2000: 141): 'genauer gesagt'.

Genialis explained that his victory was won over Semnones, also, or now, known as Iuthungi. The Augsburg inscription therefore establishes a direct link between Iuthungi and Semnones. This appears to confirm Müllenhoff's (nineteenth-century) hypothesis that the former were descended from the latter.[92] But argument does not stop here. Bakker takes 'that is to say' as indicating that the Iuthungi were the old Semnones under a different name. Castritius, aware of the tension between such an explanation and current thinking on ethnogenesis, adopted and developed Wenskus' tentative proposal that the Iuthungi were not a Suebian tribe but an offshoot of one. Their name, interpreted as *Nachkommen/Sprossen/*'descendants'/ 'offspring', makes them a breakaway group of young Semnonian warriors, a 'Jungmannschaft', which moved south-west in search of land and eventually settled on the imperial frontier. Here, their name, originally generic, became tribal.[93] However, the confirmation of nineteenth-century hypotheses and the easy attachment of old tribal labels to emerging third-century ethnic groups now appear somewhat dated.[94]

All hangs on how much weight one places on Genialis' linking of Semnones and Iuthungi. The tribal interpretation depends on the assumption that a contemporary statement must be wholly credible.[95] Genialis' complex description of his opponents hints that he was aware that he was communicating new intelligence; and

---

[92] Geuenich (1997a: 31, 39); (1997b: 75).

[93] Wenskus (1961: 509 n.533); Castritius (1998: 352, 355–6, 364). Cf. Geuenich (2000: 142, following Castritius): the name derives from 'new-born child', and the Iuthungi were a 'Jungmannschaft der altberühmten Semnonen'; similarly Neumann (2000); Pohl (2000: 104). It appears that Castritius has significantly revised his views, now (2000: 123–5) pointing out the difficulties in the concept of 'Jungmannschaft' in this respect and preferring to see the operation of the retinue: see below 60 and n.106.

[94] Cf. the remarks of Keller (1993: 85–6): warning against hunting for direct links between the Semnones and the Alamanni (made before the discovery of the Augsburg inscription but still, I feel, worthy of consideration). It is for these reasons, among others, that I am equally doubtful of Strobel's ((1996: 131–5), (1998: 86–7), (1999: 16–21); cf. above n.5, below n.101) argument. This is that in the Iuthungi we should see members of Semnonian war-bands who had moved south-eastwards, from the Elbe into (in modern terms) Bavaria and eastern Franconia, re-formed as a tribe under a label which, by proclaiming them to be 'the people of true descent', continued Semnonian claims of superiority among the Suebi.

[95] So Bakker (1993: 376).

Castritius must be right in suggesting that this came from the beaten enemy or an interested third party.[96] On the other hand, it is not necessarily true that everything that Genialis tells us here derived from the same source, in particular that the Iuthungi themselves claimed to be Semnones. What is suggestive is the order *Semnones sive Iouthungi*. Here, if Castritius' exegesis were correct, one might expect the reverse, *Iouthungi sive Semnones*. To the question 'Who are you/they?', one would expect the answer, 'We/they are Iuthungi, that is to say (i.e. but you will know us/them better as), Semnones.' It is revealing that Castritius himself, having begun with 'the equation Semnones–Iuthungi', concludes with 'the equation Iuthungi–Semnones'.[97] The phrase *Semnones sive Iouthungi* suggests rather that Genialis discovered that the force he confronted styled themselves simply, but for the first time in Roman experience, 'Iuthungi'. Baffled by this name, he introduced them as 'Semnones' in reporting his victory. In other words, Genialis or his staff drew upon their reading and inserted 'Semnones' to give substance to 'Iuthungi'. No social or anthropological significance should be attached to the association.[98] The Iuthungi may have had a relationship with the Semnones, but what this was we cannot say. All that we can really be certain of in the Augsburg inscription's 'Iuthungi' is that this is what one group of people called themselves in the rapidly changing conditions of the mid-third century. This returns us to the standard 'proof' of Iuthungian tribal feeling in the third century, in Dexippus. Assuming that we can put some trust in Dexippus' words, and not dismiss them as entirely rhetorical,[99] it is possible to interpret them differently.

---

[96] Castritius (1998: 350–1).

[97] Castritius (1998: 349, 362): 'die Gleichsetzung Semnonen-Juthungen ... die Gleichsetzung Juthungen-Semnonen'.

[98] For the literary substance and style of the Augsburg inscription see Strobel (1998: 85), (1999: 14). Bakker (1993: 376) and Castritius (1998: 349–50) explicitly reject the idea of scholarly reminiscence. Pohl (2000: 104) accepts the possibility, but concludes nevertheless that these Raetian Iuthungi were 'with some justification' ('mit einiger Berechtigung') perceived as being of Semnonian origin. However, see also Pohl (2000: 102) on the static representation of foreign peoples to be found in the sources.

[99] Cf. Castritius (1998: 353) and, more positively, Bleckmann (2002: 159); below 73.

Katharōs is better understood as referring, not to ethnicity, but to recruitment. The barbarian cavalry did not consist 'of pure Iuthungi', but 'purely of Iuthungi' (as Müller translates it, *ex Iuthungis pure*[100]). 'Iuthungi' is a mark of quality, of professionalism, indicating what, not who, the cavalrymen are. Whatever their ethnic background, they are all first-raters. Their efficiency has not been compromised by making them work with inferior horse-soldiers. Their envoys proceeded to make the same claim about their infantry, not weakened by 'mixture with others' (*tais heterōn epimixiais*).

What were Iuthungi, and how did they relate to Alamanni?[101] Genialis' Iuthungi were probably no more than raiders.[102] Like other Germanic raiding-bands, it is extremely unlikely that they were accompanied by large numbers of non-combatants. They were not coming from, travelling with or returning to an established Iuthungian 'tribe'.[103] The idea that central Germanic peoples were on the move at this time has been rejected in the case of the Alamanni, and must be similarly treated in that of the Iuthungi. The band was probably not very large, particularly if it was able to hide in imperial territory over winter and could be defeated by a scratch army. If it was a single party, it may have comprised only a few hundred warriors. Even if it was a temporary combination of two or three bands, it will have amounted to no more than about a couple of thousand men.[104] Likewise, the figure of 'thousands' of prisoners may well have been inflated by Roman boastfulness, the real number of those liberated being perhaps only in the high hundreds.[105] The disruption it caused will have been disproportionate to its own strength because it struck into regions that were not expecting

[100] Müller (1928: 632); cf. Bleckmann (2002: 158): 'ausschliesslich Juthungen'.

[101] As will be clear from what follows, I am equally (cf. above n.94) unhappy with Strobel's identification of Alamanni as a constituent of the Iuthungi—'all men': the totality of their fighting men, of their manhood in its prime. As Castritius (1998: 352) remarks, ethnic name changes, though not unknown, were not lightly undertaken, and to have three names in play in a relatively short period seems unlikely. Cf. below 64.

[102] Steuer (1998: 288).

[103] So Steuer (1998: 280) specifically criticizing such an interpretation of the Augsburg inscription.

[104] For such figures see Steuer (1997a: 150). Cf. below 331, 334: a band of 900.

[105] Cf. Jehne (1996: 188 n.18), on similar likely exaggeration of the scale of Gallienus' victory over the Alamanni at Milan.

barbarian attack. However, given that Iuthungi are mentioned by a contemporary in the context of events a decade or so later, one has to concede that, although they were not a 'tribe', there was something about the groups that made up mid-third-century Iuthungi which gave them slightly more of an identity than other Elbgermanic raiders. To explain this, and to make sense of Dexippus' Iuthungi, I offer what may be termed the 'Hell's Angels' version of the *comitatus/* retinue model. This suits Castritius' revised thinking which now inclines to place the retinue rather than the 'Jungmannschaft' at the start of Iuthungian development.[106]

I envisage groups of young warriors, each under a charismatic leader, proud of their skills and reputation and very discriminating as to those whom they allowed to join them. What they called themselves, and their tradition of high standards and exclusivity, were copied from the behaviour of a few (perhaps originally only one) such groups, the members of which had labelled themselves, or had been nicknamed, 'Iuthungi'—'Young Ones', 'Young Fighters'.[107] Each group usually operated independently of the rest, but all were aware of their common name and were prepared to act together if the opportunity presented itself. Though such joint undertakings may have resulted in significant concentrations of fighting men—10 bands each 600-strong would have produced a force larger than the traditional Roman legion—these would have come nowhere near the figures of tens of thousands found in the sources. Like other Elbgermanic raiders, from the early fourth century they settled near former imperial territory, probably up the Regnitz[108] (Fig. 4). Because they were in most respects indistinguishable from Alamanni to the west and south, in the fourth century they could be associated or confused with them: Ammianus Marcellinus calls them 'part of the Alamanni'.[109] Eventually, indeed, they merged, with 'Iuthungi' surviving as a description of a distant eastern Alamannic group. This process of integration reached completion after Aëtius' decisive defeat

---

[106] Castritius (2000).

[107] Cf. Wenskus (1961: 433, 509 n.533): 'Die Name...könnte gut *eine ursprüngliche* [my emphasis] Jungmannschaft bezeichnet haben, die sich aus dem suebischen Raum hinaus auf einen Landnahmezug begab'; Steuer (1998: 283).

[108] Below 99–100.

[109] AM 17.6.1: *Alamannorum pars*. Below 317.

of the Iuthungi in 430.[110] Overall, the Iuthungi must have been numerically much inferior to their neighbours. However, in the third century, though hardly a people, they were more 'ethnogenetically' advanced than Alamanni since their habit of flocking together under the same name and raiding into the same areas (Raetia and northern Italy) stimulated some degree of self-identity.

This brings us to the name 'Alamanni'. The question of its precise significance became less important with general acceptance of ethnogenesis *sur place*, not tribal migration, as the means by which 'the Alamanni' appeared between the upper stretches of the Rhine and the Danube.[111] However, the discovery of the Augsburg inscription has revived issues of tribal identity and re-opened debate on the derivation of the name 'Alamanni'.

There has always been agreement that 'Alamanni' is Germanic in form, being comprised of two words that bring to mind the English 'all men' and the German 'alle Männer'.[112] One view that has enjoyed wide currency is that 'Alamanni' means what it looks like: 'all men', that is people of widely differing origins. This derives from a statement by the sixth-century historian, Agathias, citing as his source the early-third-century historian, Asinius Quadratus, that the Alamanni were 'a mixed and heterogeneous people, as is shown by their very name'.[113] Such an interpretation fits well with the idea of ethnogenesis *sur place*. However, there are two difficulties. The first was encountered by those who believed that 'Alamanni' did not enter Greek and Latin until the later third century: if so, it could hardly have been known to Asinius Quadratus. The second is that 'Alamanni' has, based on analogous cases, always been accepted as a self-naming, an indispensable element in the evolution of self-identity—'das Wir-Bewußtsein'. 'Who are

---

[110] Geuenich (1998: 75). For their location see below 99–100.

[111] Above 43–5.

[112] Wenskus (1961: 510–11); Geuenich (1997a: 20), (1997b: 74).

[113] Agathias, *Hist.* 1.6.3 (=*Quellen* 2, 80): *xunēludes eisin anthrōpoi kai migades, kai touto dunatai autois hē eponumia*. The translation is that of Okamura (1984: 91). German versions include: 'zusammengelaufene und vermischte Leute'; 'zusammengewürfelte Verband von Menschen heterogener Herkunft'; 'ein zusammengewürfeltes Mischvolk'; 'zusammengespülte und vermengte Menschen'; 'zusammengelaufene und gemischte Männer': Stroheker (1975: 21–2); Keller (1993: 90–1); Geuenich (1997a: 20), (1997b: 74); Steuer (1998: 275).

you?' '*We* are the Alamanni!'[114] This makes the pejorative implication of 'mixed' (no ancient people liked to be called cross-bred) awkward to explain.[115]

Scholars circumvented the problem of Asinius Quadratus' early date by assuming that Agathias cited him incorrectly, attributing to him the knowledge and beliefs of a later age.[116] The problem of self-naming has been explained in two ways. The first, proposed by Wenskus, is that the negative interpretation of 'Alamanni' derived from a deformation of the name by Germanic neighbours.[117] Though insulting to Alamanni, it persisted because it was an accurate description of what they were. The second makes 'mixed' positive: the result as well as the origin of ethnogenesis. Steuer, for example, translates *xunēludes* as 'run together' ('zusammengelaufen'), like colours in the wash. This allows him to propose 'Alamanni' as a proud self-naming, denoting the existence of a new cosmopolitan 'warrior cooperative' ('Kriegergenossenschaft') and even eventually of 'a people under arms'.[118] Wenskus' argument is strong in its simplicity, and very easy to accommodate within the concept of ethnogenesis *sur place*.[119] It is currently the *communis opinio*. In other words, originally 'Alamanni' had a positive meaning, but came to indicate the mongrel origins of a new community comprising people from various backgrounds within the Elbgermanic world which grew up on former Roman provincial territory.[120]

There are, however, now new difficulties. Bleckmann has recently shown that Asinius Quadratus is a perfectly plausible authority for the existence of Alamanni in the first half of the third century.[121]

---

[114] e.g. Pohl (2000: 34); cf. Bleckmann (2002: 156).

[115] Wenskus (1961: 508–9); Rübekeil (1992: 218). The exception that proves the rule is, of course, that of the Romans.

[116] Cameron (1968: 126–7); Okamura (1984: 91–6); Keller (1993: 90); Strobel (1998: 87), (1999: 19).

[117] Wenskus (1961: 510–11).

[118] Steuer (1998: 275 nn.20–2). Cf. Wenskus (1961: 506) on 'Heerhaufen'.

[119] For completeness, it should be noted that Wenskus, believing that Caracalla encountered 'the Alamanni' in 213, located their ethnogenesis earlier than is now believed, and beyond the *limes*: see Pohl (2000: 103) and above 43–4.

[120] Geuenich (1997b: 74); Schach-Dörges (1997: 79); Steuer (1998: 275).

[121] Bleckmann (2002: 153–4): a contemporary of Herodian, he probably wrote his 'Millennial History' (*Chilieteris*) under Philip the Arab, though its account ends in the reign of Severus Alexander.

In addition, even before the publication of Bleckmann's article, acceptance of a later defamation of the Alamanni left unresolved the question of the meaning of the original self-naming. It has been in this respect that the discovery of the Augsburg inscription has re-opened the question of ethnic awareness.

Some scholars now want to make the original term 'Alamanni' ethnic, reflecting the transmission of a distinctly Semnonian 'core of tradition'.[122] Thus, according to Castritius, 'Alamanni' derives from 'Mannus', an ancient Germanic deity who was the divine prime man, the founder of the Germanic race. Mannus was central to the Elbgermanic tradition as the god described by Tacitus as being worshipped at the Suebian cult-centre in the territory of the Semnones. As a new western Elbgermanic grouping came into being, it expressed its common identity by adopting a name that referred to a core element of its Suebian/Semnonian heritage, its special relationship to Mannus. The 'al' prefix of 'Alamanni' was exclusive, not inclusive. 'Alamanni' signifies 'Mannus' own people', created directly by him: the 'full' or 'complete' men, in contrast to deficient others. 'Alamanni' may, indeed, have been an old generic for Suebi or Semnones, now re-deployed in different circumstances.[123] Ethnic links between Alamanni, Semnones and Iuthungi also form the basis of Strobel's recent reinterpretation of the name.[124] Strobel proposes that in the Iuthungi we should see members of Semnonian war-bands which had moved south-eastwards from the Elbe into modern Bavaria and eastern Franconia. There, in the upper Main–Regnitz region, they re-formed as a tribe under the name of 'Iuthungi'. This, meaning 'the people of true descent', was a proclamation of continued Semnonian superiority among the Suebi. An important constituent of the Iuthungi were the Alamanni, 'all men': the totality of their fighting strength, their manhood in its prime. The Romans, dealing for the most part with Iuthungian warriors, frequently encountered the term and eventually used it in preference to Iuthungi, calling almost all Suebian groups over the upper Rhine

---

[122] Above 45.

[123] Tacitus, *Germania* 2.3–4; 39. Castritius (1998: 357, 359–61) developing Wenskus (1961: 502), followed by Bleckmann (2002: 156); cf. also Rübekeil (1992: 227–9); Pohl (2000: 105) *contra*.

[124] Strobel (1996: 131–5), (1998: 86–7), (1999: 16–21). Above nn.94, 101.

and upper Danube 'Alamanni'. The exception was those in the upper Main–Regnitz region, who remained known as Iuthungi. Writers of the fourth century and later erroneously simplified matters by categorizing all Elbgermanic attacks of the third century as 'Alamannic'.

This is not the place to go into such arguments in detail.[125] The key issue remains the 'Semnones–Iuthungi equation'.[126] There can be no certainty. If the equation is authentic, and Semnonian identity survived the centuries, then ancient national and tribal affiliations were important in Elbgermanic society in the third century and beyond. If the equation is a Roman invention, and, in the general flux of the third century, Germanic social and political groupings underwent dissolution and re-formation, then, while allowing that there must

[125] Though I have to say that, although I adopt elements of Strobel's thinking below, I am not convinced by his basic explanation of the relationship between Iuthungi and Alamanni. Though it allows for the absorption of people from other communities into the warrior-bands (1996: 132), its envisaged movement of a significant number of Semnones from the Elbe to the south-west, maintaining a strong ethnic identity, appears too much like 'Völkerwanderung'. Next, Strobel is unclear as to when and where Iuthungian identity was created and maintained. He has Iuthungi making their presence felt on the middle Rhine very early, citing the Cologne inscription *Matribus Suebis* [I] *euthungabus* (*CIL* 13.8225=*ILS* 4791), dateable to the late second or early third century. However, he also has them re-forming as a tribe on the upper Main and in the Regnitz region, presumably just before they attacked the Empire, causing the surprise evident in the Augsburg inscription. Even more awkward is why Rome should have preferred 'Alamanni' over 'Iuthungi' as a name for these and related peoples. If Roman officials knew at the latest from around 260 (1998: n. 11) that the principal Elbe-*Germani* attacking the Empire were 'Iuthungi', and this had already spread to educated circles (i.e. to the drafter of the Augsburg inscription, and to Dexippus), why did they not retain the name, and apply it generally to the people involved and the area they were coming from (cf. below 69)? Furthermore, since, as Strobel rightly emphasizes, the Upper German–Raetian *limes* did not fall to Germanic onslaught in 259/60, in what circumstances did the Empire come into contact with the Iuthungian Elbgermanic *levée en masse* in which the members of the individual war-bands termed themselves, in Strobel's terms, 'Allmanner'? In addition, we can now see that the name 'Alamanni', as referring to a significant group of people, was certainly not as new as Strobel implies. Everything we know points to the fact that, in the third century, Alamanni and Iuthungi, though related, were still distinguishable from each other—just as they are described in 297 (*Pan. Lat.* 4(8).10.4). Finally, it should be noted that the archaeologist whose work was the inspiration for Strobel's thinking is at pains to distinguish between Alamanni and Iuthungi, and, though allowing them links with the Semnones, stresses the novelty of the emergence of the Iuthungi in the 'crucible' of the Upper Main: Haberstroh (2000a: 128).

[126] Above 60.

have been some general Elbgermanic/'Suebic' affiliation between Semnones, Alamanni and Iuthungi, one must seek the origin of 'Alamanni' beyond this circle. I believe that the Augsburg equation was a Roman construct, and that a distinct Semnonian identity did not survive into the third century.[127]

The original Alamanni comprised mixed bands of Elbgermanic raiders. Pursuing the virile military connotations suggested by Steuer, Castritius and Strobel, I propose that in the early Germanic phrase 'all men', 'all' was similar in meaning to the 'all' in the modern English phrase 'all man'. 'Alamanni' denotes its bearers' claim to all the manly virtues, to be warriors *par excellence*: like 'Iuthungi', a generic, not an ethnic.[128] Among the Elbgermanic warrior-bands that, from around 200, began raiding westwards was one which called itself 'Alamanni'—'he-men'. Its success encouraged others to adopt its name, but the spread of 'Alamanni' allowed their many Germanic victims to twist the meaning of the title to sneer at those who bore it as 'mongrels'. By 260, 'Alamanni' was being applied indiscriminately by those attacked to any band of attackers, whatever these called themselves. In response, more discriminating groups of warriors sought to distinguish themselves from their predecessors by referring to themselves as 'Young Ones', 'Iuthungi'.

This returns us to Asinius Quadratus. Since Asinius was writing around 30 years after Rome's first known encounter with Alamanni, and allowing time for these to come into existence and for the Empire to notice them, the de-formation of the meaning of their name will have occurred between, say, 200 and 240, that is relatively quickly.[129] Bleckmann suggests that the slight was the work of proud Semnonian Iuthungi, who wanted to draw attention to the non-exclusive, increasingly non-Semnonian, composition of Alamanni.[130] This is unconvincing because it is unlikely that 'Iuthungi' or 'Alamanni' were ethnic labels, and because it makes the Iuthungi appear too early. The Romans' first introduction to the name Alamanni is much more likely to have been through so-called

[127] Ibid.
[128] Above 62.
[129] Cf. Bleckmann (2002: 156 n.40): against Castritius' view that 'Alamanni' may have been a very old name.
[130] Bleckmann (2002: 158–60).

Rhine–Weser *Germani* in the Tauber/Upper-Main–Regnitz areas.[131]
Generally cooperative with Rome, these must have been more
affected by early Elbgermanic raiding than the Empire, and so had
every reason to resent their tormentors. The derogatory interpretation of 'Alamanni' could have been picked up by Asinius Quadratus
from Roman troops who participated in Caracalla's campaign.

Indeed, we should never forget the existence of an interested and
powerful third party. There is now strong acceptance of Wenskus'
view that 'Alamanni' and 'Alamannia' were far more useful to the
Romans, who needed to classify their neighbours on an imperial
scale, than to the people to which they were attached, who, in their
everyday lives, would have seen themselves more as members of small
communities.[132] This raises the question as to whether the name,
though Germanic in form and origin, was wholly Germanic in
the manner in which it was deployed. 'Alamanni' and 'Alamannia'
come from imperial sources: again, we have no idea what the south-
western Elbe-*Germani* called themselves in the third century.[133] In
such circumstances, a single name could have been taken up and
manipulated by the one people that needed to come to terms with
the new phenomenon—the Romans.[134]

There was an important precedent. Much earlier, the Romans had
hit upon the name *Germani* as a useful catch-all for those living over
the Rhine.[135] Three centuries on, from 261/2, imperial officials
would have needed a convenient term for territories now occupied,
under sufferance, by outsiders. 'Former Upper Germany and Former
Raetia' would have been a mouthful, and an unwelcome reminder of
Roman withdrawal. 'Marcomanni' and 'Marcomannia' had long
been in existence to act as models.[136] It would have required no
more than an awareness of the existence of 'Alamanni', of the insulting interpretation of this name by Germanic neighbours, and a

[131] Frank (1997); Schach-Dörges (1997: 95–7 and Fig. 81).

[132] Wenskus (1961: 502); Geuenich (1997a: 19), (1997c: 144); Hummer (1998: 16);
Steuer (1998: 276); Pohl (2000: 103).

[133] Above 4.

[134] Cf. Gillett (2002b: 120) on the role of 'Roman labelling' in the case of Goths,
Vandals and Franks.

[135] Pohl (2000: 3–4, 50–6).

[136] Cf. Okamura (1984: 287): third-century Italians erroneously applied the name
Marcomanni to early Alamanni.

rudimentary knowledge of early German on the part of a Roman on the Rhine/upper Danube frontier to come up with 'Alamannia' as a disparaging but accurate description of the lost lands. The most likely place for this would have been on the Rhine, well away from the less numerous but more distinctive Iuthungi; otherwise, instead of 'Alamannia', we might have had 'Iuthungia'.[137] 'What is that? Where are we/they being sent?' 'That is we/they are being ordered to, Alamannia, rabble-land' (the haunt of many war-bands, not just those of 'authentic' Alamanni).[138] 'Who are they?' 'They—all those between the upper Rhine and upper Danube[139]—are the Alamanni, the rabble,' would have followed immediately after.

Like *Francicus* ('Conqueror of the Franks'), *Alamannicus* ('Conqueror of the Alamanni') took some time to appear as an imperial title alongside the established *Germanicus*. The first known bearer of *Alamannicus* is Constantine II, no earlier than 331.[140] A little later, in 354, when according to a carefully worded and detailed inscription it was taken by Constantius II, it was glossed as *Germanicus*.[141] This must reflect the Roman establishment's continuing reluctance to adopt neologisms and especially, in this case, those derived from military vocabulary. As Elton notes, until the fifth century, barbarian tribal names were used by Rome to indicate where her enemies came from, not precisely who they were, and to clarify and enhance victories over relatively small groupings.[142] Until the fourth decade of the fourth century, emperors and their advisers may have felt that in most cases this task was fulfilled perfectly adequately by *Germani/Germanicus*.[143]

---

[137] Cf. above n.125.

[138] For the early imperial shift of emphasis from peoples to the lands they occupied (in line with classical ethnography: Amory (1997: 18)), see Burns (2003: 178–9).

[139] Below 83, 125.

[140] *CIL* 3.352=7000; *ILS* 6091; *MAMA* 7.305; *Quellen* 6, Inscriptions no. 61. *Francicus* appears first in 361: below 252.

[141] *Germanicus Alamamnicus* (sic) *Maximus, Germ. Max.* etc. (note the repetition of *Germanicus*). *CIL* 3.3705; *ILS* 732; *Quellen* 6, Inscriptions no. 64. Cf. Zotz (1998: 390) and Bleckmann (2002: 168 and n. 94) on the odd mixing of titles.

[142] Elton (1996a: 37).

[143] See Bleckmann (2002: 167–9, esp. 167–8) on the likely politico-dynastic reasons for the innovation: Constantine I wanted to honour Constantine II, but to reserve *Germanicus* to himself. Cf. below 198–9.

In the period 261/2, therefore, as the result of the partition of
the western Roman Empire between Postumus and Gallienus, the
Upper German/Raetian *limes* was abandoned.[144] Elbgermanic warrior-bands were able to move into former imperial land east of the
Rhine and north of the Danube and were tempted to cross these
rivers and plunder Gaul and Italy. During the next decade or so such
raiding was a chronic problem. For the most part it must have been
on a relatively small scale, but when conditions were favourable
(usually due to imperial political strife), such groups could amal-
gamate and undertake more daring attacks. Though probably not
involving huge numbers of warriors, these could, thanks to the
availability of the imperial road network and the lack of defences in
the interior, be wide-ranging and must have caused great panic.[145]
Literary sources tell of a Frankish incursion deep into Spain.[146]
Archaeological evidence for Alamannic attacks into Gaul, one at
least of which reached southern Aquitania, is provided by finds of
Roman metalware at Hagenbach and Neupotz, near Speyer. These are
interpreted as booty lost by raiders while attempting to cross the
Rhine.[147]

In the military and political chaos which followed the capture of
Valerian, two large groups made their way into Italy, one through
Gaul and the other by way of Raetia.[148] Neither was a 'tribe' or even
an 'army'. Those who took the Raetian route appear to have called
themselves Iuthungi. Later generations called the others Alamanni.
Unorganized and disorganized, both groups would have faced difficulties arising out of success. With no commissariat and carrying
quantities of booty, both inanimate and animate, they were vulnerable to counter-attack.[149] Probably, as was to happen again in 268
and 271, neither went far into the peninsula.[150] Few probably got

[144] Cf. Witschel (1999: 248 n.56), though, at 211–12, he sees the process as
gradual, taking from 260 to 265.

[145] Witschel (1999: 205, cf. 214–15).

[146] Above 52.

[147] Hiernard (1997); Nuber (1997: 64 and Figs 42–3); Carroll (2001: 138 and
plate 23).

[148] i.e. following Jehne (1996: 189–92, 196–201), though with a revised chronology: cf. above 54–5.

[149] Okamura (1984: 273, 289).

[150] Below 71, 76.

beyond the Po valley. Zosimus' report of the Senate's raising a militia to defend Rome suggests reaction to panic rather than to assault.[151] There is no sign of serious fighting near the city, and it is likely that the main body of attackers began to withdraw irrespective of any challenge from this quarter. Gallienus returned from putting down usurpation on the Danube to deal with the Alamanni at Milan. Imperial propaganda made this a major set-piece battle, with 10,000 Romans supposedly overcoming 300,000 barbarians.[152] As Okamura observes, such figures are 'impossibly high'. The Alamanni who fell to Gallienus probably amounted to no more than several thousand. Given the fissile nature of their alliance, a similar number probably simply avoided battle and fled homewards.[153] This is probably what also happened with the Iuthungi: evading the imperial forces, they dispersed and headed north. One group was caught and destroyed the following year by Genialis.

The next major incursion involving Alamanni that we know of began in 268. This again occurred in strained political circumstances, following the assassination of Gallienus and his replacement by Claudius II. There was a battle near Lake Garda, fought probably in 269.[154] Claudius may have left its direction to one of his generals, possibly Aurelian.[155] The eastern location of the conflict suggests Iuthungian involvement.[156] However, this is unlikely since Dexippus does not make Aurelian refer to this battle when he reminds the Iuthungi of recent Roman successes at the start of his reign.[157] Claudius did not last long as emperor. He died of disease late in the summer of 270 and his death was, as usual for the time, followed by civil war. His brother, Quintillus, succeeded him but was soon challenged by his senior general, Aurelian, and quickly overthrown. Aurelian was emperor by the end of 270. The reign of Aurelian returns us to the fragment from Dexippus recording this emperor's dealings with the Iuthungi.

---

[151] Zosimus 1.37.2. Cf. Jehne (1996: 190–1): those who threatened Rome were Iuthungi. On the basic reliability of Zosimus' report see Bleckmann (2002: 166).

[152] Zonaras 12.24. See now Bleckmann (2002: 164).

[153] Cf. Okamura (1984: 273): 'Gallienus ... intercepted one large group ....'

[154] *Epitome* 34.2. Okamura (1984: 275–6); Watson (1999: 43).

[155] Watson (1999: 43).

[156] Okamura (1984: 283); Watson (1999: 220).

[157] Below 74.

The chronology, location, course and even number of Aurelian's barbarian wars are very difficult to reconstruct from the available sources, which are obscure and, in the case of the *Historia Augusta*'s 'Life' of Aurelian, suspect. The question of his Iuthungian wars has recently been reviewed by Saunders and Watson.[158] Both note that pioneering scholarship had Aurelian wage two Iuthungian wars, for the first of which Dexippus' fragment 6 was regarded as sole evidence.[159] However, the *communis opinio* of the last 60 years or so has been that there was only one such conflict, of which Dexippus' fragment 6 describes the final stage, on the Danube.[160] But modern thinking appears to be returning to the older version of events, either in its traditional form (Saunders) or with modifications (Watson). Watson proposes that one Iuthungian invasion, undertaken jointly with Alamanni, took place under Claudius II and was defeated by the emperor and Aurelian on Lake Garda in 269. It was this war, and the defeat they suffered while working with Alamanni, that later produced the Iuthungian ambassadors' deprecating assessment of the value of 'mixed' forces. Watson's second, far more serious, incursion happened under Aurelian, in 271, while the emperor was absent fighting Vandals in Pannonia. The Iuthungi invaded alone, through Raetia and into Italy. Dexippus' fragment 6 describes events in the middle of the war, which occurred on the Metaurus not the Danube. In support of his interpretation of the 271 invasion, Watson adduces the Augsburg inscription. He dates the events it describes to 261, and uses the fact of a Iuthungian invasion of Italy in this year to argue that the Iuthungi were capable of mounting a second major attack on Italy in 271.

Problems arise as to how much credence can be given to Dexippus' account of the encounter. Fragment 6 consists for the most part of two speeches (one Iuthungian, one Roman) and therefore inevitably falls under the suspicion of having resulted more from Dexippus' Thucydidean reconstruction of what ought to have been said in the circumstances than from what was actually spoken. In this respect, it has to be conceded that Aurelian's response to the Iuthungi, though

---

[158] Saunders (1992); Watson (1999: 216–20 (with 43, 50–2)).

[159] See, e.g. Homo (1904: 61–4, 73–6).

[160] See, e.g. Alföldi (1939: 156–7).

much longer than their speech, is far less substantial. It is just a reaction to the points they raise, heavily rhetorical and couched in terms of the usual Roman disparagement of barbarian impudence and unreliability. It has to be used with great caution. Elsewhere, on the other hand, rich circumstantial detail offers hope of some degree of authenticity. For example, Dexippus' account of Aurelian's theatrical staging of the meeting rings true. In other respects, such as the walling of Rome, his great triumph and his building of a magnificent temple to the Sun, Aurelian demonstrated a keen understanding of the power of display.[161]

As far as the speeches are concerned, the Iuthungian envoys' insistence on the distinction between the people they represented and other Germanic raiders, however interpreted, and its apparent acceptance by the imperial authorities, also rings true. Likewise, the envoys' recollection of recent cash payments from the Empire and their claim that the renewal of these subsidies would bring about a mutually beneficial peace (6.5, 7) appear to be more than rhetoric. These points are substantial and unexpected, give the Iuthungi remarkable courage in dealing with Aurelian, and excite the emperor's most barbed comments. It was probably because of them that the passage was excerpted from Dexippus' *Scythica* for inclusion in a tenth-century compilation of extracts 'On foreign embassies to the Romans' (*De legationibus gentium ad Romanos*).[162] In addition, the possibility of discrete groups of Elbgermanic warriors serving in third-century imperial forces has been strengthened by finds of Roman artefacts and gold coins in rich burials in Thuringia (the so-called Haßleben–Leuna grave-group, from type-sites near Erfurt). These have been interpreted as indicating payment by Postumus and his successors to leaders of war-bands.[163] Other groups could have agreed to serve the Central Empire. The Iuthungian claim therefore

---

[161] Cf. Watson (1999: 176–7).

[162] Saunders (1992: 320).

[163] Drinkwater (1987: 225), from Werner (1973); Steuer (1997a: 150–1), (1998: 290–1). See also Martin-Kilcher (1993), concerning the rich burial of a Germanic officer in Cologne *c.*300, and others elsewhere along the Rhine and Danube, which she associates with the Haßleben-Leuna graves; likewise Pirling (1993: 109), for 'Frankish' graves at the fort at Gellep, between Cologne and Xanten, from the third century. Cf. below 145.

deserves to be examined closely; but first it must be set within a precise chronological and historical context.

The events described in fragment 6 must come relatively early in Aurelian's reign. This derives from what Aurelian is made to say to the Iuthungi. The emperor makes no allusion to any earlier victory of his over Iuthungi. As recent examples of the success of Roman efficiency over barbarian brute strength, he cites only defeats suffered by 'Scythians' and 'Galmionoi'(?) (6.11: the text appears corrupt). I follow Saunders in interpreting these as victories against Goths and Alamanni won by Claudius II.[164] I also follow Saunders in placing Aurelian's first brush with the Iuthungi as emperor before his war with the Vandals (as described in fragment 7), and so accept that at the start of Aurelian's reign there were two Iuthungian 'wars', the second of which followed the Vandal campaign.[165] Inverted commas are important here. In assessing the strength of Alamanni and Iuthungi, one must establish what is meant by 'war': full-scale invasion or a series of irritating raids? Taking seriously the idea of some earlier alliance with the Empire, I propose that the state of hostility described in fragment 6 was not a major attack on Italy. The Iuthungi refer to destructive incursions into Raetia and deep into Italy as a boast and as a threat, but not as their current activity. In other words, contrary to the usual interpretation, they should not be seen as claiming that they had just penetrated Italy with 40,000 first-class cavalrymen, but rather that this is what they had achieved on a previous occasion.[166] Their point is not that they currently dispose of such men. On the contrary, at 6.6–7, they concede the weakness of their position: having divided their strength and having been defeated in a major battle they now face a larger force confident of victory. Rather, the large numbers that they throw about represent the avenging force that Aurelian will bring down on himself if he destroys them. Such numbers are, of course, grossly inflated.[167] Much of this may have been put into the Iuthungian envoys' mouths by Dexippus to explain the apparent effrontery that follows.

[164] Saunders (1992: 322–3).
[165] *Contra* Watson (1999: 320–1), I accept Saunders' argument that fragments 6 and 7 are probably in chronological order and should not be transposed.
[166] e.g. Okamura (1984: 297); Saunders (1992: 311, 327); Watson (1999: 51, 218).
[167] So Saunders (1992: 324 n. 64).

Here we have the substance of what was said. What was really happening is to be found in the envoys' justification of their recent actions. These, they say, did not amount to raiding, but to foraging. This they regarded as legitimate: they were not aware that they were acting wrongly until they found themselves attacked by Aurelian (6.5). What they say suggests movement into Raetia and just over the provincial border into Italia Transpadana, but no further. It appears that the imperial government had earlier come to terms with the Iuthungi after a major incursion by them into Italy, agreeing to pay them to keep the peace and to act as allies if called upon. This agreement had been kept, until payments were ended by the Romans, without consulting the Iuthungi, who then simply helped themselves. For the Iuthungi to get used to such subsidies, the major invasion and consequent agreement must have come much earlier. I propose that this incursion was that of 260. An agreement with Iuthungi who had escaped Roman retribution was made by Gallienus, who is known to have favoured such arrangements.[168] This was maintained by Claudius but collapsed in the turmoil following his death in 270.[169] Aurelian probably dealt with the ensuing trouble immediately on coming to power, that is without first going to Rome.[170] This need not have taken long, since disturbance was confined to Raetia. Indeed, if, as subsequently happened in the case of the Vandals, Iuthungian cavalry had been recruited directly into Roman service, some of the unrest described in fragment 6 may have begun on imperial soil. In other words, if the cessation in the supply of money affected pay, not subsidies, what occurred may have been more in the nature of a mutiny than an attack.

---

[168] Aurelius Victor, *Caesares* 33.6; *Epitome* 33.1; Zosimus 1.30.2f. Cf. Witschel (1999: 218 and n.195).

[169] Cf. Okamura (1984: 297): Gallienus or Claudius. Castritius (1998: 353, 356 n.28), following A. Radnóti ((1967), *Die germanischen Verbündeten der Römer* (Deutsch–Italienische Vereinigung Heft 3), Frankfurt/Main: 1–20) and the implications of the Augsburg inscription, suggests that the Iuthungian claim to a Roman alliance was based on an understanding with Postumus and his successors as 'Gallic' emperors, i.e. that the Iuthungi may be equated with the Haßleben-Leuna warriors (above 73). I consider this unlikely, but since I have not been able to obtain a copy of Radnóti's publication I cannot be certain in this respect.

[170] Cf. Saunders (1992: 319): from Sirmium.

Having dealt with the Iuthungi, and established his own position, Aurelian moved to Pannonia to face raiding Vandals. As Saunders says, the statement in Dexippus' fragment 7.4, that he had to interrupt this campaign to return to Italy because the Iuthungi were attacking 'again', marks the beginning of the second 'war'. However, this, too, may have been no major conflict. The sole trustworthy account says simply that Aurelian was victorious in three battles in Italy, at Piacenza, on the river Metaurus just beyond Fanum Fortunae, and finally near Pavia.[171] Such an itinerary is odd, involving an engagement on the upper Po, a dash south-eastwards along the Via Aemilia and Via Flaminia down to the Umbrian coast, and another chase back along the same roads to a final confrontation just west of the site of the first engagement. Even if Aurelian had won the initial battle at Piacenza he had not won the war. News of barbarians heading south, albeit still on the northern side of the Apennines, must have shaken the peninsula, and may have caused a wave of opposition to Aurelian in Rome.[172] The highly imaginative writer of the *Historia Augusta* developed this series of events to produce an exciting but confused tale of Roman defeat, despair and final victory.[173] This reconstruction has been developed and reinforced by those who take Dexippus' fragment 6 as evidence for a massive contemporary Iuthungian invasion of Italy and locate its events in the course of a single great 'Iuthungian war'.

The evidence of the *Historia Augusta* is best ignored. Aurelian's swift movement from north to south and back again may be interpreted as his having to deal with relatively small bands of highly mobile opponents—troops of horsemen—able to do a fair degree of damage and difficult to bring decisively to battle.[174] On the other hand, the fact that the Iuthungi were unable to cross the Apennines to the south or take a route other than the one they had come in by to the north hints that Aurelian had the overall situation under control.

---

[171] *Epitome* 35.2: *Iste in Italia tribus proeliis victor fuit, apud Placentiam, iuxta amnem Metaurum ac fanum Fortunae, postremo Ticinensibus campis.*

[172] Zosimus 1.49.2; Saunders (1992: 319).

[173] *Historia Augusta*, *V. Aureliani* 18.3–21.4. Cf. Saunders (1992: 314): that the *Historia Augusta* author 'extensively reworked' his material at this point (though without accusing him of outright fraud).

[174] Cf. Okamura (1984: 290).

It seems that, as a demonstration of firmness at the start of his reign and as a punishment for making trouble, he kept to the threat that he would not renew earlier agreements which he had made to the Iuthungi on his first confrontation with them; and this was still causing unrest. The wider Alamanni were not involved. Zosimus' statement that in the second war Aurelian faced 'the Alamanni and their neighbours' and defeated them decisively on the Danube appears to derive from ignorance and carelessness: specifically, the common confusion between Alamanni and Iuthungi and the transposing of events of the first war to the second.[175] Much the same may be said of Aurelius Victor's laconic observation that Aurelian returned to Italy to deal with raiding Alamanni after campaigns against Palmyra and Persia and before his defeat of Tetricus in Gaul, in which events of 271 are transferred to 273.[176] It is likely that, following his victory at Pavia, Aurelian moved directly to deal with the troubled situation in Rome.[177]

The threat posed to Italy by Elbgermanic peoples was small. By Aurelian's reign the Alamanni had ceased their raiding and the harm done by the Iuthungi was relatively minor and confined to the north. After Aurelian's victories, the peninsula suffered no further barbarian incursions until the early fifth century. This security resulted from the dedication and skill of individual emperors, and from the enormous underlying strength of the Roman Empire.[178] However, it is also a measure of the nature of the Germanic menace. The raiders were not migrating tribesmen but bands of young warriors exploiting current Roman weaknesses to win fame and booty: not 'the Alamanni' or 'the Iuthungi' but 'Alamanni' and 'Iuthungi'. In chaotic conditions they enjoyed success but against coordinated Roman resistance they were helpless. That Aurelian regarded his Iuthungian victories as small beer may be reflected in the fact that though he took the title *Germanicus*—'Conqueror of the Germans'—he did not advertise it widely on his coinage.[179] However, such diffidence may also be interpreted as embarrassment. Though Alamanni and

---

175 Zosimus 1.49.1; cf. Saunders (1992: 318).
176 Aurelius Victor, *Caesares* 35.1–3; cf. Dufraigne (1975: 169–70).
177 Watson (1999: 218–19).
178 Drinkwater (2005: 62–3).
179 Okamura (1984: 300).

Iuthungi never posed a threat to Italy, it is certain that they were perceived as having done so. Anti-Germanic prejudice, the *terror teutonicus* and *terror germanicus*, had been burned into the Roman soul by the Cimbric invasion and the Varian disaster. Marcus Aurelius' Marcomannic Wars will have confirmed such feelings; and the incursions of 260, 268/9 and 270/1 must have touched a raw nerve. Aurelian's re-walling of the city of Rome, begun immediately after the second Iuthungian conflict and arguably the greatest monument to the uncertainty of the third-century 'Crisis',[180] may be seen as a political more than a tactical move. It resulted from Aurelian's recognition that he needed to be seen to be doing something, especially in order to distinguish his regime from that of the supposedly negligent Gallienus, who had also allowed Germanic raiders onto Italian soil. His Roman walls were imposing but, in military terms, superfluous and flawed in design.[181] However, they were useful in projecting the image of Aurelian as a man of action; and they continued to remind people, wrongly, of the danger from the north.

Although there was, as far as we know, no further Alamannic or Iuthungian raiding into Italy in the third century, there were still incursions into Raetia and Gaul. Since 260 Gaul had been protected from both Alamannic and Frankish depredations by the attention of Postumus and his successors as Gallic emperors, Victorinus and Tetricus, all based in the Rhine/Moselle area. This privileged position was lost in 274 when Aurelian overthrew Tetricus; and the situation was made worse by the severity with which Aurelian re-imposed imperial authority and by the uncertainty that followed his assassination in 275.[182] Franks and Alamanni raided over the Rhine.[183] Their direct effect was probably overestimated by ancient writers.[184] However, there was undoubtedly looting and slaughter throughout the Gallic provinces. The finds at Hagenbach and Neupotz have already been noted.[185] In addition, at least 13 inhabitants of the villa at

---

[180] Watson (1999: 143): 'the most emblematic and the most enduring monument of Aurelian's age.'

[181] See Watson (1999: 150–1), on the weaknesses of the original Aurelianic circuit.

[182] Okamura (1984: 304); Drinkwater (1987: 44, 202); Witschel (1999: 217–18, 229).

[183] Grünewald and Seibel (2003: xii–xiii).

[184] Okamura (1984: 304–9).

[185] Above 70.

Regensburg-Harting were brutally killed and their bodies dismembered, partially scalped and dumped into two wells. Likewise, remains of a late-middle-aged man and a teenage girl, both of whom had suffered burning and dog-bites, were found in a well at the villa of Mundelsheim.[186] As earlier in Italy, the perceived danger will have been very great, causing panic and, in some regions, with the appearance of indigenous rural rebels, the 'Bagaudae', social disruption.[187] After the short reigns of Tacitus and Florianus (275–6), the situation was taken in hand by Probus (276–82). He campaigned in the west in 277 and 278, apparently giving his personal attention to the area over the Upper and High Rhine and the upper Danube, that is precisely where Alamanni and Iuthungi were to be found, though Zosimus, in a very muddled section, in this respect mentions only Vandals and Burgundians.[188] Significant raiding into Gaul, and the disruption that this caused there, ended under Probus' successors, Carus and Carinus (282–5) and Diocletian and Maximian (as 'dyarchs', 285–96). Though there were still some barbarian incursions, these do not appear to have been serious, and some may even have been exaggerated to enhance the reputation of the ruler who dealt with them.[189]

The absence of any attempt to reconquer the lands lost between the Rhine and Danube and the old Upper German/Raetian *limes* at this time should not be seen as the measure of a prevailing Germanic 'threat'. The Empire had other concerns, and the new line of demarcation worked well enough—to the extent that it was being fixed in a line of fortifications.[190] Inertia had set in. As from the early first century, the area could serve as a useful source of external 'danger' and military glory.

---

[186] Wahl, Wittwer-Backofen, and Kunter (1997: 345–6); Witschel (1999: 104, 106 and n.26); Schröter (2000: 180–1); Carroll (2001: 138).

[187] For the Bagaudae, see Drinkwater (1984: 363–8).

[188] Zosimus 1.67, 1.68.1; Paschoud (1971: 173–5); Okamura (1984: 313). Cf. below 108.

[189] Okamura (1984: 321, 325, 333); below 181.

[190] Below 192.

3

Settlement

There is very little evidence for Germanic settlement over the Upper German/Raetian *limes* before about 300. However, this could be an artefact of archaeology, perhaps due to frequent changes of simple settlements, the wooden structures of which are invisible to current techniques of surveying and excavation.[1] Where early settlement affected Roman masonry buildings, as at the Wurmlingen villa, it can be detected.[2] We may therefore presume some early activity of this type, if only to explain what followed.[3] But what were its mechanisms?

In the first instance, war-bands raiding into and through former provincial territory would have had little inclination to settle. Their warriors were accustomed to returning home, and are unlikely to have had the wish or the expertise to turn to farming. As settlers, they would also have been open to attack by the Empire and by other bands. On the other hand, continued success and the difficulties involved in carrying booty and prisoners over long distances would have encouraged them to put down roots further west. Just beyond the mouth of the 'invasion-funnel' into the Rhine–Danube re-entrant, to the west of early Elbgermanic settlement around Bamberg,[4] there are signs of later-third-century Elbgermanic settlement down the Main, around Würzburg[5] (Fig. 4). Further into the funnel, conditions would have been more difficult. Here, the 'invasion-corridor'

[1] Geuenich (1997b: 76).
[2] Fingerlin (1997b: 127–30); and below 86.
[3] Cf. Schach-Dörges (1997: 96): to the early fourth century, Alamannic settlement was slow, but not non-existent.
[4] Above 48–9.
[5] Steidl (2002: 108); cf. below 92.

would have to turn into a 'living-room'.[6] But this could only happen from west to east, since any east to west settlement would have run the risk of being destroyed by continuing new arrivals.[7] Germanic settlement in Alamannia indeed appears to have begun in the north-west, close to the Roman frontier.[8]

How many 'proto-Alamanni' are we talking about? Alamannia, however defined (it is commonly thought of as being bounded by the old *limes*, but this is not precisely the case[9]), was not large, being about the same size as a small Roman province. As a funnel into the Empire it could have taken considerable through-traffic, but once raiders started to settle numbers would have been more restricted. An average war-party of 600-strong,[10] once stationary and acquiring dependants, would have placed a substantial burden on the local economy, and the more so if this economy was centred upon a damaged and degraded agricultural system.[11] Furthermore, if, as seems likely, such bands were prone to quarrel, they could not have settled in close proximity to each other. The region cannot have supported very many such groups. Below I propose a maximum resident population of *c*.120,000 for the fourth century. The third-century figure must have been considerably lower.

Crucial must have been Roman acceptance and indeed encouragement of a Germanic presence.[12] From the imperial viewpoint, withdrawal from the Upper German/Raetian *limes* had created a re-entrant in the frontier which left Italy and central Gaul vulnerable to Germanic raiding. The corner had to be taken off and the best way of achieving this was to persuade some bands to help the Empire against the rest. Rome demonstrated its overwhelming strength by restoring the frontiers.[13] Having blocked the raiding-bands, what could the Roman Empire offer to get some to stay? The obvious answer is pay or subsidies, in precious metal coin or bullion. Such payments are attested in the literary sources in respect of the Iuthungi, and in the archaeological in the case of the Haßleben-Leuna warriors. Similar ones were probably made to Alamanni, though it is strange that Roman silver and gold coins are rare in

---

[6] Nuber (1990: 52).   [7] Below 106.   [8] Below 83; Stribrny (1989: 437).
[9] Below 110–11.   [10] Above 49.   [11] Below 90.
[12] Nuber (1993: 103), (1998: 376–7).   [13] Below 192.

elite graves and hill-sites.[14] Rome could also offer toleration of occupation of former imperial territory. Finally, Rome could give group-leaders access to imperial goods, opportunities for service within the Empire, status to help them maintain their positions and, when necessary, help against rivals: 'management', not suppression.[15] Against Nuber, early Roman policy cannot have extended to the encouragement of the growth of a dependent population required to provide men and *matériel* sufficient to make up for the lost tax revenues of the region. How could these lands, their agriculture disrupted and their population diminished, have satisfied such demands?[16] Such a reconstruction of events is heavily 'tribal' in conception, and overinfluenced by details found in the unreliable *Historia Augusta*.[17] It smacks of anachronism, of fourth-century conditions under which, as we shall see, there was some restoration of a Roman presence and Roman exploitation of natural resources over the Rhine.

Whatever uncertainties there may be about developments in the second half of the third century, it is now accepted that from around 300 an increasing number of Elbgermanic warrior-bands settled permanently in Alamannia.[18] However, it is very difficult to perceive this process. Our best information is from burials, but this is unrepresentative and its interpretation controversial.[19] The problem is compounded through difficulty in dating what has been found. Consequently, the course of permanent settlement, for example whether it happened at once or in stages, is disputed.[20] As far as geographical distribution is concerned, our understanding is not helped by a lack of correlation between such groupings as can be established, such as those of the hill-sites, the coin-finds, the 'sub-tribes' of Ammianus and the *Notitia Dignitatum* and the gold-hilted sword burials.[21]

---

[14] Below 105–6, 131. Cf. Reuter (1997: 69): that the earliest 'Alamanni' were mercenaries in the pay of the Gallic Empire.

[15] Below 145–6, 178, 189.

[16] For the condition of Alamannic agriculture see below 90–1.

[17] *Historia Augusta, V. Probi* 15.2–6.

[18] Steuer (1997a: 149), (1998: 281–3, 285).

[19] Above 4, 48–9.

[20] Cf. Fingerlin (1997b: 125).

[21] Steuer (1997a: 152); cf. below 96, 126, 130, 135, 169–74, 341.

As far as the speed of settlement is concerned, those scholars prepared to express a view favour a gradual process.[22] Prior to around 300, Alamannic settlement (inferred from small clusters of ceremonial burials of group-leaders and their dependants) was to be found along the lower Main, the lower and middle Neckar, and in the area of the Nördlinger Ries at the eastern end of the Swabian Alp[23] (Fig. 6). In the course of the fourth century, settlement was extended to the upper Rhine and upper Danube as immigrants were drawn to the favourable conditions they found there[24] (Fig. 7). These conditions were good agricultural land, already opened up by Roman settlement, and Roman sufferance of newcomers. The availability of land explains Alamannic settlement in or near former forts, towns, villages

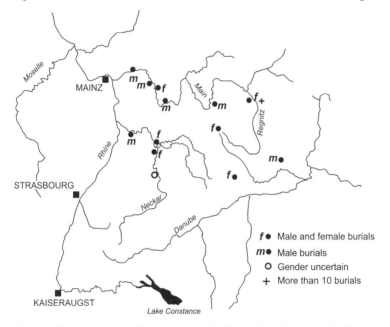

Fig. 6 Elbgermanic burial sites to *c.*300 [from Schach-Dörges (1997: 96 Fig. 82); © Archäologisches Landesmuseum Baden-Württemberg].

---

[22] Fingerlin (1993: 79); Schach-Dörges (1997: 98); Bücker (1999: 18 and n.25); Steidl (2000: 108); Schmauder (2002: 199).

[23] Schach-Dörges (1997: 96 and Fig. 82). Cf. above 80.

[24] Schach-Dörges (1997: 97 and Fig. 83); cf. (for the Breisgau) Fingerlin (1993: 69), (1997a: 106); Bücker (1999: 192–3, 197, 217).

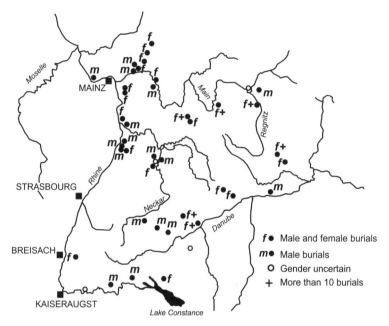

Fig. 7 Elbgermanic burial sites *c.*310–75 [from Schach-Dörges (1997: 97 Fig. 83); © Archäologisches Landesmuseum Baden-Württemberg].

and, especially, villas.[25] Such practice, which was continued when the Alamanni moved further into imperial territory in the fifth and sixth centuries,[26] indicates that they did not systematically destroy or even (contrary to a canard based on a misreading of Ammianus Marcellinus) sedulously avoid former Roman sites.[27] But Alamannic settlement was not restricted to the neighbourhood of former Roman

[25] The pioneering study was Weidemann's (1972); see now Planck (1990: 71, 82, 84, 92, 94); Fingerlin (1993: 64–5 and nn. 16–17), (1997b: 127–31, 136); Schach-Dörges (1997: 96); Bücker (1999: 23). (*Limes* forts/associated *vici*: Jagsthausen; Osterbürken; Unterböbingen; Weltzheim. Hinterland forts/associated *vici*: Heidenheim; Ursprings; Walheim. *Vici*: Köngen, Ladenburg. Villas: Hechingen-Stein; Lauffen-am-Neckar; Wurmlingen.)

[26] Bücker (1997: 320).

[27] AM 16.12.2. Accepted, for example, by Stroheker (1975: 33); Martin (1997a: 121 and n.9), (1998: 409–10). Cf. Fingerlin (1997b: 128); Nuber (1998: 375); Sommer (1999: 191). Zotz (1998: 394) notes that caution would anyway be needed in dealing with Ammianus' statement since he says much the same about the Huns: 31.2.4. On this, see further below 218.

structures. Examples of free-standing sites are also increasingly coming to light. Some of these were agricultural, but others were developed to exploit mineral resources, specifically iron.[28] Access to, and between, all sites will have been helped by the survival of many of the Roman roads of the region.[29]

Though we now know that there was direct continuity of settlement (between 'Rhine–Weser' and 'Elbgermanic' artefact users) at existing Germanic sites beyond the old *limes*,[30] there is less certainty about what happened within it. The question as to whether there was a residual 'Roman' population will be considered below.[31] Much has been made of Ammianus' reference to Alamannic villas, built after the Roman fashion and destroyed by Julian's troops in his campaign in the Main valley in 357.[32] Matthews, for example, finds confirmation of Ammianus' observation in the site of Ebel-bei-Praunheim, west of Nida-Heddernheim near Frankfurt-am-Main (Fig. 4). Here, a Roman villa abandoned during the later third century underwent Germanic reoccupation in the later fourth century, with stretches of drystone wall and posts being added to the structure. Matthews sees this as the work of 'an Alamannic optimate'.[33] However, the patching up of a century-old ruin hardly smacks of careful restoration in the Roman style; and I argue below that Ammianus' 'native' villas may anyway have been Roman.[34] Further, how or whether the buildings concerned functioned as the centre of a Roman-style estate remains unclear; and as far as 'Alamannic' nobles are concerned, a nearby weapon-grave has been interpreted as Eastgermanic (specifically, Burgundian), of a man who achieved success by serving in the Roman army in Gaul.[35] What we have here are signs not of prosperous

---

[28] e.g. Großkuchen (iron); Lauchheim (late seventh century, but very instructive); Mengen; Schleitheim; Sontheim-im-Stubental (fortified): Bücker et al. (1997: 318–20); Planck (1990: 82–4, 87–90); Stork (1997: 304, 306); Wahl, Wittwer-Backofen, and Kunter (1997: 340). See now Trumm (2002: 218), for the settlement of marginal agricultural land in eastern Swabia, probably in connection with the extraction and working of iron ore.

[29] Fingerlin (1997b: 131). For the network see Fig. 4. Cf. below 135.

[30] Schmauder (2002: 199–200).

[31] Below 126–8, 136.

[32] AM 17.1.7. Cf. below 226.

[33] Matthews (1989: 310), with Werner (1965: 77–80 and Fig. 1).

[34] Below 134, 241.

[35] Schulze-Dörlamm (1985: 560–1).

Alamannic aping of Roman ways, but of tension in the region.[36] Likewise, to take a somewhat earlier example, around 250 a smallish villa at Wurmlingen (Kreis Tuttlingen) on the upper Danube was finally abandoned. About 10 years later it was reoccupied by Germanic incomers. Their 'reoccupation' consisted of no more than the insertion of timber structures, 'Grubenhäuser', into the Roman complex, sometimes in the shells of rooms, which were re-roofed using Germanic techniques. The precise use of the new structures is unknown.[37] The primitive roofing of Germanic structures is particularly significant in distancing these from those 'built after the Roman fashion', because it is precisely the splendour of Roman roofs that Symmachus evokes in his description of Valentinian I's military strongpoints.[38] What we find, therefore, is that Alamannic presence on former villa sites shows association with but not continuity of these places.

The newcomers ignored the previous Roman economic, social and administrative structures. Indeed, though we have no clear idea of the northern and eastern limits of Alamannia, Elbe-*Germani* with close links to 'Alamanni' also settled to the north and east of the old *limes* on land that had never been part of the Upper German or Raetian provinces.[39] In the south and west, the survival of Roman roads did not prevent Alamannic settlement from being broken up by natural features, in particular the Black Forest.[40] Unlike, for example, what happened in post-Roman Gaul, here there is absolutely no sign of any survival of the *civitas*-organization or the juridical framework.[41] The evidence is difficult to find and interpret, but there is a general consistency and the main concentrations of archaeological material of the fourth and early fifth centuries are to be found in (Fig. 8): (a) the lower Main valley, near the confluence with the Upper Rhine; (b) the lower Neckar valley around the

[36] Cf. below 112, 114–16, 190, 324.
[37] Fingerlin (1997b: 130); Reuter (1997).
[38] Symmachus, *Orat.* 2.20. Cf. below 300.
[39] Keller (1993: 110–11); Schach-Dörges (1997: 97–8 and Figs 83–4). Cf. below 125.
[40] Cf. Fingerlin (1990: 103) and (1993: 65–7) on the relative isolation of the Breisgau.
[41] Fingerlin (1997b: 125–6).

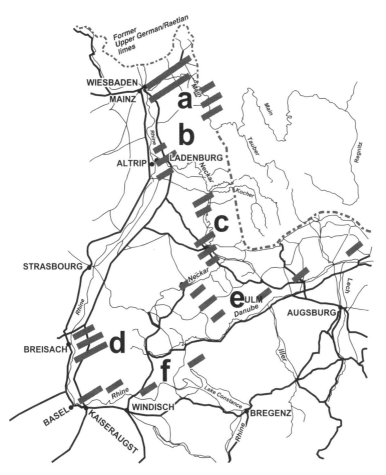

Fig. 8   Alamannia: main concentrations of archaeological remains. Key:
a lower Main; **b** lower Neckar; **c** middle Neckar; **d** Breisgau; **e** Swabian Alp;
f High Rhine.

confluence with the Upper Rhine; (c) the middle Neckar; and (d) the Breisgau. Lesser concentrations are situated along: (e) the Swabian Alp, north of the Danube; and (f) the High Rhine, between Kaiseraugst and Lake Constance.[42] Settlement was also clearly attracted to

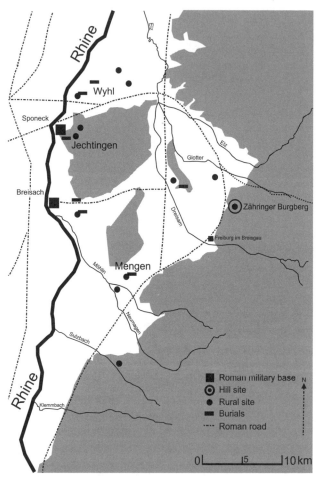

Fig. 9 The Breisgau [from Bücker (1999: 15 Fig. 1); © Jan Thorbecke Verlag, Ostfildern].

[42] Schach-Dörges (1997: Fig. 83). Cf. Roeren (1960: Fig. 2); *Germanen* (1986: 345–6 and Fig. 69); Planck (1990: 92); Schmid (1990: 18).

Roman military installations, which offered access to imperial manufactured goods and service in the imperial army.[43] A number of important sites, for example those at Mengen and the Zähringer Burgberg, are found near the imperial frontier[44] (Fig. 9). This must reflect a desire on the part of those who lived there to be neighbours of the Empire, and a belief that they would not be subjected to Roman harassment.

This attitude was based on experience. Though Ammianus is usually interested only in Roman frustration of Alamannic hopes in this respect, Symmachus shows that the Roman side was not averse to cooperation.[45] Here too, however, there are currently anomalies. For example, Germanic finds over the Rhine from Kaiseraugst, though significant, do not fully match the Roman or, indeed, reflect what we know from written sources was a strong Roman interest in the area.[46] Given what was happening opposite Breisach, Giesler's explanation for the phenomenon—that the region lay distant from the main lines of Alamannic expansion and was exposed to the threat of Roman military intervention—is unconvincing.[47]

The land that Rome in effect ceded to local Elbgermanic leaders by tolerating the settlement of their groups was probably distributed by them among their followers, according to rank. On this land developed the rural sites and the 'Höhensiedlungen'.

Alamannic settlement was almost entirely rural. The vast majority of the population lived in small villages or hamlets, or on isolated farms. They would have used simple wooden-framed buildings, some, at ground level, for habitation, others, slightly below (the typically Germanic 'Grubenhäuser'), for storage and artisanal activities. The decay of such timber structures would have forced relocation probably every 30–50 years. They are hard to detect and excavate. Since very few such sites are known, we have little idea of

[43] Cf. below 163; Bücker (1999: 217–18). For the similar effect of Roman bases on the Danube on Marcomannic settlement in the second century see Burns (2003: 231).

[44] Cf. Fig. 8 for the concentration of Alamannic settlements along the Upper Rhine near the confluences of the Main and the Neckar and around Breisach during the fourth century.

[45] e.g. AM 27.10.7 (368); cf. Symmachus, *Orat.* 2.10 (369), and below 217–18, 290. *Contra* Pabst (1989: 331), it would appear that the Alamanni chose to settle near forts, and not that the forts were built to face concentrations of Alamanni.

[46] Cf. below 219.

[47] Cf. below 101; Giesler (1997: 209–11).

the dynamics of their distribution: for example, their relationship to Roman settlements and roads,[48] or the local densities or overall level of population. However, a population level low in comparison with that of the Roman period is suggested by other studies. This is crucial, for it returns us to the enormous disparity in strength between Alamannic society and the Roman Empire. Aurelius Victor and Ammianus Marcellinus famously describe the Alamanni as being many in number.[49] There appears to be no basis in fact for such an assertion. What we have is prejudice: general, in that both authors pick up the ancient ethnographical tradition that viewed all northern barbarians as inordinately prolific; and particular, in that both wished to maximize Julian's Alamannic victories.[50]

The occupants of Alamannic settlements regularly smelted and forged iron and so had relatively good access to iron tools. Indeed, it has been claimed that their scythe and plough show signs of innovation—taking them beyond Roman standards.[51] On the other hand, the evidence for such improvement suggests a relatively late date, during the fifth century,[52] and it may be explicable in terms of developments specific to the period.[53] The overwhelming impression is that, during the fourth century, Alamannic agriculture was significantly different from its Roman predecessor.

The Romans cultivated specialized crops (for example, spelt wheat) on large estates for sale into a distant market. The Alamanni appear to have grown a wider range of produce on individual farms for subsistence. Barley (a summer crop, the cultivation of which generated useful free time in autumn and winter and would have allowed fallow pasturage) predominated. In short, the Alamanni practised a typically Germanic (as opposed to Celtic or Roman) form of agriculture, earlier characterized by Tacitus as being centred on pastoral farming.[54] However, there was some divergence from this

[48] Bücker et al. (1997); Bücker (1999: 208–11); Fingerlin (1990: 112), (1997a–b: 107–8, 125, 127–9, 133).

[49] Aurelius Victor, *Caesares* 21.2: *gens populosa*; AM 16.12.6: *populosae gentes*.

[50] Below 141–2, 176, 237–8.

[51] Henning (1985); Planck (1990: 87–90); Amrein and Binder (1997: 360); Bücker et al. (1997: 318); Bücker (1999: 198–201); Fingerlin (1993: 69), (1997a–b: 108, 131–3).

[52] Henning (1985: 590).

[53] Cf. below 338.

[54] Tacitus, *Germania* 5.2. I am very grateful to Dr A. Kreuz for her comments on this section, the responsibility for which, of course, remains entirely mine.

model. Other cereals and plants were grown, including species which demanded a degree of care, such as protein-rich lentils, and garden plants (various vegetables and herbs, mustard, cherry, fig, grape) brought in by the Romans. The presence of the latter category suggests some element of continuity in food production between the two periods.[55] Elsewhere we find evidence for a similar pattern of major discontinuity accompanied by minor continuity.

In the Breisgau, there may have been a move to more pastoral farming, with the average size of cattle gradually declining to that of the Germanic norm. On the other hand, smaller animals introduced under the Romans (for example, duck and goose) continued to be raised.[56] The sense of regression in agricultural activity receives confirmation from pollen analysis. There was a long period of significant reforestation in the fourth century, the sign of a smaller population failing to maintain previously cultivated land.[57] One has to be careful with such evidence. It is not totally generalizable: in some places reforestation did not occur.[58] And the failure to find settlements does not necessarily mean that these did not exist. As ever, 'voids' on maps may be due to lack of archaeological activity or expertise rather than to distribution of population. In the Breisgau, recent advances in archaeology have revealed many more sites than were previously known, and have indicated a significant growth in the Germanic population of the area from the early fourth century.[59] However, this is best treated as exceptional, caused by the area's proximity to Roman military bases.[60] Generally, the size of population that Alamannic agriculture could support must have fallen well below the Roman level, a level not reached again until the seventh century.[61]

[55] Rösch (1997: 323–4, 326); Bücker (1999: 204–5).
[56] Bücker (1999: 202–4); Kokabi (1997: 331–3, and 334: the relative modesty of sixth and seventh-century meat offerings in graves). Kreuz (1999: 82–3), however, prudently warns against taking big as 'good' and little as 'bad': much depends on the needs of society.
[57] Rösch (1997: 324, 327–9 and Figs 357–8), pollen diagrams from Hornstaad and Moosrasen, by Lake Constance. For the presence of beech pollen as a general indicator of reforestation and of the associated return of 'prehistoric settlement strategies' in the late Antique and medieval periods, see Küster (1998: 79).
[58] Stobbe (2000: 213): of three sites investigated in the Wetterau, two showed signs of reforestation, one did not.
[59] Fingerlin (1990: 101–3), (1997a: 107, 131).
[60] Fingerlin (1990: 110–12), (1993: 67); Bücker (1999: 217–18).
[61] Rösch (1997: 324, 327–9).

Despite frequent signs of iron-working, early Alamannic rural sites do not appear to have been great producers of manufactured items, or commercial centres. Their occupants made basic subsistence-goods which comprised, along with iron objects, hand-formed (not wheel-thrown) pottery, textiles, and other everyday items in leather, bone and horn.[62] The exchange of goods between settlements, though it existed, was small and over short distances: a maximum of 30 km (*c*.18 statute miles) has been proposed.[63] What is even more remarkable is that such sites consistently yield very few imported Roman wares, even at relatively important locations, such as the fortified settlement at Sontheim-im-Stubental, and in places, such as Mengen, in close proximity to the Empire. This is in stark contrast to the relatively large amounts of such material and evidence for highly-skilled artisanal activity found on the hill-sites (discussed next).[64] This is not to disparage Alamannic rural skill entirely. There are examples of bronze-working away from the hill-sites, for example at the Wurmlingen villa.[65] And though Alamannic hand-formed pottery resembles the late Iron Age pottery of the region, which has confused its interpretation, recent investigation has revealed that it was significantly better produced, perhaps as a result of the copying of Roman techniques.[66] It is also being increasingly realized that, despite the prevalence of hand-formed pottery, in the vicinity of rural sites and hill-sites there were local attempts to produce wheel-thrown vessels, again copying Roman forms.[67] There are, indeed, interesting incidences of larger-scale production of Roman-style fineware, along with Germanic pottery made by Roman methods and influenced by Roman style, in Free Germany (at Haarhausen, south of Erfurt, and at Eßleben, north of Würzburg) in the late third century[68] (Fig. 4). Such fairly sophisticated operations

[62] Bücker (1999: 198–202).
[63] Bücker (1999: 160).
[64] Below 95. Generally: Bücker (1997: 139); Hoeper (1998: 330–1, 339–40). Iller–Danube region: Planck (1990: 94). Breisgau: Fingerlin (1997a: 106–8); Bücker (1999: 167–8, 216–17), noting that at Mengen only 6 per cent of the ceramics found were Roman imports, as against 39 per cent on the Zähringer Burgberg.
[65] Reuter (1997: 67).
[66] Bücker (1999: 158–9, 216).
[67] Bücker (1999: 152, 158–9 and nn.436, 452: Lauffen; Runder Berg).
[68] Teichner (2000).

(which included the manufacture of food preparation vessels: *mortaria*[69]) can only have been the work of Romans, free or slave.

However, attempts at more sophisticated ceramic production remained local and marginal; the Haarhausen–Eßleben experiments appear to have lasted no more than a generation.[70] The Alamanni continued to manufacture and use predominantly hand-made pottery, and the production of high-quality ceramics, and glassware, remained a Roman speciality. As Matthews remarks, 'Alamannic technology was not advanced.'[71] It has been suggested that a major shift in the siting of their farms closer to water sources, which began around 400, was due, inter alia, to the failure of the Alamanni to maintain Roman irrigation systems.[72] Given the likely weaknesses in their agriculture, level of population and technology, it is improbable that they could have borne the sorts of demands that some have suggested were imposed upon them in the late third century.[73]

Not all Alamanni, however, lived exclusively on the land. We now know of small-scale but significant habitation on prominent hill-tops: the so-called 'Höhensiedlungen'—'hill-settlements' or, as I prefer to call them to avoid implying permanent residence or uniform function, 'hill-sites'[74] (Fig. 10). The modern pioneer in the field was Werner. In the early 1960s, he was able to list about a dozen probable sites; this number has since grown to over 60.[75] However, only a very few have been subjected to close archaeological scrutiny. By the late 1990s, indeed, just 10 of 62 proposed sites had been confirmed as Alamannic 'Höhensiedlungen'.[76] Of these, only that of the Runder Berg, near Urach (1)[77] had been fully excavated. Near the Rhine frontier, significant work has been done on the Zähringer

[69] Schallmayer (1995: 58); cf. above 36.
[70] Bücker (1997: 135–6, 139–40); Steuer (1998: 290); Steidl (2002: 87–9, 98–111). Cf. below 140.
[71] Matthews (1989: 312).
[72] Weidemann (1972: 114–23, 154); Keller (1993: 97–100).
[73] Above 82.
[74] Cf. Hoeper (1998: 341): 'Höhenstationen'.
[75] Werner (1965: 81–90 and Fig. 2), citing earlier work by Dannenbauer; Steuer (1990: Catalogue [45 sites]: 146–68); Fingerlin (1997b); Steuer (1997a: esp. 149 and Fig. 145); Hoeper (1998: Catalogue [62 sites]: 344–5); Haberstroh (2000a: 47–52).
[76] Hoeper (1998: 325).
[77] Numeration from Steuer (1990), Hoeper (1998).

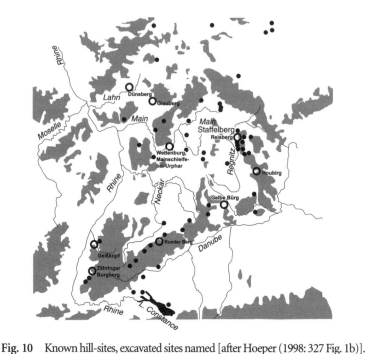

Fig. 10   Known hill-sites, excavated sites named [after Hoeper (1998: 327 Fig. 1b)].

Burgberg, near Freiburg (2), and on the Geißkopf near Offenburg (49); and, in the Alamannic hinterland, at Dünsberg, near Gießen (4), Glauberg, in the Wetterau (5), on the Wettenburg, Mainschleife-bei-Urphar (3), at Reisberg, near Scheßlitz (12), Houbirg in Franconia (7), and Gelbe Bürg, near Dittenheim (6).[78] It is certain that more hill-sites will be found, and that excavation of the ones we know will expand understanding of their form, distribution, dating and function. In addition, it may be that in non-hilly areas other sites will be recognized as having served a similar purpose.[79] For the moment, analysis will have to proceed based on the little we know.

Some hill-sites were constructed anew; others were built over Iron Age hill-forts. They were occasionally walled, as at Glauberg and Staffelberg (near Staffelstein) (10), but heavy defences are not one of their chief characteristics.[80] They vary greatly in area, from *c.*0.5

---

[78] Steuer (1990); Fingerlin (1997b: 127); Steuer (1997a: 154–7); Hoeper (1998: 329). See also Haberstroh (2000a: 48–9).

[79] Below 98.

[80] Steuer (1990: 169, 172); Haberstroh (2000a: 47, 49–50).

to over 10 ha (1.5–25 acres), though the largest were never fully occupied.[81] Common to all, despite their differences, and, as we have seen, sharply distinguishing them from rural settlements, are signs of material prosperity and specialized military and artisanal activity. Finds include weaponry, ornaments of male and female dress (for example, Roman-style military belt-fittings, brooches), Roman ceramics and glassware, and evidence of local craftwork (often using Roman scrap).[82] Alamannic technology was unsophisticated and the only sources of such items were the Roman Empire or craftsmen trained in Roman techniques. Though clearly esteemed by the Alamanni, these goods are unevenly distributed from hill-site to hill-site, and not particularly remarkable in the context of the full repertoire of Roman manufactures.[83] The lifestyle of those who used them was rich by local but mediocre by imperial standards. Hill-sites began to be built in the late third and early fourth centuries and continued in use until the Frankish takeover, early in the sixth.[84] They experienced various shifts in fortune. The Runder Berg, for example, began life in the early fourth century, was destroyed around 400, but recovered and was finally abandoned in panic around 500.[85] The Zähringer Burgberg was settled in the early fourth century, remodelled in the course of that century and occupied until the mid-fifth century.[86] Glauberg was built on a prehistoric site around 300, and persisted until c.500.[87]

Explanation of the hill-sites has ranged from refuges and guard-posts to army-camps and cult-centres.[88] A widely held view is that the largest 'Höhensiedlungen' were the seats of power of local leaders: 'Herrschaftszentren'. They contained the residences of chiefs and

[81] Steuer (1990: 68–9).

[82] Fingerlin (1997b: 126–7); Steuer (1990: 170, 195), (1997: 157); Hoeper (1998: 330–2).

[83] Bücker (1999: 152), (1997: 136), concerning glassware but, I believe, with equal relevance to ceramics etc.); cf. Hoeper (1998: 330).

[84] Steuer (1997a: 153–4).

[85] Steuer (1990: 147); cf. Fingerlin (1990: 106), (1993: 65); Koch (1997a: 192); Hoeper (1998: 329).

[86] Steuer (1990: 148–9), (1997: 154–7); Hoeper (1998: 334).

[87] Steuer (1990: 153). The late-third-century dating of Glauberg is based on the find of a coin of Tetricus I (AD 271–4): Werner (1965: 87–8). However, coins of this type remained in circulation until around 300: Drinkwater (1987: 202).

[88] For variations in size and likely use see Fingerlin (1990: 136), (1997: 126); Steuer (1997a: 158); Hoeper (1998: 341–3).

their military entourages, with their families, and separate quarters for dependent artisans. It has been suggested (using names taken from Ammianus Marcellinus) that the Zähringer Burgberg may have been the residence of Gundomadus or Vadomarius, and the Glauberg that of a king of the Bucinobantes.[89] As in the case of the rural settlements, buildings were probably simple timber structures, which rotted away completely in the course of time.[90] The lesser hill-sites have been interpreted as subordinate elements in local power structures.[91] Such a model is derived from Ammianus Marcellinus' description of the hierarchy of Alamannic kings and nobles in the mid-fourth century.[92] This is plausible. Ammianus' account of Alamannic society is consistent with barbarian society in general;[93] and there is no reason to suppose that it was subject to much change. As Hoeper says, though we cannot be certain that the Runder Berg was the seat of a *rex*, this seems likely.[94]

However, the interpretation of archaeological data directly from historical data is not without problems. There is no direct connection between Ammianus' Alamannic rulers and the hill-sites;[95] and it has to be conceded that hill-sites cannot be securely identified in his narrative. The nearest he comes to describing them are his ambiguous accounts of the defended 'lofty height' at Solicinium, stormed by Valentinian I's army in 368, and the 'sheer rocks' defended by 'obstacles like those of city walls' encountered by Gratian in his attack on the Lentienses in 378.[96] Most striking is the absence of any mention of such structures in Ammianus' narratives of Julian's close dealings with a series of Alamannic chiefs in 357–9.[97] Ammianus has his problems as a source,[98] but his omission of hill-sites seems to reflect an authentic historical phenomenon. Mapping known or

[89] Zähringer Burgberg: Fingerlin (1990: 136), (1997: 127); cf. Steuer (1997a: 158); Hoeper (1998: 334). Glauberg: Werner (1965: 895). Cf. below 173–4, 206.

[90] Steuer (1990: 169, 196).

[91] Steuer (1997a: 149–51).

[92] Below 118.

[93] Elton (1996a: 32–3).

[94] Hoeper (1998: 330–1).

[95] Fingerlin (1993: 72).

[96] AM 27.10.8–9: *mons praecelsus*. Cf. Matthews (1989: 311–12). AM 31.10.12–13: *velut murorum obicibus*. Cf. Haberstroh (2000a: 23). Below 282, 288, 311, 314.

[97] Below 224–7, 242–3, 246–7.

[98] Above 3, below 177–8.

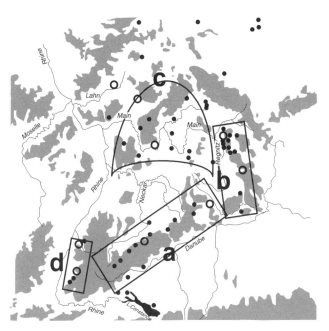

Fig. 11 Known hill-sites: main lines of distribution. Key: **a** Swabian Alp; **b** Franconian Alp (Regnitz area); **c** Odenwald/Steigerwald/middle Main; **d** Breisgau [after Steuer (1990: 144 Fig. 1a)].

likely hill-sites produces three clear concentrations (Fig. 11): (a) a narrow line running south-west/north-east, along the Swabian Alp, north of the upper Danube, inside the old Upper German/ Raetian *limes*; (b) a narrow line running roughly north/south, along the Franconian Alp, outside the Upper German/Raetian *limes*; (c) a broad crescent spanning the middle Main, from the Odenwald into the Steigerwald, outside the old Upper German/Raetian *limes*. (I will deal with (d), the local concentration in the Breisgau, below.) These patterns might well represent only the last phase of hill-site development in the fifth century. However, there are grounds for believing that they existed earlier. In the Swabian Alp, Runder Berg (1) was occupied from the early fourth century; and in the Wetterau, a date of around 300 has been suggested for the first Germanic use of Glauberg (5). If all three stretches of sites were present in the fourth century, Julian's activities in the later 350s would have taken him through only one, on the Main, in 359.[99] It therefore seems likely that Ammianus did not mention hill-sites on the middle Rhine because they were not a feature of the area.

Did Alamannic *reges* living away from hilly areas make use of alternative power centres, such as stockades or even river islands? And what sort of dealings did Rome have with those lines of hill-sites that do not figure in the sources? As far as the first of these questions is concerned, there must be a type of settlement not yet detected in the archaeology. As the Iron Age produced lowland *oppida*, so must the early Alamannic period have seen centres of power other than at hill-sites.[100] However, none of these can yet be identified. 'Superior' rural sites, for example at Lauffen and Mengen, are distinguished by the presence of rich, especially female, graves;[101] and the settlement at Sontheim-im-Stubental stands out by virtue of its size and complexity, and its fortifications.[102] But none of these locations has produced the wealth of imported material found, for example, at the Runder Berg. It seems likely that they were not 'Herrschaftszentren', but the rural residences of Alamannic notables (perhaps, in the case of Sontheim, of a man who was not close to the local *rex* and who therefore spent much of his time away from the local main 'Höhensiedlung').[103] Probably, with their timber buildings gone and their artefacts indistinguishable among the general spread of Germanic and Roman material, lowland centres are currently invisible to archaeologists. From the literary material, however, we have the name 'Bucinobantes', recently interpreted as 'people of the quick-set hedge'; Symmachus' description of a likely lowland 'Herrschaftszentrum' under Roman attack in 369; and the possibility that when Roman troops sent to arrest Macrianus near Wiesbaden in 372 ran amok, they were led astray by the treasures of a royal power centre.[104]

---

[99] Below 249.

[100] Cf. Werner (1965: 71–2): in Free Germany, where no hill-sites have been found, the usual residence for *principes* must have been estates; and in the west, hill-sites are not a feature of Merovingian and Carolingian life.

[101] Planck (1990: 71); Bücker (1999: 211–14).

[102] Planck (1990: 82–4).

[103] Below 120. Cf. Werner (1965: 74–5) on the difficulties of determining precisely where kings and *optimates* lived.

[104] Below 173, 290, 308.

With regard to the second question, of prime importance was the relationship between the imperial authorities and the hill-sites north of the upper Danube, which commanded routes into Alamannia and, at their western end, were close to roads into Italy.[105] The string of sites along the Swabian Alp might suggest confrontation with the Empire; and the impression of tension between the two sides is reinforced by the rarity of late-Roman bronze coinage here in comparison with the Rhine valley.[106] However, the notion that lines of hill-sites represent direct reaction to the Empire is contradicted by that in the Franconian Alp, at right-angles to the imperial frontier.[107] Further, the very existence of the Swabian Alp line, parallel to a frontier that shielded Italy, suggests that here was something that the Empire was prepared to tolerate; and the Raetovarii of the region produced crack troops for the imperial army.[108] Related diplomatic activity may have been channelled through the hall complex at the fort of Kellmünz, interpreted as a place for the reception of Alamannic envoys[109] (Fig. 12). Roman toleration may also have affected the Odenwald/Steigerwald concentration, spanning the sensitive Main valley.[110] Imperial authorities may have seen such sites as one means of turning the invasion 'corridor' into a 'room'[111]—protecting Alamannia from further incursions by outsiders and buttressing the power of those with whom they were now doing business, while discouraging the rise of supra-regional leaders. The breadth of the Odenwald/Steigerwald crescent, and its extension up the Main, could have resulted from the leaders of a 'marblecake' of Elbgermanic and Eastgermanic communities using hill-sites to defend themselves against outsiders and each other, so again discouraging the rise of supra-regional groupings.[112] A similar role could have been played by hill-sites along the Franconian Alp, which may also indicate the

---

[105] Cf. below 206, 210.

[106] Fig. 16.

[107] Haberstroh (2000a: 132).

[108] Below 170–2.

[109] Mackensen (1999: 223–8, 239). Cf. below 157, 212. See also below 282, on Alamannic dealings with a Roman *dux* at Mons Piri.

[110] Above 36, 51 n.47, 85–6; below 113–14, 132, 190.

[111] Cf. above 81.

[112] See Haberstroh (2000a: 132), for the likely expansion of Burgundian influence up the Main during the fourth century. Also below 114.

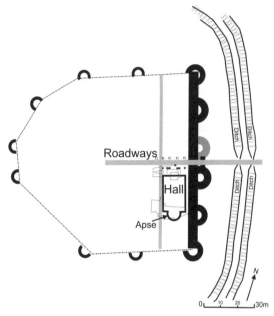

Fig. 12   Kellmünz fort [from Mackensen (1999: 224 Fig. 7.16); © *Journal of Roman Archaeology*, Portsmouth RI].

location of Iuthungi.[113] This would put these people between the Danube and the Main, east of the Burgundians and bordering other Elbgermanic settlements on the middle Main.[114]

Rome may even have encouraged the building of specific hill-sites with subsidies and technical help. Werner drew attention to the skills required to build the massive drystone 'Ringwall' that sealed the approach to Alamannic Glauberg. He proposed that the work was done by Roman prisoners. I suggest rather that it was constructed by Alamanni under Roman instruction. The site lies close to the old fort at Altenstadt, on a route from Mainz into Thuringia in an area which was important to the Empire in political and military terms and in which coin-finds indicate a relatively high degree of continuing Roman involvement.[115] A strong Alamannic ally would have been

[113] Cf. Steidl (1997: 76); Strobel (1999: 17–18); and esp. Haberstroh (2000a: 128, 132).
[114] Below 112–14; Steidl (1997: 76), (2000: 108). Cf. Strobel (1999: 17–19).
[115] Below 129–30.

useful in protecting the region. This takes us to the concentration of hill-sites in the Breisgau.

The group of hill-sites in the Breisgau (Fig. 11) (d) may well appear unexceptional: simply another concentration useful to Rome in policing the Rhine border. However, it is odd. It occurs in an area directly adjacent to the imperial frontier where events took place described by Ammianus and in which the coin-finds suggest a strong Roman presence into the fourth century;[116] and, above all, it is centred on the Zähringer Burgberg (2). This is a massive hill-site, built on a height in the Rhine valley, within sight of Breisach, a major Roman military base then attached to the left bank of the river.[117] Some have interpreted it as an Alamannic response or even challenge to Roman power, a 'counterweight' to neighbouring imperial forts and towns.[118] This is unlikely. Throughout the fourth century, Roman military strength and political confidence remained formid- able; no neighbouring barbarian would have dared open defiance. Moreover, the Zähringer Burgberg is characterized by its pretentious- ness and the skill deployed in its construction. With the exception of only a central prominence, a hilltop was completely levelled and the massive amount of spoil this generated was packed between huge, radiating drystone ribs and wooden shuttering in order to increase the area of level ground to *c*.5 ha (12.5 acres)[119] (Figs 13–14). Such a high level of building science was, to judge by what they showed themselves capable of elsewhere in their region, well beyond the knowledge and competence of contemporary Alamanni and, as in the case of Glauberg, hints at Roman guidance.

The gift of such a magnificent 'Herrschaftszentrum' suggests that the beneficiary was a local leader (or family of leaders) who had shown exceptional loyalty to Rome and from whom the Empire expected even more in the future. The individual or individuals involved should not, however, be thought of as 'Brisigavi',[120] and they probably lived much later than Gundomadus or Vadomarius.

[116] Ibid.

[117] On Breisach see Bücker (1999: 22–3) and below 192, 295.

[118] Steuer (1990: 176), (1997: 156): response, challenge. Fingerlin (1990: 136), (1993: 69): counterweight.

[119] Steuer (1997a: 156 and Figs 152, 153); Hoeper (1998: 332).

[120] Below 170–1.

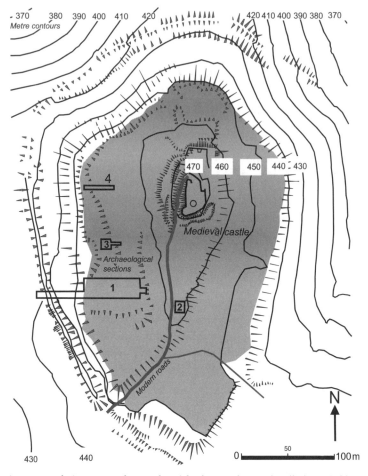

Fig. 13 Zähringer Burgberg: plan (shading indicates levelled area) [from Steuer (1997a: 154 Fig. 153); © Herr Prof. H. Steuer].

They may even have been of a family that replaced that of these two brothers under Valentinian I.[121] The Zähringer Burgberg, indeed, helped articulate a complex interaction between Alamannic and Roman military elites which amounted to more than that of fierce

[121] Below 287. An inexplicable oddity here is that the Zähringer Burgberg, though much closer to the Empire than the Runder Berg, has yielded many fewer imported Roman artefacts: Bücker (1999: 152).

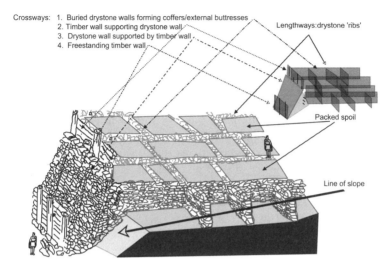

Fig. 14 Zähringer Burgberg: techniques of construction [from Steuer (1997a: 154 Fig. 152); © Herr Prof. H. Steuer].

enemies or mutually suspicious allies. Both sides were involved in a symbiotic relationship, examined in more detail below.[122] For the moment, there may be much in Steuer's suggestion that the difference between Roman forts and their garrisons on the upper Rhine and upper Danube and neighbouring Alamannic hill-sites may have become indistinct.[123] Both were eventually manned by Alamannic warriors whose interest lay in defending the Empire that gave them money and the goods on which to spend it. Both provided high-status locations for the chiefs of such warriors, confirming their power and ensuring continuity and reliability in their service—producing leaders with whom the Empire could do business.[124]

This returns us to the general character of the hill-sites. They reflect the continuing military nature of early Alamannic society, inherited from the hierarchically structured warrior-bands.[125] But the 'Höhensiedlungen' also embody discontinuity. They do not appear to have been a feature of wider Germanic society.[126] They reflect

[122] Below 133–5, 179, 290–2, and esp. 359–62.
[123] Steuer (1997a: 152); cf. below 157.   [124] Cf. below 303, 327–8.
[125] Steuer (1997a: 149, 152).   [126] Werner (1965: 71–2).

a switch from movement to semi-permanent settlement and may even have been generated by this change. External difficulties, as settled bands determined their ranking through squabbles over territory or found themselves challenged by newcomers from the east, would create the need for refuges and redoubts.[127] Internal strains, as leaders struggled to maintain themselves in conditions quite different from those of the raiding-party (consider, for example, the pressure put on Gundomadus and Vadomarius in 357[128]), would make hill-sites become 'Herrschaftszentren'. Against such a background, the spontaneous emergence of such places is hardly surprising. There is no significance in similarities between Alamannic hill-sites and others of the same period within the Roman Empire.[129] 'Höhensiedlungen' appear well away from the imperial frontier. All resulted from similar human behaviour in similar circumstances: neighbouring Alamanni did not simply copy Roman models.

The major hill-sites, as 'Herrschaftszentren', came to dominate the surrounding territories as seats of power rather than as citadels.[130] Each of these territories must have witnessed some degradation of the newcomers' warrior culture. Crops had to be grown and animals tended, if not directly by Alamanni then under their supervision. Not all fit males could be fighters all the time. Other hill-sites, the so-called 'army-camps' ('Heerlager'), may have been used as places to reconstitute the old warrior-bands—as rendezvous points for occasional 'wapentakes' or *levées en masse*.[131] In contrast, finds in the major sites reflect the development of a smaller specialized warrior class, permanently at the disposal of its leaders.

Such a class had to be supported by a developing peasantry or external income, in the shape of booty or pay from the Roman Empire, or both. (By 'pay' is meant sums given to Alamanni under the terms of the treaties struck at various times with the Empire. This is likely for the later third century and probably continued as a feature of imperial diplomacy.[132]) Archaeological evidence suggests

---

[127] Cf. Werner (1965: 84): hill-sites distant from the imperial frontier acted as 'Gauburgen . . . Stammesmittelpunkte'; Steuer (1997a: 149); below 106.

[128] Below 230.

[129] *Contra* Steuer (1990: 141–3, 176).

[130] Steuer (1990: 168, 197).

[131] Heerlager: e.g. Geißkopf. Cf. Steuer (1998: 290); Hoeper (1998: 334–9).

[132] Above 81; Gutmann (1991: 40).

an unhealthy dependence on external income. The enormous variation in the occurrence of imported items between the hill-sites and the rural settlements must have resulted from a process that brought expensive items to local power centres but did not allow them to circulate further afield. This suggests that the rural settlements were too weak economically to obtain such items through trade. It appears that the hill-sites did not stimulate their local economies, for example, by methodically collecting rents and taxes, so provoking local communities to produce surpluses that could be used in commerce: the 'Höhensiedlungen' were economically sterile.[133]

The hill-sites also lacked architectural dynamism. Unlike the Iron Age *oppida* which they superficially resemble, they cannot be regarded in any way as 'townlike',[134] not even the Zähringer Burgberg. The major excavated sites have produced some evidence for central structures, but this is poor because to the end such structures were simple wooden affairs resembling Free Germanic farmsteads ('Großgehöfte').[135] There is no evidence for new masonry building in Alamannic territory from the later third to the seventh century,[136] and this despite the fact that models for such building were close to hand over the Rhine and Danube, and that during the fourth century a number of important Alamanni must, through their service in the Roman army, have seen the wonders of the Empire's Mediterranean core.[137] In the south-western sites, both rural and 'Höhensiedlungen', imported pottery consists overwhelmingly of fine tableware. For other food uses, for example storage and preparation, all classes appear to have been content with native wares. Thus, even though this region was adjacent to the Empire, there appears to have been no major change in eating habits, a common feature in Germanic settlements throughout the Roman period.[138] Finally, in striking contrast with the *oppida*, the hill-sites reveal no developing coin usage, and so no evolving market economy and all that this

[133] On the dependence of the northern peoples in general on the Empire see Shaw (1999: 159).
[134] Thus *contra* Fingerlin (1993: 72): 'stadtähnlich'; cf. (1997b: 126).
[135] Steuer (1990: 170–1, 173–7); cf. (1997a: 154).
[136] Planck (1990: 94).
[137] Below 153.
[138] Bücker (1999: 170); Carroll, *pers. comm.*, cf. above 36.

entails for social change.[139] It is tempting to interpret such behaviour as the result of Alamannic cultural deficiency that made Alamanni, unlike Franks, unreceptive to 'civilized' ways. This is mistaken, and will be discussed further below.[140]

Finally, under settlement, we have to consider those whom, apart from Romans, Alamanni had as their neighbours.

Some would have been only temporary. With the realization that there was no single Alamannic invasion has come acceptance that *Germani* continued to drift in and out of Alamannia from the late-Roman into the early-medieval period. There are indications of the maintenance of links between Alamanni and people living in the vicinity of the Elbe: the use and production of Germanic-style artefacts in the south-west was to some degree matched by that of Roman-inspired objects in the north-east. Here, the most significant aspect of this phenomenon are the implications of protracted movement into Alamannia by users of Elbgermanic artefacts.[141] On the middle Main, for example, Elbgermanic artefacts did not entirely replace Rhine–Weser goods until the early fourth century.[142] Such new arrivals, actual or potential, permanent or transitory, must have acted as a destabilizing element, which should be taken into account in all discussions of Alamannic development.[143]

With regard to permanent neighbours, mention must first be made of the Franks. These are currently held to be the product of another process of ethnogenesis as, again due to the strains of the internal conflict of the third century, Germanic tribes on the Lower Rhine, long known to the Empire (as Bructeri, Chamavi, Ampsivarii etc.), dissolved and re-formed as new, more aggressive communities to which the Romans attached the general label of *Franci*.[144] Given the Frankish conquest of Alamannia around the end of the fifth century, one might expect a fair amount of contact between

[139] Below 130. Cf. Heinrichs (2003: 296–7), on the economic and social implications of the absence of coin usage among *Germani*.

[140] Cf. Martin (1998: 409–11: 'differences in outlook' ('Mentalitätsunterschieden')); Schmauder (2002: 201) citing Keller. See further below 350, 356.

[141] Schach-Dörges (1997: 85); Steuer (1997a: 150–2), (1998: 281–309).

[142] Steidl (1997: 76).

[143] Cf. above 81, 100–1, below 189, 338.

[144] Pohl (2000: 108–9).

Alamanni and Franks, but this is not the case. We hear of individual conflicts. Julian set the bandit-turned-mercenary-turned-Roman-general, Charietto, who may have been Frankish, against Alamanni.[145] Likewise, Gratian employed the Frank, Mallobaudes, as a general against Lentienses.[146] Mallobaudes later appears as a native leader, slaying the Alamannic king, Macrianus, who, after facing down Romans and Burgundians, perished while raiding into Frankish territory. This shows how, once they were beyond imperial control, Rome's allies were quite capable of destroying each other.[147]

Beyond this, however, there are few signs of regular Franco-Alamannic interaction during the fourth century. This could be an artefact of the sources, but there are good reasons for accepting it is an authentic historical phenomenon. Camille Jullian described Franks and Alamanni as occupying two different worlds, separated by the Taunus and the Main.[148] Frankish ethnogenesis, by which is meant the crystallization of Franks around Salian leaders of the Merovingian dynasty, was less rapid than Alamannic; and its centres were relatively far north, around Cologne and, for the Salians, in Toxiandria by the Lower Rhine.[149] The Franks were also probably isolated from Alamannia by continuing Roman interest in the area over the Rhine from Mainz.[150] Macrianus' attack on the Franks was, presumably, from north of the Main, after his exclusion from south of the river.[151] On the other hand, Macrianus' activities show that such isolation was not absolute, and the existence of north–south routes across the Taunus is indicated by the location of Augustan military operations and bases.[152]

More important during the fourth century was another group of people, described as positively hostile to the Alamanni, the

---

[145] Zosimus 3.7.1–6; AM 17.10.5, 27.1.2. Cf. below 267. Charietto: *PLRE* 1.200; Waas (1971: 80–1); Heinzelmann (1982: 578).

[146] AM 31.10.6. Cf. below 311.

[147] AM 30.3.7. Mallobaudes: *PLRE* 1.539; Waas (1971: 92); Heinzelmann (1982: 643). For Macrianus, see below 248, 304–9; Gutmann (1991: 41).

[148] Jullian (1926: 412).

[149] James (1988: 39, 51); Périn (1998: 59–62). For Toxiandria, see below 200. Cf. below 355, 356.

[150] Cf. above 85, below 134, 241, 296.

[151] Below 309.

[152] Gechter (2003: 149).

Burgundians. The Burgundians occur much earlier than the Alamanni in the Greco-Roman sources, and played a much more direct role in European history.[153] To deal with their later development first, in 411, in the chaos which followed the Vandal/Alan/Suebian invasion of 406/7, a number of Burgundians crossed the Rhine and supported the elevation of the ephemeral Gallo-Roman usurper, Jovinus, at Mainz.[154] In 413, following the fall of Jovinus, they were granted territory across the middle Rhine in Gaul, probably in the vicinity of Mainz.[155] This first Burgundian kingdom lasted until 436, when it was destroyed by the imperial general Aëtius and his Hunnic allies.[156] Around 443, the surviving Burgundians were resettled by Aëtius in Savoy, north of Geneva.[157] The second Burgundian kingdom went on to become a major force in fifth-century Gaul, being the only countervailing force to the Visigoths who were threatening to take over the country. Like the Alamanni from 496/7, and the Visigoths in 507, in 534 the Burgundians fell victim to the late expansion of Frankish power.[158]

We find Burgundians mentioned for the first time in the first century AD, when Pliny the Elder described them as being part of the Vandal nation. A century or so later, Ptolemy located them east of the Semnones, between the middle Oder and the Vistula[159] (Fig. 5). In the later third century, Probus is reported as having fought with Burgundians and Vandals, probably on the river Lech (running north, past Augsburg, into the Danube).[160] An imperial panegyric of 289 describes Burgundians, alongside Alamanni and others, raiding into Gaul. However, a similar speech of 291 tells of deep hostilities

[153] Indispensable for what follows is Anton (1981). See now also Favrod (1997) and Wood (2003).

[154] For full discussion of these events, see below 321, 324.

[155] Anton (1981: 239–40); Pohl (2002a: 156): near, but not at, Mainz, since there remained a regular Roman military presence on the Rhine (below 327), and definitely not in Worms.

[156] Anton (1981: 231–5).

[157] Anton (1981: 241); Wood (1994: 8); Pohl (2002a: 157–8).

[158] Anton (1981: 245–6).

[159] Pliny, *Nat. Hist.* 4.99; Ptolemy, *Geog.* 2.11.8. Goetz and Welwei (1995: 1.108–9, 180–3); Anton (1981: 235–6); *Germanen* (1986: 361).

[160] Zosimus 1.68.1–2. Cf. above 79; Paschoud (1971: 175); *Germanen* (1986: 371–2); Pohl (2002a: 155).

between Burgundians and Alamanni over territory, the former provoking fierce reprisals by the latter.[161] By the later fourth century, indeed, according to Ammianus Marcellinus, the Burgundians had become the permanent neighbours of the Alamanni, and intractable enemies, as a result of their laying claim to salt springs and other territory.[162] It was this animosity that, in 370, enabled Valentinian I to recruit the Burgundians as allies in his vendetta against Macrianus.[163]

Though he mentions the Burgundians only in passing, Ammianus may be taken as suggesting that Burgundian identity was built around a 'kernel of tradition', manifested in the institutions of a temporary sacred king (*hendinos*) and a permanent chief priest (*sinistus*).[164] This, together with their early appearance in the sources, hints that, unlike the Alamanni, the Burgundians were a true 'people', a discrete *gens*, and that their appearance near the Rhine was the result of authentic migration. However, there are indications that this is not the case. 'Burgundian' appears to have been a general description of a varied and fissile set of groupings of which the 'western' Burgundians were only a part.[165] Indeed, there are signs in Ammianus that by the mid-fourth century the identity of this western group was being manipulated by Rome for the Empire's own ends. Ammianus tells us that the prime reason why the Burgundians helped Valentinian against Macrianus was that they were convinced that they were sprung from ancient Roman stock.[166] As most scholars now agree, this descent is likely to have been an invention of Roman diplomacy.[167] Their use of a sacred kingship has also been questioned.[168]

[161] *Pan. Lat.* 2[Galletier](10).5.1; 3(11).17.3. Cf. below 190.

[162] AM 28.5.11: *salinarum finiumque causa Alamannis saepe iurgabant.*

[163] AM 28.5.8–11. Cf. below 305–6.

[164] AM 28.5.14; cf. above 45. Anton (1981: 240–1).

[165] Anton (1981: 236–7). Cf. Haberstroh (2000a: 130); Favrod (1997: 39, 44).

[166] AM 28.5.11: *prima quod iam inde a temporibus priscis subolem se esse Romanam.*

[167] Anton (1981: 238); Matthews (1989: 310); Wood (1990: 58). Matthews notes how this story was taken to fanciful etymological extremes by Orosius (*Hist.* 7.32.11–12), 'perhaps making the best of a bad job'.

[168] Pohl (2002a: 155–6); Wood (2003: 244). Cf. Goffart (2002: 64).

Overall, the evidence suggests that the western Burgundians were not a full tribe but rather, at best, a splinter of a tribe. This had managed to preserve its name and something of its culture, but found itself adrift in a sea of wider ethnogenesis. In other words, 'the Burgundians' consisted of a group of warrior-bands among other warrior-bands.[169] However, while most of these others were Elbgermanic in culture, the Burgundians were eastern *Germani* and so harder to absorb. This made them dangerous to Alamanni and Romans alike, but also, because they were different, accessible and useful to Rome as a counterweight to the Alamanni. This would explain the 'special relationship' between Romans and Burgundians. (The survivors of Probus' victory over the Burgundians and Vandals were sent to Britain, presumably as troops, and these and their descendants may have acted as useful contacts with 'free' Burgundians.[170])

Probus faced the western Burgundians in Raetia. Ammianus' Burgundians are, however, further north. There is general agreement as to where they were to be found, based on two passages in Ammianus. The first concerns the dispute between Alamanni and Burgundians over salt springs. This would put the area of contention in the Kocher valley, the site of a flourishing medieval salt industry, with its centre at Schwäbisch-Hall[171] (Fig. 4). The second is to do with Julian's campaign of 359. Having marched across Alamannia, Julian's forces reached an area where 'boundary stones' (*terminales lapides*) marked the borders of 'Romans' and 'Burgundians'.[172] These boundary stones are currently usually associated with the old *limes*, which crossed the Kocher between the forts of Jagsthausen and Öhringen. It is assumed that the Burgundians were settled just to the east of its line, north of Schwäbisch-Hall, between the Kocher and the Main.[173] Such an interpretation is debatable. Support for the association of the boundary stones with the *limes* has been sought in the name that

---

[169] 'Group' because Ammianus specifically mentions 'kings', in the plural (e.g. 28.5.10).

[170] Zosimus 1.68.3; for possible fourth-century Alamannic links, see below 206.

[171] Anton (1981: 287); cf. below 134.

[172] AM 18.2.15.

[173] Anton (1981: 237–8); *Germanen* (1986: 372–3); Matthews (1989: 307–10); Lorenz, S. (1997: 60–1).

Ammianus gives the region: 'Palas or Capellatii'. It has been proposed that the former was derived from *palus*, 'stake' or 'paling'.[174] But the argument is tenuous and unable to explain Ammianus' reference to 'boundary stones' which, whatever these were, cannot mean any sort of wall. There is also the question as to whom the boundary stones separated. The manuscript tradition has 'Romans and Burgundians', but this is odd of a region deep in Alamannia a century after Roman withdrawal. Since the sixteenth century, some have preferred to read '*Alamanni* and Burgundians'.[175] However, the use of artificial markers was infrequent between *Germani*. When such demarcation occurs, it is based on linear earthworks;[176] boundary stones (*horoi/ termini*) were a feature of Mediterranean society. The current trend is to revert to 'Romans'.[177] But who were these? One answer is that they were a residual Roman population.[178] However, the Celto-Roman popula-tion of the area was probably very quickly expelled or absorbed; and coin-finds are rare along the southern stretch of the old *limes*, which suggests only a few visitors from the imperial population exploiting the area's resources.[179] The alternative is that 'Romans' is a reference not to a particular set of people but to the totality of the Empire, which still saw itself and was still recognized by *Germani* as exercising nominal sovereignty over the region.[180]

Interaction between Romans and Burgundians therefore probably took place somewhat further north than is usually accepted. Julian's march of 359 is likely to have taken him north-eastwards, reaching the Burgundians on the middle Main, between the old Roman forts of Großkrotzenburg and Miltenberg, which in their day had policed a river, not an artificial, frontier[181] (Fig. 21). Such a point of contact is more suited to Ammianus' narrative. His *terminales lapides* do not conjure up a picture of a palisaded *limes* but one of an open area in

[174] Matthews (1989: 309–10 and n.9); Lorenz, S. (1997: 60 and n.227).
[175] Matthews (1989: 308 and n.8); cf. Lorenz, S. (1997: 61 and n.229).
[176] e.g. Tacitus, *Annales* 2.19.3 (the *agger* separating Angrivarii and Cherusci).
[177] Anton (1981: 237); Lorenz (1997: 61 n.228).
[178] Anton (1981: 237).
[179] Below 127, 129–30, 136.
[180] Witschel (1999: 212 and n.159). Cf. below 132, 190, 299. Since, as Isaac (1992: 396) points out, imperial boundary markers are otherwise unknown, these are best seen as demarcating 'provincial' and 'client' territory.
[181] Below 249.

which people were warned off, not fenced off, from each other. This puts the western edge of main Burgundian settlement on the Main, between the line of the old *limes* and the Tauber, in a region which had been occupied by *Germani* until the disruption of the third century.[182] Burgundians settled on the middle Main might expand downriver to Mainz, a possibility of concern to local Alamanni and Romans in Gaul, and the more so for the latter because of their continuing presence east of the Rhine. I propose that the boundary stones were set up by the Empire across the Main corridor as a means of controlling the area.[183]

To what degree is this mainly historical reconstruction supported by the archaeological evidence? If early Alamannic archaeology is difficult, Burgundian is worse. In the one place that we can be fairly sure from the literary sources that the Burgundians were present at some stage in the fourth century, the Kocher valley, no artefacts or sites have been identified as belonging to them.[184] Most of the little material we have comes from funerary deposits and presents the usual difficulties of interpretation. However, it is suggestive.

There is a small number of burials characterized by weapon-deposits, including swords, in the case of males, and by jewellery and toilet articles, in the case of females, and dated to the period from the later third to the early fifth century. These are found from the middle Main down to the Rhine confluence, up the Rhine to the Neckar, and across the Rhine into northern Gaul. Apart from the fact that those who made them practised inhumation as opposed to cremation, they show close affinities to grave-clusters between the Elbe and the Vistula.[185] (The deposition of useable weaponry was, in this period, not part of Alamannic funerary rites. Instead, we find two or three token arrow-heads, in bronze or silver (Fig. 15).[186]) The idea that weapon-burials resulted from Roman practices moving eastwards appears to have been abandoned.[187] Currently, there seems to be a reversion to the older view

---

[182] Schach-Dörges (1997: 96 and Fig. 81); Steidl (1997), (2000).

[183] Cf. below 190 for the proposal that such stones were originally set up by Maximian; cf. Höckmann (1986: 379).

[184] Cf. Steidl (1997: 76).

[185] Schulze-Dörrlamm (1985: 548–9, 552–6 and Figs 1, 32–4); Schach-Dörges (1997: 88, 94 and Fig. 78); Martin (1997b: 163–4 and Fig. 163).

[186] Quast (1997: 186–7); cf. below 341–2.

[187] Schulze-Dörrlamm (1985: 509–10, 549, 555).

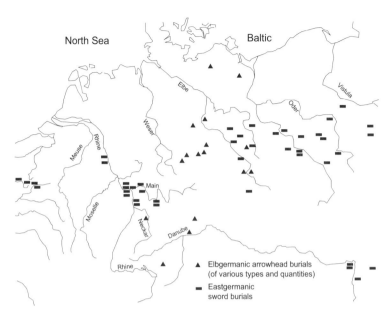

Fig. 15 Elbgermanic and Eastgermanic grave-goods *c.*300–400 [from Schach-Dörges (1997: 94 Fig. 78); © Archäologisches Landesmuseum Baden-Württemberg].

that these graves reflect Eastgermanic customs spreading westwards, but responding to Roman influence by substituting inhumation for cremation.[188] However, there is debate over the mechanisms of such movement. Steuer proposes that all we can see is a new form of funeral rite travelling westwards along an ancient line of communication.[189] Schulze-Dörrlamm, on the other hand, concludes that the graves reflect some movement of individuals or groups—in particular, Burgundians, but sometimes Vandals—along an established east–west route.[190] Given what the literary sources say about the presence of Burgundians near or in the Rhine–Main area from the late third to the early fifth century, the latter explanation is preferable.

More recent work has revealed the introduction of artefacts of an Eastgermanic character in the middle and upper Main

---

[188] Schulze-Dörrlamm (1985: 509–10, 549–51).
[189] Steuer (1998: 286–7 and Fig. 1).
[190] Schulze-Dörrlamm (1985: 509–10, 549, 555–6, 561).

valley, between the old *limes* and the Regnitz region, from the late
third century. These have been identified as Burgundian, and used to
locate the heartland of the Burgundian presence on the middle
Main.[191] The small hill-site at Wettenburg, Mainschleife-bei-Urphar
(3), founded in the later fourth century on the Main beyond the old
limes line, has been interpreted as an important Burgundian
'Herrschaftszentrum'.[192] Roman, or Roman-style, artefacts (in particular, *terra nigra* pottery) found here and throughout the area
reflect significant contact with the Empire.[193] The spread of Eastgermanic artefacts deep into the upper Main–Regnitz region during
the fourth century has been interpreted as reflecting the expansion of
Burgundian influence (though not Burgundian conquest) upstream
into Elbgermanic areas.[194]

The archaeology of the Main–Regnitz region appears to support
the hypothesis that the heartland of western Burgundian settlement
was on the middle Main, and confirms the idea of the Main corridor
as an artery of communication.[195] The artefacts indicate the ability of
the Burgundians to extend their military and political influence
eastwards; and some burials are sufficiently late to confirm the
impression given by the literary sources of Burgundian movement
westwards, as far as the Mainz bridgehead, in the late fourth and early
fifth century.[196] A thinning-out of settlement in the upper Main–
Regnitz area has been associated with this movement, though other
late finds suggest that not all were involved. Some may have remained
on the middle Main into the fifth century, while the region reverted
to Elbgermanic control.[197]

The presence of ambitious Burgundians must have unsettled local
Alamanni. No wonder there was friction. Disputes over salt were
probably the manifestation, not the direct cause, of mutual suspicion.

---

[191] See the works cited by Haberstroh (2000a: 29). Haberstroh (132) himself
prefers the neutral 'Eastgermanic' to 'Burgundian' (while not expressly ruling out
the latter), and a slightly later date—from *c*.300.
[192] Steuer (1990: 150), (1997: 158); Haberstroh (2000a: 133), citing Rosenstock.
Cf. above 94.
[193] Haberstroh (2000a: 131–2).
[194] Ibid.
[195] Haberstroh (2000a: 13, 131–2).
[196] Martin (1997b: 164). Cf. below 174, 324.
[197] Haberstroh (2000a: 133); Steuer (1990: 150), (1997: 158).

Burgundians may also have disrupted Alamannic life along the Main by inviting further Roman interference. From the Roman viewpoint, the lower Main had to be guarded as an important transverse route to and from the Empire.[198] To manage the area Rome relied mainly on agreements with incoming Elbe-*Germani*, but this was not entirely sufficient. In addition, therefore, Rome sent regular patrols into the region, indicated by coin-finds on the main routes; and, as in the case of boundary markers, in certain areas made deals with neighbouring Burgundian communities. Funerary archaeology suggests that individual Eastgermanic warriors were also brought in.

The dangers of identifying the ethnicity of the occupant of a single burial site are increasingly being recognized. 'Diagnostic' artefacts might just as easily be objects of desire, acquired through travel or by purchase.[199] Again, however, one must be pragmatic. The graves concerned are very distinctive, and can be related to the wider Burgundian settlement pattern. As Schulze-Dörrlamm and Stribrny propose, they probably indicate the movement of East-*Germani* who came to serve in the Roman army.[200] For burials west of the Rhine, this is unexceptionable. The regular use of Germanic troops by Rome began in the third century and continued well into the fifth.[201] A complication is that certain patterns of grave-goods suggest that some individuals may have served in the Roman army on the Danube before being posted to the Rhine/Main area,[202] which suggests that they did not come down the Main corridor into Gaul. This need not detain us here; the phenomenon may result from individuals' acquiring 'exotic' possessions by travel or purchase, as noted. The main puzzle springs from weapon-burials found east of the Rhine, in Alamannia, which amount to just over half (10/19) of pertinent sites. These could belong to men who had died on active service or while returning home after retirement, but this is unlikely. In this respect, the most suggestive site is that of Ebel-bei-Praunheim/Frankfurt, with its native farm and associated Eastgermanic grave of

---

198 Cf. above 51, below 190.
199 Cf. Bowlus (2002: 253); Brather (2002: 173); Pohl (2002b: 236).
200 Schulze-Dörrlamm (1985: 561); Stribrny (1989: 432).
201 See above 73–4; below 327.
202 Schulze-Dörrlamm (1985: 553–5, 561).

a man, probably a Burgundian, who had served in Gaul before dying and being buried in Alamannia.[203] This has a look of permanence: of being the last resting place of a warrior who had chosen to live where he died, and who had decided to be buried there in a particular fashion. The Ebel-bei-Praunheim grave was dug in the second half of the fourth century, but the pattern of which it is part began much earlier: the earliest known weapon-burial, Stockstadt I, near a former *limes* fort on the Main frontier, dates from the late third/early fourth century.[204] Who were these people? I am reluctant to accept Stribrny's proposal that they were part of a regular transrhenish militia.[205] I prefer to see them as veterans who were allowed, and, perhaps, through the promise of protection, encouraged, by Rome to settle in the Main area as a further means of controlling the region. The Ebel-bei-Praunheim villa lies not far from the Main and the Nidda, and so in an emergency could have received naval support.[206]

In the three-sided relationship between Romans, Alamanni and Burgundians, it was the Alamanni who tended to come off worst. Instructive are Julian's actions during his Alamannic campaign of 359. It is clear from Ammianus that even Julian, renowned for his merciless treatment of barbarians, took care that his troops, eagerly terrorizing Alamanni, did not extend their bloodlust into Burgundian territory.[207] Such cooperation puts into perspective the invention of the myth of a common origin which was probably a creation of the early fourth century.[208] It also explains the inscription commemorating Hariulfus, son of a Burgundian king, Hanhavaldus, who died while serving as *protector domesticus* in the imperial court at Trier, probably under Valentinian I: 'probably the finest epigraphic monument to integration between Roman and German in the late imperial army'.[209] In the Main valley, the Alamanni, facing both Romans and Burgundians, found themselves between a rock and a hard place.

---

[203] Schulze-Dörrlamm (1985: 555–61, Fig. 39 and list 5 (556)); cf. above 85.

[204] Schulze-Dörrlamm (1985: 537–46, esp. 545).

[205] Below 130–3.

[206] Cf. below 241, 297–8.

[207] AM 28.2.15. Cf. below 249.

[208] Anton (1981: 238).

[209] *CIL* 13.3682 (*ILS* 2813). Hoffmann (1978: 317, quotation). For *protector* (officer cadet), see below 147.

4

Society

This chapter offers no complete 'Life and Times' of the Alamanni. There is simply not enough material, textual or archaeological, with which to construct a solid ethnographic account.[1] Other than that their warriors had long hair, dyed red, and liked strong drink we know little about them.[2] As far as, for example, the lives of women are concerned, we know nothing; and all that can safely be said of Alamannic religion is, as Agathias remarked in the sixth century, that it was solidly and unsophisticatedly pagan.[3] (Christianity did not penetrate Alamannic society to a significant degree until the seventh century.[4]) This is despite the fact that, though Ammianus says more about the social organization of Alamanni than that of any other barbarians, unlike the rest he passes no comment on their sexual *mores*, dress, general diet etc.[5] What follows, therefore, is mainly, though not exclusively, a review of political and military aspects of the life of the various Elbgermanic communities living in Alamannia.

The feature of Alamannic political life most frequently mentioned in the sources is the presence of 'kings': *reges/basileis*. Of these, Crocus figures in the *Epitome* in an early-fourth-century context,[6] and many others are prominent in the accounts of Julian, Libanius and, of course, Ammianus Marcellinus. Their names (Chnodomarius, Fraomarius, Gundomadus, Hariobaudes, Hortarius, Macrianus, Priarius, Serapio, Suomarius, Urius, Ursicinus, Vadomarius, Vestralpus, Vithicabius)

---

[1] Cf. Pohl (2000: 7) on such difficulties in respect of Germanic society in general.
[2] AM 16.12.36; 27.2.2; Matthews (1989: 313).
[3] Agathias, *Hist.* 1.7.1 (=*Quellen* 2, 80).
[4] Lorenz, Sönke (1997: 442).
[5] Cf. Guzmán Armario (2002: 216, 135–60).
[6] *Epitome* 41.3. Below 146.

are rhythmic and memorable. The kings were part of a social hierarchy. This is seen most clearly in Ammianus' account of the Alamannic host before the battle of Strasbourg in 357 and of Hortarius' entertainment of Alamannic leaders facing Julian in 359.[7] Combining these narratives, we find superior kings (*excelsiores ante alios reges*), kings (*proximi reges*), lesser kings (*reguli*) and princes (*regales*).[8] The same passages tell us that beneath the kings were nobles (*optimates*) and beneath the nobles were warriors (*armati*). This hierarchy has attracted a good deal of attention; but we should note Elton's point that it is very similar to what the sources relate of most other northern barbarian societies,[9] and that Ammianus uses much the same terms when describing the Sarmatians.[10] Ammianus probably envisaged all northern societies in this way, and we should not expect his account to contain much in the way of anthropological subtlety. Indeed, in most cases it is probably best not to worry too much about precise distinctions and think simply of 'kings', 'nobles' (a number of whom were probably related to the kings[11]) and 'warriors'.

I have so far employed the term 'king' since this is the usual translation of *rex/basileus*. However, since Alamannic leaders were clearly not kings in the same sense as, say, Philip of Macedon or Herod the Great, it may be better to think of them as 'chieftains'. Yet even this term needs to be treated with care. Were the *reges* established 'chiefs' (succeeding '. . . to a hereditary position in a context of social hierarchy', their power 'ascribed' and coinciding 'with privileged control of wealth') or competing 'big men' (manipulating wealth to achieve their positions of power)?[12] A related possibility is that they were anyway only temporary, wartime, leaders.[13]

The crucial question is whether Alamannic 'royal' power was hereditary and permanent; and the *communis opinio* is firmly that it was. Geuenich, for example, is confident that dynastic kingship was a

[7] AM 16.12.23, 26; 18.2.13.

[8] For *regales* as men of royal blood see Werner (1965: 75); Geuenich (1997b: 77); Zotz (1998: 402–3). Cf., in a context which suggests Alamanni, *Historia Augusta, V. Probi* 14.1: *reguli*.

[9] Elton (1996a: 15–19, 32–7).

[10] AM 17.12.1: *subreguli, optimates*; 18.2.13: *reges omnes et regales et regulos*.

[11] Zotz (1998: 403).

[12] Curta (2002b).

[13] Geuenich (1997a: 49).

normal part of Alamannic government, noting the cases of Chnodomarius and Serapio (uncle and nephew), Gundomadus and Vadomarius (brothers), Macrianus and Hariobaudes (brothers), and Vadomarius and Vithicabius (father and son).[14] One has to be careful: some of these links, especially those between brothers, may have been contemporary, the result of related challengers' cooperating to topple a dominant 'big man'. However, dynastic succession is the most likely convention, at least for those communities living close to the Empire. Rome would have preferred it because it offered more stability and the chance of influencing future generations.[15] Roman deposition of an Alamannic king must have been a policy of last resort.[16] Very telling, in this respect, is the case of Serapio's father, Mederichus. He was taken by Rome as a hostage for what seems to have been a considerable period of time, before returning to the Rhineland where he probably preceded his son as a local king.[17] If there had been a significant danger of his absence damaging his status in Alamannic society, that is if his position had not been assured by birth and could have been open to challenge by an ambitious big man, it would not have benefited the Empire to detain him. We may envisage the Alamannic kings as chiefs, and interpret Hortarius' feasting of border Alamannic leaders in 359 in these terms: not as a big man creating a power base but as an established chieftain and fellow chieftains demonstrating (feigned) unity in difficult circumstances, after a fashion that was as much Roman as Germanic.[18] However, Rome also made sure that no such chieftain became a 'Great King'.[19]

According to Ammianus, the *reges* ruled over discrete territories: *regna* ('kingdoms') or *pagi* ('districts'/'cantons'). *Pagi* were probably discrete geographical areas, such as major valleys.[20] It appears that a

---

[14] Geuenich (1997a: 45, 49–50); cf. Zotz (1998: 402). Chnodomarius and Serapio: AM 16.12.25. Gundomadus and Vadomarius: AM 14.10.1, 10; 16.12.17; 21.3.4. Macrianus and Hariobaudes: AM 18.2.15. Vadomarius and Vithicabius: AM 27.10.3; 30.7.7.

[15] Cf. Burns (2003: 242–3).

[16] Cf. the case of Macrianus and Fraomarius, below 150–1, 284, 353.

[17] Below 155.

[18] AM 18.2.13. Cf. below 251.

[19] Below 124.

[20] Elton (1996a: 32).

kingdom might comprise more than one *pagus*.[21] The inheritance of constituent *pagi* would explain how brothers might come to share power, with the office of king being seen as divisible rather than the kingdom.[22] From Ammianus' accounts of Roman campaigns it appears that the kingdoms were small—much smaller than, say, the average Gallic *civitas*—from which one may infer that they generally comprised no more than a couple of *pagi*.

Subordinate to the kings were the nobles. These could prove troublesome subjects, but from them the kings must have drawn their most trusted helpers, their *comites*, 'companions'. In 357, Chnodomarius surrendered with 'three very close friends'.[23] In 358, Julian detained Hortarius' four *comites*, 'on whose aid and loyalty he chiefly relied'.[24] In 361, Julian's officials arrested Vadomarius but released his *comites*.[25] Ammianus does not specify the number of Vadomarius' attendants and clouds our conception of royal companions in general by reporting that Chnodomarius surrendered not only with his close friends but also with 200 *comites*. I propose that the kings' intimates were few in number, and that Chnodomarius' '200' was the garrison of his 'Herrschaftszentrum', under himself and three 'captains'. The 800 or so warriors that I suggest formed the remainder of a *pagus*-army of *c*.1,000[26] will have been dependants of *optimates* living elsewhere. If each, like Chnodomarius and his cronies, provided around 50 *armati*, they will have been about 16 in number. Kings would therefore have depended on *optimates* for their main military strength.

Optimate allegiance may have been flexible, with successful kings winning new supporters at the margins of their realms.[27] It appears that in times of great need kings could strengthen their power and authority by calling in help from outside their territories;[28] but this must have been unusual, and the more so because, by disturbing the current order, it was potentially dangerous for kings and *optimates*

[21] Zotz (1998: 400–1) referring to AM 18.2.8.
[22] Elton (1996a: 33); Zotz (1998: 402). Both cite the example of Gundomadus and Vadomarius.
[23] AM 16.12.60: *amici iunctissimi*.
[24] AM 17.10.8: *quorum ope et fide maxime nitebatur*.
[25] AM 21.4.5.
[26] Below 238.
[27] Elton (1996a: 31–2).
[28] Below 238.

alike. *Optimates*, as well as generally supporting their chiefs, were expected to fight alongside them in battle—even, when necessary, as berserkers.[29] They were also used as envoys in dealings with the Empire (and, presumably, with other *regna*).[30] On the other hand, it appears that any king who was perceived to be failing would face trouble from his *optimates*. In 357 Gundomadus was murdered and Vadomarius forced to accept anti-Roman policies. Ammianus puts this down to their respective *populus* and *plebs*, but we are probably justified in ascribing the 'plots' involved to leading *optimates*.[31] This raises questions concerning the mechanism of succession. It seems likely that, on Gundomadus' death, Vadomarius was able to join his brother's kingdom to his own.[32] However, if Vadomarius and his family had been killed, from whom and how would a new king have been chosen? One can only guess at some meeting of warriors, its decisions reflecting the political scheming of leading *optimates*.

This brings us to the little we know of the character of Alamannic society: that it was violent. This is in line with the martial nature of barbarian society in general, and the habitual violence and feuding of Germanic society in particular.[33] The latter is visible in early medieval Alamannic laws, which reveal a highly competitive warrior-society, based on family groups.[34] The cause of such violence was probably social insecurity resulting from chronic poverty rather than population increase or natural catastrophe.[35] Under such circumstances, warriors would fight each other and the Roman Empire not out of malice or long-term political strategy but simply because they felt they had to. And it seems that brutal practices, such as head-hunting, were encouraged by Rome for imperial ends.[36] It would not be surprising if the urge to raid remained a feature of even settled Alamannic society. This would help explain excessive Alamannic

[29] AM 16.12.49.

[30] AM 14.10.9–10 (357); 26.5.7 (365); 28.2.6 (369); 28.5.11–12 (370).

[31] AM 16.12.17: [Gundobadus] *per insidias interemptus.* Cf. Zotz (1998: 404).

[32] Cf. above 119. I take Ammianus' later (21.2.3: 360) *a pago* [singular] *Vadomarii* to be just a generalization, with *pagus* as equivalent to *regnum*.

[33] Hedeager (1993: 122); Elton (1996a: 46–7); cf. Heather (2001: 41).

[34] Steuer (1997b: 275–8); Pohl (1998a: 641), (2002a: 65).

[35] Gutmann (1991: 14); cf. above 49.

[36] Libanius, *Orat.* 18.45; cf. Zosimus 3.7.2, which Paschoud (1979: 79) relates to *Historia Augusta, V. Probi* 14.2.

enthusiasm to 'aid' Constantius II against Magnentius in the 350s and, generally, spasmodic trouble indicating that even friendly chiefs had difficulties in controlling their own warriors.[37]

Though the most able and ambitious *optimates* may have been removed from local politics by entering imperial service,[38] one suspects that it was never easy to be an Alamannic chief. This explains the attractiveness of Roman support[39] and is also likely to have affected Roman terminology.

The derivation and meaning of *Alamanni* and *Alamannia* have been dealt with. Here, it is sufficient to repeat that we do not know what the Alamanni called themselves. However, it is reasonable to suppose that people identified themselves and where they lived according to the name of their current chief: 'the people of *n*' or inhabitants of 'the *pagus* of *n*'.[40] From a Roman viewpoint this would have been unsatisfactory because kings were bound to change. For its purposes, the Empire needed more permanent names, which brings us to the question of the 'Teilstämme'.

Striking in Ammianus' accounts of how the Alamanni organized themselves for war are his references to two regional groupings. These comprise the Lentienses, just north of Lake Constance, whose name is plausibly associated with the medieval 'Linzgau';[41] and the 'Bucinobantes', in the area of the lower Main, approached by way of Wiesbaden.[42] To Ammianus' groups modern historians have added two more, found in the *Notitia Dignitatum* alongside mention of the Bucinobantes, which appear to reflect the same sort of organization. These are the 'Brisigavi', associated with Breisach/Brisiacum in the Breisgau on the upper Rhine; and the 'Raetovarii', understood as 'men of the (*sc.*) lost territories of Raetia', that is north of the upper Danube.[43] All are now generally referred to as 'constituent'- or

[37] Cf. Stroheker (1975: 30); Gutmann (1991: 14); Elton (1996a: 74). Below 203, 222, 262 and 286.

[38] Below 154.

[39] Cf. above 82.

[40] Wenskus (1961: 498); Geuenich (1997a: 29–30, 46), (1997b: 74–5); Zotz (1998: 401). Cf. Ammianus 16.12.17; 18.2.8.

[41] AM 15.4; 31.10.1. Zotz (1998: 393).

[42] AM 29.4.3, 7. de Jonge (1939: 97).

[43] *Not. Dig.* Or. 5.58; Occ. 5.201/7.25, 5.202/7.128. Zotz (1998: 401); Steuer (1998: 276); Geuenich (1997a: 29).

'sub'-tribes ('Teilstämme'), not in a past ('this is how the Alamanni arrived in Alamannia') or even contemporary ('this is how the fourth-century Alamanni were organized') sense, but as emerging aggregates of *pagi* which would eventually coalesce to form 'the Alamanni'.[44]

It has been suggested that the 'Teilstämme' were originally Roman constructs. 'Lentienses', 'Raetovarii' and 'Brisigavi' seem Celto-Roman, not Germanic, in form.[45] They are locational, indicating where people lived, not necessarily what they called themselves. They therefore could have been applied to Germanic newcomers by outsiders already acquainted with the areas in which these people had settled. They have the air of having been given to provide permanent descriptions of groupings irrespective of who led them. It has been further suggested that such outsiders could have been Roman recruiting officers, raising Alamannic units for the imperial army.[46] I consider these issues below, and propose modification of current thinking. In brief, 'Lentienses', 'Brisigavi' and 'Raetovarii' were even more Roman than has been accepted so far: they should not be seen as permanent indigenous geopolitical entities in any state of development. An exception is provided by the 'Bucinobantes', the only group we know with a Germanic name. These may have exploited the identity given to them by Rome to create a temporary miniature empire on the Main.[47]

Another controversy concerns the existence of a Great King. This is important for events during the fifth century,[48] but debate begins with the fourth. In describing the Alamannic alliance of 357, Ammianus calls Chnodomarius and Serapio 'kings higher than the rest in authority'. Further, his narrative has Chnodomarius clearly in charge of operations.[49] The alliance was destroyed by Julian, but the question arises as to whether Chnodomarius' position indicates that, despite political division, Alamannic communities already had the potential to unite under a single leader. In short, are we in the presence of the first stage of development of a single Alamannic monarchy, like

---

[44] Geuenich (1997a: 29–31).
[45] Wenskus (1961: 498).
[46] Geuenich (1997a: 29–31), (1997b: 74–5); Steuer (1998: 276); Zotz (1998: 401).
[47] Below 174, 250, 304, 324.
[48] Below 335–7.
[49] Below 236.

that of the Salian Franks under the Merovingians? Some express doubt by pointing out that, though the confrontation of 357 was dominated by Chnodomarius, nominally at least he shared power with Serapio; that not all Alamannic communities were directly involved; and that the alliance was shattered following military defeat. The enterprise should therefore be regarded as partial and temporary.[50] Others are more positive, interpreting the collapse as reflecting the extent of Chnodomarius' influence and proving that there were means by which an individual might gain prominence in Alamannic society.[51]

We should not overlook the obvious. Though there is a case for suspecting that Ammianus exaggerated the extent of Chnodomarius' standing,[52] he was clearly a key player and he was followed by other Alamannic leaders with more than local influence, such as Macrianus.[53] We must also take into account the militaristic and competitive nature of Alamannic society, likely to produce warriors willing to challenge the leaders of their own community or, as kings themselves, other kings. History has produced enough examples of such men creating great empires for us to be familiar with the type. Why not among the Alamanni? The problem for such people in the fourth century was that the Alamanni were in a cultural and strategic cul-de-sac. For a leader to emerge, he would have to be victorious in battle, and the sole worthy opponent was Rome. But Alamannic leaders relied on Rome for pay and goods; and Rome was anyway all-powerful: able and willing to nip any such aspirations in the bud and, if this failed through imperial inadvertence, distraction or incompetence, to crush anyone who managed to emerge.[54] There was potential, but this could be realized only after the removal of imperial power. Without such leadership, in the fourth century there could be no clear Alamanni and indeed no clear Alamannia.

Like the 'Teilstämme', in the Roman period Alamannia was a geographical expression, not a geopolitical entity. There is no reason to assume that the old *limes* formed a frontier. The traditional case

---

[50] Geuenich (1997a: 49), (1997b: 77); cf. Stroheker (1975: 36).
[51] Zotz (1998: 395–6, 402).
[52] Below 236.
[53] Below 304. Zotz (1998: 402).
[54] Cf. Heather (2001: 42–6); below 358.

for this as the Burgundian 'border' is not convincing; and anyway hill-sites extend far beyond its line.[55] In addition, at Gaukönigshofen, further up the Main, recent research has shown Elbe-*Germani*, who may have been Alamanni or Iuthungi, rubbing shoulders with residual Rhine–Weser *Germani* and probably also Burgundians.[56] The region was not administratively and politically integrated until the Merovingian ducate of the sixth century.[57] *Allemagne/Alemania* entered modern European languages from Alamannia's status as a Frankish dependency, not from its original designation as an area just outside the Roman Empire. In fact, relative to its fourth-century position, Frankish Alamannia appears to have 'slipped' significantly southwards and westwards.[58] Medieval Alamannia came into existence as a result of the perception and needs of outsiders, and the same may be said of its earlier relationship with Rome.

Rome can have been interested only in people near the borders of its Empire. This gave Roman Alamannia a definite shape in the south-west, where it abutted the Empire, but in the north-east its boundaries are unknown and were probably never clear. It is likely that people became or ceased to be Alamanni in Roman eyes as they moved in and out of the region.[59] So, again, as in the case of the 'Teilstämme', such shape as Alamannia had was Roman-imposed, like so much else in developing Germanic society.[60] It is hardly surprising that in the fourth century, as in the third, we find no Alamannic unity or even aspiration to unity.[61] There had been progress. The settled kingdoms were more sophisticated and, presumably, more in contact with each other on a regular basis than itinerant war-bands; and, as with the Franks, Roman-inspired ethnogenesis will have fostered fellow-feeling. However, integration was still weak and liable to be disrupted by fresh raiders from the east,[62] and so was not expressed in political or military terms. There was still no more than a mosaic

---

[55] Above 94, 110–11.
[56] Steidl (1997: 76), (2000: 108–10); cf. above 100.
[57] Geuenich (1997a: 92); cf. below 347.
[58] Geuenich (1997d: 204–7).
[59] Keller (1993: 100–1); cf. Zotz (1998: 401). Cf. above 48.
[60] Geary (1988: vi); cf. Pohl (1998b: 2).
[61] Wenskus (1961: 503); Geuenich (1997b: 77–8); Pohl (2000: 30–1).
[62] Below 313.

of kings and *pagi* (although, unlike the Franks, there is curiously little direct evidence for Alamanni fighting each other), incapable of acting together on a grand scale. 'The Alamanni' posed no direct threat to Roman territorial integrity. Alamannic raiding could be distressing, but despite the impression given by the sources, especially Ammianus, there were no really dangerous attacks on the Empire.

Against this background, it is hardly surprising that the groupings we know about, or think we know about, form no tidy pattern. Thus, while the Bucinobantes and Brisigavi fall neatly into the coin-using areas, the Lentienses and the Raetovarii do not. And while the hill-sites along the Swabian Alp might take in the Raetovarii, they lie north of the Lentienses.

The question as to whether Alamannic settlements comprised a significant proportion of the original imperial population and its descendants is much debated. Some scholars reserve judgement; others are hotly opposed to the idea.[63] However, before dealing with this directly, we need to consider the proposal that, under Gallienus or the 'Gallic' emperors, the people of the region were formally evacuated and settled in north-eastern Gaul.[64] This is based on two observations. The first is that an operation of this nature was later put in train for the inhabitants of Dacia. These were settled south of the Danube in two 'new' provinces of Dacia Ripensis and Dacia Mediterranea. Second, the part of Upper Germany that was lost to Alamannia was known as the *Agri Decumates*, 'The Ten Canton Lands'.[65] In the late Roman period, we find a similar name, *Decem Pagi*, 'The Ten Cantons', referring to a place but perhaps originally designating a district, to the west of Strasbourg. The evacuation hypothesis has won support,[66] but I reject it here.

The evacuation of Dacia was put in hand by Aurelian, a strong-minded ruler under no direct threat, with the confidence to take a painful but necessary decision and the wit to obscure imperial contraction in a confusing new nomenclature.[67] Any evacuation of the *Agri Decumates* would have fallen in the early stages of protracted

[63] Schach-Dörges (1997: 101). Cf. the observations of Sommer (1999: 190–1).
[64] Hind (1984).
[65] Cf. above 32–3.
[66] e.g. Matthews (1989: 308); Jehne (1996: 204); Witschel (1999: 211–12).
[67] See Watson (1999: 143, 155–7).

civil war, in an area which had the attention of at least two interested parties. Its effective loss did not need to be so carefully disguised. The abandonment of Dacia was the abandonment of a huge province, conquered by the mighty Trajan. The abandonment of the *Agri Decumates* could be projected as the partial withdrawal from a marginal area of Upper Germany which had been annexed only after it had been colonized unofficially, under the reviled Domitian, by the 'riff-raff' of Gaul.[68] The similarity between *Agri Decumates* and *Decem Pagi* is fortuitous.

What happened to the Roman population of what was to become Alamannia? It is likely that, at the same time as the military abandonment of the region, if not earlier, those provincials who could moved to territory that was still under imperial protection.[69] Alamannic raiding and settlement, however gradual, cannot have been pleasant. One thinks again of signs of torture and murder at Harting.[70] But others must have chosen, or felt compelled, to remain behind. Choice would have been easier for the poor: the reluctance of peasants to leave their land is notorious.[71] As for compulsion, one may assume, for example, that Germanic warriors detained and supported a number of provincial females and their joint offspring. Generally, chances of demographic continuity would have been much higher if Germanic settlement was a piecemeal process, not a sudden, violent conquest. There may even have been a phase when indigenous peasants and warrior newcomers lived alongside each other.

Early upper-class flight is, it has been suggested, revealed in inscriptions showing the presence of *civitas*-elites of the area in Mainz.[72] Alternatively, these might simply reflect the propensity of 'country' decurions to spend their money in the regional capital.[73] As far as lower-class reluctance to move is concerned, the picture is even more obscure. There is no sign of the continued use of Roman-style goods in rural settlements. However, this may be because a Roman

---

[68] Tacitus, *Germania* 29.4 (cf. below 140 n.146).
[69] See, e.g. Trumm (2002), for the area around Schleitheim.
[70] Above 78–9.
[71] Drinkwater (1992: 214).
[72] Nuber (1997: 64); Carroll (2001: 138 and Pl. 8).
[73] Witschel (1999: 345–6).

residual population would have been forced to use what was to hand, that is Germanic products.[74] Scholars inferred the existence of such a population from the assumption that incoming war-bands, lacking time and agricultural expertise, would have depended for the necessities of life upon the work of a servile Roman labour force, made up of residual inhabitants and people seized during raids into the Empire.[75] Another suggestion is that Alamannic remains at or near former non-rural Roman sites do not signify Germanic settlement, but Germanic control of a residual Roman workforce that supplied the newcomers with goods and services they were unable to provide for themselves.[76] However, neither idea is sustained by archaeological evidence. As far as the first is concerned, pollen studies indicate a decline in the rural population. A slave population descended from resident provincials, if it existed, could not have been large. With regard to the second, there is no sign of settlements at former Roman forts, towns and *vici* acting as significant centres of exchange. Alamannic rural sites yield few luxury items, which suggests that these were scarce and expensive, and generally available only in the 'Höhensiedlungen'. On the other hand, thanks to the work of Stribrny, we can now see a very curious local coin-pattern.

Investigation of stray finds of Roman bronze coins in Alamannia has shown that these continued to circulate throughout the fourth century.[77] There is no doubt that this is an authentic circulation pattern, and not, say, the result of the 'churning' of coins obtained from booty or brought in by imperial campaigns in the region. On the contrary, the pattern of coin loss (and, therefore, of coin availability and usage) closely resembles that of Roman provinces (Germania I and Maxima Sequanorum) to the west of Alamannia.[78] Within the general pattern, Stribrny has identified two significant variations. These are areas of 'major' and 'minor' circulation, with the latter similar to the former but with a distinctly smaller volume of coins (Fig. 16).

[74] Steuer (1990: 199–201).
[75] Keller (1993: 98–9). Cf. above 93, below 139, 243.
[76] Keller (1993: 97–8); Fingerlin (1997b: 131).
[77] Weidemann (1972: Figs 1–12); Stribrny (1989).
[78] Stribrny (1989: 423, 426).

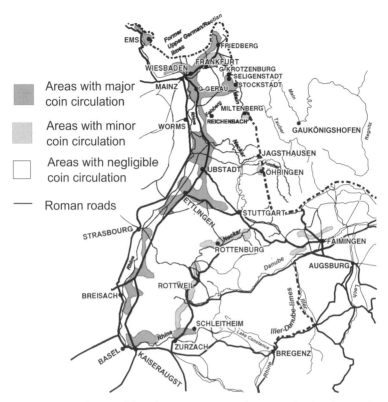

Fig. 16 Circulation of fourth-century Roman bronze coins in Alamannia [after Stribrny (1989: 401 Fig. 19); Trumm (2002: 217 Fig. 11)].

The largest area of major coin circulation consists of a strip, *c.*20 km (12 statute miles) wide, running, with small breaks, along the old military highway from the Mainz bridgehead to the major base at Kaiseraugst.[79] From this sprout three eastward projections. The most prominent echoes the route of a pair of roads that left the main north–south highway at Ubstadt and Ettlingen respectively, joined at Stuttgart and then ran as a single road to the Danube at Faimingen. Another runs parallel to the route of the Roman road

[79] For this and the following details see Stribrny (1989: 375–97).

north of the river Main, from Mainz by way of Wiesbaden to Friedberg, formerly an important *limes* fort. The third projection runs south of Mainz, from Groß Gerau to Seligenstadt and Stockstadt, also former *limes* forts. It seems influenced by a road to the Main, to the south of which is a region, the Felsberg, of fourth-century Roman quarrying. A detached stretch of the Rhine corridor is discernible to the north of Mainz, around Bad Ems. The areas of minor circulation, though more scattered, seem also to be related to Roman structures and sites. Three such areas form another broken strip, running north–south, roughly parallel to the Rhine strip, along the middle and upper Neckar and roads from Rottenburg by way of Rottweil to the Rhine at Zurzach and on to Windisch. This cuts across the Stuttgart–Faimingen road. Trumm has recently shown that it terminates in a major area of circulation, between Schleitheim and Windisch.[80] Two other areas of minor coin circulation mark the end of the east–west route, between Faimingen and, to the west, the confluence of the Iller and the Danube. A fourth area of minor coin circulation is sandwiched between the two northernmost projections of major circulation, around Frankfurt-am-Main. Two islands of minor coin circulation lie on the line of the former *limes* around Miltenberg and Öhringen.

Coin circulation east of the Rhine was at its most intense under the house of Constantine, especially early in the reign of Constantine I. In common with the Gallic pattern, there is a break in supply from *c.*350 into the early 360s, as a result of the revolt of Magnentius. Supplies were renewed under Valentinian I, but much less strongly than west of the Rhine.[81] Since Roman bronze coins do not figure prominently in the finds from accepted Alamannic sites, I do not agree with Nuber that the newcomers could have been taught how to use coins by earlier Germanic immigrants, that is that the coin-pattern reflects Alamannic usage.[82] Precisely what it means is open to debate.

The main engine of coin supply must, as always, have been the Roman state, in particular its payments to the army. Stribrny proposes

---

[80] Trumm (2002: 36–8 and Fig. 11, 217).
[81] Stribrny (1989: 375–7, 400–2, 407–8).
[82] Cf. Stribrny (1989: 426 and n.186): only two post-260 coins were found during the Runder Berg excavations. Nuber (1993: 102), (1998: 375, 379).

that the bronze was paid to a local militia, acting as a defence screen. He argues that such a militia was not required east of Basel since this frontier had been heavily fortified under Diocletian. The meandering course of the old Rhine had, however, hindered the building of defences from Basel to Coblenz.[83] Stribrny envisages this militia as a disciplined force, comprising both men from a residual Roman population and some resident Alamanni, stationed along the right bank of the Upper Rhine and, in places, on the old *limes*. Thus Alamannic control did not extend close to the Rhine.[84] The coins were spent by the soldiers and their dependants on Roman provincial imports, as is reflected in finds of Roman ceramics in these areas.[85] While elsewhere dismissing the activity of Roman traders as a cause of the areas of major circulation, Stribrny accepts this as an explanation for the existence of the isolated area of minor circulation on the old *limes* around Öhringen.[86] The system worked well until the revolt of Magnentius.[87] It was made redundant by Valentinian I's fortifying the Upper-Rhine frontier. It was only then that Alamanni took control of territory adjacent to the Upper Rhine.[88] Stribrny's ideas deserve serious consideration.[89] I agree that the coins reflect important imperial activity, but propose that this amounted to more than just payments to irregular troops.

Although there were such troops available to Rome in Alamannia, these did not constitute the organized force envisaged by Stribrny. They would have been Alamannic warriors put in the service of the Empire by their chiefs under treaty agreements.[90] But if the chiefs received a monetary reward, this would have been in gold and silver, and it is unlikely that they or the Empire would have paid out bronze to their men. This is the implication of the near-absence of such pieces from the hill-sites.[91] Eastgermanic veterans appear to have

---

[83] Stribrny (1989: 417, 422, 430–1).
[84] Stribrny (1989: 432–3, 436).
[85] Stribrny (1989: 403).
[86] Stribrny (1989: 388, 450).
[87] Below 201.
[88] Stribrny (1989: 436).
[89] There is curiously little said about them in, e.g. *Alamannen* (1997), though Witschel (1999: 217) takes up the idea of a 'Grenzmiliz'.
[90] Above 81.
[91] Cf. above 130.

been settled in the Main valley.[92] These may have brought bronze coinage with them, and perhaps received more from the Empire, but their numbers must have been small and restricted. Finally, there is no other indication of an imperial *cordon sanitaire* east of the Rhine during the early fourth century. Ammianus gives no hint that Alamannic kings mentioned as being on the Rhine from 350 were recent unwelcome arrivals: charges against them amount to their having crossed, or threatened to cross, the river, not having reached it.[93] A better explanation for finds of Roman coinage in Alamannia is a more orthodox Roman presence in the area.

It is unlikely that Rome ever renounced its claim to sovereignty over the region, out of pride but also because it was important for the security of Gaul and, especially, Italy.[94] To uphold this claim regular forces continued to be sent on routine missions into Alamannia. This began early, in the making-good of abandoned military sites and the reusing of their remains.[95] It is also visible in the establishment of major bridgeheads and bases—at Mainz/Kastel[96] and at Wiesbaden. The latter was an important military and civil site into the second half of the fourth century with a coin-pattern identical to that of Mainz and may have supplied regiments for the imperial army.[97] Smaller military bases may also have been maintained up the Main in the early fourth century, providing a model for Valentinian I's river-supplied forts over the Rhine.[98] Though rivers were important, it would also have been prudent to monitor the old imperial roads. Such interest might explain the inclusion in the Peutinger Table of the route from Zurzach to Günzburg, important for Julian in 361.[99] The concentration of coin-finds near important highways, especially in areas of minor circulation, may indicate reconnaissance

---

[92] Above 116.

[93] Thus Gundomadus, Vadomarius; Chnodomarius, Serapio; Suomarius, Hortarius: see below 204, 236, 242, 247.

[94] Strobel (1999: 12–13); Witschel (1999: 212); Pohl (2002a: 63). Cf. below 190, 299. Italy: above 78.

[95] Above 53.

[96] Schoppa (1974: 93). Cf. below 364.

[97] Schoppa (1974: 48, 91, 95–101); Stribrny (1989: 377–9). Cf. below 135, 171.

[98] Below 241.

[99] Benedetti-Martig (1993: 360–1); cf. below 256–7.

patrols.[100] (The coin-pattern suggests that this activity involved troops from the Upper Rhine: the garrison on the High Rhine and upper Danube was secure behind the Danube–Iller–Rhine *limes*.[101]) None of this amounted to a full re-establishment of Roman control. There are signs of the pragmatic securing of key areas, but no more. Against Stribrny, there is no convincing epigraphic or literary evidence for the restoration of Roman administration in Alamannia.[102]

Low-key imperial military presence in western Alamannia may have been reinforced by exploitation of the region's resources. The most dramatic evidence we have of this comes from Trier cathedral. Here, a major refurbishment of the building, planned around 330 but completed only later in the century, led to the commissioning of four massive granite pillars (each *c.*12 metres long and weighing 30 tonnes) and marble capitals. The complete set came from quarries over the Rhine to the east of Worms, near Reichenbach, in the Felsberg (or 'Felsenmeer'). The working of such quarries and the transporting of their products into the Empire must have required the long-term presence of significant numbers of people—engineers, labourers, supervisors, guards, and ancillary personnel.[103] Those who were not slaves would have been paid, and so have attracted a further set of people offering goods and services. In this way, coinage would have been circulated and lost. In addition to stone, we may envisage the collection of other raw materials for export into the Empire. Ammianus Marcellinus and Libanius indicate that Alamannic territory was a good source of building timber. Equally suggestive, in the light of archaeological evidence for widespread working of the metal, is Libanius' report that Julian compelled Alamanni to provide him with iron.[104] Ammianus' knowledge of the dispute between

---

[100] I note that this interpretation resembles that of Schönberger, as cited by Trumm (2002: 35–6 and n.124).

[101] Above 131, below 192, 295.

[102] Stribrny (1989: 390, 434–6). The Heidelberg gravestones (*CIL* 13.11735, 11737) are unofficial and, to judge from their form and content, were probably erected before 260. The Victorinus leaguestone at Illingen is generally accepted to have been erected on the west bank of the old Rhine: Drinkwater (1987: 121). Generally, Stribrny puts too much trust in the *Historia Augusta*.

[103] Cüppers (1990: 634). Cf. Elbe (1977: 125–6); Höckmann (1986: 387–8); Stribrny (1989: 382–5, 432).

[104] AM 17.10.9, 18.2.3–6; Libanius, *Orat.* 18.78; cf. Symmachus, *Orat.* 2.15. Below 243.

Alamanni and Burgundians over access to salt deposits may also have derived from the shipment of salt to the Empire.[105] The presence of provincials involved in this in the Kocher region would explain coin concentrations at Öhringen. Ellis has proposed similar late-Roman interest in the salt trade along the river Mures, in western Romania; she has also drawn attention to a continuation of both a sedentary population and maintenance of Roman military and economic interests via control over the left bank of the Danube in the neighbouring Banat region.[106]

Alamannic farming was primitive, but close to the Rhine large-scale agricultural production may have been maintained by resident provincials. There is evidence for the continuation of Roman *villae rusticae* around Wiesbaden;[107] and Trumm has recently proposed the existence of a late-Roman rural population on land over the High Rhine.[108] Ammianus reports that, when Julian campaigned over the Rhine in 357, his troops plundered farms 'rich in cattle and crops', with houses 'built quite carefully in the Roman fashion'.[109] It is usual to take Ammianus at his word and interpret these buildings as evidence for Alamannic occupation and reuse of Roman structures.[110] However, this fits uncomfortably with what we know about Alamannic use of villa sites and with the generally unsophisticated standards of Alamannic building. Much more in keeping with the 'Großhöfe' and 'Grubenhäuser' of the 'Höhensiedlungen' and rural sites are, from a Roman viewpoint, the 'flimsy huts' that Ammianus mentions in the context of Julian's campaign of 359.[111] I suggest that the villas that Julian's troops destroyed in 357 were Roman: the property of a Roman population over the Rhine which, during the first half of the fourth century, had managed to survive

---

[105] Cf. Guzmán Armario (2002: 221).
[106] Ellis (1998: 231–2).
[107] At Erbenheim, Bierstadt and Igstadt: Schoppa (1974: 86–7, 91, 95–8, 101); Stribrny (1989: 379).
[108] Trumm (2002: 218–19).
[109] AM 17.1.7: [*sc. miles Romanus*] *opulentas pecore villas et frugibus rapiebat, nulli parcendo, extractisque captivis, domicilia cuncta, curatius ritu Romano constructa, flammis subditis exurebat.*
[110] Matthews (1989: 310); above 85.
[111] AM 18.2.15: *saepimenta fragilium penatium.* Cf. above 85, 89, 104, below 290.

and enjoy some modest prosperity. Ammianus' villas appear to have lain along the road from Wiesbaden to Friedberg, in an area of major coin circulation. Nominally ruled by Alamannic kings, but looking to the Empire, those who worked them would have helped to bring together imperial and Germanic society.[112] The road system may also have made Wiesbaden a centre of slave trading.[113]

Thus, the coin-pattern of parts of Alamannia resembles that of the Empire because it was part of it. But the areas concerned were small, and most imperial economic activity was probably state-controlled, with no chance of achieving its own momentum. The number of people involved cannot have been great, nor did the mass of Alamanni participate meaningfully. The rarity of coinage on all Alamannic sites and the scarcity of imported goods in rural settlements suggest negligible involvement in monetary transactions. Even Alamannic communities that grew up close to the frontier from a relatively early date, such as at Mengen, do not appear to have benefited from this exchange.[114] If Alamannic leaders directed their people to supply goods or services, they alone enjoyed the reward, in a form other than that of minted bronze.

It is strange that a small but appreciable number of late-Roman bronze coins following Stribrny's pattern has been found beyond old imperial territory at the Elbgermanic site of Gaukönigshofen, near the Main[115] (Fig. 16). While this, too, has been interpreted as losses from money paid to *Germani* in the service of Rome,[116] I see it as reflecting trading activity, along the lines proposed for Öhringen.[117] The presence of coins in all three areas may be a sign that on the fringes of Alamannia, perhaps beyond the reach of the major chiefs, Elbe-*Germani* were capable of participating in a monetary economy.[118]

---

[112] Below 356.

[113] AM 29.4.3–4. Matthews (1989: 312); Geuenich (1997a: 36). Cf. below 307.

[114] Fingerlin (1993: 69); Bücker (1999: 208–11).

[115] Steidl (1997: 77).

[116] Schmauder (2002: 193–4 n.55).

[117] Above 131. Such usage would represent direct continuity of economic activity from the second and third centuries: Steidl (1997: 76); Trumm (2002: 38); cf. above 36.

[118] Cf. above 105, 119, below 358.

The ending of the circulation of bronze coins east of the Rhine is obscured by the cessation of supplies to the western provinces generally in the late fourth and early fifth centuries.[119] Though Stribrny's histograms show new issues failing to arrive after *c*.400,[120] this dearth was not exclusive to Alamannia. One might argue that preceding activities could have continued using old coins. However, Stribrny claims an authentic break on the grounds that old coins did not stay long in circulation,[121] and that well before the general shortage there was a sharp diminution in Alamannia.[122] Against this, we now know that imports of Roman ceramics into the Wetterau and beyond did not break off in this period, so there may have been continuing contact, albeit in very changed circumstances.[123]

The coins indicate that there was, for a time, a small resident imperial population in parts of the former provincial territory. However, this did not endure, and it must be distinguished from the original provincial population. Of this, the upper classes and some of the peasantry had gone. Some of the latter must have stayed: only the presence of such people, supplemented by others, slave and free, brought in from the Empire, can explain how early Alamanni were able to sustain themselves. However, this 'real' residual class is invisible to us.

Mention of slaves brings us to consideration of their role in Alamannic society. All ancient communities exploited slaves. The *Germani* in general were no different,[124] and for the third century we now have direct contemporary evidence for Elbe-*Germani*, Iuthungi, fleeing the Empire with prisoners whom they no doubt hoped to use as slaves.[125] Without further proof, one might state confidently that the Alamanni must have employed servile labour.

---

[119] *RIC* 10, 26–30.

[120] e.g. Stribrny (1989: 398–9).

[121] e.g. Stribrny (1989: 411).

[122] Stribrny (1989: 413–14). This interruption Stribrny ascribes, of course, to the demobilization of the local militia consequent upon Valentinian I's fortifying the upper Rhine (while conceding that Friedberg, with its relatively large number of Valentinianic coins, hardly fits his case).

[123] Steidl (1997: 77); cf. below 174, 324, 327.

[124] See Tacitus, *Germania* 24.4–25.1, for slavery, bond and chattel, in Germanic society.

[125] Above 53.

However, Alamannic slave exploitation is of particular interest because of the emphasis laid on it by ancient authors.

In 361, just after leaving the country, Julian catalogued his achievements in Gaul, beginning: 'Three times, while I was still Caesar, I crossed the Rhine; 20,000 persons who were held as captives on the further side of the Rhine I demanded and received back.'[126] Shortly afterwards, Libanius recorded extensive Alamannic slaving in the chaos caused by Constantius II's machinations against the usurper Magnentius in the early 350s. While Alamanni occupied and worked provincial land in Gaul, Roman prisoners were sent as slaves to farm theirs.[127] Later, Julian forced Alamannic captors to return those whom they had taken, and to prove that those they did not give up had died in captivity.[128] Eunapius records 3,000 prisoners held by Vadomarius, retained until after the return of his son, held as a hostage by Julian.[129] Zosimus, writing much later but drawing on Eunapius, provides interesting details about such prisoner handovers. Julian was able to confound the Alamanni by consulting lists of the missing, and naming those who had not appeared.[130] Ammianus mentions such events in his account of Julian's campaigns of 358 and 359.[131] All accounts are probably exaggerated and, deriving from the same pro-Julian tradition, cannot be said to corroborate each other.[132] However, their common interest indicates that they considered the recovery of prisoners significant, and suggests that they offer a grain of truth.[133] This has stimulated speculation concerning links between Alamannic slaving and the needs of Alamannic society: briefly, the Alamannic economy was so short of skilled and unskilled manpower that it needed regular injections of outside labour to keep it viable.[134] Is this plausible?

---

[126] Julian, *Ep. ad Ath.* 280C. Cf. Lorenz, S. (1997: 63 n.245).

[127] Libanius, *Orat.* 18.34. On Magnentius, cf. below 200–1.

[128] Libanius, *Orat.* 18.78–9, cf. 17.14.

[129] Eunapius, *Hist.* fr. 19 (Blockley).

[130] Zosimus 3.3.4–7.

[131] AM 17.10.7–8; 18.2.19. Below 243, 244–5, 247.

[132] Cf. below 178.

[133] On the basic veracity of Zosimus' account see Paschoud (1979: 72).

[134] So Werner (1965: 73–4); Geuenich (1997a: 36–7). Most recently, Heather (2001: 44).

According to our sources, all the Roman prisoners concerned were taken in the troubles following the revolt of Magnentius. This is consistent with the general development of Romano-Alamannic relations during the first half of the fourth century, which were generally peaceful, with little opportunity for routine Alamannic slaving in imperial territory.[135] Thus, in 358 and 359,[136] Julian purportedly freed a large group of people taken in the short period from 351 to 355 (when Constantius II began to re-establish order in Gaul after Magnentius) or to 356 (when Julian first began to re-establish order in Gaul after the revolt of Silvanus).[137] Julian therefore liberated a distinct set of people who had been captured in unusual circumstances and who were, apparently, still available for mass repatriation very close to Roman territory—certainly in the territories of Suomarius, Hortarius and Vadomarius (on the Rhine) and very probably in those of Urius, Ursicinus and Vestralpus (on the Main artery).[138]

These had not been dispersed into Alamannia or beyond; they had not become part of the slave trade. At this point one begins to suspect that the people involved were not run-of-the-mill enslaved war captives but rather, as Curta has suggested (albeit via a different line of reasoning), hostages, acquired for ransom or for bargaining in future negotiations.[139] Those from upper levels of society would have fitted this bill better than peasants and slaves, and would be the sort of people to figure on relatively hastily prepared lists. Both Libanius and Eunapius refer to the high birth of the prisoners.[140] The taking of hostages in large numbers, though at the most in thousands, not tens of thousands, would indicate a fair degree of political acumen on the part of Alamannic war-leaders, but this is hardly surprising given their long contact with Rome.[141] As part of this cunning, one might adduce the fact that they did not threaten to

[135] Below 200.
[136] See Lorenz, S. (1997: 56 and nn.210–11), for problems in establishing the precise chronology of events.
[137] Cf. below 204, 212, 219.
[138] Below 223 Fig. 18, 250.
[139] Curta (2002b).
[140] Libanius, *Orat.* 12.50; Eunapius, *Hist.* fr. 19.
[141] Cf. below 145–6.

kill their prisoners before the battle of Strasbourg, or do so after their defeat. But this leads to another issue.

All these prisoners of the Alamanni would have needed food and shelter. How was this provided? Surely not in camps, an anachronistic concept, well beyond the capacity of the local economy. An alternative is their being held on rural sites and set to work to feed themselves. This would have been all the more necessary because Alamanni occupying land on the left bank were growing crops there with the help of, one presumes (though Libanius says they worked 'with their own hands'), labour brought over from the right.[142] It would explain the complaints of the sources that they were treated like slaves, which well-born hostages would have found hugely humiliating. However, the notion of hard work suggests a further group of potential hostages more used to labour. A significant proportion of Roman prisoners held by the Alamanni in 358 may have been people who had been working on the right bank of the Rhine, supervising production for export into the Empire. These could have been seized when the political situation deteriorated from 351, and not released after Magnentius' fall in 353. They were again the sort of people whom authorities might well have been able to list. The possible exceptional nature of the prisoners held by the Alamanni in the 350s must change our interpretation of sources. What happened cannot be generalized to yield conclusions about Alamannic society as a whole: it is not proof that the Alamanni were peculiarly short of labour.

So what was the nature of day-to-day Alamannic dependent labour? A simple model of how this may have developed may be constructed from what has been touched upon.[143] In the late third and early fourth centuries, young warriors overwintering in Alamannia needed a subservient agricultural workforce and drew this from a residual peasantry or from prisoners taken in raiding into the Empire, or both. In the fourth century, as permanent communities developed, Alamanni continued to use slaves for agriculture, for practical (the advantages of a subservient workforce) and cultural (the satisfaction derived from the existence of social inferiors and the belief that the meanest

---

[142] Below 227, 235–6; Libanius, *Orat.* 18.34.
[143] Cf. above 104.

tasks were fit only for the unfree) reasons. However, given the low level of population, such slaves were not present in massive numbers. Even less numerous, but equally significant, were the skilled outsiders who served the elites of the hill-sites. In the later third century, such outsiders may have been slaves, acquired through raiding and introducing new skills.[144] In the fourth century, such people would have been less accessible and recourse may have been had to dependent freemen: we know of a much later Alamannic leader employing free craftsmen.[145]

In the fourth century, free Roman craftsmen were available over the Rhine. Indeed, it may have been that a number of these were voluntary exiles, with no wish to return to Roman jurisdiction. In other words, the exploitation of transrhenish resources may, in opening up the Rhine frontier, have encouraged imperial emigration. From what later writers, such as Salvian, say about deteriorating social conditions in the west in the fifth century, which drove the desperate to flee to the barbarians, there is the possibility that the fourth century saw imperial migrants trickling into Alamannia, escaping problems with landlords, tax-collectors, judges and recruiting officers.[146] It is significant that legislation of Valentinian I recognized the possibility that, in time of barbarian attack, people might go over to the enemy of their own accord.[147]

Overall, we may envisage the population of Alamannia during the fourth century as being a rich mix of Germanic warriors (Elbgermanic and eastern), Roman provincials of various backgrounds and

---

[144] Cf. above 93. Steidl (2000: 109–10), (2002: 107–10) notes a rise in Germanic technical expertise in the later third century—visible in the Haarhausen–Eßleben 'experiments'—and attributes it to a single generation of Roman craftsmen, taken as slaves in third-century raiding, who were unable to pass on their skills to succeeding generations.

[145] Steuer (1990: 201), citing Eugippius, *V. Severini* 8.3: Giso, wife of the fifth-century Alamannic king, Feletheus, foolishly subjected barbarian goldsmiths brought to work at court to unlawful arrest.

[146] Salvian, *De Gub. Dei* 5.22. As already noted above (127), according to Tacitus, *Germania* 29.4, in the first century the *Agri Decumates* were colonized in advance of formal annexation by 'all the riff-raff of Gaul': *levissimus quisque Gallorum*.

[147] *CT* 5.7.1; cf. below 278. On the forces that encouraged desertion (excessive taxation, extortion by soldiers and civil officials, the demands of landowners etc.), see Gutmann (1991: 20). For the possible presence of Roman or Roman-trained workers on Germanic soil in the Early Roman Empire see Stupperich (1997: 19).

conditions, the products of interbreeding between these, and dependants brought from Free Germany. As far as these last are concerned, leaders probably had their families with them from the start.[148] If having a Germanic wife was seen as a mark of high status, others would have striven to bring one in under the easier conditions of permanent settlement, along the lines of communication that linked the Vistula, the Oder and the Elbe to the Main and the Rhine.[149]

This returns us to the thorny problem of population. If Alamanni were few in the later third century,[150] were they more numerous in the fourth? Much has been made of Aurelius Victor's description of the third-century Alamanni as a 'populous nation who fight wonderfully well from horseback'.[151] These words have done much to shape modern popular conceptions of the Alamanni;[152] but they are open to question. It has been suspected that the sources' projection of the population of the 'free' Germanic territories as massive, as a potential flood tide of immigrants, is mistaken, a reflection of imperial propaganda.[153] The idea of Alamanni as numerous and exceptionally skilled horsemen is likewise explicable as, in modern jargon, an urban myth: a piece of conventional wisdom which appears plausible until subjected to scrutiny. Such wisdom may have been derived, for example, from the ancient belief that cold northern climes naturally produced an excess of population.[154] A related and perhaps more likely explanation is that Victor used this belief to point up Julian's recent victory at Strasbourg.

This famous defeat of the Alamanni took place in summer 357, just under four years before Victor's publication of his *Caesares* in spring 361.[155] Victor had a high opinion of Julian, a feeling that was reciprocated when Julian, having moved eastward from Gaul, made him governor of Pannonia II in summer 361.[156] Before this, however,

[148] Above 49.
[149] Cf. above 46 n.20.
[150] Above 80–1.
[151] Aurelius Victor, *Caesares* 21.2: *gens populosa ex equo mirifice pugnans* [trans. Bird (1994)].
[152] e.g. Südwestfunk (1997).
[153] Wolfram (1990: 28); Drinkwater (1997: 1 and n.2). Cf. below 169.
[154] Pohl (2002a: 15).
[155] Below 224–5; Bird (1994: xi).
[156] Bird (1994: ix).

as he was completing the *Caesares* and dealing with contemporary matters, Victor had been under the authority of Constantius II and therefore had to be careful in what he wrote. Thus Julian is praised, but briefly and with no mention of Alamanni; and his successes are credited to the 'good fortune and planning' of the senior emperor.[157] But the story of Julian's victory at Strasbourg must have spread quickly through the Empire, and have been made more dramatic by the detail that the day had almost been lost thanks to the failure of the Roman cavalry, which Julian had to rally, and later punished.[158] I propose that Victor, unable to comment directly on the battle in its place, made indirect reference to it when describing Caracalla's Germanic campaign of 213. Recording this first contact with Alamanni, he enhanced Julian's victory in two ways. First, helped by ancient preconceptions of northern barbarian fecundity, he made the Alamanni generally dangerous by asserting that they were many in number.[159] Second, he made them particularly dangerous, and excused Julian's lapse as a commander, by transposing their unexpected cavalry success at Strasbourg into the past and categorizing them, incorrectly, as horsemen of renown.[160]

What may safely be said about Alamannic numbers? In truth, nothing. The archaeological evidence does not suggest a massive population, but as far as precise figures are concerned we can only speculate. The most direct statements concerning the strength of a Germanic 'Volk' come from Victor Vitalis and Procopius. Combined, these suggest that in 429 Geiseric led 50–80,000 Vandals and others across to Africa.[161] As Pohl says, citing Wolfram for *c.*100,000, including 15–20,000 warriors, as the maximum number for 'a major people', this is not implausible.[162] Alamannic numbers at the battle of Strasbourg may be calculated at around 15,000, made up of *c.*1,000 warriors from each of 11 known or likely *pagi* and 4,000 from

[157] Aurelius Victor, *Caesares* 42.18.

[158] Below 239.

[159] On Alamannic numbers at Strasbourg, see below 237–9.

[160] i.e. *contra* Springer's view: that Victor used Julian's achievements to enhance Caracalla's campaign. This is discussed and refuted by Bleckmann (2002: 161–3), though Bleckmann still believes Victor on the quality of Alamannic cavalry. See further below 175–6.

[161] Pohl (2002a: 76–7).

[162] Wolfram (1990: 28): 'ein großes Volk'.

elsewhere.[163] Wolfram's multiplier of about four dependants for each warrior produces a total associated population of *c*.75,000. Though not all Alamanni were involved, this figure approaches the proposed maximum of 80–100,000 and suggests that the population of those areas which stayed completely aloof from the conflict amounted to no more than *c*.5–25,000.

But these sums require adjustment. First, the 4,000 outsiders and their dependants have to be subtracted from the 75,000 'involved' Alamanni, bringing these down to *c*.55,000; and some at least of the former have to be re-allotted to nominally neutral communities. The 4,000 may have included warriors from the wider Elbgermanic triangle. Alamannia was probably still visited by bands raiding westwards over long distances from within this region. Though normally a danger for settled communities, in 357 these could have supplemented Alamannic fighting strength.[164] On the other hand, such recruitment could not have produced the whole 4,000. Given the rapid turn of events that led to conflict, local Alamanni must have been driven very much on their own resources.[165] A small number— three or four—roving bands of Elbe-*Germani* could have contributed, say, half the extras.[166] This leaves *c*.2,000 drawn from Alamannic *pagi* nominally uninvolved in the conflict. With their *c*.8,000 dependants, these raise the total population of these communities to *c*.15–35,000. But, second, this is not enough. At *c*.5,000 people per *pagus*, these figures produce only three to seven additional *pagi*, which is too few. There were about five north of the Main (those of the 'three kings'; and of Macrianus and Hariobaudus);[167] a clutch, say three, north of Lake Constance;[168] perhaps a couple along the Swabian Alp;[169] and, say, another three belonging to the Iuthungi.[170] This makes 13, or an additional 65,000 people, bringing the total population of 'Greater' Alamannia to around 120,000 (55,000 + 65,000)—large for a people on the move but plausible for a group

[163] Below 238–9; for *pagus*, see above 119–20.
[164] Steuer (1998: 288), his explanation for Alamannic 'populousness'. Cf. below 238–9.
[165] On the antecedents to Strasbourg, see below 236–7.
[166] Above 49.
[167] Below 226, 240, 246, 249.
[168] Below 207, 209, 211–12.
[169] Above 88, 97.
[170] Above 97, 99–100.

of relatively settled communities. Though these other *pagi* had a greater total population than those which found themselves facing Julian, they were, with the exception of those on the Main, probably more scattered and larger in area. The main concentrations of population were, as the archaeological material and the historical record suggest, probably along the Rhine, the lower Main and the Neckar.

To set all this in perspective, against *c.*120,000 Alamanni there was a population in the neighbouring Three Gauls and Germanies of around 10,000,000—a ratio of about 80:1 in favour of the Empire.[171]

[171] Drinkwater (1983a: 170–1).

5

Service

The Alamanni are best known for fighting Rome, and conflict will be the subject of the following three chapters. However, they also served Rome, and an understanding of this service is essential for reconstructing the relationship between Alamanni and Romans in war and at peace.

Alamannic service was essentially military service. As such it was hardly unusual. The use of outsiders to augment Roman armed strength went back to the Republic; Julius Caesar hired Germanic cavalry;[1] and earlier emperors, for example Tiberius and Caracalla, employed Germanic warriors as bodyguards.[2] Wider recruitment of *Germani* began in the later third century[3] and became a matter of course. Current thinking is not to view such 'barbarization' as overwhelming or as a threat to the security of the Empire. *Germani*, officers and men, served Rome well.[4] Military service was, indeed, the traditional means by which *Germani* profited peacefully from the later Roman Empire.[5] From the later fourth century, the most successful were able, through intermarriage, to produce children who were accepted into the topmost levels of the imperial aristocracy.[6]

It is helpful to distinguish between officers and other ranks. As Zotz remarks, thanks to the work of Stroheker, Waas and Martin, we

---

[1] Above 14.

[2] Tacitus, *Annales* 1.24.3; Dio 78.6.1; Herodian 4.7.3. Geuenich (1997a: 34).

[3] Above 73, 75, 77 (Postumus, Gallienus, Aurelian).

[4] On the 'normal' and positive side of Germanic recruitment, see Elton (1996a: 136–52); Witschel (1999: 235). Cf. Jones (1964: 620–2).

[5] Martin (1998: 407).

[6] e.g. the Vandal father of Stilicho and, indeed, Stilicho himself: *PLRE* 1.853; and probably also Bauto the Frank: see below 152–3.

are now much better informed about certain high-ranking Alamanni in the service of Rome during the fourth century.[7] These are now dealt with in chronological order.

CROCUS[8]

Following the death of Constantius I in York in 306, prominent among those who urged his son, Constantine, to replace him was Crocus, a king of the Alamanni and a military ally of Constantius.[9] Caution is necessary since the *Epitome* is a relatively late (early fifth century) and quirky source, which here is clearly embellishing the account of Aurelius Victor,[10] and since an even later account mentions another Alamannic king Crocus raiding deep into Gaul in the mid-third century.[11] 'Crocus' may therefore have become a legendary 'bogeyman', with the name of the 'earlier' being applied to the 'later', or even vice versa. The *Epitome*'s reference may, indeed, be pejorative, suggesting unhealthy barbarian influence at the court of Constantine I.[12] However, there is no reason to doubt the basic historicity of what it says, that is that an Alamannic leader played a role in the elevation of Constantine I.[13]

LATINUS, AGILO, AND SCUDILO[14]

The next three important military Alamanni occur in 354, in Ammianus Marcellinus' account of Constantius II's campaigning

[7] Zotz (1998: 388); Stroheker (1961), (1975); Waas (1971); Martin (1997a), (1998). Cf. Geuenich (1997a: 28–35).

[8] Waas (1971: 82); *PLRE* 1.233.

[9] *Epitome* 41.3: *Alamannorum rex; auxilii gratia Constantium comitatus.*

[10] Aurelius Victor, *Caesares* 40.4.

[11] Gregory of Tours, *Dec. Lib. Hist.* 1.32, 34; cf. Fredegarius, *Chron.* 2.40, 60.

[12] Festy (1999: 186).

[13] Festy, ibid., following *PLRE* 1.233, even accepts that this Crocus may have been a descendant of the Crocus of Gregory of Tours.

[14] Latinus: *PLRE* 1.496; Waas (1971: 88). Agilo: *PLRE* 1.28–9; Waas (1971: 68–9). Scudilo: *PLRE* 1.810; Waas (1971: 103–4).

near Kaiseraugst. According to Ammianus, at that time they exercised enormous influence in the running of the Empire.[15] All three were, presumably, members of the imperial privy council, the *sacrum consistorium*.[16]

In 354, Latinus was *comes domesticorum*.[17] This meant that he commanded the *protectores domestici*, elite troops, the cream of the imperial bodyguard.[18] These men attended directly upon the emperor and were used by him for special errands. They were close to the centre of power and could expect accelerated promotion. Their unit has been described as a 'corps of officer-cadets' and 'a kind of staff college'.[19] Latinus was, therefore, 'a senior general'.[20] He was also an imperial politician with important connections, and in his dealings with Constantius had already shown some spirit. In 351, during the manoeuvring that led up to Magnentius' defeat at the battle of Mursa, Constantius II had thrown a great banquet. Latinus, already *comes domesticorum*, and Thalassius, an imperial *comes*, refused to attend to express their concern about Constantius' acceptance of Magnentius' treatment of an envoy. Thalassius was from a rich Antiochene family and was related to the famous rhetor, Libanius. He was a long-standing lieutenant of Constantius II and by the time of his death in 354 had become praetorian prefect of the east and played a role in the fall of Gallus.[21] Zosimus describes Latinus and Thalassius in 351 as 'the emperor's closest associates'.[22] Latinus was, indeed, mixing with the cream of imperial society.[23]

In 354, Agilo was *tribunus stabuli*,[24] in charge of the imperial stables and remounts.[25] He then became commander of a regular regiment of the imperial guard (*schola*), but his career only really

---

[15] AM 14.10.8: *qui tunc ut dextris suis gestantes rem publicam colebantur.*
[16] Cf. Elton (1996a: 176).
[17] AM 14.10.8.
[18] Jones (1964: 1.372, 2.636–40).
[19] Jones (1964: 2.638), (1966: 224); Tomlin (1987: 115).
[20] Tomlin (1987: 114).
[21] Thalassius: *PLRE* 1.886; Waas (1971: 88).
[22] Zosimus 2.48.5: *ta prōta para basilei pherontes* [trans. Ridley]; cf. Paschoud (1971): 'qui exerçaient les plus hautes fonctions auprès de l'empereur'. See de Jonge (1939: 104).
[23] Paschoud (1971: 257).
[24] AM 4.8.10; de Jonge (1939: 105).
[25] Jones (1964: 1.372–3, 2.625), (1966: 141); de Jonge (1939: 104–5).

took off in 360 when he replaced Ammianus' patron, Ursicinus, as senior general in attendance (*magister peditum praesentalis*) in the east. Ammianus viewed this as unreasonably rapid promotion.[26] In 361, he was recalled to help Constantius against Julian.[27] Though Julian emerged victorious he kept Agilo in his service, trusting him to end resistance in Aquileia.[28] Even more surprisingly, Agilo was then appointed a judge in the trials of the enemies of the new regime at Chalcedon.[29] Around 362 he left the limelight and settled in the east where he married Vetiana, daughter of Araxius, a friend of Julian and Libanius and holder of a number of important imperial posts.[30] Agilo thereby became a member of a prominent eastern family. In 365, he reappeared as one of the usurper Procopius' senior generals.[31] Due to his influence, indeed, Araxius became Procopius' praetorian prefect of the east.[32] However, he played a crucial role in the usurper's downfall by going over to Valens at the battle of Nacolia in 366 and so suffered only mild punishment for his treachery.[33] His was a career remarkable in any circumstances, and unique among the Alamanni known to us.[34]

In 354, Scudilo commanded a *schola* of imperial guards (*scutariorum rector/tribunus*).[35] If, as seems generally accepted, he is to be identified with Zosimus' 'Skolidoas', he had, while already a colonel of the guards (*taxiarchos*), like Latinus, distinguished himself before the battle of Mursa.[36] Later in 354, he went to Antioch to persuade Gallus, under suspicion, to move west to see Constantius. He was remarkably successful, laying stress on Constantius' merciful disposition. Ammianus Marcellinus, somewhat grudgingly, praises his diplomatic talents, 'a skilled artist in persuasion, under the cloak of a somewhat rough nature'.[37] He died of a painful illness soon after

---

[26] AM 20.2.5; Hoffmann (1969: 290–1).
[27] AM 21.13.8.
[28] AM 21.12.16–18.
[29] AM 22.3.1.
[30] AM 26.7.5–6; 10.7. Vetiana: *PLRE* 1.954; Araxius: *PLRE* 1.94; Waas (1971: 69).
[31] AM 26.7.4. *PLRE* 1.29 has him 'retired', then 'induced to return to office'.
[32] AM 26.7.6.
[33] AM 26.9.7, 10.7.
[34] Stroheker (1975: 35).
[35] AM 14.10.8, 11.11, 11.24.
[36] Zosimus 20.5.2, 3; de Jonge (1939: 105); *PLRE* 1.811.
[37] AM 14.11.11: *velamento subagrestis ingenii, persuasionis opifex callidus.*

Gallus' execution, according to Ammianus, as punishment for his part in the affair.[38]

GOMOARIUS[39]

Gomoarius was Agilo's colleague on the general staff of Procopius and, like him, soon deserted his commander. In 350, he had been colonel of a guards regiment (*tribunus scutariorum*) under the usurper Vetranio, whom he is also supposed to have betrayed. Constantius named him Julian's *magister equitum* in Gaul in 360 but Julian, distrusting him, replaced him with another. Also like Agilo, he must then have taken up residence in the east. Though nowhere explicitly described as such, it is likely that he was Alamannic in origin.

HARIOBAUDES[40]

In 359, he was a colonel without regimental attachment (*tribunus vacans*). Julian used him to spy out the land preparatory to an Alamannic campaign, which suggests that he was Alamannic by origin. He proved worthy of the trust shown to him.[41] It is unlikely that he was the brother and fellow king of Macrianus.[42]

VADOMARIUS[43]

Vadomarius first appears in 354 as an Alamannic *rex*.[44] He was a loyal client of Constantius II, which strained his relationship with other Alamannic leaders and, later, with Julian. In 361, indeed, he was

---

[38] AM 14.11.24.
[39] *PLRE* 1.397–8; Waas (1971: 84–5).
[40] *PLRE* 1.408; Waas (1971: 85).
[41] AM 18.2.2.
[42] Cf. below 248; *contra* Geuenich (1997a: 45).
[43] *PLRE* 1.928; Waas (1971: 108–10).
[44] AM 14.10.1.

arrested on Julian's orders while attending a military banquet on the left bank of the Rhine. He was exiled to Spain.[45] Subsequently, however, he was appointed *dux Phoenices.*[46] As military commander in an important border province, Vadomarius had real responsibility.[47] It may be significant that two units composed of (or originally raised from) Alamannic troops were stationed here as *limitanei.*[48] In 365/6 Vadomarius served Valens against Procopius, playing a leading role in the siege of Nicaea, though this turned out badly.[49] He survived the setback and reappeared in 371 in a high position, fighting Persians.[50] Hoffmann suggests that Vadomarius was appointed *dux Phoenices* by Jovian, in 363. After Valens came to power, he dismissed Vadomarius but then re-employed him as general without portfolio (*comes rei militaris vacans*). It was as such that he fought Procopius in Bithynia and the Persians in 371.[51] His son, Vithicabius, was freed by Julian, became king, but was troublesome; Valentinian I had him assassinated in 368.[52]

FRAOMARIUS, BITHERIDUS, AND HORTARIUS[53]

These were three Alamanni serving in the army in the west in 372, under Valentinian I, as tribunes and regimental commanders. The Romans had made Fraomarius king of the Bucinobantes in an abortive attempt to depose Macrianus.[54] After internal troubles

    [45] AM 21.3, 4.1–6. Cf. below 256.
    [46] AM 21.3.5; 26.8.2: *ducatum per Phoenicen regens/ex duce et rege Alamannorum.* *PLRE* 1.928 dates the ducate to 361–6.
    [47] Jones (1964: 609); Elton (1996a: 139).
    [48] Waas (1971: 110); cf. below 164.
    [49] AM 26.8.2–3.
    [50] AM 29.1.2.
    [51] Hoffmann (1978: 308–9). For a different interpretation (of Vadomarius as the *vicarius* of the *magister peditum praesentalis* Arintheus) and chronology see Woods (2000: 693).
    [52] AM 27.10.3–4; 30.7.7; Eunapius, *Hist.* Fr. 19 (Blockley); *PLRE* 1.971. Cf. below 281.
    [53] Fraomarius: *PLRE* 1.372; Waas (1971: 82). Bitheridus: *PLRE* 1.162; Waas (1971: 79). Hortarius: *PLRE* 1.444; Waas (1971: 86); Hoffmann (1978: 309).
    [54] On Macrianus see below 304–9.

forced him to stand down, he received command of a large Alamannic *numerus* in Britain.[55] Bitheridus was another Germanic noble who was given a military command. Although nowhere explicitly described as Alamannic, all that Ammianus says about him points in this direction.[56] Hortarius is paired with Bitheridus by Ammianus, who records that he was executed for treacherous dealings with Macrianus and other Alamanni.[57] He may have been the son of the king Hortarius who joined in the alliance against Julian in 357.[58]

These three are the latest fourth-century Alamanni whom we know by name. After them, we can identify no one else until the enigmatic king (or kings) Gibuldus/Gebavultus in the mid-fifth century.[59]

In assessing the historical significance of these Alamannic officers it is important to understand their background and upbringing, particularly those of the high-fliers: Crocus, Latinus, Agilo, Scudilo and Gomoarius. Were they primarily Alamannic warriors, or Roman officers? A direct answer to this question is impossible, since we do not know enough about them. On the other hand, something may be inferred from other evidence.

This is the career of a high-ranking Germanic soldier who was not Alamannic: the Frank, Silvanus, who supposedly seized the purple in Gaul in 355.[60] His father, Bonitus, helped Constantine I against Licinius.[61] Assuming that Bonitus flourished around 320, and calculating a generation at about 30 years, we can estimate when his ancestors and descendants were in their prime:

*c.*260: Bonitus' grandfather=Silvanus' great-grandfather
*c.*290: Bonitus' father=Silvanus' grandfather
*c.*320: Bonitus=Silvanus' father
*c.*350: Bonitus' son=Silvanus.

This approach looks promising because it produces the 'right' date for Silvanus. We may guess that Silvanus' great-grandfather was

---

[55] AM 29.4.7. Below 170, 309, 353.
[56] AM 29.4.7.
[57] Ibid.
[58] *PLRE* 1.444; cf. below 236. Geuenich (1997a: 55) identifies him as Hortarius.
[59] Geuenich (1997a: 73–5), (1997c: 144); cf. below 331–2.
[60] *PLRE* 1.840–1; Waas (1971: 105–7).
[61] AM 15.5.33. Bonitus: *PLRE* 1.163.

among the leaders who first raided the Roman Empire in strength following the capture of Valerian. Silvanus' grandfather would have been among the Frankish chiefs brought to heel by the Tetrarchy. He may have provided troops for the Empire and given up his son, Bonitus, as a hostage. This would have allowed Bonitus to learn Roman ways, and so aided his rise through the military hierarchy.[62] It is likely that he remained on imperial territory while raising his family: we are told, indeed, that Silvanus was born in Gaul.[63] Thus Silvanus, for all his 'Frankish' origin, would have been brought up a Roman. We know that he was a Christian;[64] and Festy notes his 'complete assimilation into Roman civilization'.[65]

This helps us make sense of Silvanus' 'usurpation' against Constantius II in 355. His enemies at court had striven to undermine his position by making it seem as if he were plotting to become emperor.[66] This was ludicrous. Apart from Silvanus' loyalty to Constantius II, his barbarian blood disqualified him from donning the purple. Silvanus was cleared of the charges in his absence. Unfortunately, this came too late to prevent him from acting out of self-defence: either (according to Ammianus Marcellinus) by going against tradition and proclaiming himself emperor, or (more likely) by working to proclaim another.[67] Nevertheless, the fact that the original accusation had found some credence confirms that Silvanus never looked or acted the Frankish warrior: he was, to all appearances, fully Roman.[68] Silvanus had a legitimate son, pardoned by Constantius II.[69] If he had completed his imperial career, that son, flourishing around 380, would have enjoyed enormous opportunities. One thinks, for example, of the Frank Bauto, a leading general

---

[62] Cf. above 119, below 154, 187.

[63] Aurelius Victor, *Caesares* 42.15; cf. below 153.

[64] AM 15.5.31.

[65] Festy (1999: 203).

[66] AM 15.5.4–5.

[67] AM 15.5.15–31; Drinkwater (1994).

[68] Cf. *Epitome* 42.11: *quamquam barbaro patre genitus, tamen institutione Romana satis cultus et patiens.* It is interesting that the Epitomator, unlike Victor, gives Silvanus only one barbarian parent which, given the propensity of leading Germanic soldiers to marry Roman wives, appears more likely. Cf. below 322 (Stilicho). In this case, his Christianity probably came from his mother.

[69] Julian, *Orat.* 1.49A; 2.98C–99A.

under Gratian and Valentinian II, whose daughter, Aelia Eudoxia, married the emperor Arcadius.[70]

This model of long-standing *Romanitas* also fits those early-fourth-century Alamanni we know, and allows us to envisage them as integrating into the imperial aristocracy. Crocus, of Silvanus' grandfather's generation (his original association was with Constantius I, not Constantine I), would have been among the first Alamanni to commit his future to Rome (though the Epitomator, hostile to Constantine I, may have exaggerated the extent of his 'barbarian' influence on the events of 306). Latinus, Agilo, Scudilo and Gomoarius were of Silvanus' generation and may, like him, have been born and brought up in the Empire and owed their success not just to their abilities but to the influence of Romano-Germanic families.[71] They lived dangerous but generally successful lives as Roman grandees. Their descendants may have gone on to do even greater things—hidden from us by Roman names. The main lesson of all this is that we must constantly bear in mind the likelihood of a considerable degree of 'Roman-ness' on the part of leading fourth-century 'Alamanni'. As A. H. M. Jones remarked, Julian's choice of Hariobaudes as a good linguist makes no sense 'unless many of the German officers in Julian's command were at least rusty in their mother-tongue'.[72]

To answer the question posed above, we should envisage such men primarily as Roman officers. This will be important in assessing Romano-Alamannic relations as a whole.[73] However, 'primarily' is not 'exclusively'. A. H. M. Jones went too far in concluding that, 'Those Germans of whom we know anything, those that rose in service and made names for themselves, certainly became thoroughly romanised, and quite lost contact with their homes.' Recent research has shown that, during the Early Empire, Batavians serving in the Roman army were capable of keeping in touch with home.[74] The same may be expected of Alamannic officers and men in the fourth century. Ammianus treats Alamannic home-leave as a matter of

---

[70] *PLRE* 1.159–60, 2.410; Waas (1971: 77–8). Cf. Bury (1923: 1.108): that Eudoxia's mother 'had doubtless been a Roman'.

[71] Cf. Tomlin (1987: 115) on the importance of nepotism.

[72] Jones (1964: 622).

[73] Below 176, 207, 358.

[74] Derks and Roymans (2003).

course;[75] and even the most highly Romanized of military Alamanni could exploit links with their communities of origin.[76] Constant exposure, via Romanized Alamanni, to the Roman view of 'Alamannia' must, indeed, have been an essential element in the region's population coming to accept themselves as 'Alamanni', that is in the process of Alamannic ethnogenesis.[77] Such links would also have assured the Empire of a stream of good recruits from families with long records of service.

But the system was dynamic. First-generation recruitment was also a feature of the fourth century, as in the case of Hariobaudes, Vadomarius, Fraomarius, Bitheridus and Hortarius. The most typical of these appear to have been Hariobaudes, Bitheridus and Hortarius. As tribunes ('colonels'), they were mid-way through the standard career of high-ranking foreign recruits to the Roman officer-corps, probably having held protectorships and looking forward to being promoted *dux*.[78] But this raises the question of their status in Alamannic society, and why they decided to serve Rome. These issues are partly resolved by the careers of Vadomarius and Fraomarius. These show that *tribuni* and *duces* could be recruited from the highest levels of Alamannic society: in their case, from kings. However, Vadomarius and Fraomarius were recruited in abnormal circumstances, without much choice. Furthermore, it is unlikely that recruitment of established kings—which would have disrupted Alamannic society and so not have been helpful to Rome—was ever 'normal'. More likely is that men like Hariobaudes, Bitheridus and Hortarius were recruited from princes and superior nobles, otherwise unable to progress further in their own society.[79] Such recruitment would have been helped by the Roman habit of taking young upper-class males hostage to guarantee the behaviour of their parents. For some, this was a death sentence.[80] For others,

[75] Below 160.
[76] Jones (1964: 622); below 176, 207. I agree with Barlow (1996: 224) that Jones' interpretation is probably too rigid (for instances of Alamannic and Frankish cross-border contact see below 160, 312, 318) and that Germanic soldiers maintained regular links with their home communities.
[77] See above 68–9, 119.
[78] Hoffmann (1978: 316).
[79] Above 122.
[80] Below 282–3.

however, probably the majority, sojourn in the Empire was a valuable education. The best known example is Mederichus, father of the king Serapio who opposed Julian in 357[81] and probably Serapio's predecessor, who spent a long time in Gaul and changed his son's name from Agenarichus to Serapio after being initiated into Greek mysteries there.[82] Presumably, Serapio also learned Roman ways. Their position as heirs is likely to have prevented both from following imperial careers. However, their experience shows how young, well-connected Alamanni were exposed to the Greco-Roman world.

New Alamannic recruits, whom service took into the Empire and who managed to survive the perils of war and politics, will, like their predecessors, probably have distanced themselves from Alamannic society, founding new, Roman, families. Thus, as Hoffmann has commented, Ammianus is correct in describing Vadomarius towards the end of his career as 'former *dux* and former king of the Alamanni': he will have had no direct involvement with his former life.[83] As always, however, the likely role such people played in bridging the gap between *Germani* and Romans should constantly be acknowledged.

In this respect, it is worth giving further attention to Vadomarius, who was a major player in the events that brought Julian to power in Gaul and therefore figures prominently in Ammianus' narrative. Prior to his arrest, Vadomarius was already no simple Alamannic chief, but a prominent imperial politician. We first hear of him in 354 when he made a formal agreement with Constantius II.[84] However, if from *c.*352 Constantius set Alamanni on to Magnentius and Decentius,[85] it is unlikely that this was the first time Vadomarius had dealings with him. In 352, Constantius could not have had formal agreements with the Alamannic leaders involved, since any treaties that existed would have been made by Constans and then, after his overthrow in 350, by Magnentius. Furthermore, confined to Italy,

---

[81] Above 119.

[82] AM 16.12.25. For the opposite experience see AM 18.2.17: living far from the frontier, Macrianus was astonished by his first sight of the Roman army on parade (presumably in the manner of Aurelian: above 73).

[83] AM 26.8.2; Hoffmann (1978: 308–10), making the same point about the Frankish 'count and king' Mallobaudes.

[84] Below 204–5.

[85] Below 201–2.

Constantius would have had to deal with them over a distance, through the territory of Vadomarius and his brother. Vadomarius may, from an early stage in Constantius' direct involvement in the west, have acted as broker between the imperial authorities and fellow Alamannic leaders (as he did later, under Julian).[86] The 354 agreement simply formalized an existing relationship.

If, subsequently, all had gone well for Constantius, we would probably have heard no more of Vadomarius. However, the rise of Julian and Vadomarius' decision to stand by Constantius caused the game to continue. Vadomarius was probably intimidated into joining the Alamannic coalition of 357 and may even have supplied troops for the battle of Strasbourg.[87] However, his influence with Constantius (and the likelihood that he avoided personal participation at Strasbourg) saved him from retaliation. He then continued to act as an agent of Constantius in unscrambling the omelette of the defeat of Constantius' former allies at Strasbourg,[88] and then in keeping an eye on Julian (supposedly even attempting to hamstring Julian's war-effort).[89] This suggests that Vadomarius was in regular contact with Constantius' court. As the employer of professional secretarial staff and the sender and recipient of imperial messages, both public and private, he may even be seen as a 'corresponding member' of the sacred consistory.[90] Like Latinus and his peers, though without formal office, Vadomarius should be regarded as 'Roman'. And, again like Latinus and the others, this must have been based on some cultural foundation. Ammianus emphasizes his acquaintance with Roman ways and with Roman officials on his border.[91]

Here we may consider the topic of dress. Our evidence for Germanic dress in general is scarce. We know of no significant difference between Alamanni and other western *Germani* in this respect.[92] What the poor wore remains a mystery. The inhumations of the well-to-do show that while women wore native clothes, men

[86] Below 247, 251–2.
[87] Below 239.
[88] Below 247.
[89] Below 257–9.
[90] Cf. Szidat (1981: 93–4: Vadomarius' possession of a secretarial staff, on the imperial model).
[91] AM 18.2.17; 21.4.3. Cf. below 255–6.
[92] Brather (2002: 153).

adopted a version of Roman military uniform.[93] The modern parallel is the similarity between the camouflage smocks, baseball caps and assault rifles of guerrilla fighters and the combat fatigues and weaponry of their regular opponents. When Vadomarius and his entourage crossed the Rhine to visit members of the imperial garrison, probably at Kaiseraugst,[94] guests and hosts would have looked similar, would have talked about the same things in the same language—soldiers' Latin—and would have eaten off much the same crockery.[95] This returns us to the cultural foundation of Vadomarius' dealings with the Empire. A high level of Romanization is likely to have been true not just of Vadomarius but also of his parents and grandparents. As in the case of Latinus, Agilo and Scudilo, this would help explain his ability to operate in the east. It is also worth observing that Vadomarius must have been admired not just for his diplomatic but also for his military skills, explaining his ducate and his career as an imperial general. Overall, he emerges as a complex and imposing figure, certainly no brute barbarian.

The earlier career of Vadomarius underlines a particular aspect of Alamannic engagement with the Roman Empire. It is likely that Rome actively promoted control of the border *pagi* by established chiefs.[96] The work of such people, Ammianus' 'kings', will have been as important as that of Alamannic officers within the regular army. Though a number of ruling kings will probably, as hostages, have lived on imperial territory in their youth, once in power most must have been encouraged not to pursue imperial careers.[97] However, it appears that they continued to have direct contact with the Empire—both as a matter of routine with local military commanders at major border installations (such as Kaiseraugst and, perhaps, Kellmünz[98]) and, on special occasions, with high imperial officials and emperors. The latter occurred when they travelled to court to receive personal gifts marking the establishment or renewal of alliances.[99] Their

---

[93] Fingerlin (1993: 79); Steuer (1998: 313), citing Böhme.
[94] Below 255.
[95] For eating-habits, see above 105.
[96] Above 119.
[97] Above 154.
[98] Above 99.
[99] Below 271, cf. 246.

reception would have been the responsibility of the *magister officiorum*, from whom they might expect due deference and generous hospitality. (Complaints of Alamannic ambassadors against the *magister officiorum* Ursacius in 365 derived from their not having received the welcome they had come to expect.[100]) In short, they too, like their military cousins, must have had stirring experiences of imperial life, and, through their acceptance of the imperial perspective, have helped to foster local acceptance of the identity of 'Alamanni' and 'Alamannia'.

If they were so highly Romanized, why did leading Alamanni not do more to Romanize their immediate environments, for example by building villas and 'proto-towns'?[101] I will return to this in Chapter 9.[102] Of more immediate concern is the question of the mid-fourth-century 'exclusion'. A strong body of opinion, voiced most recently by Martin, holds that the disappearance of high-ranking Alamanni from imperial service in the later part of that century is not simply the result of the deterioration in the quantity and quality of our sources, but is a real historical phenomenon, caused by a change in policy on the part of Valentinian I. Valentinian, to demonstrate that he was a strong emperor, decided to 'get tough' with Alamanni, provoking them to retaliate and causing them to be seen as the enemies of Rome. As a result, their leading men were excluded from high office. In the second half of the fourth century, Frankish, not Alamannic, generals rose to leading positions in the Roman army.[103]

We have to be careful. The changing fortunes of regional groups within the Roman Empire were not new. The 'Spanish' emperors of the late first and early second centuries came and went, as did the 'Danubians' of the late third and early fourth. This is unexceptional. The rise and fall of cliques is normal in any social structure and does not necessarily indicate the operation of flagrant favour or

---

[100] AM 26.5.7. Below 267; Jones (1964: 1.369), (1966: 140). *Contra* Lorenz, S. (1997: 75 n.15), I see no reason to suppose that attendance at the imperial court was forced on those concerned.

[101] Cf. above 105.

[102] Below 358.

[103] Geuenich (1997a: 53–6); Martin (1997a: 122–4), (1998: 409–18). Cf. Böhme (1998: 40); Heather (2001: 53–4).

prejudice.[104] As the career of Silvanus shows, Franks were prominent before Valentinian; and then, like Alamanni before them, Frankish generals did well for a couple of generations or so only to be eclipsed by other Germanic leaders and even Romans. It took almost another century for Franks to return to play a major role in western affairs, but no one suggests that this was due to their being the victims of exclusion. Though there was a decline in the number of Alamanni in high positions from the middle years of the fourth century, this would probably have happened anyway. This development may have been hastened by events which made Alamannic communities the enemy of choice for Roman commanders, though arising out of Julian's need to save himself from destruction and not from the accession of Valentinian I.[105] Yet, even then, there was no brutal curtailment in the recruitment of Alamannic officers, as the careers of Hariobaudes, Vadomarius, Fraomarius, Bitheridus and Hortarius show. It simply faded away, suggesting that instead of exclusion we should think of 'accelerated evolution'.

Traces of more extensive Elbgermanic/Alamannic service in the Roman army, that is that of 'other ranks', are sparse but significant. They occur from the later third century. Archaeological finds may be interpreted as evidence for the Gallic emperors' having recruited Thuringians.[106] Likewise, around 260, Gallienus may have made an agreement with Iuthungi which included them undertaking to provide military help to the Empire.[107] The first direct indication of such activity comes from the early fourth century, when we hear of Crocus exercising significant influence at the court of Constantius I as a provider of auxiliary military support.[108] A. H. M. Jones describes him as 'an Alamannic chieftain, commanding a body of his countrymen in Britain'.[109]

After Crocus there is a long gap until we reach Julian's report that, in the course of two battles and a siege, he captured a considerable

---

[104] Cf. Elton (1996a: 144), on the rise and fall of other 'regional cliques' into the sixth century.
[105] Below 264–5, 272.
[106] Above 73.
[107] Above 75.
[108] *Epitome* 41.3: *Alamannorum rex, auxilii gratia Constantium comitatus.*
[109] Jones (1964: 2.612).

number of men of fighting age and his intimation that he drafted
them into his own forces.[110] If one of these battles was that of
Strasbourg, these prisoners would have included young Alamanni.[111]
More explicit is Ammianus' statement that, following Julian's raid on
the territory of Vadomarius in 361, he received a certain number of
prisoners of war as *dediticii*, which must mean that he took them into
his army.[112] Next is Ammianus' account of the career of Fraomarius.
Here it is not the career of the colonel which is of interest but the
existence of his regiment which, we are told, was at that time fully
up-to-strength and doing well.[113] Ammianus also relates the story of
an Alamannic soldier who served in Gratian's guard and went home
on leave to his native Lentienses.[114] His loose talk is supposed to have
precipitated the Lentienses' rising of late 377, and contributed to
their defeat at the battle of Argentovaria in 378. After Argentovaria,
Gratian launched a campaign of vengeance against the Lentienses,
and then made a peace with them by which they provided recruits for
distribution throughout the Roman forces.[115] It is probably this
incident that Gratian's tutor and minister, Ausonius, touched upon
when he wrote poetically of Franks and 'Suebi' contending to supply
troops to Rome.[116] About a dozen years later the anonymous author
of the so-called *Historia Augusta*, writing the 'Life' of the emperor
Probus, described dealings with *Germani*—by whom (given his references to the Neckar and the Swabian Alp) he must mean
Alamanni—which appear better suited to late-fourth than to late-
third-century conditions.[117] (Similarities have been noted between
this account and Symmachus' second panegyric to Valentinian I,
delivered on 1 January 370.[118]) Probus, having driven Germanic

[110] Julian, *Ep. ad Ath.* 280C–D.

[111] Hoffmann (1969: 141).

[112] AM 21.4.8: *dediticios cepit.* See Elton (1996a: 129–30); cf. below 166.

[113] AM 29.4.7: *potestate tribuni Alamannorum praefecerat numero, multitudine
viribusque ea tempestate florenti.*

[114] AM 31.10.3: *quidam inter principis armigeros militaris.* See further below 310.

[115] AM 31.10.17: *post deditionem, quam impetravere supplici prece, oblata
(ut praeceptum est) iuventute valida nostris tirociniis permiscenda.*

[116] Ausonius 20 (*Precationes*).2 [Green], 29–30; Green (1991: 535). Cf. Hoffmann
(1969: 143), giving it a more general application.

[117] *Historia Augusta, V. Probi* 13.5–14.7.

[118] Okamura (1984: 316), citing Norden. Okamura refers to Symmachus' third
panegyric, but this must be a mistake, perhaps resulting from a confusion between the
second panegyric and Valentinian's third consulship, which it celebrated. Cf. below 289.

invaders from Gaul, forced their leaders to give him hostages and provisions, and then recruits for his army. These amounted to 16,000: '... all of whom he scattered through the various provinces, incorporating bodies of fifty or sixty in the detachments or among the soldiers along the frontier; for he said that the aid that the Romans received from barbarian auxiliaries must be felt but not seen.'[119] In 400, Stilicho held his first consulship. Claudian, in a poem celebrating this event, refers to Alamannic offers of military aid courteously declined.[120]

The most direct source for Alamannic military service is the *Notitia Dignitatum*, an official schedule of senior positions in the civil service and army around 395. The *Notitia* is quirky, being in places lacunose, and generally uneven in its state of revision. Its eastern section reflects the situation just before 395, its western that of *c*.420.[121] Among a range of eastern frontier regiments named after Germanic 'tribes', there are units, infantry and cavalry, of Alamanni and Iuthungi.[122] Among the eastern household regiments (*auxilia palatina*: each with a nominal strength of *c*.1,200 men) is a unit of 'Bucinobantes'.[123] The Bucinobantes are known as an Alamannic 'tribe', living opposite Mainz, from Ammianus Marcellinus' account of Valentinian I's vendetta against their king, Macrianus.[124] On the basis of this reference, other household regiments, both eastern and western, with names that appear to derive from Alamannic districts, have been accepted as having been raised from communities making up the wider 'Alamanni'. Thus 'Raetovarii' were recruited from

---

[119] *Historia Augusta*, *V. Probi* 14.7: *Accepit praeterea sedecim milia tironum, quos omnes per diversas provincias sparsit, ita ut numeris vel limitaneis militibus quinquagenos et sexagenos intersereret, dicens sentiendum esse non videndum cum auxiliaribus barbaris Romanus iuvatur.*

[120] Claudian, *De Cons. Stil.* 1. 233–6: *Quotiens sociare catervas/oravit iungique tuis Alamannia signis!/Nec doluit contempta tamen...*; Hoffmann (1969: 143).

[121] Jones (1964: 1.347, 351, 354, 395–413). Cf. Hoffmann (1969: 525) and, most recently, Kulikowski (2000b), proposing the dates 386 and *c*.419 respectively.

[122] *Not. Dig.* Or. 28.43 (cohors IV Iuthungorum, Egypt); Or. 31.63 (cohors IX Alamannorum, Egypt); Or. 32.36 (ala I Alamannorum, Phoenice); Or. 32.41 (cohors V Pacata Alamannorum, Phoenice); Or. 33.31 (ala I Iuthungorum, Syria).

[123] *Not. Dig.* Or. 6.58; Elton (1996a: 89).

[124] AM 29.4.7: *Bucinobantes... quae contra Mogontiacum gens est Alamannica.* Above 122–3, below 283, 304–10.

former northern Raetia, and the 'Brisigavi' *seniores* and *juniores* from
the neighbourhood of Breisach in the Upper Rhine valley.[125]

The *Codex Theodosianus* preserves a constitution of 30 January
400, somewhat peevish in tone, from the emperor Honorius to
Stilicho as senior general (*magister utriusque militiae*), concerning
the attempts of various classes of people to evade military service. It
was probably to do with the contemporary defence of Italy.[126] In a
short list of miscreants, mention is made of *laetus Alamannus*.
If, following the current *communis opinio*, 'laetus' is taken with
'Alamannus' ('Alamannic laetus'), and we are not dealing with two
distinct categories (of 'laeti' and 'Alamanni'), this document provides
evidence for Alamanni serving as *laeti*, that is some sort of tied
troops.[127] This topic will be pursued further below.[128]

The evidence is thin and patchy, and presents no immediately
obvious pattern. One can only propose a set of possibilities and
then assess the extent to which each of these is supported by what
we know, that is to use models. However, we first need to establish a
working terminology. Ancient writers did not categorize foreigners
in imperial service as precisely as we would wish. It is best to follow
Elton in considering what such people did—how they were recruited
and employed—rather than what they were called.[129]

The basic distinctions were length of service and identity of leaders. We may envisage two broad classes of recruits. The first comprised men serving under their native leaders for specific campaigns.
They were not part of the Roman army and therefore not subject to
its regulations. The second consisted of men who, at least nominally,
volunteered for service in the Roman army subject to these regulations. They might serve in ethnic units or be distributed among
ethnically-mixed regiments. If they found themselves under
Germanic officers, these would be full members of the Roman

---

[125] Raetovarii: *Not. Dig.* Or. 5.58; Brisigavi *juniores*: Occ. 5.201/7.25 (Italy); Brisi-
gavi *seniores*: Occ. 5.202/7.128 (Spain). Generally see, e.g. Stroheker (1961: 40), citing
Schmidt and Wais; Geuenich (1997a: 29). For the location of the 'Raetovarii' 'um
Nördlingen' see Hoffmann (1969: 1.165).

[126] *CT* 7.20.12; Jones (1964: 2.620).

[127] Lorenz, S. (1997: 15 n.35).

[128] Below 166–9.

[129] Elton (1996a: 92).

officer-corps. These distinctions are not wholly exclusive: one can envisage ways in which men of the first group joined the second. However, they are generally valid. Both groups could serve as the result of formal agreements between their communities and Rome: *foedera* ('treaties'). Both might therefore legitimately be termed *foederati* ('federates'). This confuses the picture, and I will term the first group 'allies' and the second 'auxiliaries'.[130]

The easiest type of general Elbgermanic/Alamannic service to envisage is that of the 'allies'. Under Model I, we may imagine Romans hiring itinerant war-leaders (not yet adjacent territorial chiefs or kings) and their bands on a short-term basis. These would have fought as instructed, then returned whence they had come. Their mercenary activities were an extension of their normal long-distance raiding. This is presumably how 'Thuringians' and Iuthungi served Postumus and Gallienus and their successors. This category is likely to have been a very early phenomenon, before the Alamannic 'corridor' became a 'room'.[131]

The emergence of Alamannic settlements on the imperial frontier is likely to have generated another type of allied service. While it is unlikely that Rome encouraged kings to abandon their responsibilities, princes and nobles would have been welcome military associates. Under Model II, one can imagine sons of kings and their *comites*, or ambitious *optimates*, forming war-bands from the local youth and serving the Empire as short-term allies under the terms of treaties.[132] The Epitomator's likely exaggeration of the role of Crocus in 306 makes it possible that for 'king' Crocus we should understand 'prince' Crocus.[133] And, whatever his status, as Martin says, Crocus was probably not alone in serving Rome in this fashion.[134]

As a variant of both Model I and Model II, it is possible to visualize cases where, for various reasons, war-parties did not return home as

---

[130] For 'allies' I follow Elton (1996a: 96). My 'auxiliaries' he calls 'federates' (92), which returns us to potential confusion.

[131] Above 80–1.

[132] Cf. Elton (1996a: 33, 35), on subordinate *reguli*, *subreguli* and *optimates*.

[133] Above 146. Cf. Zotz (1998: 387 (Fürst), also 388: Crocus' position may have helped the rise of other Alamanni at this time). (For a somewhat different view of Crocus' position and background, see now Drinkwater (forthcoming).)

[134] Martin (1998: 408).

planned. One may imagine an isolated group ceasing to be 'allied' and, perhaps, becoming an auxiliary unit in the Roman army. This process would have been helped by the similarity in size and behaviour between barbarian raiding-bands and standard Roman army units of the period.[135] Such 'detached' groups are not visible in the sources. It is likely that, like the auxiliary 'native' units of early Roman Gaul,[136] they were originally called after their leaders ('the *manus, cohors* or *ala* of *x*'), but such names are not found in the *Notitia Dignitatum*. They may, however, have formed the basis of the 'broadly ethnic' Alamannic and Iuthungian regiments of the eastern frontier, dated to the late third and early fourth centuries.[137]

It must have been possible for individuals to cross into the Empire and to join the army on their own initiative. This is my Model III. Auxiliaries raised in this way would have been posted to existing units.[138] One text is conventionally regarded as directly confirming such recruitment. In the winter of 359–60, Julian is supposed to have objected to Constantius II's removal from Gaul of Germanic troops who had volunteered for service under special terms:

One thing, however, he could neither overlook nor pass over in silence, namely, that those men should suffer no inconvenience who had left their abodes beyond the Rhine and come to him under promise that they would never be led to regions beyond the Alps; for he declared that it was to be feared that the barbarian volunteer soldiers, who were often accustomed to come over to our side under conditions of that kind, might on having knowledge of this thereafter be kept from so doing.[139]

These could have been Franks or Saxons, or even *Germani* from much further afield, but they may also have included Alamanni. The fact that such conditions of service could be bandied about at the

[135] Elton (1996a: 72, 79, 99, 94).

[136] Drinkwater (1978: 829).

[137] Jones (1964: 611 and n. 7); Hoffmann (1969: 140); cf. Stroheker (1961: 35–6). Cf. also Kuntić-Mativić (1996: 187–8), on the imperial military's taste for ethnic—in this case 'internal' ethnic—labels during the fourth century.

[138] Elton (1996a: 140).

[139] AM 20.4.4: *Illud tamen nec dissimulare potuit nec silere: ut illi nullas paterentur molestias, qui relictis laribus transrhenanis, sub hoc venerant pacto, ne ducerentur ad partes umquam transalpinas, verendum esse affirmans, ne voluntarii barbari militares, saepe sub eius modi legibus assueti transire ad nostra, hoc cognito deinceps arcerentur.*

highest level of imperial politics suggests that they were plausible. Ammianus' report is usually interpreted as direct proof of the recruitment of individuals, as envisaged in Model III.[140] However, on practical grounds this is unlikely.

Individual recruits must have been posted to a wide variety of units, and the presence in the same units of men recruited on different terms would have been impossible to manage. It is more likely that what we have here is reference to conditions negotiated between war-leaders and the Empire, that is that we are still dealing with the 'allies' of Models I and II. According to Hoffmann, during the fourth century the use of Germanic allies was a characteristic of western usurpers from outside the imperial family, such as Carausius, Magnentius, Magnus Maximus, Eugenius and Constantine III. However, all of these were ultimately losers and are treated as such in the historical tradition: it suited the winners to emphasize their opponents' scandalous use of *barbari*. The winners, on the other hand, may well themselves have employed such forces—it would have been madness for them not to—while ensuring that this received little publicity. Constantius II probably used allied Alamanni against Magnentius.[141] It suited Julian to criticize Constantius' actions, but this made it difficult for him to justify his own use of Germanic allies. It would have been in his interests to confuse the issue by conflating potential (and legitimate) complaints of the allies and current (and quasi-mutinous) objections by certain regular regiments: that by moving south of the Alps they would expose the families they left behind to barbarian attack.[142]

This leaves the most likely example we have of an individual volunteer as Gratian's Lentiensian guardsman, loyal enough to be allowed leave. However, even he may have been promoted into the guards from a unit raised, say, according to Model V (below). The youths posted to Roman regiments as a result of Gratian's arrangement with the Lentienses cannot have been treated differently

---

[140] e.g. Hoffmann (1969: 142, 151); Heather (2001: 33).

[141] Below 201–2.

[142] So AM 20.4.10, 16. On this see further below 254. Cf. Martin (1998: 413): that Julian's army would have contained many Germans—though he assumes that most of these would have been 'laetic' in origin.

from their new companions, and so must have been regarded as volunteers. The same was probably true of Julian's forced recruits of 20 years earlier. Possible archaeological evidence for this sort of recruiting into the Rhine and Danube armies from young men from throughout the Elbgermanic triangle is in the form of finds of male cloak-brooches, after the Roman military style and dated to the later fourth and early fifth centuries, throughout the region.[143]

Models I–III concern nominally voluntary service by 'free' Alamanni. Different from this is the recruitment of Alamanni living on Roman soil as prisoners of war (*dediticii*) or refugees (*laeti*), dealt with here as Model IV. The general issue of Gallic *laeti* is difficult and controversial. In taking them to be Germanic in origin I follow den Boeft et al.[144] In return for being granted their lives and/or permanent residence in the Empire, both *dediticii* and *laeti* appear to have been placed in discrete settlements under the supervision of imperial 'prefects'. Though the *Notitia Dignitatum* lists only *praefecti laetorum*, a reference by the emperor Julian suggests that both *laeti* and *dediticii* were viewed in much the same manner.[145] The fine line between the two sorts of communities, especially in later generations, may have led to both eventually being treated as laetic.[146] They were obliged to maintain themselves and supply recruits to the Roman army. However, such recruits were not formed into their own regiments but posted in the usual way to existing units.[147]

A localized and obscure institution, *laeti* have caused uncertainty and confusion among historians, ancient and modern. Zosimus saw them as a 'tribe'.[148] Ammianus Marcellinus has *laeti barbari* making an unsuccessful attack on Lyon in 357.[149] In his Loeb edition of Ammianus, Rolfe followed Zosimus in translating the phrase containing *laeti barbari* as 'the Laeti, a savage tribe, skilled in seasonable raids'. By treating *laeti* as a proper noun and the 'Laeti' as a tribe he by-passed the issue of the existence of a semi-servile population in

---

[143] Schach-Dörges (1997: 82); cf. above 160.
[144] den Boeft, den Hengst, and Teitler (1987: 202–4).
[145] AM 20.8.13.
[146] Cf. Lorenz, S. (1997: 14–15, 65): *laeti* were the offspring of *dediticii*.
[147] Elton (1996a: 131).
[148] Zosimus 2.54.1.
[149] AM 16.11.4. Below 225.

Gaul. In Rolfe's version, the Laeti appear to be an Alamannic tribe or sub-tribe. This interpretation reflects a long-standing misinterpretation in anglophone studies, reinforced by Rolfe's description of the recruits whom Julian offered Constantius in 360 as 'of the Laeti, a tribe of barbarians on this side of the Rhine'.[150] As is being increasingly recognized, Ammianus' *laeti* of 357 cannot be interpreted in this way.[151] They are just 'barbarian *laeti*': certainly not a tribe, probably not Alamannic, perhaps not principals in the events of 357, and maybe not hostile to Rome.[152] One may imagine the inhabitants of one or more Germanic laetic settlements west of the Rhine, having weathered the political storms of the early 350s, now finding themselves caught between Alamanni and Romans. Suspected by both sides, they fled deeper into Gaul. However, their flight was interpreted and dealt with as an attack.

Thus, there is no secure mention of tied Alamannic recruits in the Roman army in Ammianus. All that remains is a reference to Alamannic prisoners of war being sent to farm in the Po valley in 370, after count Theodosius' Raetian campaign.[153] This has been connected with the Alamannic *laeti* of the *Codex Theodosianus*.[154] However, the latter and their fellow draft-dodgers seem to have been a relatively sophisticated group of people, evading their responsibilities by obtaining documents exempting them from service, and may have been relatively few in number. It looks as if the Po-dwellers had done exceptionally well for themselves as farmers, and were now hardly down-trodden semi-free dependants of the Empire. (The fact that neither they, nor any of the other groups of potential recruits mentioned, appear to have been destined for any particular sort of unit must be a strong indication against the existence of specifically 'laetic' units.[155]) In the end, the best evidence for 'normal' laetic

---

[150] AM 20.8.13: *adulescentes Laetos quosdam, cis Rhenum editam barbarorum progeniem.* See, e.g. Browning (1975: 84): 'Another German group, the Laeti...'; Elton (1996a: 131): '*Laeti* was also the name of an Alamannic canton.' Generally, Lorenz, S. (1997: 15 and n. 35).

[151] Nixon and Rodgers (1994: 142 n. 76).

[152] *Contra* Lorenz, S. (1997: 40): that these *laeti* were hostile Alamanni.

[153] AM 28.5.15: *quoscumque cepit ad Italiam ... misit, ubi fertilibus pagis acceptis, iam tributarii circumcolunt Padum.* Cf. below 283, 304.

[154] Above 162; Hoffmann (1969: 142 and n. 90).

[155] Elton (1996a: 131).

communities composed of Alamannic settlers in the Empire is the *Notitia Dignitatum*'s indication of the presence of *laeti gentiles Suevi* in Gaul.[156] But this too is questionable. Later Roman writers used 'Suebi' as a synonym for Alamanni, but the usage tended to be poetical, with a view to style and metre.[157] Soldiers and administrators dealing with Germanic settlers would have been subject to no such constraints and would, like the legal draftsman who composed *CT* 7.20.12, probably have preferred the prosaic Alamannus. 'Suebi' are more likely to have been other Danubian *Germani*.[158] This finds some confirmation in the fact that the *Notitia Dignitatum*'s reference to the (few) Suebi settled in Gaul is followed by that of the (many Danubian) Sarmatians settled in Italy.

There is also the question of the number of *dediticii/laeti* available for service. Hoffmann proposed that the later Roman army in Gaul consisted for the most part of western *Germani*. During the fourth century, the bulk of these came from laetic settlements. Unit names which appear to reflect regional (e.g. *Gallicani*) or *civitas*-based (e.g. *Ambianenses, Bituriges, Picatavenses*) recruitment of native Gauls are deceptive. They indicate only where laetic units were originally stationed.[159] Gauls could still be recruited into legions and, occasionally, into other units; but where the latter occurred it was only of secondary importance.[160] This is controversial, and Hoffmann's views have been disputed.[161] It returns us to the question of numbers. To resolve the issue as to the importance of the *laeti* we need to know far more than we do about: the number of laetic settlements; the size of their populations; the distribution of such populations by gender and age; the quality of their land; the level of their agricultural expertise; the housing, tools, seed crops, work animals etc. made available to them; and the proportion of working males they were obliged to give up to the army, and for how long. Such questions can be answered only by means of archaeology, and currently archaeology is not in a

---

[156] *Not. Dig.* Occ. 42.34 (Baiocasses/Bayeux), 35 (Cenomanni(?)/Le Mans), 44 (Arverni(?)/Clermont-Ferrand); Stroheker (1975: 39).

[157] Green (1991: 535); Heinen (1995: 82). Cf. above 46.

[158] Castritius (2005: 195–6); cf. above 48, below 324, 335.

[159] Hoffmann (1969: 142, 145–54, 160, 164, 168, 180, 196, 200).

[160] Hoffmann (1969: 177, 154 (citing *ILS* 9215: below 171 n.177)).

[161] Cf. Elton (1996a: 150–1).

position to do so. However, what we now know about Gaul and Germania tells against Hoffmann's reconstruction.

The population of the Free Germanic territories was not massive: there were no many thousands of pairs of hands ready to be put to the service of Rome.[162] Some *dediticii* and *laeti*, like those settled in the Po valley, succeeded.[163] For others, however, life must have been hard. Living near the frontier, many must have been exposed to raiding by their free cousins. And the lands they worked, though previously farmed, are likely to have gone to waste. It would have required enormous amounts of skill and energy to re-instate even basic subsistence farming—the best that Alamannic farming expertise could offer. But most *laeti* and *dediticii* will have been young men with limited experience of and interest in wresting a bare living from the soil. The acquisition of wives and children may have increased their commitment but, like Romulus' Romans of old, they would have faced difficulties in obtaining womenfolk. And one can hardly imagine the Roman authorities taking a close interest in their problems. *Laeti* appear to have survived in some fashion, since the term is used, somewhat enigmatically, of troops employed by Merovingian kings.[164] However, during the fourth century, most laetic communities must have found it a struggle to survive; and overall they could hardly have been numerous or strong enough to meet the regular manpower needs of the western army.[165]

Models I–IV envisage Alamannic warriors coming into Roman service and being used, dismissed or absorbed as the occasion demanded. Now, however, we have to consider a situation in which Rome went to Alamanni and hired them under longer-term commitments. This is dealt with as Model V, involving units which we appear to know most about and which therefore should be the easiest to understand: the 'regionally ethnic' regiments of the *Notitia*

[162] Above 39.
[163] Above 167.
[164] Wood (1994: 64).
[165] MacMullen (1963: 9–13, 19–21) has argued vigorously for farming as the part-time occupation of full-time soldiers and soldiering as the part-time occupation of full-time farmers in the later Roman Empire. However, despite his direct comparison (14), this was hardly the same as the use of barbarians, who would have needed constant surveillance and support.

Dignitatum, Bucinobantes, Raetovarii and Brisigavi. These have attracted a great deal of attention in the past because they appear to give the names of constituent elements of the Alamanni—their 'Teilvölker' or 'Teilstämme'.[166] Attempts have been made to connect this putative 'tribal' history with the political history of Ammianus' narrative. For example, Vadomarius is frequently termed king of the Brisigavi.[167] But this reconstruction is not as straightforward as it might seem.

These units were significant components of the imperial military establishment. The formation of permanent regiments was a serious business because of the implied cost. It was not something that can have been taken lightly. Hoffmann has shown that such increases in imperial strength happened in waves, when, presumably, the normal sources of troop recruitment were unavailable or inappropriate. Hoffmann suggests that this happened in circumstances of exceptional need, when just a few western commanders-in-chief—Julian, Valentinian I and Stilicho (for Honorius)—rapidly raised new regiments to pursue particular objectives.[168] This is clearest in the case of the Bucinobantes and Raetovarii. Hoffmann sees these as a linked pair of units, and dates their formation from the career of king Fraomarius, sent to Britain to take command of the Bucinobantes in 372/3.[169] Both the Bucinobantes and the Raetovarii had been raised by Valentinian I in the tense period after his arrival in Gaul in 365. In 368, they were transferred to Britain to help deal with the 'Barbarian Conspiracy' of 367.[170]

Similarly, if we accept Hoffmann's dating, the formation of the twin units of Brisigavi occurred during the acute political and military unease at the beginning of Honorius' reign. At this time, his regent, Stilicho, prudently increased his strength by recruiting from western *Germani*. He formed at least 18 new regiments, two of which were Alamannic: the Brisigavi Seniores and Brisigavi Juniores.[171] In this instance, however, the Alamannic connection is less strong. The

---

[166] e.g. Stroheker (1961: 40); Hoffmann (1969: 167). Above 122–3.

[167] e.g. Stroheker (1961: 46: 'zweifellos'); Lorenz, S. (1997: 78: Vadomarius' son, Vithicabius, also as 'König der Brisigavi').

[168] Hoffmann (1969: 141–3, 159, 165–8).

[169] For the date, see below 285.

[170] Hoffmann (1969: 165–6). On the troubles of 367 and later, see below 237.

[171] Hoffmann (1969: 143, 168); cf. Bury (1923: 1.118), for Stilicho's visit to the Rhine in 397. Below 320, 322.

Brisigavi are accepted by historians as Alamannic because of the similarity between their name and the modern name of the area on the right bank of the Rhine, immediately west of the town of Breisach/Brisiacum: the Breisgau.[172] But it should be remembered that late Roman Brisiacum was a military base guarding a Rhine crossing, and lay on—or, at least, attached to—the river's left bank.[173] In principle any regiment taking its name must have been raised in its immediate, left-bank neighbourhood, and so need have been little different from the many others recruited in or from Gallic communities, from *dediticii/laeti* or native Gauls, or both. The association of Brisigavi in the *Notitia Dignitatum* with regiments bearing the 'tribal' names Atecotti, Marcomanni and Mauri is not helpful. Though the first of these is likely to have indicated an authentic tribal affiliation,[174] the other two are suspiciously vague, and may be fanciful.

If the Brisigavi are still to be regarded as in some way Alamannic, a supposition supported by archaeological finds suggesting a strong Germanic presence in and around Breisach in the later fourth century, similar interpretation ought to be extended to the several household units of 'Mattiaci' found in the *Notitia Dignitatum*.[175] These must have been raised around Wiesbaden/Aquae Mattiacorum, on the right bank of the Rhine in an area of Romano-Germanic activity. Hoffmann, indeed, locates their formation in the late third or early fourth century, when such activity was gaining strength.[176] He suggests that they were recruited from prisoners of war or recruits from the high imperial tribe of the Mattiaci which was somehow, despite the turmoil of the third century, still in existence; but this is implausible. More likely is that they were raised from a mixed transrhenish population, consisting of provincials and incoming Alamanni, and perhaps Burgundians.[177]

---

[172] Matthews (1989: 306); Bücker (1999: 22).

[173] Bücker (1999: 23).

[174] Hoffmann (1969: 154).

[175] In the east, Mattiaci seniores, *Not. Dig.* Or. 5.53 and Mattiaci juniores, Or. 6.53; in the west, Mattiaci seniores, Occ. 5.164/7.15 (Italy), Mattiaci juniores, Occ. 5.165/7.64 (Gaul) and Mattiaci juniores Gallicani, Occ. 5.209/7.77 (Gaul). Above 101.

[176] Hoffmann (1969: 156–7); above 130.

[177] Cf. above 168 n.160. *ILS* 9215 suggests Gallic recruitment into the Mattiaci. However, this could have taken place long after the original formation of the units.

The *Notitia Dignitatum* does not mention the one Alamannic grouping which we know provided recruits, the Lentienses.[178]

'Urgency', 'rarity', mixed populations and awkward omissions raise other questions about the areas from which units derived their names. We return to the extent to which the names we have denote 'Teilvölker' or 'Teilstämme'. Current thinking is that most of these names were not coined by the people they referred to. 'Men of the Linzgau', 'men of [the old province of] Raetia' (I omit 'Brisigavi' and 'Mattiaci' for reasons obvious from my remarks above, and also 'Bucinobantes' to which I will return below) is not what Germanic newcomers are likely to have called themselves but what they were called by outsiders already acquainted with the areas in which they had settled and their old, Celto-Roman, names. Such outsiders have been tentatively identified as Roman recruiting officers, raising Alamannic regiments but unwilling to heed Alamannic self-labelling based on the names of kings.[179] This interpretation requires some adjustment.

First, it must have been the case that Roman regional names for the Alamanni existed independently of and probably long before the raising of regular regiments from these regions. As in the case of 'Alamannia',[180] Roman soldiers and administrators would have needed ways of describing the people they found themselves dealing with which avoided the names of individual rulers. So they hit upon regional names. This explains the existence of 'Lentienses'.[181] Second, when it came to regimental recruitment, the question of the impermanency of particular Alamannic rulers cannot have been an issue. The Late Empire did not name its regiments after anyone outside the imperial family.[182] In addition, it is unlikely that a full regiment could have been raised from a single *pagus*. The removal of around 1,000 of his best warriors, even if he had that number at his disposal,

---

[178] AM 31.10.17.

[179] Above 122.

[180] Above 68–9.

[181] AM 15.4.1, listing Constantius' Alamannic opponents in 355 (... *et Lentiensibus, Alamannicis pagis*: below 207), appears to suggest that the Lentienses were a single *pagus*. But he obscures the sense of the word by using it in the plural; and at 31.10.2–3 he represents the Lentienses as a *populus* and then a *natio*.

[182] Cf. above 164.

would have seriously weakened any *pagus* chief. Thirdly, these regiments were apparently raised in a hurry, outside the regular system of recruitment. Rome would have wanted as many suitable recruits as possible in the shortest time. Overall, such activity, though it would need to have been agreed with individual kings and princes, cannot have been organized by them and would probably have had to cover several *pagi*. It is these wider areas, already identified, which were targeted by Roman recruiting officers, and it is these areas which are reflected in the names of the regiments formed in this way. They were indeed Roman constructs, not indigenous geopolitical entities.[183] On the other hand, such regional groupings may have affected Alamannic political and social structures. Ambitious local leaders, whose help Rome would have welcomed in raising regiments, may have attempted to exploit the boundaries and names given by Romans to increase their power. This takes us to the Bucinobantes.

Of Brisigavi, Bucinobantes, Lentienses and Raetovarii only 'Bucinobantes' appears to be basically Germanic in form. It has been interpreted as 'the people of the area of the defensive quickset hedge'.[184] If this is correct, the hedge in question will have been a real and considerable feature of the landscape, creating some form of redoubt. This suggests an interesting alternative to the 'Höhensiedlung'.[185] A hedge also fits well with the little we know of the middle Main, where the careful defining and defending of areas seems to have been an important issue in a region in which Romans, Alamanni and Burgundians confronted each other.[186] 'Bucinobantes' therefore appears, uniquely, as more than a neutral imperial label. Is it an indication of a 'Teilstamm'? Probably not: 'Bucinobantes' is another, albeit different, example of a spurious 'constituent tribe'.

We first hear of a king of the Bucinobantes, Macrianus, not long after the likely date of the formation of the unit of this name.[187] Though Ammianus makes out that Macrianus was highly inimical to Valentinian I, this is probably overstated. Macrianus appears generally to have been well-disposed to Rome, using the relationship to

---

[183] Cf. van Driel-Murray (2003: 204) on the Batavi, as interpreted by comparison with the modern Gurkhas: 'Tribal boundaries were established by Roman administrators, tribal identities registered by Roman census officials.'

[184] Neumann (1981): 'Knick, Verhau, verflochtene Heckenschutzwehr'.

[185] Above 98.   [186] Above 112.   [187] AM 28.5.8.

expand his influence down the Main valley.[188] A decade or so before, Macrianus had been cultivated by Julian,[189] and it takes little to envisage him creating a Lilliputian empire on the middle Main, useful to Rome as a buffer against neighbouring Burgundians. Likewise, we may imagine the people of Macrianus' empire taking their name from the nature of their chief stronghold. As Macrianus took over other Alamannic *pagi*, the name was retained: the Bucinobantes drove westwards. Valentinian's need to raise a new regiment, recruited along the middle and lower Main and called, accordingly, 'Bucinobantes', caused him to continue to cooperate with Macrianus, allowing the latter to come closer to the Rhine and so increase his power and prestige. However, once Valentinian's position was secure, he decided to break Macrianus, now seen as a threat to the Mainz crossing.[190] This was eventually only partially achieved.[191] Macrianus' empire continued, but did not survive the death of its founder at the hands of the Frank, Mallobaudes.[192] This helps explain the Burgundian presence at Mainz by the early fifth century.[193] Overall, the Bucinobantes were a temporary political construct, not a constituent tribe.

Ammianus' report of Gratian's diffusion of Lentiensian recruits and the *Historia Augusta*'s approbatory account of Probus having done the same thing in the later third century hint that by the end of the fourth century there was concern in educated circles about the recruitment of external *Germani* into their 'own' regiments.[194] Yet recruits into such units would, in the longer term, have been even more subject to the integrating pressures outlined in respect of Models I and II. Immediately enrolled on the permanent strength, they could have soon been transferred far from home, as happened to the Bucinobantes.

A final model, Model VI, may be used to postulate a situation in which, in changed circumstances, the Empire handed over the guarding of the Rhine to Germanic kings and princes. Roman allies thus became Roman agents, serving in Roman installations on Roman soil. Though this is more a feature of the fifth century than the

---

[188] Below 304–5.   [189] Below 248–9.   [190] Below 286–7, 304–5.
[191] Below 304–9.   [192] Below 318.   [193] Below 324.
[194] Above 160–1.

fourth,[195] the process may have begun before 400. This is suggested by finds of artefacts dated to the later fourth century in the military cemetery at Sponeck, near Breisach. These are indistinguishable from those of neighbouring Alamannic settlements, and may indicate that the men of the garrison were recruited from Alamanni or had very close links with local villages.[196] However, there are problems in this interpretation. The presence of Alamannic artefacts could result from the garrison's having been supplied by the local community, in the process adopting something of its lifestyle (including permanent liaisons with its womenfolk). Further, even if the garrison were Alamannic, our current inability to localize Alamannic artefacts means that we cannot tell if it was recruited locally. Finally, thanks to Roman views on the recruitment of barbarians during the fourth century, it is likely that any local recruits, if there were any, were fed into what was still at least nominally a Roman unit.

Alamannic warriors served Rome in significant numbers from the late third to the early fifth century, from almost as soon as both were in close contact to the beginning of the dissolution of the western Empire. Unlike that of Alamannic officers, the pattern of recruitment of other ranks continued unchanged throughout this period. What was the proportion of Alamannic recruits in the Roman army as a whole? This is impossible to establish with any precision, but the impression is that it was not overwhelming. In the sole area for which one can perform simple calculations, the *Notitia Dignitatum*'s listing of guards-regiments and *comitatenses*, Alamannic representation is not high. In A. H. M. Jones' tables, the overall proportion of Alamannic units is 3 per cent including the Mattiaci and 1 per cent without them.[197] This, together with the fact that known Alamannic first-class regiments (the *auxilia palatina*) were infantry regiments, provides no comfort for Okamura's suggestion that Aurelius Victor's description of the third-century Alamanni as a *gens populosa ex equo mirifice pugnans* was an anachronism, based on his knowledge of their contemporary army service.[198] The absence

---

[195] Below 327.

[196] Fingerlin (1990: 123), (1997a: 104); Steuer (1997a: 152–3); Bücker (1999: 160, 217). Cf. below 328.

[197] Jones (1964: 364 Tables V, VI).

[198] Aurelius Victor, *Caesares* 21.2; Okamura (1984: 90).

of archaeological evidence for the Alamanni numerous or keen horsemen likewise tells against the idea that Victor's statement reflected fourth-century experience of them.[199] In Ammianus' account of Constantius II's 355 campaign, there is passing mention of Lentiensian cavalry, but the associated fighting does not seem to have amounted to a cavalry battle.[200] Victor was probably referring cryptically to Julian's recent victory at Strasbourg.[201] Finally, it should now be clear that we must resist the temptation to treat Roman regimental names as tribal names.

Appreciation of the extent and nature of Alamannic service as a whole helps in understanding the events of the following chapters. For example, as we have seen, Latinus, Agilo and Scudilo were, though nominally Alamanni, probably raised in the Roman Empire. They pursued careers in the Roman army, probably Constans' army of Illyricum, which came to Constantius II through Vetranio, but possibly even Constantius' own army of the east. In culture, experience and outlook they were a long way from Alamannia. However, if their origins lay in the relatively few proximate *pagi* that Rome knew best, they may have been able to maintain blood ties with their home communities. One can envisage how, when Constantius II reached Italy, the idea of using these connections to turn the Alamanni on Decentius and Magnentius came from 'court' Alamanni like Agilo; and a key intermediary in this could have been Vadomarius.[202] Ammianus' report that in 354 Latinus, Agilo and Scudilo 'betrayed' Constantius' invasion plans to 'their own people' may contain a grain of truth:[203] that they originated from the region over the Rhine from Kaiseraugst, the *pagi* of Gundobadus and Vadomarius. However, their 'treason' was no more than their involvement in negotiation, aimed at securing peace without bloodshed on the High Rhine.[204]

---

[199] Keller (1993: 90). Cf. Whittaker (1994: 214), on a similar lack of evidence for the Huns as horse-riding nomads; below 340.

[200] AM 15.4.12. Below 210–11.

[201] Above 141–2.

[202] Above 155–6, below 207.

[203] AM 14.10.8: *populares suos.*

[204] Below 204, 207.

6

Conflict 285–355

Fighting—by Rome against Alamanni and by Alamanni against Rome—features most prominently in the literature, ancient and modern. We can now examine this against the background of Alamannic development established in preceding chapters.

Precisely how one constructs the overall picture is determined by the extent to which one believes that the Alamanni posed a real danger to the security of the Empire. I propose that, whatever either side may have felt or claimed, there was no substantial 'Germanic threat' on the Rhine from the later third to the early fifth centuries. Alamanni and Franks were never a menace to Rome. The Empire exploited them much more than they could ever have damaged it.[1]

A more sceptical view of the Germanic menace derives from a more questioning attitude to the sources, in particular from a more critical assessment of Ammianus Marcellinus. Since the publication of Edward Thompson's pioneering study in 1947, many scholars have contributed to the identification and examination of the vagaries of Ammianus' narrative, and of what he does not say quite as much as what he does.[2] Stroheker, for example, noted Ammianus' intense dislike of Alamanni, and his constant projection of a negative image of these people, especially in respect of their duplicity.[3] Stroheker explained this by reference to Ammianus' feelings of resentment against Constantius II for his rough treatment of Roman

---

[1] Drinkwater (1996: 26–8); cf. above 125, 133–5, below 360.

[2] See Drinkwater (1997: 1 n.5). Fundamental is now Sabbah (1978). Among English-language studies, particular mention should be made of Elliott (1983) and Barnes (1998). Cf. most recently Rollinger (2001).

[3] Stroheker (1961: 32–3, 48–9).

officers and for his promotion of Alamanni, and to Ammianus' strong bias in favour of Julian. The latter came from both Ammianus' own feelings and his sources, comprising a discrete and easily recognizable pro-Julian tradition.[4] Other earlier work on the same lines, for example by Bitter and Rosen, has been collected by Zotz.[5] This, again, tells against Ammianus' objectivity with regard to Alamanni, whom he consistently portrays as a constant and untrustworthy enemy. More recent investigations have pursued the same vein. Barceló registers the same hostility to Constantius II and the same 'Tendenz' in favour of Julian.[6]

But few historians have carried criticism of Ammianus on the Alamanni to its logical conclusion.[7] They have noted Ammianus' flaws, but have accepted the broad accuracy of his account and the general validity of his argument. So, for example, Rosen, Barceló and Zotz, while conceding that Ammianus' narrative needs qualification, are ready to accept the reality of the Franco-Alamannic threat.[8] Acceptance of barbarian 'pressure' has most recently been expressed by Heather, despite his contention that barbarians were susceptible to 'management' and his identification of aspects of Rome's dealings with them which allow a different interpretation. These are: age-old hostility to barbarians which justified and even encouraged the perpetration of atrocities against them; emperors' need for successful wars; and the fact that major barbarian attacks tended to occur only when the Empire was damaging itself through civil war.[9] Bluntly, as far as the Alamanni and Rome are concerned, Ammianus grossly exaggerates the danger posed by the former to the latter. His admiration of Julian was profound, and led him to present him in the best possible light and to give the worst impression of his enemies. So he depicted Alamanni as formidable foes, able to get the better of Constantius II but unequal to Julian's military genius.[10]

---

[4] Stroheker (1961: 50). Cf. Guzmán Armario (2002: 542 and, esp. on Ammianus' hatred of the barbarians as a moral menace, 218, 228, 285, 539–42).

[5] Zotz (1998: 385–7, 400–4).

[6] Barceló (1981: 24, 31–3).

[7] Recent exceptions are Burns (2003) and Guzmán Armario (2002).

[8] Rosen (1970: 91); Barceló (1981: 12, 26, 37); Zotz (1998: 384–7).

[9] Heather (2001: 18–20, 50–2, 54).

[10] Cf. below 204–5, 209.

Hostility to the barbarians and a genuine, if misguided, conviction that they posed a real danger to the Empire is evident in all our sources, epigraphic and numismatic quite as much as literary. The Empire needed external enemies to bind it together. In particular, the notion of 'barbarian pressure' helped justify the imperial administrative and military structure in the west, and the taxation that was necessary to sustain it.[11] The Empire needed its bogeymen; and so, apparently, does modern scholarship.[12] The reason for this is sometimes evident when we consider historical context. Camille Jullian, for example, a patriotic Frenchman, published the last two volumes of his monumental *Histoire de la Gaule* in 1926 when, after the humiliation of the Franco-Prussian War and the agony of the First World War, the threat from Germany was a painful memory and a potential reality. In discussing the Rhine barbarians, he deals with Franks, Saxons and Alamanni. However, it soon becomes clear that the villains of the piece are the Alamanni. Here we can see the resonance of Alamanni/ Alamannia, 'les allemands'/'Allemagne'. While the Franks were soon cooperating with the Roman Empire and manifesting signs of a greatness that would find its first embodiment in Clovis, the Alamanni were hostile to Greco-Roman culture, arrogant, and intent on conquest: dangerous.[13] On the other hand, it is less easy to explain why historians of the era of the European Union find it difficult to abandon the concept. There can be no doubt that the impression of the *Germani* as numerous, warlike, only temporarily cowed by Roman campaigns of retribution and ever ready to renew wide-scale plundering and devastation retains enormous strength.[14]

I will deal with Romano-Alamannic conflicts in chronological order, establishing a narrative and indicating how events may have been 'spun' for the benefit of imperial politics, beginning with the period 285–355—from the accession of Diocletian to Julian's arrival in Gaul.

For all its problems, Ammianus' account remains our only extensive source. Until we reach its first extant book (Book 14), which

---

[11] Drinkwater (1996: 26–7); see also now Heather (2001: 51). See esp. below 361.
[12] Below 359.
[13] Jullian (1926: 169–71, 174–6).
[14] e.g. *Germanen* (1986: 340–1); cf. Drinkwater (1997: 1).

concerns the events of 353/4, we have to rely on lesser authors, inscriptions and coins. This causes problems. For example, the reconstruction of campaigns from imperial titles found on inscriptions has attracted criticism.[15] However, the situation is not quite as bad as these observations may suggest. Down to 321 we are fortunate to have the evidence of nine Latin panegyrics: speeches in honour of emperors or (in one case) imperial officials. Given that these take a close interest in campaigns, and that they are at pains to relate events of the present to those of the past, by frequently employing the flashback, we may be fairly confident that we know the major incidents on the Rhine in this period, even if their details are often obscure. Further, the little that we do know about Rome's dealings with the Alamanni can be made to yield more when seen in the context of Rome's dealings with Rhine barbarians in general, especially the Franks. Overall, the broad peaks and troughs of Romano-Alamannic interaction in this period may be accepted as authentic historical phenomena, and not condemned as the deceptive creations of the source material.

Diocletian began his challenge for the throne in the east in 284, and by 285 was leader of the whole Empire. He sent Maximian into Gaul as commander of the west, and before the end of the year had recognized him as Caesar. In 286 he made Maximian fellow Augustus: the 'dyarchy' (rule-of-two) was born.[16] Maximian was sent to Gaul in the first place to deal with Bagaudae, not Franks or Alamanni. The Bagaudae were internal dissidents, created by the dislocation of the third-century 'Crisis' and by government measures intended to overcome it.[17] Only after these had been suppressed did he turn to deal with the 'Germanic problem'.

Late in 285 or early in 286, he supposedly faced serious barbarian invasion.[18] A panegyric of 289 tells us that the invaders were in two groups: Chaibones and Heruli; and Burgundians and Alamanni. Maximian left the Burgundians and Alamanni to succumb to hunger and disease, but engaged the Chaibones in person, though with only

[15] Lippold (1981: 362–3).
[16] Kienast (1996: 272).
[17] Jullian (1926: 51); Stroheker (1975: 26); Drinkwater (1984: 364–8).
[18] *Pan. Lat.* 2(10).5.1. Date: Barnes (1982: 57); Kolb (1987: 41); Nixon and Rodgers (1994: 61 n.23).

part of his forces.[19] The panegyrist's naming of Chaibones and Heruli is odd, since the first are otherwise unknown and the second a long way from their normal geographic location. They are, however, mentioned again in a panegyric of 291.[20] It is probably best to treat both as being associated with the Franks on the Lower Rhine.[21] Maximian gave another dramatic demonstration of his energy and personal courage on 1 January 287, the date of his inauguration into his first consulship, at Trier. Receiving news of barbarian raiders in the vicinity, he dashed out to deal with them in person, returning victorious on the same day.[22] It is reasonable to suppose that these raiders, too, were Franks.[23]

Each of Maximian's first two 'campaigns' may be explained as resulting from his desire to re-establish his reputation as a general. Success against the Bagaudae was admirable, but it was success against fellow citizens and simple peasants to boot: not something to boast about. Real success could be gained only through victories against external enemies, leading to recognition as 'conqueror of the barbarians' (*debellator gentium barbararum*: Constantine I) or even (to draw on the vocabulary of modern film) 'terminator of the barbarians' (*barbarorum extinctor*: Julian).[24] However, both these early efforts were small-scale and unfocused.

Maximian showed that he had identified a more promising target when, later in 287, he campaigned over the Rhine.[25] If this is the same expedition in which Constantius I participated before he became Caesar, it took Roman forces from Mainz to Günzburg[26] (Fig. 4). Maximian thus traversed Alamannia. His campaign was bloody, destructive and triumphalist.[27] Two years later, a Gallic orator, celebrating the emperor's success, declared, 'All that I see across the

[19] *Pan. Lat.* 2(10).5.2–3.
[20] *Pan. Lat.* 3(11).7.1.
[21] Jullian (1926: 60–1, as 'allies').
[22] *Pan. Lat.* 2(10).6; Nixon and Rodgers (1994: 42–3).
[23] Drinkwater (1996: 22 n.10); Runde (1998: 660).
[24] *RIC* 7, Trier no. 356; *AE* 1969, 631 (=*Quellen* 6, Inscriptions no. 66).
[25] *Pan. Lat.* 2(10).7.2–3.
[26] *Pan. Lat.* 4(8).2.1. Stroheker (1975: 26–7); Nixon and Rodgers (1994: 110 n.6).
[27] *Pan. Lat.* 2(10).7.6; 3(11).5.4, with Nixon and Rodgers (1994: 89 n.33); *Pan. Lat.* 4(8).2.1.

Rhine is Roman.'[28] Also in 287, probably just before the Alamannic campaign, Maximian was involved with Franks on the Lower Rhine, leading to the submission of king Gennobaudes. This appears to have been achieved through intimidation more than force.[29] Gennobaudes may have sensed that Maximian was looking for trouble and prudently avoided a full-scale war with him. Others may have followed suit, perhaps after a token show of strength, as is hinted at in a brief notice of Constantius' capture of another Frankish leader.[30] We hear of Gennobaudes probably only because Maximian needed a 'royal' supplication to match that by the king of Persia to Diocletian.[31] For all its display of his Herculean 'vigour and activity',[32] Maximian's success was already hollow. Probably even before he had set out on his Alamannic campaign, a major crisis had erupted in the west.

This was the usurpation of Carausius, probably during the winter of 286/7.[33] Carausius' rebellion was dangerous not so much because it posed an immediate military challenge—he showed himself eager to cooperate with his imperial 'colleagues'—but because it threatened Diocletian's new political order. The uncontrolled proliferation of rulers risked a return to the recent Crisis. The imperial *collegium* was not open to gate-crashers.[34]

Diocletian returned from the east at this time. In 288, he fought his own campaign against the Alamanni, attacking 'that part of Germany which lies opposite Raetia'.[35] From a later reference to the borders of

[28] *Pan. Lat.* 2(10).7.7: *quidquid ultra Rhenum prospicio Romanum est.*

[29] *Pan. Lat.* 2(10).10.3–6, cf. 3(11).5.4.

[30] *Pan. Lat.* 4(8).2.1; Nixon and Rodgers (1994: 110 n.6).

[31] *Pan. Lat.* 2(10).10.6, with Nixon and Rodgers (1994: 68 n.36), and Drinkwater (1996: 28 n. 35). Cf. below 188.

[32] Rees (2002: 47).

[33] Nixon and Rodgers (1994: 107): 286; Kienast (1996: 278): late 286 or winter 286/7. The dating is difficult. One might suppose that the occurrence of Maximian's Alamannic war during the campaigning season of 287 offers a reliable *terminus post quem* for the rebellion, on the grounds that Maximian would not have embarked upon such a venture with danger threatening him in the rear. But the earlier dating, however imprecise, seems well founded, and what happened provides further evidence of Maximian's characteristic impetuosity.

[34] Kolb (1997: 44); Rees (2002: 65, 91–2).

[35] *Pan. Lat.* 2(10).9.1; 3(11).5.4. Date: *Quellen* 6, 43; Stroheker (1975: 26–7); cf. Nixon and Rodgers (1994: 66 n.31) 288 or 289.

Germany and Raetia being extended to the source of the Danube (*ad Danubii caput*) in this period, it would appear that Diocletian was operating to the west of Lake Constance, presumably—like Constantius II in 356—moving from Italy into Raetia and Maxima Sequanorum, where he crossed the Rhine.[36] The precise extent of Diocletian's foray and the reason for it are nowhere explained. Given the emphasis on imperial harmony and 'similar virtue' at this still very early—and now, thanks to Carausius, rather tense—stage in the development of the dyarchy, he may have wished to show his approval of Maximian's Alamannic venture.[37] In practical terms, he may have intended to extend the lesson taught by Maximian to the area west of Günzburg.[38] The two emperors conferred. The precise date and even the venue of this meeting are unknown, but its main business is evident: how to deal with Carausius.[39]

From 288 and into 289 and possibly 290, imperial attention was focused on defeating Carausius. Preparations consisted of the building of an invasion fleet on Gallic rivers, and action against Franks on the Lower Rhine. The former Maximian supervised himself, the latter he left to his generals.[40] The Frankish campaigns show how attention had been diverted from the Alamanni, and demonstrate how Romano-barbarian relationships could be shaped by Roman perceptions of a threat rather than by the real nature of the threat itself. The panegyrics down to 313 consistently portray Franks as ferocious and untrustworthy demons, a fair target for savage Roman reprisals: bogeymen *par excellence*.[41] For the most part, this resulted

[36] *Pan. Lat.* 4(8).3.3. Below 208–9 and Lippold (1981: 352); cf. below 294.

[37] Cf. Rees (2002: 55, 60–4, 67).

[38] Below 189.

[39] Date: Barnes (1982: 51): 288, following Diocletian's Raetian campaign; Nixon and Rodgers (1994: 43, 66 n. 32): summer/autumn 288, before Diocletian's Raetian campaign. Location: Nixon and Rodgers (1994: 66 n.32).

[40] *Pan. Lat.* 2(10).12.3–5; 2(10).11.4, with 2(10).11.7. Nixon and Rodgers (1994: 71 n.39).

[41] *Pan. Lat.* 2(10).11.4 [289]: 'that pliant and treacherous race of barbarians'; 5(9).18.3 [298]: 'Frankish ferocity'; 6(7).4.2 [307]: 'the slippery faith of the whole race'; 7(6).10.1 [310]: the Franks as 'contemptible' perpetrators of 'brigandage'; 7(6).11.2 [310]: Frankish 'audacity'; 7(6).11.4 [310]: the Franks as possessors of 'that famed ferocity... that ever untrustworthy fickleness'; 7(6).21.1 [310]: the Franks as practitioners of 'barbarian perfidy'; 9(12).22.3 [313]: the Franks as 'fickle and flighty'; 9(12).24.2 [313]: 'The grim Frank filled only by the flesh of wild beasts'. Nixon and Rodgers (1994: 137 n.60); Drinkwater (1996: 22).

from wilful confusion between Carausius and the Franks. Carausius
was a Gaul, a Menapian, from an area north of his Continental
bridgehead at Boulogne (Fig. 17). Still further north, between the
Waal and the Rhine, lay Batavia, now being occupied by Franks.[42] By
the end of the third century, it was normal for the Roman army to
recruit Germanic troops in various ways.[43] It comes as no surprise to
learn that Carausius' forces contained Frankish elements.[44] Given his
agreements with rulers such as Gennobaudes, Maximian's army must
have done the same. However, imperial rage, picked up and articu-
lated by the panegyrists, caused the position to be presented entirely
differently. Carausius' revolt was politically intolerable, but for a long
time nothing could be done to end it. The emperors' frustration
caused Carausius to be vilified. The admiral whose command had
been against pirates was himself labelled a 'pirate'. And the provincial
whose homeland lay close to the Franks of the Lower Rhine was
accused of recruiting Franks as allies and fellow pirates. The war
against Carausius thus became a war against the Franks, and vice
versa.[45] This made Frankish communities at the Rhine mouths fair
game for Roman military action. In other words, Maximian sent his
generals against these people mainly because this was the only way in
which he could demonstrate that he was doing something against
Carausius, not because they were, in fact, Carausius' particular allies.

However, all these preparations, and the accompanying brave
anticipation of victory,[46] were in vain. The panegyrics, naturally,
say nothing about what occurred but, in 289 or 290, the strike against

[42] *Pan. Lat.* 7(6).5.3. Cf. below 200.

[43] Above 145.

[44] e.g. *Pan. Lat.* 4(8).17.1–2.

[45] *Pan. Lat.* 2 (10).12.1; 3(11).7.2, with Nixon and Rodgers (1994: 92 n.49); 4(8).6.1,
with Nixon and Rodgers (1994: 120 n. 27). Cf. 2(10).11.4, with Nixon and Rodgers
(1994: 71 n.31); and 5(9).18.3, with Nixon and Rodgers (1994: 169 n.71): the close
association of events in Britain and Gaul; 7(6).5.3: the Frankish occupation of Batavia
was 'led' by Carausius. Later reference to the third-century 'Batavian' destroyers of
Autun (*Pan. Lat.* 5(9).4.1; cf. 5(9).21.1–2, with Nixon and Rodgers (1994: 172, n.80))
may be seen as an anachronistic reference to these Franks. Other, unpleasant, Frankish
memories that were being stirred at the time included recollection of 'cheeky' Frankish
piratical raiding under Probus (*Pan. Lat.* 4(8).18.3. Cf. Zosimus 1.71.2; *Historia
Augusta, V. Probi* 18.2–3), perhaps with the implication that similar raiding would
have come out of Britain if Carausius had not been defeated. Cf. *Pan. Lat.* 4(18).4–5:
Carausius *could* have attacked Gaul, Spain, Africa; Drinkwater (1996: 22–3).

[46] *Pan. Lat.* 2(10).12.8.

Fig. 17　The north-western provinces, fourth century.

Carausius failed or was permanently postponed.[47] The intolerable had to continue to be tolerated. In the west, all major military activity was suspended.[48] There is a possible hint of the defensive attitude that this provoked in a panegyric delivered to Maximian in 291. With its emphasis on the dyarchy rather than on Maximian's personal qualities, this is much more subdued than that of 289.[49] The speaker claims that it is of no concern that Diocletian and Maximian are both away from the frontier.[50] Referring to their previous campaigns, he claims that further action is anyway unnecessary, since the barbarians are tearing themselves to pieces: '... inspired by madness, they re-enact on each other your expeditions in Sarmatia and Raetia and across the Rhine.'[51] He continues: 'The Goths utterly destroy the Burgundians ... The Burgundians have taken over the land of the Alamanni but obtained it at great cost to themselves. The Alamanni have lost the land but seek to regain it.'[52]

One cause of imperial absence from the frontiers was a second summit meeting in Milan, at the end of 290 and the beginning of 291.[53] We do not know what Diocletian and Maximian discussed, but it must have included Carausius.[54] The meeting may also have led to the formation of the Tetrarchy, though this is debated.[55] Certainly, however, the situation was radically changed in March 293, when the rule-of-two became the rule-of-four (tetrarchy), with Constantius I and Galerius being appointed as the imperial helpmates of Maximian and Diocletian. Shortly afterwards, in a brilliant campaign which must have been long in the planning, Constantius took Carausius' base at Boulogne, and then started building a new invasion fleet on the Seine.[56] In the meantime, as Maximian had done, he attacked

[47] Nixon and Rodgers (1994: 73 n.45, 102 n.90, 130 n.46). Date: Barnes (1982: 58); Nixon and Rodgers (1994: 42, 79, 93 n.53); Kienast (1996: 272).

[48] Barnes (1982: 58); Nixon and Rodgers (1994: 79); Rees (2002: 69). *Contra* Lippold (1981: 351, from Ensslin): that Maximian campaigned against the Alamanni *c*.292.

[49] Rees (2002: 76, 92).

[50] *Pan. Lat.* 3(11).14.1.

[51] *Pan. Lat.* 3(11).16.1.

[52] *Pan. Lat.* 3(11).17.1, 3. Below 189.

[53] *Pan. Lat.* 3(11).11.3–4. Barnes (1982: 58); Nixon and Rodgers (1994: 74 n. 46).

[54] Nixon and Rodgers (1994: 80, 93 and n. 53).

[55] Nixon and Rodgers (1994: 70 n.38).

[56] *Pan. Lat.* 4(8).6.1, 13.1; 4(8).7.3, 14.4.

Carausius' purported Frankish allies, named as Chamavi and Frisii, on the Scheldt and Lower Rhine, defeating them and settling the survivors in Gaul.[57] In Britain, Carausius, having lost Boulogne, had been overthrown by Allectus. Allectus fell in 296, when Constantius finally retook Britain. Vilification of the enemy and his barbarian allies persisted to the end. Allectus' troops were described as barbarian or, at least, dressed like barbarians.[58] Franks are specifically described as being slaughtered by Constantius' forces when they took London.[59] During the recovery of Britain there was, we are told, no trouble on the Rhine, secured by the presence of Maximian.[60]

On his return to Gaul, Constantius put his energy into civil projects, aimed at restoring morale and prosperity.[61] He may also have sanctioned Frankish occupation of Batavia.[62] In a panegyric of 310 there may be some hint that Constantius fought Franks on his return from Britain, but this is brief and obscure. If a campaign took place, it cannot have been on any grand scale.[63] Then come clear references to severe fighting with Alamanni.

A panegyric of 310 relates that, though wounded, Constantius won a great victory among the Lingones; that he left the field of Windisch strewn with enemy dead; and that he defeated a 'huge multitude of Germans from every nation' venturing onto the frozen Rhine.[64] This report is supplemented by Eutropius, who records that Constantius, campaigning near Langres, was suddenly overwhelmed by invading barbarians. Seeking refuge in the city he found its gates closed and had to be hauled over the walls on a rope. However, on the same day, the arrival of the Roman army allowed him to kill almost 60,000 of the enemy.[65] Eutropius identifies these as Alamanni, which squares with the panegyrist's reference to Windisch as the site of another

[57] *Pan. Lat.* 4(8).8.1, 4; 9.3; 6(7).4.2.
[58] *Pan. Lat.* 4(8).16.4.
[59] *Pan. Lat.* 4(8).17.1.
[60] *Pan. Lat.* 4(8).13.3.
[61] e.g. Autun: *Pan. Lat.* 4(8).21.2; 5(9).4.1–3, 14.4, 18.1.
[62] Jullian (1926: 85–6).
[63] *Pan. Lat.* 7(6).6.2; Barnes (1982: 61) dating it to 300 or 301; Nixon and Rodgers (1994: 225 n. 24) dating it to *c.*296.
[64] *Pan. Lat.* 7(6).4.2, 6.3–4.
[65] Eutropius 9.23.1.

major conflict. This fighting is conventionally dated to the late 290s, but there is a case for putting it between 301 and 305, when the number of times Constantius was hailed as *Germanicus Maximus* rose from two to five.[66]

These disturbances were clearly exaggerated: 60,000 Alamannic dead is an impossible figure. Much was made of them probably in order to sustain Constantius' military reputation against that of Galerius, who in 297 or 298 won a spectacular victory over the Persians. Diocletian's Persian success may earlier have prompted Maximian to make much of a minor Frankish chief. Though Constantius had defeated Allectus, this was an internal affair; he needed a 'foreign' victory and Alamanni could be pressed into service.[67] These events amounted to the closest that the Alamanni ever came to affecting the course of world history. If Constantius I had been disabled or killed, it is unlikely that his son, the future Constantine the Great, would ever have become emperor. They deserve attention.

In the first place, they should not have happened. Such conflicts had been a feature of the third-century Crisis, but this was now over. Under the Tetrarchy, Alamanni should not have been allowed to penetrate so deeply into the Empire; and a Roman emperor should not have been able to find himself in such danger on imperial soil. It will, indeed, have been easy to relate events in a way which damaged Constantius' reputation. Being hauled to safety on a rope is hardly heroic. The rope incident could, of course, have been a later embellishment, which means that we cannot attach any importance to its absence from the panegyric. But the panegyric admits that Constantius had been wounded, which could have exposed him to the charge of professional negligence. On the other hand, it is clear that the story was, in fact, 'spun' very positively. The panegyrist, reminding Constantine I of the exploits of his father, tackles it head on, having mentioned Constantius' great victory at Windisch only in passing.[68] There are more indications of Constantius' general confidence. Above all, there is no sign that he embarked on a punitive

---

[66] Lippold (1981: 362); Barnes (1982: 61); Nixon and Rodgers (1994: 225 n.25).

[67] Above 182, with *Pan. Lat.* 5(9).21.2–3 (Britain and Persia). Cf. Lippold (1981: 363); Barnes (1982: 63); Nixon and Rodgers (1994: 176 n.85).

[68] *Pan. Lat.* 7(6).4.2 (allowing for the correctness of an emendation: Nixon and Rodgers (1994: 223 n.17)).

campaign over the Rhine. And, having defeated those *Germani* (who, from the context, must be Alamanni) who had attempted to cross the Rhine, he showed remarkable clemency, not slaughtering or enslaving them, but taking captives by lot and freeing the rest. He did not even bother to strengthen the line of defence from Basel to Strasbourg.[69]

How can we explain these events? The answer may lie in the wider context of Romano-Alamannic relations and contemporary imperial politics. Rome probably encouraged permanent friendly Elbgermanic settlement on the border.[70] We may assume that this was under way from around 300,[71] but it was uneven, affecting the upper Rhine and upper Danube later than other areas.[72] Alamannia was constantly subject to population movement eastwards and westwards.[73] At the close of the third century, there must still have been war-bands raiding deep into the region and beyond. The Alamannic frontier therefore needed constant attention, with friends supported, foes undermined, and stray raiders ejected: Heather's 'management'.[74] This may explain Diocletian's campaign of 288, to the east of settled, friendly Alamannic leaders, directing its worst terror against those who were not Rome's direct neighbours.[75] In the heady days following the defeat of Allectus, attention may have slipped, allowing raiders to gain entry over the Upper Rhine where Roman military installations were less dense and where there were as yet no established right-bank allied communities.[76] The result was Constantius' brush with death at Langres. This was a nasty surprise but, thanks to a little luck, no great disaster. Numbers were, as usual, overestimated. We should think in terms of a few thousand, not tens of thousands, Alamannic warriors. Once Constantius had marshalled his resources he had no difficulty in pushing back the raiders and decisively defeating them as they sought to return over the Rhine. Settled Alamanni further north on the

[69] Below 192.
[70] Above 81.
[71] Above 82.
[72] Above 83.
[73] Above 106, cf.115–16, below 338.
[74] Heather (2001).
[75] Above 183.
[76] Cf. below 295. Lorenz, S. (1997: 160) suggests a crossing over the Swiss Rhine, around Basel, where the river is narrower.

frontier may have provided useful help: this could have been the time when Crocus began his association with Constantius.[77] There was no call for a punitive campaign.

One spring of contemporary Alamannic unrest may be found in references linking Alamanni and Burgundians.[78] Although mention of the Burgundians is found in the sources from the first century, they remain shadowy until their move into Gaul early in the fifth century.[79] However, they may have played more of a part in fourth-century politics than is usually allowed. What always needs to be taken into account is the sensitivity of the Main valley, down which the Burgundians might spill to discomfit Romans and Alamanni alike.[80] Rome may have sought to manage the situation by encouraging Alamannic-Burgundian hostility while, through alliances with local leaders, taking care to ensure that neither side gained a significant advantage over the other.[81] That such management developed very early is hinted at by the panegyrics' knowledge of ill-feeling between Alamanni and Burgundians well before the end of the third century. Maximian's campaign of 287 may therefore have been more than self-advertisement. His march across Alamannia could have taken him up the Main and then southwards, down the longest stretch of the abandoned Upper German/Raetian *limes*. This would have asserted Rome's claim to sovereignty over its old territories while giving the local barbarians a practical demonstration of the length of the Empire's reach. As was said of the later recovery of Britain: 'The Roman state holds in a comprehensive embrace of peace whatever at any stage in the vicissitudes of time was ever Roman.'[82] Intimidation would have been directed against those Alamanni who were not Rome's direct neighbours and also possibly against hostile Burgundians. Ammianus' *terminales lapides*, or, at least, their oldest predecessors, may have been set up at this time.[83]

[77] For Crocus see above 146.

[78] *Pan. Lat.* 2(10).5.1; 3(11).17.3. Cf. above 186.

[79] Above 108.

[80] Cf. above 112.

[81] Above 112, 115.

[82] *Pan. Lat.* 4(8).20.2. For habitual Roman refusal to concede sovereignty over lost land see Pohl (2002a: 63, 135). Cf. above 111, 132.

[83] Above 112.

The same campaign could also have provided the inspiration for the later 'Lyon medallion'.[84]

Neglect of the Alamannic-Burgundian situation in the later 290s could have been dangerous. Uncontrolled hostilities on the Main may have stimulated wider raiding. Some bands could have reached the Rhine 'knee' and then moved into Gaul. It is possible that it is Constantius' success at Windisch which is commemorated on a monument at Nicaea, bearing the inscription *Alamannia*. However, heavy damage to the structure makes this uncertain.[85]

Constantius fought no more Alamannic campaigns as Caesar; and when Diocletian and Maximian retired and he became the senior emperor in the west in May 305, he confirmed his position by fighting far from the Rhine, in northern Britain.[86] Romano-Alamannic relations appear settled. One of Constantius' allies and counsellors on this expedition was king Crocus.[87] Overall, western rulers from 285 to 306 appear to have been more concerned with Franks than with Alamanni.

This situation remained unchanged after 306, when Constantius died at York and Constantine I improperly replaced his father as ruler of the north-western provinces. In doing so, he precipitated a long period of political instability and civil war until his victory over Licinius in 324 gave him sole control of the Empire. From 306 to 312, when his responsibilities were exclusively north-western, Constantine gave great attention to the Franks, characterized by 'perfidy'. In 306/7, Constantine supposedly avenged Frankish attacks which began around the start of his reign. His conduct was vengeful. Spectacular punishment was wreaked on two Frankish chieftains, Ascaric and Merogaisus.[88] The campaign of 308 was equally violent, consisting of an all-out assault over the Rhine against the Bructeri.[89] All this is explicable in terms of Roman politics rather than of any

---

[84] Below 364–7.
[85] *Quellen* 6, Inscriptions no. 59 (=*AE* 1939, 292).
[86] Cf. *Pan. Lat.* 7(6).7.2, on Constantius' location at the edge of the world.
[87] Above 146.
[88] *Pan. Lat.* 6(7).4.2; 7(6).10.1–7, 11.5; 10(4).16.5–6, 17.1; Eutropius 10.3.2. Barnes (1982: 69). I follow Nixon and Rodgers (1994: 213–14) for the chronology of 306–10.
[89] *Pan. Lat.* 7(6).12.1–4. Barnes (1982: 70); Nixon and Rodgers (1994: 235 n.54).

Frankish threat. Constantine's first campaign provided him with a welcome opportunity to move himself from Britain—marginal to imperial politics and embarrassing as the location of what, after all, was a usurpation—to the Rhine.[90] The second further confirmed his abilities as the conqueror of foreign foes. In 309, although there was no fighting, Constantine continued to pressure the Franks by initiating the building of the fortified bridge complex at Cologne/ Deutz: an early example of imperial 'busy-ness'.[91]

Here we may review late-third/early-fourth-century imperial defence works. Following Roman withdrawal from the Upper German/ Raetian *limes*, a major development under Diocletian and Maximian had been the commencement of the creation of a new demarcation and defence line, comprising waterways and fortifications, along the High Rhine (centred on Kaiseraugst)—the Danube–Iller–Rhine *limes*.[92] However, the Upper Rhine, from Basel to Mainz, was not heavily fortified. Constantine I's development at Breisach helped to remedy a weakness exposed by his father's disaster at Langres, but major development of this sector was not begun until Valentinian I.[93] One reason for the different treatment of these two stretches of the Rhine was undoubtedly hydrology: the meandering and unreliable course of the old Rhine downstream from Basel impeded large-scale riverine construction.[94] However, a more important element in imperial thinking was probably the protection of Italy. Fear of the Alamannic bogeyman will have persisted, and Diocletian and his colleagues would have been as careful as Aurelian to show themselves attending to the defence of the peninsula and the imperial capital.[95] Yet, again, such action was hardly necessary: Alamanni never again raided deep into Italy. The decision not to lavish resources on the Upper Rhine was, as events turned out, justified. With rare exceptions, Gaul remained undisturbed by Alamanni until Roman intrigue precipitated the crisis of the mid-350s.

---

[90] So Seeck (1921: 1.74); Barceló (1981: 13).

[91] *Pan. Lat.* 7(6).11.4, 13.1, 5; Grünewald (1989: 175–8); Nixon and Rodgers (1994: 213). Below 296, 361.

[92] Garbsch (1970); Petrikovits (1971: 181–2); Mackensen (1999: 203–22), arguing against the view that this began under Probus.

[93] Fingerlin (1990: 107), (1997a: 103–6); Lorenz, S. (1997: 138). Below 295.

[94] Cf. below 231.

[95] Cf. Stroheker (1975: 29).

Constantine first allied himself with Maximian and his family—who had used the situation created by his usurpation to re-establish their own claims to imperial power. Initially this worked well, but in 308 a quarrel between Maximian and his son, Maxentius, brought the former from Italy to Gaul into impossibly close proximity to Constantine. Their relationship deteriorated and in 310 Maximian revolted against Constantine in Arles. Constantine moved quickly, and captured Maximian after besieging him in Marseille. In the same year, Constantine again faced Frankish raiding.[96] The order of events is difficult to establish. Some follow Lactantius in having Constantine face Frankish trouble before the revolt of Maximian.[97] However, Lactantius' account is contrary to the panegyric of 310 and is highly tendentious, determined to denigrate Maximian. It is more plausible to place the Frankish attack after Constantine's move to southern Gaul, causing him to return hotfoot northwards.[98] The severity of this 'attack' must have been minimal. In the event, the danger simply evaporated, allowing Constantine to visit the shrine of Apollo at Grand, where he enjoyed a vision of the god.[99] This looks like more exploitation of the Frankish 'threat'. Invocation of Frankish 'perfidy' allowed Constantine to distance himself from his embarrassing prisoner at Marseille, and to be absent from the scene of Maximian's suspicious end: he was found hanged.[100] Other than this, Constantine's military concerns may have taken him to Britain in 307 and 310.[101]

We know of no conflict between Constantine and the Alamanni in the period 306–12. In the panegyric of 310 the emphasis is still on the Frankish bogeyman. There is no mention of the Alamanni apart from the references to Constantius' victories years earlier.[102] It is significant that there were no barbarian attacks when Constantine moved against Maxentius in Italy, in 312.[103]

In 312, Constantine defeated Maxentius at the battle of the Milvian bridge and became ruler of the western Empire. Until 324, he

[96] *Pan. Lat.* 7(6).21.2.
[97] Lactantius, *De mort. pers.* 29.3. e.g. Jullian (1926: 103); Barnes (1982: 70).
[98] So Barceló (1981: 15).
[99] *Pan. Lat.* 7(6).21.3–4. Nixon and Rodgers (1994: 247–8 nn.89, 91).
[100] Lactantius, *De mort. pers.* 30.5.
[101] Barnes (1982: 69–70); Kienast (1996: 298).
[102] *Pan. Lat.* 7(6).5.3–6.4; 11.
[103] Jullian (1926: 105).

continued his Frankish campaigns. In 313, he fought Franks after returning to Gaul from Italy.[104] As usual, the Franks were condemned as 'fickle and flighty' breakers of their word;[105] the fighting was punitive and patently contrived to give Constantine a great victory.[106] His prisoners were put to death in triumphal games.[107] These details come from a panegyric of 313. A later treatment, of 321, offers further particulars, including the names of the barbarians involved: Bructeri, Chamavi, Cherusci, Lancionae, Tubantes and (actually fifth in this list) Alamanni.[108] Though some have been prepared to take this additional information about the 313 campaign seriously, it is best to treat it as a rhetorical flourish.[109] The speaker, Nazarius, is more concerned with atmosphere than accuracy, confusing events of the distant past with those of the present to underline the Frankish threat.[110] His list should be seen as an imaginative hotchpotch, made up of tribal names that he believed were appropriate to the area. None can be given credence, least of all that of the Alamanni. These are most unlikely to have been involved in the fighting.[111] As was so often the case, the 313 campaign suggests Roman exploitation of, not vulnerability to, the Frankish menace. For Romans a 'good' foreign war was the best remedy for the bitter taste in the mouth left by civil strife, however successful; and Constantine's presence in Italy would have been repugnant to Licinius.[112] It would have been in Constantine's interest to move to confirm his reputation as a general able to defeat foreign foes, and to integrate elements of Maxentius' army into his own.

Inevitably, Constantine's attention was increasingly drawn to the wider Empire. In 315–16, he wintered for the last time in Trier.[113] Supervision of the north-western provinces was delegated to his son,

[104] *Pan. Lat.* 9(12).21.5–22.5. I take the date from Nixon and Rodgers (1994: 326 n.138, 328 n.145); Barnes (1982: 71–2) suggests 313 and 314.

[105] *Pan. Lat.* 9(12).22.3.

[106] *Pan. Lat.* 9(12).22.3–6; Barceló (1981: 17).

[107] *Pan. Lat.* 9(12).23.3.

[108] *Pan. Lat.* 10(4).18.1.

[109] Barceló (1981: 18).

[110] *Pan. Lat.* 10(4).17.1: Franks in Spain; cf. 4(8).18.3.

[111] Jullian (1926: 112 and n.1). For further references and general discussion see Nixon and Rodgers (1994: 363–4 and nn. 79, 81).

[112] Nixon and Rodgers (1994: 326 n.137 and 295 n.7).

[113] Barnes (1982: 73); cf. Heinen (1985: 228).

Crispus (born *c.*300 and proclaimed Caesar in March 317).[114] Before 321, Crispus had successfully fought against Franks.[115] The details, from Nazarius, are again obscure. All that we are told is that Crispus gained 'the first fruits of an enormous victory'.[116] It is likely that Franks were used to enable the young prince to win his spurs, to confirm his right to imperial office, and to secure his family's traditional Gallic power base.[117] It is immaterial whether the credit for the victory should go to Crispus or to the experienced generals who must have been advising him.[118]

After Nazarius' speech of 321 there is a gap of over 40 years until the next panegyric, that of Mamertinus to Julian. Until we reach the beginning of Ammianus' extant narrative, with the events of 353/4, we have to infer Rome's dealings with the western *Germani* from coins, rare inscriptions and odd scraps of information from lesser literary sources.

Coins produced in Trier from 322 to 323 suggest contemporary campaigning on the Rhine. Gold pieces (*solidi*, with fractions and multiples) hail Constantine I as 'conqueror of the barbarians' (*debellator gentium barbararum*).[119] Others associate him and Crispus with named representations of Alamannia and Francia, defeated and dejected, and the triumphalist legend 'rejoicing of the Roman People' (*gaudium Romanorum*).[120] Barnes has used these types to propose campaigning by Crispus against both Franks and Alamanni around 323.[121] This is odd, given that the panegyrics indicate that there had been little or no trouble between Rome and the Alamanni for almost a generation. It becomes odder when we take into account that the *gaudium Romanorum*/vanquished Alamannia and Francia types were introduced much earlier than the 320s, from 310 to 313, when Trier issued them on *solidi* in the name of Constantine I.[122]

---

[114] Kienast (1996: 305–6).
[115] Date: Nixon and Rodgers (1994: 362 n.77).
[116] *Pan. Lat.* 10(4).17.2.
[117] Cf. *Pan. Lat.* 10(4).37.1–4.
[118] Barceló (1981: 18); Nixon and Rodgers (1994: 362 n.77).
[119] *RIC* 7, Trier nos 356–7.
[120] *RIC* 7, Trier nos 365 [Constantine I: Francia]; 362–3, 366 [Crispus: Alamannia and Francia].
[121] Barnes (1982: 83).
[122] *RIC* 6, Trier nos 823–4.

Serious fighting between Rome and Alamanni, as well as Franks, from relatively early in Constantine I's imperial career is unlikely.[123] The slight literary evidence we have to support this interpretation is garbled.[124] The established 'default' position of the late-third and early-fourth-century rulers vis-à-vis Franks and Alamanni was to harass the former and, unless severely provoked, to leave the latter alone. In 309/10, with events coming to the boil in his relationship with Maximian and other rulers and pretenders, it is improbable that Constantine would have embarked upon any major new military initiative over his own borders. Finally, the *solidus* was no ordinary coin. It was a new denomination, introduced from 309. At 72 to the Roman pound, it was slightly lighter than the old *aureus* (at 60 to the pound), and it suffered a shaky start: but it recovered and went on to become the keystone of the Empire's monetary system throughout the fourth century and beyond. It was an important coin, and the bulk of its initial series celebrated important imperial achievements: the subjection of Alamannia and Francia; Constantine's defeat of Maxentius; and his welcome from the Roman senate.[125] Barceló's explanation—that the coins referred to successes by Constantine's generals, which therefore did not receive mention in the panegyrics[126]—is therefore unpersuasive. The first numismatic references to Alamannia and Francia were probably retrospective. Constantine needed to impress upon the political nation of the north-western provinces that the frontiers were secure, and would stay so if and when he moved from the Rhine to Italy. This security came from both his own activity, against the Franks, and that of his father, Constantius I—the darling of Gaul—against both Franks and Alamanni. *Alamannia devicta* and *Francia devicta* were faits accomplis, not contemporary achievements. From 306 to 312, there was general peace with the Alamanni.

A further series of *gaudium Romanorum*/vanquished Alamannia and Francia *solidi* and multiples in the names of Constantine I and Crispus was issued from Trier in 319–20. In these, Constantine is

---

[123] Thus *contra* Stroheker (1975: 27 and n.12); Nixon and Rodgers (1994: 364 n.81).

[124] *Pan. Lat.* 10(4).8.1 (above 195); Eutropius 10.3.2. Barceló (1981: 18–19).

[125] *RIC* 6, 40–1, 100, 158. Jones (1964: 439–44); Demandt (1989: 77).

[126] Barceló (1981: 20).

associated with Alamannia, Crispus with Francia.[127] Crispus' types appear occasioned by the Frankish victory celebrated by Nazarius, hence the usual dating of this campaign to around 319.[128] However, a similar explanation cannot be applied to Constantine's types, since during this period he was in the Balkans.[129] As both types form a long established numismatic pair they should be explained as such. I propose that, as in 309–13, they merged past and present. They proclaimed that the Rhine frontier was safe in the hands of the new Caesar, whose father and grandfather had done sterling work in pacifying neighbouring barbarians and in whose steps the young prince, through his current success over Franks, was following.

Returning to the 322–3 coins, the idea that they indicate contemporary warfare should be treated with equal circumspection. Again, wider political events were coming to a head, as the decisive conflict between Constantine I and Licinius drew near in which Crispus would play an important role as a naval commander. It was probably in preparation for this that Constantine 'brought on' Crispus' much younger half-brother, Constantine II (born 316/17, created Caesar 317[130]) on the Danube, in a war against the Sarmatians.[131] Crispus, in the meantime, settled the Rhine frontier. He may have made contact with Frankish and Alamannic chieftains, but in receiving homage not waging war. All this was put out on martial coin-types as the subjection of Sarmatia, Alamannia and Francia. It follows that the *gaudium Romanorum*/Alamannia, Francia issues from Trier—supposedly more sympathetic to the conquered than those of Pavia and Sirmium—should not be taken as promoting a local policy of persuading leading Franks and Alamanni to integrate into the Empire. Such cultural sensitivity was not a feature of imperial Rome.[132] Whatever their meaning, the designs on the Trier *solidi* were aimed at imperial not barbarian users.

[127] *RIC* 7, Trier nos 237–9, 243, 240–1.
[128] Nixon and Rodgers (1994: 362 n.77); cf. Barceló (1981: 20–1).
[129] See Barnes (1982: 74).
[130] Kienast (1996: 310).
[131] *RIC* 7, Trier nos 358–61, 364, 364A, 367 [Constantine II receives credit for his father's Sarmatian victories].
[132] *RIC* 7, Ticinum nos 28, 37 [315], Sirmium nos 49–52 [324/25]. *Contra* Martin (1998: 409). Cf. Drinkwater (1998b: 235).

The products of the Sirmium mint are, however, important in indicating a change from 324, when the traditional pairing of Alamannia and Francia was broken. Bronze coins (*folles*) of 324/5 from Sirmium associate Crispus and Constantine II with the legend *Alamannia devicta*, with no mention of Francia.[133] Likewise, *solidi* (with fractions) in the name of Constantine II, issued from Trier in 328–9, repeat the *gaudium Romanorum* type in respect of Alamannia but not Francia.[134] In addition, we know from an inscription from Orcistus in Phrygia that Constantine II had been granted the title 'Conqueror of the Alamanni' (*Alamannicus*: the earliest known attestation of this name) by 30 June 331.[135] It appears that, after a gap of almost 40 years, Alamannia had again become the western target of choice. We are back to the exploitation of barbarians for the building of an imperial name. The person who benefited most from Alamannic campaigns will have been Constantine II, still young and needing to demonstrate his fitness for the purple. After Constantine I's victory over Licinius, he took over the running of the whole of the Empire, and needed as many of his sons as possible in a position to share the load, especially in the west. As Constantine I had brought on Constantine II on the Danube against the Sarmatians, Crispus could be charged with doing the same on the Rhine against the Alamanni.[136] In 328, Constantine II's need for military success would have been even greater. The family feud that led to Crispus' execution in 326 will have shaken the dynasty and removed an able military leader. Constantine II needed all the standing that he, his father (the autumn and winter of 328–9 were the time of Constantine I's last sojourn in the west[137]) and their

---

[133] *RIC* 7, Sirmium nos 49–52.

[134] *RIC* 7, Trier no. 516.

[135] *CIL* 3.7000; *ILS* 6091; *Quellen* 6, Inscriptions no. 61.

[136] Cf. Barnes (1982: 84): Crispus had returned to Trier by March 325 (although Barnes, ibid., provides no evidence for Constantine II's being in the west in 324/25).

[137] Barnes (1982: 77–8). I note Barnes' argument (84 n.159) that because Constantine I was not called *Alamannicus*, he could not have been present for the campaign, which therefore should be dated slightly later, to 330. I have kept the earlier dating because it suits the coinage and because it appears to me that *Alamannicus* and, indeed, *Francicus* were for a long time oddly regarded by the Roman establishment. Cf. above 69. Though *Alamannicus* was, eventually, coined for a young prince (who went on to make much of it), for a long time it was held unsuitable for a senior emperor. As Zotz (1998: 389) points out, Constantine II's victory may have given Constantine I the title *Germanicus Maximus IV*, which he held by 328/9.

advisers could create for him. The result was another campaign against the Alamanni, a much-trumpeted victory, and the title *Alamannicus*. This is the most likely occasion for Constantine I's sanctioning of 'Alamannic Games' (*ludi Alamannici*), held in Rome from 5 to 10 October of each year.[138]

The precise identity of the Alamanni involved and how Rome justified its attack on them are unknown. Generally, it may have been that Alamanni were now judged a more worthy foe than Franks, already the victims of many Roman 'victories'. Memories of the third-century Crisis and the belief that Alamanni still constituted a threat to Italy may also have been called upon. The 322/3 and 328/9 campaigns were unusual. It was not in Rome's interests casually to disturb Alamannic communities on her borders, and the more so since this was the period when Roman economic exploitation of the right bank of the Rhine was in full swing.[139] On the other hand, neither campaign was extensive; and there is no reason to suppose that they were repeated. A *gaudium Romanorum*/Alamannia-type on *solidi* and multiples in the name of Constantine II was issued from Trier in 332 and 333,[140] but it was accompanied by others recalling the Caesar's earlier success in Sarmatia[141] and may be regarded as retrospective. Yet the fact that Alamannia could twice be singled out as a target is ominous. It was not long before it was under attack again.

Constantine I died on 22 May 337. After a short period of uncertainty, involving dynastic murder, he was succeeded by his three surviving sons. Constantius II (born 317, proclaimed Caesar 324) supervised the eastern provinces and Constantine II the western. However, while Constantius ruled alone, Constantine shared power with Constans (born 320, proclaimed Caesar 333), responsible for Italy, Africa and Illyricum. All three needed to assert themselves, and there is a strong indication that Constantine II waged another Alamannic campaign in 338.[142] However, in 339 he quarrelled with Constans and early in 340 he was killed at Aquileia. Constans became

---

[138] *Calendarium Furii Dionysii Filocali* ('Calendar of 354'), *ad loc.* (=Riese (1892: 9.97)); Salzman (1990: 135, 137–8).

[139] Above 130, 133.

[140] *RIC* 7, Trier no. 535.

[141] *RIC* 7, Trier nos 532–3, 536.

[142] *CIL* 3.12483; *ILS* 724; *Quellen* 6, Inscriptions no. 63: *Maximus* added to Constantine's title of *Alamannicus*. Barnes (1993: 218 and n. 4).

Augustus of the west. Soon he, too, predictably waged a Germanic war, but against Franks, not Alamanni. This campaign of 341/2 was much trumpeted. It is possible that it was at this time that Constans permitted Salian Franks, under pressure from Saxons, to drift from Batavia, at the mouth of the Rhine (where they had been allowed to settle by Constantius I), a little deeper into the Empire, finally arriving in Toxiandria, just over the Meuse west of Cologne. Here, in 358, they were encountered by Julian.[143] Henceforth, though Constans certainly did not neglect the west, he could not give it his undivided attention. The huge and awkwardly shaped territory that was under his jurisdiction and a state of more-or-less permanent hostility towards his brother caused him to spend much time in northern Italy and the Balkans. The Rhine frontier fell quiet.

What conclusions may we draw concerning relations between the Alamanni and Rome in the period 285–350? Barceló accepted that the Rhine-*Germani* posed an authentic threat, but his reconstruction of Rome's Frankish policy early in this period, based on 'demonstrations of power', 'police actions' and punitive attacks, suggests that the initiative lay with the Empire.[144] As he indicates, what we know about the Alamanni, though less, points in the same direction.[145] Thus, the first half of the fourth century was hardly a period of total peace between the Alamanni and Rome.[146] There were occasions when Roman rulers, especially Constantine II, threatened to extend traditional exploitation of Franks to Alamanni. However, compared with the Franks, the border Alamanni appear to have been relatively unmolested. This tallies with continuing Roman involvement in their trans-Rhine territories, and with the employment of high-ranking Alamanni as army officers.[147] During this period Alamanni may have felt themselves coming closer to the Empire.

The Flavian dynasty edged closer to extinction early in 350, when Constans was deposed and killed in Gaul by a court conspiracy that

---

[143] Libanius, *Orat.* 59.127–36 [= Riese (1892: 9.63)]; Socrates 2.13; AM 17.8.3; Zosimus 3.6. Jullian (1926: 146 and n.2, cf. 171, 199); Barceló (1981: 38); Heinen (1985: 230); Barnes (1993: 225); Périn (1998: 59–61 and Fig. 1). See also below 218, 226, 242.

[144] Barceló (1981: 13–18).

[145] Barceló (1981: 20–1).

[146] *Contra* Martin (1997a: 120–1), (1998: 408–10). Cf. Zotz (1998: 389 and n.35).

[147] Above 133–5, 145–6.

put a senior field officer, Magnus Magnentius, on the western throne. Magnentius moved quickly into Italy. He was recognized throughout Constans' territory except in the Balkans, where power was seized by another army officer, Vetranio. The sole remaining Flavian emperor, Constantius II, appeared to be destined to become part of a triarchy. However, by the end of the year he had removed Vetranio; and in September 351 he defeated Magnentius at Mursa, on the Drava, forcing the usurper to flee. He seized Italy in 352, and Magnentius withdrew to Gaul. On 10 August 353, Constantius finally overcame Magnentius at Lyon. Magnentius committed suicide, as did his Caesar, Decentius.[148]

This was a bitter civil war, one of the results of which was that Germanic barbarians wreaked havoc in Gaul. Their attacks began during Magnentius' reign, and continued well after his fall. Both Franks and Alamanni were involved. The seriousness of the situation is reflected in the fact that by the end of 355 they controlled the Rhine valley.[149] As far as the Alamanni are concerned, coin-hoards indicate that sporadic, small-scale raiding over the entire length of the Rhine took place in 350/1. The first large-scale localized attacks, over the Rhine-knee into the area of modern Switzerland, occurred in 351/2. These attacks then spread down the Rhine, affecting the modern Palatinate in 352 and the Mainz–Trier–Cologne region from 352/3 to 355.[150] Perhaps the most dramatic incident of the troubles was the defeat of Magnentius' Caesar, his brother Decentius, who was based in Trier, by the Alamannic chieftain, Chnodomarius, probably in 352.[151]

The crucial issues are whether Constantius II was responsible for turning Alamanni on Gaul and, if so, what he promised them as reward. There is an apparently strong tradition that says that he was, and that he gave the Alamannic leaders written undertakings that

---

[148] *PLRE* 1.532; 244–5; Kienast (1996: 319–21).

[149] Cf. below 219–20. For the seriousness of the Frankish attacks over the Lower Rhine see Grünewald and Seibel (2003: xiii).

[150] Wigg (1991: 101 and Maps 9–14).

[151] AM 16.12.5. Lorenz, S. (1997: 23–4); Zotz (1998: 391); Bleckmann (1999). Lorenz's location of this battle at Bingen—Ausonius' (*Mosella* 1–4) 'Gallic Cannae'—is ingenious but not compelling. So early a reference to so recent (and so ambiguous—Decentius was, after all, a usurper) a disaster strikes me as an unlikely way of beginning the poem. Green (1991: 464) relates the comparison to events in 70. But cf. below 237.

they would be given land on the left bank of the Rhine.[152] However, the authors concerned are not independent witnesses, but Julian and his champions, all harsh critics of Constantius. Recent studies have tended (albeit far from unanimously) to doubt the validity of the charges.[153] The developing new *communis opinio*, influenced by current inclinations to rehabilitate Constantius II,[154] is that this emperor was too aware of his wider responsibilities: he would never have put the suppression of internal over that of external enemies.[155] This is questionable. Conscientious though he was, Constantius II was also exquisitely sensitive to any slight to his family and resolutely unwilling to share power with men of inferior status. This is reflected in his behaviour elsewhere. Unlike other emperors, he never took a commoner to be his colleague in the consulship.[156] And throughout 350, when he might well have conceded a new political order and accepted Magnentius and Vetranio as colleagues, he never forgot his Flavian heritage and toiled to establish his position as sole ruler.[157] Contemporary defamation of Magnentius as a barbarian and the friend and recruiter of barbarians (Franks and Saxons) may have derived from the Constantian court's uneasiness about its use of Alamanni.[158] In short, Constantius, ready to use anything to defeat his enemies, may well have encouraged Alamanni to attack Magnentius' administration in Gaul, probably from late 352, when he had direct access to their leaders from northern Italy.[159]

Imperial exploitation of Rhine-*Germani* was standard behaviour. However, it is also important to see events from the Alamannic perspective. Chnodomarius and the chieftains associated with him came from *pagi* near the Rhine well within the Roman sphere of influence indicated by the pattern of coin circulation.[160] They and

---

[152] Libanius, *Orat.* 18.33–4, 52 (with Socrates 3.1.26, Sozomen 5.1.2); Zosimus 2.53.3. Cf. AM 16.12.3.

[153] For a summary of the debate see Lorenz, S. (1997: 22–3); Zotz (1998: 391). Martin has recently (1998: 411) decided against Constantius.

[154] See, e.g. Henck (1998).

[155] Lorenz, S. (1997: 43).

[156] AM 16.10.12.

[157] Stroheker (1975: 33–4); Drinkwater (2000: 142, 154, 159).

[158] Julian, *Orat.* 1.34D. Drinkwater (2000: 142).

[159] Wigg (1991: 101); Drinkwater (1997: 5); cf. Libanius, *Orat.* 18.33.

[160] Above 129.

their dependants would have enjoyed long and no doubt profitable contact with the Empire. There is every reason to suppose that they saw themselves as close friends, if not subjects, of Rome and its ruling dynasty: faithful followers of Constantius II against a usurping regime. In addition, by the mid-fourth century a number of Alamannic males, integrated into imperial life, were serving as colonels and generals in the Roman army.[161] There was every reason for the central authorities to accept such men as loyal servants, and the people these were still in touch with in Alamannia, and whom they could recommend for action against Magnentius and Decentius, as welcome allies.[162]

Even if the Alamannic attacks had been contrived by Constantius, it would have been easier for him to turn them on than turn them off; but he did his best to deal with the problem, though not immediately. From Lyon he moved south, to winter in Arles.[163] It was here that he dealt with the surviving supporters of Magnentius and associated religious issues, before transferring to Milan in 354. He may have felt that, with the east still demanding his main attention and disputes between Arian and Nicene Christians soon requiring his presence in Italy, he could not run the risk of becoming tied down in north-east Gaul. However, his indecision shows that he did not consider the region to be in exceptional danger. His solution was to appoint Silvanus *magister peditum* and give him charge of the military situation in the west. Silvanus established his headquarters in Cologne, probably because Trier and its region had suffered severe damage in 352/3.[164] He came of a distinguished military family which, though Frankish in origin, had a long history of service to the Empire.[165] He had initially followed Magnentius, but had deserted him at Mursa, giving Constantius the opportunity for victory.[166] He may have known the Rhine well, and he was loyal. He did a good job.[167] But

---

[161] Above 153.
[162] Above 176.
[163] Barnes (1993: 221).
[164] Heinen (1985: 233); Drinkwater (1997: 5); and below 213, 273.
[165] Above 151–2.
[166] On Silvanus see generally Drinkwater (1994); on the date of his appointment see Wigg (1991: 26).
[167] AM 15.5.4.

Constantius did not ignore the Alamanni. In 354, instead of proceeding directly from Gaul to Italy, he went out of his way to confront those on the High Rhine. With Ammianus' narrative now available, we can follow the course of this campaign, and those that followed, in some detail.

Constantius moved against Gundomadus and Vadomarius, brothers and kings of the Alamanni, who had been raiding adjacent Gallic territory.[168] There was some delay due to problems with supplies, but the army eventually reached the High Rhine around Kaiseraugst, where Constantius intended to cross.[169] (Opinion is divided as to whether by 'Rauracum' Ammianus means the old city of Augst/ Augusta Rauracorum or its fourth-century successor, the adjoining Diocletianic fort of Kaiseraugst/Castrum Rauracense. Here, and in what follows, I opt for the latter.[170]) The current *communis opinio* is that a crossing was not made because Alamanni opposed the building of a bridge and subsequent Roman plans to ford the river were revealed to them by the treachery of certain Alamanni in the Roman army—according to rumour, Latinus, Agilo and Scudilo. The Alamanni therefore sought peace before a crossing could be attempted.[171]

Recently, however, Lorenz has revived a suggestion of Jankowski that Ammianus should be understood as saying that the Rhine was forded, but the attack was suspended because the Alamanni then sued for peace having learned of the incursion from their countrymen in Roman service.[172] This is persuasive. A valid claim that he had dealt with the enemy on their own soil better explains Constantius' subsequent celebration of a great victory. It also helps us understand the rumoured Alamannic 'treachery'. Informing one's fellow countrymen that a crossing might take place would have been very dangerous if those informed had decided to attack as the attempt was being made. On the other hand, informing one's fellow countrymen of a crossing that was a fait accompli involved much less

[168] AM 14.10.1.
[169] AM 14.10.2–6.
[170] de Jonge (1939: 103); Lorenz, S. (1997: 26 and n.5); Schwarz (1998: 108); Zotz (1998: 392). For an accessible plan see Cornell and Matthews (1982: 132).
[171] See AM 14.10.6–8.
[172] Lorenz, S. (1997: 26–7).

danger and, if the officials concerned were being used as go-betweens, may have been part of Constantius' plan. Ammianus' report that the Alamanni may have been persuaded by unpropitious omens and sacrifice not to continue their opposition hints that important people on both sides may have been working for peace.

At any rate, the Alamanni requested peace and forgiveness, and their request was accepted by Constantius, though he put the final decision to his army.[173] A *foedus*, that is a positive agreement involving alliance, not just non-aggression, was established, and Constantius moved to winter at Milan.[174] It was this success on the High Rhine which appears to have prompted Constantius, also in 354, to adopt the title *Germanicus Alamannicus Maximus*.[175] Historians are inclined to disparage Constantius' 'bloodless victory'.[176] However, his was a rare and remarkable campaign,[177] which deserves closer consideration.

Constantius could have travelled from Arles to Italy much more quickly by other routes. He could also have moved north later in the year: he began in early spring and had finished by late May or early June, at a time when the Gallic campaigning season normally began in July.[178] His Rhenish expedition, with a full army in poor conditions, cannot therefore have been undertaken lightly by a man who, by his own reckoning, was 'cautious and prudent'.[179] Why did he take the risk? Part of his motivation must, again, have been to use *Germani* to bolster the imperial office. Like his father and grandfather before him, he needed a 'foreign' success to remove the sour taste of civil war and bind the army to him as its leader. The Alamanni, in reality no great threat, fitted the bill. But why pick on those of the High Rhine?

Ammianus makes much of the Alamanni of the Upper Rhine who, on Constantius' orders, made trouble for Decentius in the final period of Magnentius' rule. But at an earlier stage, and equally

---

[173] AM 14.10.9–16.
[174] AM 14.10.16; Lorenz, S. (1997: 28).
[175] *CIL* 3.3705, *ILS* 732; *Quellen* 6, Inscriptions no. 64; above 69.
[176] So Zotz (1998: 393).
[177] Martin (1998: 411).
[178] Barnes (1993: 221); Lorenz, S. (1997: 28); AM 17.8.1.
[179] AM 14.10.11: *cunctator et cautus*.

important for Constantius' tactic of unsettling Magnentius, must have been the need to pressure Magnentius and to weaken his defence of Italy against Constantius' invasion from the east.[180] This would have meant encouraging attacks on Magnentius' southern territory: not on Italy, which would have been unthinkable, but on Gaul through the Belfort Gap or the central Swiss Plateau, threatening Magnentius from the rear and separating him from Decentius. This explains Wigg's 'Rheinknie' hoards of 351/2.[181] To judge from these hoards, Alamannic aggression was short-lived, which suggests that it was under control. However, Constantius needed to show that he had brought it to an end and to demonstrate that these Alamanni posed no threat to Italy.[182] Constantius II therefore made in person for the High Rhine, intent on a demonstration of his authority.

But again it is important to see events as they are likely to have appeared from the other side of the river. The Alamanni of the southern Upper and High Rhine had settled relatively late and were isolated, poor and heavily exposed to Roman power and influence.[183] These conditions are likely to have encouraged young males to serve in the Roman army while retaining links with their home communities.[184] Their leaders cannot have been ignorant of Roman politics, or have been inclined to make trouble for the Empire. The chieftains that Constantius encountered on his arrival at Kaiseraugst, Gundomadus and Vadomarius, may have already been known to the Roman authorities, and may have won respect for their control of the situation in 351/2.[185] Neither side will have wanted trouble; each will have preferred respectable shows of strength followed by agreement.[186]

As far as Gundomadus and Vadomarius were concerned, their best policy was to deal with the emperor through the same high-ranking, and possibly related, officials who had earlier encouraged them to

[180] Cf. Wigg (1991: 108).
[181] Above 201.
[182] Cf. Heinen (1985: 234–5).
[183] Above 83, 88, 129–30.
[184] Above 176.
[185] Cf. AM 18.2.16: the letter of recommendation presented by Vadomarius in 359 (below 247) could therefore have been drawn up in 352, not 354. This would fit the following phrase: *olim ab Augusto in clientelam rei Romanae receptus.*
[186] Cf. Lorenz, S. (1997: 27).

raid in his name. Thus, we return to Latinus, Agilo and Scudilo. These should not be seen as 'traitors'. They were too important and too successful: vilification of medium or low-ranking Alamannic officers would be much more credible. There is no sign of ethnic 'Alamannic solidarity'.[187] The false charges against them should be seen as part of a culture of accusation at the court of Constantius II, which led nowhere if the emperor chose not to believe it.[188] Rather, what we have is facilitation. Constantius II wanted a military success and stability. Gundomadus and Vadomarius wanted peace, and will maybe (in a warrior culture where it was often difficult to rein in men who had tasted blood) have welcomed Roman intervention to support themselves and their pro-Roman policies. High-ranking Alamannic officers, with links to local leaders, were on hand to arrange all this.[189] The treaty was kept until the murder of Gundomadus, apparently at the hands of an anti-Roman faction, in 357.[190]

In 355, Constantius II returned to the High Rhine. According to Ammianus, war was declared on two Alamannic *pagi*, one unknown (the text is corrupted here) and the other the Lentienses, both notorious raiders of Roman territory.[191] Constantius took his army to Campi Canini in Raetia. He then sent his *magister equitum*, Arbetio, ahead around Lake Constance. Arbetio was caught in an Alamannic ambush, but recovered and defeated the enemy. Constantius returned triumphantly to Milan.[192]

The 18 months or so following his 354 campaign proved momentous for Constantius II. One of his major worries in the east was his Caesar, Gallus, appointed before he moved westwards against Magnentius in 351. Gallus soon showed himself to be dangerously self-willed, unsettling the region and raising the spectre of usurpation. It became clear that he could not be left as he was. Later in 354 he was persuaded to travel to northern Italy to meet Constantius, and

---

[187] *Contra* Zotz (1998: 393).
[188] Drinkwater (1983b: 362–3); and cf. the failed accusations against Arbetio in 356/7: AM 14.16.6.
[189] Cf. Barceló (1981: 25); Lorenz, S. (1997: 27): Latinus, Agilo and Scudilo as 'Vermittler'. Cf. above 176.
[190] AM 16.12.17. Below 230.
[191] AM 15.4.1. Rollinger (1998: 166): two *pagi*; cf. above 172 and n.181.
[192] AM 15.4.1, 7–13.

was executed en route, near Pola. But this was not the end of Constantius' problems. Gallus' death and the subsequent prosecution of his supporters intensified the atmosphere of fear and distrust at Constantius' court. In addition, Constantius now had to find a way of dealing with Gallus' half-brother and his own cousin, Julian, apart from himself the last surviving male in direct descent from Constantius I. There remained growing tension with Persia. And Constantius still had to resolve bitter differences between eastern and western bishops which twisted doctrinal disputes, issues involving Church careers and secular politics, and hunger for imperial patronage into a maddeningly complex knot.

The religious problem was tackled at the Council of Milan, held probably in July and August of 355. This must have been long in the planning, and Constantius kept a close eye on its proceedings. However, it still proved difficult, and did not get him the agreement he had hoped for.[193] As the council ended, the emperor suffered a further reversal in fortune when Silvanus 'usurped' in Gaul and had to be deceived and killed by one of Constantius' agents, Ammianus' patron, the senior general Ursicinus.[194] This left Roman military and civil administration on the Rhine in tatters, and prompted further raids by Franks and Alamanni.[195] After much heart-searching, Constantius, still bent on returning to the east, decided to make Julian his representative in the west. On 6 November 355, he commended his cousin to his troops at Milan, and with their approval named him Caesar. On 1 December, Julian left for Gaul. As he left Italy, Ammianus tells us, he received the dreadful news that Cologne had been besieged and taken by barbarians.[196]

Establishing the basic framework of Constantius' 355 campaign is difficult. Though Ammianus implies a date fairly late in the year, with his reference to the emperor's returning to winter quarters,[197] it is generally agreed that fighting must have taken place in late spring or early summer because it is impossible to allocate it reasonably to

[193] Barnes (1993: 117).
[194] Kienast (1996: 322): Silvanus 'reigned' 11(?) August to 8(?) September. Cf. above 152.
[195] Below 213.
[196] AM 15.8.1–18.
[197] AM 15.4.12.

any other period in the year.[198] Constantius and Arbetio probably travelled to Lake Constance over the Splügen pass, establishing the imperial headquarters near the transportation centre and important naval base of Bregenz.[199] It is possible that en route, at Como, Constantius met Julian making his first visit to the west.[200] Proposed alternative locations of Campi Canini further south are implausible.[201] Arbetio's advance is likely to have been to the north of Bregenz, not along the southern shore of the lake which was Roman territory.[202]

This location of the campaign raises some difficulties about the relationship between the Lentienses and the early medieval 'Linzgau', with which they are now commonly associated.[203] The Linzgau is usually taken to be the area just to the north of the western arms of Lake Constance. The now vanished stream of the Linz, whose name links the 'Gau' and the Lentienses and which survives in that of the settlement of Linz, near Pfullendorf,[204] ran *c.*60 km (36 statute miles) as the crow flies to the north-east of Bregenz.[205]

Ammianus gives a very negative impression of the aims and achievements of the campaign. A preliminary protracted council of war suggests indecision; division of the army implies lack of nerve; ambush hints at incompetence; and subsequent vacillation at further lack of leadership. He attributes final success to the bravery of the troops, not the skill of their generals. Most modern commentators have taken their tone from him.[206] Again, however, what he says has to be handled carefully. Though the 355 expedition was no enormous venture, it is a wonder that Constantius bothered with it at all when he had so many other worries; and, as in 354, he seems to have been

---

[198] Barnes (1993: 221): around June; Lorenz, S. (1997: 28): probably June; Rollinger (1998: 188–91): mid-May to mid-June.

[199] Rollinger (1998: 180–4).

[200] Rollinger (1998: 188).

[201] Rollinger (1998: 168–79); cf. Lorenz, S. (1997: 175–6, 179, 183).

[202] So Rollinger (1998: 179), *contra* Lorenz, S. (1997: 30–1), though, certainly, as Lorenz says, we should not envisage Arbetio as crossing the Rhine at the western end of the lake.

[203] e.g. Rollinger (1998: 178 and n.65), from Staehelin (1948: 291).

[204] Zotz (1998: 393).

[205] On the Lentienses, see further below 310–15.

[206] e.g. Demandt (1989: 84); Lorenz, S. (1997: 31).

very pleased with what he achieved.[207] It cannot be true that the 355 campaign was 'probably of no major military significance', and that it was of interest to Ammianus only because he happened to be in Milan.[208] The key, as ever, is context; and the context was still that of 354. Ammianus' wording suggests that the cause of the 355 expedition, raiding, was recent and perhaps even contemporary.[209] However, like that under Gundomadus and Vadomarius, it could have taken place earlier, occasioned by Constantius' invitation to make trouble for Magnentius. Indeed, like that around Kaiseraugst, the hoard-pattern south of Lake Constance indicates raiding in 351/2 which then more or less ceased.[210] Constantius therefore, in his methodical manner, moved to deal with an important but not critical problem. Again, he needed to show that he had his allies under control and that they posed no threat to Italy. Ammianus' use of *collimitia* and the evidence of the coin-hoards suggest that the Alamanni had not penetrated beyond Raetia. However, since the affected area lay in the diocese of Italia Annonaria at the end of a first-class route leading directly into the Po valley, Constantius must show that the safety of the peninsula was now assured.[211] Success would also further enhance his military reputation.

In respect of Constantius' tactics, Ammianus' detail both illuminates and obscures. Though Ammianus does not say so directly, and indeed in one place appears to indicate the contrary, Arbetio was sent ahead with a small but elite cavalry force.[212] His orders were to engage the enemy around Lake Constance. However, Ammianus' phrasing, though unclear, does not suggest a direct attack.[213] Arbetio's job was therefore probably to locate Alamanni. As at Kaiseraugst, this was to be followed by a show of strength,[214] followed in turn by a peace agreement. Despite Ammianus' emphatic double mention of

---

[207] AM 15.4.13: *ovans.*

[208] *Contra* Rollinger (1998: 192), (2001: 150, quotation).

[209] AM 15.4.1: *collimitia saepe Romana latius irrumpentibus.*

[210] Wigg (1991: 103–7 Maps 10–14).

[211] Cf. Rollinger (1998: 183).

[212] Rollinger (1998: 172–4): note especially the alternative translation of *validiore* [15.4.1] as 'very strong' not 'the larger part of'.

[213] AM 15.4.1: *relegens margines lacus Brigantiae pergeret protinus barbaris.* I interpret *relegens* as 'going through again', 'combing'.

[214] Cf. Barceló (1981: 27); Rollinger (1998: 73).

'war',[215] all-out fighting was not Constantius' intention. That combat occurred may be explained by poor reconnaissance on both sides: Ammianus reports that Arbetio moved without waiting for news from scouts.[216] One can easily envisage each side running into the other without warning, and both panicking and coming to blows: a major skirmish but not a pitched battle.[217] It is clear that the violence was relatively short-lived, and that both sides reached an agreement.

This agreement is likely to have involved treaties.[218] These are not mentioned by Ammianus, but again we have to exercise care; and this returns us to the question of why Ammianus described these events as he did. Ammianus was hostile to Constantius because of the emperor's treatment of Ursicinus, Ammianus' patron,[219] and it was in 354/5, following the fall of Gallus, that Ursicinus suffered his first disgrace. He cleared himself only by removing Silvanus, but then again fell under suspicion.[220] However, even deeper than Ammianus' regard for Ursicinus was his regard for Julian, and it is likely that he ignored the Alamannic treaties of 355 not only because he wanted to bury anything that would redound to the credit of Constantius but also because, unlike those of 354, these were not going to figure in his account of Julian's encounters with Alamanni.[221] He also used the 355 campaign to point up the immensity of the threat faced by Julian in Gaul.

Ammianus includes a relatively long excursus on the upper reaches of the Rhine and Lake Constance.[222] This, however, is entirely untrustworthy, being highly stereotyped and derivative.[223] Alamanni are depicted as wild people in a wild, ruined land; and wilderness and ruin begin south of the frontier. Ammianus thus disregards centuries of development in the original province of Raetia.[224] Finds from

---

[215] AM 15.4.1, 7: *bellum, aspera... bellorum.*
[216] AM 15.4.7.
[217] So Rollinger (1998: 173).
[218] Benedetti-Martig (1993: 356–7): these were the treaties still operational in 378 (AM 31.10.2); below 310.
[219] Above 178.
[220] Above 208.
[221] Cf. above 155.
[222] AM 15.4.2–6.
[223] Rollinger (2001: esp. 136–8, 140, 144, 149–50).
[224] Rollinger (2001: 132–3).

the area to the north and north-east of Lake Constance do not indicate intensive Alamannic settlement or particularly intimate contact with the Empire; and it lies outside Stribrny's regions of coin circulation.[225] On the other hand, the Lentienses, living close to the Iller-*limes*, must have had some dealings with Rome. A Lentiensian could become a member of Gratian's guard and could return home on leave; and having fought with Gratian, the Lentienses were required to supply recruits for the army.[226] Though Lentienses were never formed into full, permanent regiments, this service was provided, probably under Gratian's father, by Raetovarii, who could not have been distant from them.[227] In this region lies the fort at Kellmünz, with an unusual apsed structure that may have been built to facilitate dealings with local Alamanni.[228] All this suggests decades of relatively peaceful interaction between Alamanni and Romans. The leaders of the Lentienses and their allies would hardly have recognized themselves in Ammianus' description of 'wild' Alamanni.

There remains one issue concerning Roman military activity on the Rhine in 355. Ammianus records that in 356, Julian, preparing to move from Autun to Reims, learned that Silvanus had gone 'not long before' (*paulo ante*) by a shorter route with 8,000 men.[229] This has been taken to indicate that, at about the same time as Constantius was campaigning by Lake Constance, Silvanus was active near or on the Rhine frontier. It has been suggested that both campaigns were ordered by Constantius in a move that was a prototype of pincer attacks of 356 and 357.[230] This is unlikely. The signs are that Constantius' 355 campaign was short and localized. The theatres of operations were too distant to allow practical liaison. In early 355, Gallus had fallen and Julian looked well on the way to being discredited. But Silvanus was trusted, and under his charge Gaul appeared to be in safe hands.[231] He was left to manage things on

[225] *Germanen* (1986: 343 Fig. 69); Stribrny (1989: 401 Fig. 19).
[226] Above 160.
[227] Above 170–3.
[228] Above 99, 157.
[229] AM 16.2.4.
[230] Jullian (1926: 166 and n.1); Drinkwater (1997: 5 and n.27); Lorenz, S. (1997: 35 and n.73).
[231] AM 15.5.2: *efficax ad haec corrigenda.*

his own. Ammianus suggests that he drove out the invaders.[232] However, an earlier disparaging description of his activities by Julian has it that he

plundered the cities of their wealth and distributed it among the invading barbarians, paying it down as a sort of ransom, though he was well able to take measures to win security by the sword rather than by money. But he tried to win them over to friendliness by means of money.[233]

Troop movements, expulsions and subsidies suggest that Silvanus' policy, like that of Constantius, was to solve 'the Alamannic problem' by a blend of aggression and conciliation, not full-scale war. This should have included treaties with Alamannic communities on the Upper Rhine and the lower Main.[234] It could well have been that some left-bank settlement by Chnodomarius and his neighbours was tolerated at this time.[235]

The situation soon deteriorated.[236] Trier, capital of the west since the third century, had suffered badly during the revolt of Magnentius. Possibly subject to Alamannic and Frankish attack, it had thrown up its own leader, Poemenius, in opposition to Decentius, only to be retaken by the latter before he himself succumbed to Constantius II. It seems likely that the city had ceased to be a viable base before Constantius II recovered Gaul.[237] This is probably why Silvanus set up his headquarters in Cologne.[238] However, in the summer of 355, Cologne was closely involved in his usurpation and its suppression by Ursicinus. Silvanus' death made Ursicinus de facto imperial vice-roy in Gaul, responsible for its defence.[239] Thanks to Silvanus and Constantius, Ursicinus did not have to deal immediately with any sort of barbarian crisis. Some indication of the restoration of order may be seen in the fact that he and his small retinue do not appear to have taken raiding by Alamanni or Franks into account on their

---

[232] AM 15.5.4: *barbarosque propellans.*
[233] Julian, *Orat.* 2.98C–D.
[234] See AM 17.1.3.
[235] Cf. below 217–18, 228. *Contra* Lorenz, S. (1997: 35 n.73), from Gilles: that Silvanus had to deal with attacks from Chnodomarius at this time.
[236] The following linking narrative is a revised version of Drinkwater (1997: 6–8).
[237] Drinkwater (1997: 5–6).
[238] Above 203.
[239] So Frézouls (1962: 674–5); cf. Matthews (1989: 38).

journey to Cologne to meet Silvanus, and that after Silvanus' fall Ursicinus was able to arrest his accomplices and send them to Milan for interrogation.[240] Yet Ursicinus was in an unenviable position.

He was physically isolated, with very few trustworthy followers in an area he did not know. He must have been constantly on the defensive against both the followers of the man he had just betrayed and an emperor who remained uneasy about his loyalty, who was soon to complain about the misuse of public funds in Gaul, and who was never, by promoting him from *magister equitum* to *magister peditum*, to make him the full successor of Silvanus in Gaul (the post went to Barbatio).[241] Ursicinus left Cologne. He could not move to Trier—by late 355 not only badly damaged but also compromised by the support Poemenius had given Silvanus.[242] Ursicinus therefore transferred his headquarters and, I would argue, most of the forces he commanded, including the main strength of the Rhine garrisons, westwards, to winter in the vicinity of Reims. Here, Julian joined him and his successor as *magister*, Marcellus, early the following year.[243]

Ursicinus' move is entirely pardonable; but it signalled a military down-grading of the Rhineland and, worse still, was followed by complete inaction: the difficulties of his position paralysed Ursicinus' generalship.[244] It was from this time at the latest that Alamanni began to occupy land on the left bank of the Rhine; and it is arguable that Cologne, now defended by no more than a token garrison, fell to purely adventitious raiding by Franks. Contrary to Ammianus, these

[240] AM 15.5.24, 6.1f. (cf. 14.5.8: Paul's job was to take the supposed supporters of Magnentius to the imperial court for interrogation).

[241] On Ursicinus' duplicity see Drinkwater (1994); for the suggestion of embezzlement see AM 15.5.36 with Frézouls (1962: 676); and for Ursicinus' failure to gain promotion, see Frézouls (1962: 679–80). Frézouls comments usefully on Ursicinus' difficulties in the wake of Silvanus' disloyalty, but does not develop his arguments, and makes too much of Silvanus' 'Germanness'.

[242] AM 15.6.4.

[243] AM 16.2.8. Below 219. For Ursicinus' rank in relationship to Marcellus and Julian, see Frézouls (1962: 680–1). Blockley (1980: 475) explains the paralysis noted below as a result of the somewhat earlier arrival of Marcellus and the failure of Ursicinus and Marcellus to cooperate in the defence of Gaul.

[244] Cf. van Ossel (1992: 73): although in the end there was no total collapse, the political and military turmoil which accompanied the rise and fall of Magnentius appears to have led to the abandonment of a large number of rural sites in the Rhineland.

did not take the place by siege. Rather, living up to their name—the 'bold'/'impudent' ones—they just forced their way into a virtually open city, no doubt astonished by their success.[245] By late 355, the situation in Gaul was very messy but not desperate. Julian and Ammianus exaggerated the importance of the fall of Cologne to disparage the achievements of Constantius II and glorify those of his successor. The Franks posed no real threat. Their capture of Cologne did not show their overwhelming strength but resulted from their exploitation of current Roman weakness. As events were to show, once they faced a serious Roman response they gave up the city with little resistance.[246] Alamanni were the more important problem, especially now that some were settling on the Roman side of the Rhine.[247] However, they had been brought into line twice already in recent months, and could presumably be brought into line again, this time without the commitment of significant additional resources. The manner in which Ursicinus had dealt with Silvanus, though underhand, had spared the west the horrors of another civil war. Silvanus' army was intact and obedient to Constantius II and his representatives, as must have been the civil administration in Gaul. The current trouble on the Rhine frontier had been caused by irresolute leadership. Once Constantius had decided a course of action, all this could change.[248] He decided to send in Julian. This was uncomfortable for both parties, given the way that Constantius had benefited from the massacre of 337, in which most of Julian's immediate family had perished,[249] and given the problems that were bound to arise if Julian, quickly married to Helena, fathered a male heir before Constantius did.[250] In the short term, however, Constantius could take comfort in Julian's youth and inexperience; in the fact that he exercised no real power but was

[245] Zöllner (1970: 1) 'mutig, ungestüm, frech'; Drinkwater (1996: 23).

[246] AM 16.3.2. Below 220. Cf. Elliott (1983: 251 and n.9): 'so far as one can learn from Ammianus about this recapture, it was effected by walking into a deserted town.'

[247] On this, see further below 217–18.

[248] As Frézouls (1962: 683) remarks, Constantius must in the end be credited with a sensitive treatment of Ursicinus—not punished, but retained in post and eventually sent back east.

[249] Cf. above 199.

[250] Cf. Drinkwater (1983b: 357–8).

under the control of the new military *magister* and praetorian prefect
sent to replace Ursicinus and his staff; and in the expectation that, on
past form, it would not take long to restore things to normal. After
this, the 'Julian problem' could be considered afresh. Constantius did
not, therefore, as his detractors charged, simply promote Julian to
send him to death in battle.

7

Conflict 356–61

Though Julian spent fewer than six years in the west, through his own writings and those of his supporters we know more about his activities here than those of any other Roman general since Julius Caesar. This includes his dealings with Alamanni. Julian's first Alamannic campaign took place in 356, but before examining that year, we should return to the issue of Alamannic occupation of Roman territory.

When and why this came about is as important as whether Constantius set Alamanni against Magnentius in the first place. Alamanni were certainly over the Rhine by the mid-350s. In 356, Julian found Alamanni living in the territories of cities in the valley of the Upper Rhine.[1] In 357, he again encountered barbarians 'who had established their homes on our side of the Rhine', and confiscated their crops.[2] This move may have begun as early as 352, and cannot have been later than the end of 355.[3] From a Roman point of view, such a transference of population was neither unprecedented nor in principle unwelcome. The Ubii had been allowed into the Empire by Augustus; and, down to the fifth century, various emperors did not shrink from increasing the number of their subjects in the same manner.[4] For 359, indeed, Ammianus demonstrates how the idea of settling barbarians on Roman soil could be presented very positively to an emperor (albeit, in this case, by court sycophants to Constantius II): that by taking in Sarmatian Limigantes he would

---

[1] AM 16.2.12. Cf. Julian, *Ep. ad Ath.* 279A; Libanius, *Orat.* 12.44, 48; 18.34.
[2] AM 16.11.8, 11–12; cf. Libanius, *Orat.* 18.52. Cf. below 235–6
[3] Above 215. Cf. Martin (1997a: 122), (1998: 413).
[4] de Ste Croix (1981: 510–16).

'gain more child-producing subjects and be able to muster a strong force of recruits'.[5] Ammianus probably made much of this because it resulted in disaster: the barbarians attacked Constantius just as he was about to make a speech to them.[6] However, the arguments concerning the benefits of immigration ring true. Likewise, from the barbarian side, spontaneous Alamannic settlement, though impudent, should not automatically be construed as hostile.

Alamannic leaders may have been promised land, and thus had no reason not to call on this promise when the opportunity offered. Moreover, they will surely have been aware that Franks were settled over the Rhine in Toxiandria,[7] and had not been expelled despite Frankish involvement in the recent troubles.[8] And they may have known that some early-arriving Elbe-*Germani* had been allowed across by Maximian.[9] There is every reason for believing that these Alamanni did not see themselves, or expect to be seen, as enemies of Rome. They can have entertained no hope, or even concept, of 'conquering' Gaul. They must also have appreciated that any rash action would, sooner or later, be punished by the enormous resources available to the Empire.[10] In exposing themselves and their dependants to Roman power over the Rhine they cannot have believed that they were committing a punishable offence: they must have been convinced that they had sufficient authority for their actions in the documents and promises they had received from Constantius II. And in settling across the Rhine under the aegis of Rome they showed themselves willing to become Roman subjects.[11] It comes as no surprise that they did not occupy the cities of the Upper Rhine. Ammianus, famously, put this down to their superstitious dread of such places, but this is vitiated by the fact that he says the same of the Huns.[12] I propose that the Alamanni kept out of these places because they had no use for

[5] AM 19.11.7.
[6] AM 19.11.10.
[7] Above 200.
[8] Above 201.
[9] Below 366–7.
[10] Elton (1993); cf. Tacitus, *Annales* 14.33.6: British awareness of inevitable Roman retaliation at the start of the Boudiccan rebellion.
[11] *Contra* Heather (2001: 46–7): Chnodomarius as the leader of an anti-imperial movement—in modern terms, a freedom fighter.
[12] AM 16.2.12. Above 84. Zotz (1998: 394).

them[13] and, more significantly, because they recognized the cities as continuing seats of imperial power and administration. In this respect, they were more sophisticated than the Franks, who 'took' Cologne: there are strong grounds for believing that the Alamanni did not do the same with Cologne's sister-city, Mainz.[14]

Thus, it is likely that by 356 peaceful Alamannic migration over the Upper Rhine was an established and, as far as a number of leading figures on both sides were concerned, an acceptable and positive phenomenon. The Alamanni could believe in the permanency of the arrangement since there had been no action against the settlers. The problem was that Constantius II, used to the east, had misread the situation. Westerners, military and civilian, historically inclined to a forward policy based on the Rhine,[15] would have detested extensive Germanic settlement on its left bank. This explains the initial clashes in 356 on the approach to the Rhine and at Brumath, as Roman troops and settled Alamanni came into contact for the first time.[16] After this, both sides were, presumably, restrained by their leaders; but Julian, taking part in his first expedition, had noted the situation, guessed what could be made of it, and took the opportunity to act when it was offered in 357.

The year 356 saw two Alamannic expeditions. The better-known is the one in which Julian saw action for the first time. Ammianus has him move from Vienne, where he had spent the winter, to Reims by way of Autun, Auxerre and Troyes. On the way he was attacked by bands of 'barbarians' and at Autun and Troyes he found city populations which too had suffered, or feared they would suffer, violence at the hands of *barbari*.[17] Having arrived in Reims, Julian then led the Roman forces collected there against Alamanni in the Rhine valley by way of the *Decem Pagi*.[18] He was attacked by 'the enemy' en route, but recovered himself, and then proceeded more slowly and cautiously.[19] On reaching the Rhine, Julian retook Brumath, Strasbourg,

---

[13] Above 105, below 358.
[14] Below 205.
[15] Drinkwater (1987: 252).
[16] AM 16.2.10–13. Cf. below 220.
[17] AM 16.2.1, 6–7.
[18] Cf. above 126.
[19] AM 16.2.9–11.

Seltz, Rheinzabern,[20] Speyer, Worms, and Mainz, the territories of which had been occupied by the barbarians.[21] The only resistance he encountered was on the approach to Brumath.[22] After this, he moved further downstream, recovering Cologne and intimidating the Frankish kings there into making peace.[23] He then withdrew, via Trier, to winter *apud Senonas*—now no longer generally interpreted as Sens, but Senon, near Verdun, though the case for Sens still continues to attract support.[24]

The lesser-known Alamannic campaign of 356 is a third (after those of 354 and 355) by Constantius. Tucked away in Ammianus' account of the battle of Strasbourg in 357 is the information that during the previous year Constantius had invaded Alamannic territory by way of Raetia. He met little resistance, with the Alamanni eventually suing for peace. They were, in fact, in dire straits since 'the emperor was menacing them by way of Raetia, Caesar was near at hand and would not allow them to slip out anywhere, and their neighbours (whom civil strife had made their enemies) were all but treading on their necks and they were hemmed in on all sides'. After granting them the peace they sought, Constantius departed.[25]

The date of Julian's campaign is fairly easy to establish, since Ammianus provides a specific date (24 June) for Julian's arrival at Autun: it must have lasted from June into August.[26] That of Constantius is usually placed later. This is because Ammianus has the Alamanni, after early lacklustre resistance, yielding to the emperor as winter bit.[27] However, it cannot have been a true winter campaign because Constantius was in Milan on 10 November. Modern commentators place it in autumn.[28] Ammianus' reference to wintry conditions may therefore be seen as another of the literary conceits by which he depicted the Alamanni as a savage people in a

[20] See Lorenz, S. (1997: 36 n. 77): Rheinzabern not, as is usually stated, Saverne.
[21] Cf. above 217.
[22] AM 16.2.12–13.
[23] AM 16.3.1–2.
[24] Lorenz, S. (1997: 39 n.107, from Nicolle); cf. Matthews (1989: 492 n.16).
[25] AM 16.12.15–16.
[26] Barnes (1993: 227).
[27] AM 16.12.15: *sidere urente brumali.*
[28] Seeck (1921: 4.255, 7); Barceló (1981: 30); Barnes (1993: 221–2); Lorenz, S. (1997: 37).

savage land, and through which he disparaged Constantius' success: nature defeated the Alamanni, not the emperor. On the other hand, with Constantius arriving in Alamannia just as Julian was leaving, this chronology fails to explain how both can be seen as presenting a joint threat—a 'pincer movement', as some have interpreted it.[29]

To understand them, we must place these events in their political and military context. The west was now, at least nominally, in the hands of Julian; and Constantius—for all his personal failings, someone who always sought to do what he regarded as proper—must have felt the need to ensure that Julian and the régime he represented enjoyed success. Constantius II was a worrier. The man who had taken the trouble to give Julian a detailed code of conduct, 'written in his own hand', 'as if sending off a stepson to university',[30] must have been thinking of him as he faced his first major undertaking in Gaul. It is, indeed, Constantius who demands our attention.

Ammianus grossly exaggerates Julian's role at this time. Julian was only an imperial figurehead. The real directors of operations were Ursicinus and Marcellus, Ursicinus' successor, acting on orders from Constantius. Both campaigns of 356 were Constantius' campaigns.[31] Even if not the closing jaws of a pincer movement, they must have been closely related. I suggest, therefore, that Constantius' principal objective was to ensure that Julian ran into no difficulties. To bring this about, all he needed to do was to continue existing practice. There is every reason to suppose that from around 351 to 361 Constantius had important dealings with leaders of Alamannic *pagi* close to Italy and further down the Rhine.[32] In 356, he could have sent messengers alerting Alamannic communities on the Upper Rhine that Roman forces would soon be moving west in strength to reassert control over the Rhine valley and warning them not to make trouble. The positive side of this was that there was no intention of expelling Alamannic settlers on the left bank of the river: as they must not resist so they need not resist. He could also make it clear that he would be on hand in the region shortly after his Caesar,

[29] So, e.g. Bidez (1930: 142); Rosen (1970: 79–80); Barceló (1981: 31); Lorenz, S. (1997: 37).

[30] AM 16.5.3.

[31] Rosen (1970: 77–9).

[32] Above 155–6, 176.

and so be in a position to support him if the need arose. Julian's task was, therefore, made easy: police work not warfare. Not much trouble was expected, and little was encountered.

The trouble that Julian met while moving to Reims was patently not very serious, and may or may not have concerned Alamanni. It was certainly not the creation of major Alamannic chieftains. It could have involved unruly young warriors;[33] but it might have been the work of other *Germani* (e.g. Franks, Saxons), or even domestic miscreants whom it was convenient to label 'barbarians'. Uncertain times always tended to fill the uplands and forests of Gaul with army deserters, runaway slaves and even ordinary refugees driven by desperation to attack settlements and travellers.[34] Once the campaign had begun, there were just two skirmishes with Alamanni—one en route, in mist, the other before Brumath—both ascribable to nervousness on both sides. The Roman army was clearly under orders not to engage with Alamanni en masse; and Alamannic leaders were not disposed to tackle it. Operating north of the allied *pagi* of Gundomadus and Vadomarius, it quickly re-established control over cities lying in the area in which Alamanni were settling but, in line with Constantius' plans and Alamannic expectations, it did not turn on the settlers. 'Retaking' the Rhenish towns in this region was straightforward, since the Alamanni were not occupying them—not even Mainz.[35] (Further afield, as the example of the Frankish 'conquest' of Cologne showed, such cities could not be held by *Germani* even when they attempted some sort of possession.)

Constantius' route, from Bregenz to the Rhine crossing at Zurzach, by way of Windisch[36] would have taken him between the pacified Lentienses and the *pagi* of Gundomadus and Vadomarius. To support Julian, he need not have gone very far, which would have suited his cautious nature. If he took the main road from Zurzach to Rottweil or Sulz, both on the Neckar, he could threaten the rest of the Neckar valley, while being able to move down the Kinzig to the Rhine north of Strasbourg if the situation demanded (Fig. 18). Coin-

[33] Above 122.

[34] Libanius, *Orat.* 18.104 specifically mentions banditry in Gaul practised by survivors of Magnentius' army. Cf. Drinkwater (1984: 369).

[35] Above 218–19, below 240–1.

[36] Lorenz, S. (1997: 36–7).

finds show that the Rottweil road was still frequented in the fourth century.[37] This would have been useful since, by the time Constantius arrived, Julian would probably have moved north to the Lower Rhine. Thus, Constantius secured Julian's rear. Constantius' concern to prevent trouble flaring up behind the western army is indicated by the length of time he spent in the field: probably long enough to see Julian safely into winter quarters.

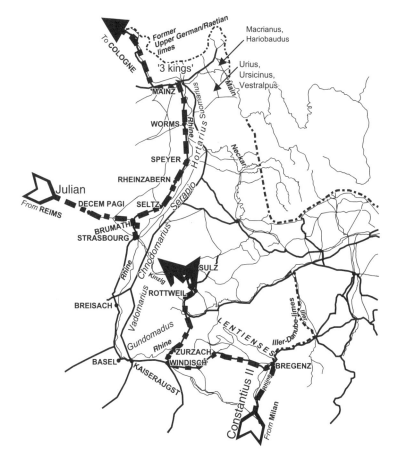

Fig. 18   Proposed routes of the 356 campaigns.

[37] Above 130; cf. Lorenz, S. (1997: 37).

A secondary objective would have been confirmation of Roman authority over the Neckar valley. The middle and upper Neckar valley was to become important in later Alamannic development.[38] This is not surprising, since it contains good land. However, we know very little about it in earlier periods. Lorenz suggests that it was the location of the *pagi* of Urius, Ursicinus and Vestralpus, allies of Chnodomarius in 357.[39] This is because Ammianus says that in the skirmishing that led up to the battle of Strasbourg in 357 the combined Alamanni recognized the shield devices of Barbatio's defeated army as those of earlier, victorious enemies.[40] Against this, Constantius would not have helped Julian's army as it moved northwards in 356 by attacking *pagus* chiefs close to powerful leaders on the Rhine. I would place the *pagi* of Urius, Ursicinus and Vestralpus closer to the Rhine, near those of Suomarius and Hortarius, and possibly along the Main, in the Groß-Gerau/Seligenstadt/Stockstadt area, another region of strong coin circulation[41] (Fig. 18). In the Neckar valley Constantius intimidated otherwise unknown communities, the inhabitants of which found themselves caught between fellow Elbe-*Germani* who, thanks to the work of 354 and 355, were now Roman federates, and an incoming Roman army. In 357, it was as allies of Chnodomarius that their warriors drew attention to Roman shield blazons.[42]

Constantius' secondary activity would have been welcome in Italy as the third and final stage in the stabilization of southern Alamannia. Again contrary to the impression given by Ammianus and adopted by modern commentators,[43] his 356 campaign may be regarded as a success. However, continued Roman toleration of the trans-Rhine settlement must have been interpreted by the Alamanni as full licence, which explains their dismay at what happened in 357.

The 357 campaigns were the most famous of Julian's career. Ammianus tells us that, during the winter of 356/7, Julian was blockaded in Senon by hostile barbarians. When the *magister equitum*, Marcellus, refused to come to his aid, Julian complained to Constantius II, who

---

[38] Below 342–3.
[39] Lorenz, S. (1997: 37–8); cf. below 247–8.
[40] AM 16.12.6. Below 225, 229.
[41] Above 130, below 250, Fig. 21.
[42] Below 238–9.
[43] Cf. Lorenz, S. (1997: 38).

cashiered Marcellus. Marcellus appealed, but Constantius stood by his decision.[44] Julian then moved to Reims, where the older and more tractable Severus was now in charge of the assembled Gallic army, which numbered some 13,000. Meanwhile, Constantius' *magister peditum*, Barbatio, brought a force of 25,000 (Libanius: 30,000) from Italy to Kaiseraugst. The plan was to drive the rampaging Alamanni 'into straits' as with a 'pair of pliers'.[45] However, *laeti* slipped between both armies and attacked Lyon. They were driven off, and Julian broke them on their return, but they were not destroyed by Barbatio.[46] At the same time, Alamanni living west of the Rhine, alarmed by the approach of the Roman armies, blockaded the roads and fled to islands in the Rhine.[47] Julian asked for seven ships from Barbatio (of those which Barbatio had collected for building pontoon bridges over the Rhine), but he was refused, and Barbatio burned all his vessels. Julian, however, found his own way of taking the islands and butchered all he could. The survivors fled east.[48] Julian re-garrisoned the fort at Saverne/Tres Tabernae, important for controlling access to central Gaul, and then, from headquarters in Strasbourg, prepared a major campaign.[49] Barbatio was hit by a surprise attack of the Alamanni and thrown back to Kaiseraugst and even beyond. He lost his baggage train and camp-followers. He abandoned the campaign and returned to Constantius highly critical of Julian.[50] Encouraged by Barbatio's failure, seven kings of the Alamanni united under Chnodomarius and commanded Julian 'to depart from the lands which they had won by valour and the sword'.[51] Julian derided their presumption and detained their envoys. He advanced against the Alamannic forces and precipitated, 'against his will' (his soldiers were keen, as was Florentius, the praetorian prefect), the battle of Strasbourg.[52] This was a hard-fought but glorious victory.[53] Julian was hailed as Augustus, but refused the honour.[54] Chnodomarius was captured, but Julian spared him and sent him to Constantius, who exiled him to Rome.[55]

[44] AM 16.4.1–3, 7.1–3, 8.1.
[45] AM 16.11.1–3, 12.2; Libanius, *Orat.* 18.49–50.   [46] AM 16.11.4–7.
[47] AM 16.11.8.   [48] AM 16.11.8–10.
[49] AM 16.11–12; 16.12.1. Geuenich (1997a: 46).   [50] AM 16.11.14–15.
[51] AM 16.12.1–4.   [52] AM 16.12.7–19.
[53] AM 16.12.20–63.   [54] AM 16.12.64–6.   [55] AM 16.12.65.

Julian pressed on. Having freed the Alamannic envoys,[56] he moved to Mainz, where he bridged the Rhine and invaded Alamannic territory in the western Wetterau.[57] The Alamanni, thunderstruck ('since they little expected that they could be molested, settled as they were in undisturbed peace'), first attempted to treat ('they sent envoys with set speeches to declare the harmonious validity of the treaties with them'), but then changed their minds and demanded withdrawal.[58] Julian trapped them in an obscure but effective pincer movement of his own devising.[59] As his forces pillaged and destroyed at will, some Alamanni living north of the Main fled to join those to the south.[60] Other Alamannic forces were, however, still hiding in the forest north of the Main, and Julian proceeded against them.[61] After marching for about 10 miles, he found the road blocked with felled timber.[62] He withdrew and re-garrisoned a *munimentum* (usually translated as 'fort') built by Trajan, 'which of late had been very forcibly assaulted'.[63] This caused the Alamanni finally to sue for peace. A 10-month agreement was made with 'three kings'—'very savage'—who had sent aid to those who had been vanquished at Strasbourg. These also agreed to respect and even provision the fort.[64] Julian then withdrew.[65] The autumnal equinox had passed around the time that he had been dealing with the *munimentum Traiani*,[66] so it was now late in the year, but this was not the end of his campaigning. En route to winter quarters in Paris, Julian laid siege to 600 Frankish raiders. These had seized the opportunity to attack while Julian was busy among the Alamanni and now fled to two abandoned forts on the

---

[56] AM 17.1.1.

[57] AM 17.1.2.

[58] AM 17.1.3.

[59] AM 17.1.4–5. This account is difficult, and possibly corrupted: de Jonge (1977: 11); Lorenz, S. (1997: 51).

[60] AM 17.1.6–7.

[61] AM 17.1.8.

[62] AM 17.1.8–9.

[63] AM 17.1.11: *dudum violentius oppugnatum*. See, e.g. Barceló (1981: 37): 'eine alte, längst verlassene traianische Festung'; but contrast Zotz (1998: 404): 'das Siegesdenkmal Traians'. (At AM 28.2.2, *munimentum* clearly means 'fort'.)

[64] AM 17.1.12–13: *immanissimi*.

[65] AM 17.2.1.

[66] AM 17.1.10.

Meuse. Julian besieged them for 54 days, from December into January. Having worn them down, he captured them, and sent them to Constantius.[67]

The chronology of these campaigns is not too difficult to establish. From Ammianus' references to the Rhine's running low and Roman confiscation of Alamannic harvests[68] it is clear that events leading up to the battle of Strasbourg occurred in high summer or early autumn. We can assume that Julian, and probably Barbatio, set out in early July.[69] Julian was campaigning on the Main well into autumn, which suggests that he crossed the Rhine at Mainz at the end of September.[70] He engaged the Franks for most of December 357 and January 358.

Less easy to answer is why major campaigning was scheduled for 357 at all. In 356, Julian, Marcellus and Ursicinus had successfully reoccupied the Rhineland. There will have remained much to be done, including difficult police work against deserters, bandits, petty outlaws and renegade barbarians, but this surely did not require a second campaign. Likewise, in 357 Constantius began to move eastwards. After a short visit to Rome, from 28 April to 29 May, he left for the Danube. From the start he headed north-eastwards, via Ravenna, well away from the route to Alamannia which he never saw again.[71] Why therefore, while Constantius was still in Italy, were two full[72] armies ordered into the Rhine valley, one under the imperial heir and the other under the Empire's most senior general, in a move which must have been long in the planning and directly authorized by the emperor?

Despite Ammianus' reference to 'Alamanni raging beyond their customary manner and ranging more afield',[73] there was no major Alamannic warlike activity at this time. The identity of the 'hostiles' who attacked Julian at Senon is just as obscure as that of those who harassed him on his way from Vienne to Reims, and the threat they posed probably just as exaggerated. Julian and his circle probably

---

[67] AM 17.2.1–3.
[68] Below 236.
[69] Lorenz, S. (1997: 40).
[70] Lorenz, S. (1997: 51).
[71] AM 16.10.20. Barnes (1993: 222). Ammianus' account of 'Suebic' raiding into Raetia presumably relates to Juthungi, dealt with by Barbatio in 358: AM 17.6. Cf. above 48 and below 242.
[72] For their sizes, see below 238; for their relatively great strength see Elton (1996a: 211).
[73] AM 16.11.3: *saevientes ultra solitum Alamanni vagantesque fusius.*

made more of the 'siege' than it merited in order to destroy Marcellus
and so improve their political position. The remorseless but, from
their point of view, indispensable efforts of Julian and his small circle
of friends in Gaul to turn the Caesar from figurehead into undis-
puted ruler of the west are too complex to be examined here, but they
drove all his dealings with the Alamanni. However, throughout this
period Julian, while doing all that was necessary, could never bring
himself to admit that he was moving towards revolt, and so for the
direct promotion of his cause relied on a few intimates. This explains
the use, in what follows, of phrases such as 'Julian and his circle',
'Julian and his advisers' and 'Julian and his supporters'.[74] More to the
point, after the success of the 356 campaigns, there is no sign of any
established Alamannic leader seeking trouble early in 357. The hostile
'grand alliance' of seven kings that Julian confronted at the battle of
Strasbourg was formed later, under different circumstances.

   The first Roman 'pincer movement' cannot have been an act of
unprovoked aggression. This would have been inconsistent with
Constantius' usual handling of Alamanni; and certainly the last
thing that he would have wanted at this time was the eruption of
full-scale war in or around Alamannia. As he returned east he needed
to leave Italy feeling safe. That Constantius planned an all-out attack,
as stated by Libanius,[75] helps justify Julian's actions to come but does
not fit contemporary circumstances. One can only conclude that the
original intention of the joint expedition was a massive display of
strength. But to what purpose, given events since 354 which had
restored Roman control over the Rhine and established a series of
alliances with Alamannic leaders? The most likely answer is that over
the winter of 356/7, perhaps influenced by information fed to him by
Julian's circle,[76] Constantius had changed his mind about Alamannic
settlement on the left bank. This had become a political embarrassment, and one that he was eager to be rid of without delay.[77] He

---

[74] Drinkwater (1983b: 372–4); cf. Matthews (1989: 84–100, esp. 93–4).

[75] Libanius, *Orat.* 18.49.

[76] The most likely agent is the eunuch, Eutherius, sent to Constantius' court to
defend Julian against Marcellus: AM 16.7.1.

[77] As Whittaker (1994: 61) notes, 'Jurisprudentially, the more powerful nation
always demands rights over the far bank.' The opposite, the giving away of rights to
the nearer bank of the Rhine, could never have been a popular policy.

could not risk war in Alamannia, but by staging a huge demonstration of military power he might compel a bloodless withdrawal. Negotiated and peaceful Alamannic evacuation of the left bank, accompanied by fresh treaties, might also retain the goodwill of communities concerned.

In Constantius' plan, much importance was clearly given to the building of the Rhine bridge, since Barbatio departed soon after this had become impossible. This raises further questions, concerning the route that Barbatio took to reach the site of the bridge, its precise function, and the reason it was never built. In this respect, Ammianus is supplemented by Libanius, in a long, rhetorically powerful, but in historical terms somewhat loose and disjointed document, presented as a funeral oration for Julian.[78] Ammianus has Barbatio proceeding to Kaiseraugst, but is obscure about his journey beyond this point. Libanius believed that Barbatio marched along the left bank of the Rhine all the way north to Julian. He says that the plan was to join forces with Julian and then build a bridge to carry the combined army over the Rhine. This failed when the Alamanni destroyed the bridge by floating tree trunks down-river against it.[79] Libanius' reconstruction is followed by most historians who have dealt closely with these events,[80] but it has difficulties.

First, how may we explain the attacks that Barbatio suffered as he retraced his steps, therefore on Roman territory, back to Kaiseraugst, and beyond?[81] Apart from the sortie made by *laeti*, there is no sign that Alamanni caused trouble in Alsace in 356 or 357: our sources indicate activity only north of Strasbourg. What we know makes better sense if we assume that, from Kaiseraugst, Barbatio turned due north, crossing the Rhine and marching along its right bank. This was a shorter route, well-known and, to judge from the coin-finds, well-used.[82] For most of its length it will have been secured by the treaties struck with Gundomadus and Vadomarius in 354. When

[78] Libanius, *Orat.* 18.

[79] Libanius, *Orat.* 18.49–51.

[80] Seeck (1921: 4.257); Jullian (1926: 191–2); Bidez (1930: 149–50); Browning (1975: 84–5); Bowersock (1978: 40–1); Lorenz, S. (1997: 40–1).

[81] Libanius, *Orat.* 18.51; AM 16.11.14. Cf. the doubts expressed by Rosen (1970: 91–2).

[82] Above 129.

Barbatio withdrew, he headed home by the same, still fairly secure, route. The burning of his boats and supplies suggests considered action and the time to carry this out: tales of a hasty and ignominious flight can be ignored.[83] Barbatio does, however, appear to have run into some trouble. This was probably nuisance raiding on the rear of his column (where he would have stationed the baggage train and camp-followers mentioned by Ammianus[84]) by Alamanni resident on the right bank reacting to apparent Roman weakness and, probably more importantly, to news of Julian's first atrocities. Such raiding occurred despite recent treaties, but southern Romano-Alamannic relations deteriorated very quickly in 357 as Gundomadus and Vadomarius were pressured by their own people to give help to their neighbours.[85] Ammianus, indeed, hints that Barbatio experienced such trouble in the south, towards the end of his journey as he neared Kaiseraugst: a possible indication of the location of the territory of Gundomadus, soon to be killed by his fellow countrymen.[86]

Barbatio's bridge was meant to serve a crucial purpose, or series of purposes. As the 'pinch point' of the Roman 'pliers', it would have allowed the two armies to join forces. However, it would also have allowed Roman troops to operate in tandem along each bank, intimidating settlers and their supporters alike. Further, it would have displayed Roman power and expertise on a stretch of the Rhine, downstream of Strasbourg,[87] that was not normally served by a bridge. Finally, it could have served as a way of removing Alamannic

---

[83] AM 16.11.14; Libanius, *Orat.* 18.51. Lorenz, S. (1997: 42); below 235.

[84] AM 16.11.14. Cf. Elton (1996a: 244). At 16.12.4, Ammianus notes Alamannic satisfaction at Barbatio's being defeated 'by a few of their brigands': *paucis suorum latronibus*.

[85] AM 16.12.17.

[86] Though AM 18.2.16 tells us that Vadomarius was 'over against the Rauraci' (*cuius erat domicilium contra Rauracos*), i.e. presumably, opposite Kaiseraugst, this was later, after the death of Gundomadus, when Vadomarius is likely to have inherited his brother's position. I do not follow Lorenz, S. (1997: 42 and n.128) who interprets Ammianus' *Gallicum vallum* as a sort of Maginot Line. As Rolfe puts it, in his Loeb translation (1963: 263), the phrase must mean just 'Gallic camp', i.e. Julian's army, now far distant from Barbatio's rear. Cf. 16.11.6: *vallum Barbationis*.

[87] Ammianus' description of the river at this point fits that of Höckmann (1986: 384–7) of the stretch between the Murg-confluence and Oppenheim.

settlers to the right bank swiftly, securely and with the minimum of fuss. Barbatio's failure to complete the bridge made it impossible for him to carry out his orders and so precipitated his withdrawal.

As for Barbatio's failure, modern historians are happy to follow Libanius' story of the floating trunks; but this is far from satisfactory. The construction of the bridge should have been easy. It was high summer[88] and the Rhine was running low and, presumably, slow: no major obstacle to engineering work. There is no sign of bad weather. The Roman army was present in force, therefore security in the immediate vicinity of the site should have been tight and warning of potential trouble further afield would be available in good time. An Alamannic party noisily cutting and dressing the tree trunks would have been very exposed and, because the river was low and non-canalized (we have to imagine the broad extent, countless meanders, multiple courses, shifting main bed, oxbow lakes, dead ends and marshy meads of the old Rhine between Strasbourg and Mainz[89]), would have faced problems in getting the trunks to deep channels. (One may note the difficulties that Chnodomarius experienced, during his attempted flight after the battle of Strasbourg, in attempting to cross the river on horseback.[90]) Once launched, the trunks would have run slow, would have run the risk of grounding, jamming those behind; and they would have been easy to spot and deal with in the long summer days. The further away the felling party was to hide its noise, the more awkward such difficulties would have been. And anyway, the bridge should have been easy to protect with a simple rope or chain boom—in modern military engineering, a routine precaution against floating weaponry and natural débris.[91] An Alamannic plan to destroy the bridge by floating down logs against it would therefore have been a long shot, and the assertion that it was one which worked is very odd.

Therefore what did happen in the first phase of the 357 campaign? I propose the following. The two armies made for their rendezvous

[88] AM 16.11.11, 14; cf. 16.12.19.
[89] See, e.g. Höckmann (1986: 369, 385–7); Bechert (2003: 1).
[90] AM 16.12.59.
[91] I am grateful for this and other important points concerning Barbatio's bridge to Lt. Col. R. G. Holdsworth T.D., R.E. (ret'd).

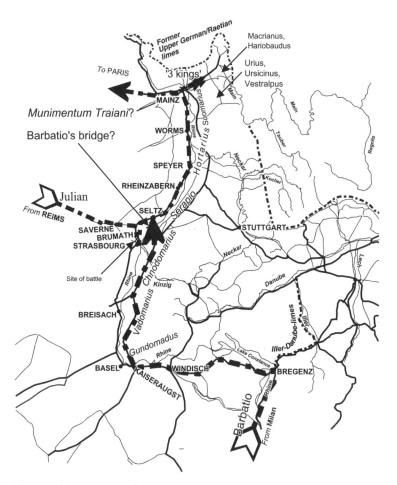

Fig. 19 The 357 campaigns.

point (Fig. 19). Barbatio's, the larger, coming from further afield and intended to do most of the work, was well supplied. It brought its own boats for bridge building, and its own rations. The boats we know of from Ammianus.[92] The rations may be deduced from Ammianus' story of Barbatio's later 'stealing' food from Julian's army:[93] he took on supplies from Gaul to replenish those he had consumed en route. This further suggests that the southern army did not, and never intended to, live off the land, in deference to Alamanni, both those bound by treaty and maybe even those further north whom Rome hoped to persuade to evacuate settlers from the left bank. The two armies met, as planned, north of Strasbourg. An advance force from Barbatio's army, which included the tribunes Bainobaudes and Valentinian (the future emperor), crossed the Rhine, presumably to prepare for the building of the bridge and to arrange for fresh supplies.[94] It is clear that these two were answerable to Barbatio, not Julian.[95] However, from the start there was tension between Julian and Barbatio because of their different personalities and experiences.[96] Added to this, Julian, for his own ends, determined to be uncooperative. This lack of harmony was first demonstrated in the laetic 'raid' on Lyon.[97] This is a very opaque episode, the opacity of which is not relieved by Ammianus' partisan attitude. Barbatio seems to have accepted the responsibility for not finishing off the troublemakers, whoever these were, by having the field commanders concerned, Bainobaudes and Valentinian, cashiered.[98] However, he cannot be blamed for the whole affair, in particular for not closing the Belfort Gap,[99] since the security of the left bank would have been the responsibility of Severus and Julian. Then followed the mysterious destruction and abandonment of the bridge.

If we accept Libanius' account, a fair number of trunks must have been cut and launched successfully and have reached the bridge; and those that got through must have caused enormous damage, not just

---

[92] AM 16.11.8.   [93] AM 16.11.12.   [94] AM 16.11.6.

[95] AM 16.11.5–6. Browning (1975: 84); Lenski (2002: 49). *Contra* Rosen (1970: 85); Lorenz, S. (1997: 40); Raimondi (2001: 24).

[96] Rosen (1970: 94); Lorenz, S. (1997: 40–1 and n. 117): Barbatio had been involved in the trial of Gallus.

[97] Above 167.

[98] AM 16.11.7.

[99] *Contra* Lorenz, S. (1997: 40).

displacing boats, which could have been retrieved, but also staving in the sides of a significant number and making them useless. This could have happened only as the result of a (from the Roman point of view) catastrophic accident: the concatenation of freaks of chance and human carelessness.

As one possible alternative to Alamannic action one is bound to consider Roman sabotage, with both parties suspect. It was clearly in the interest of Julian and his circle for the two armies not to combine for this would have given overall command to Barbatio (the most senior officer, responsible to the senior emperor). Equally, Barbatio himself, sensing that if he crossed he was bound to clash with Julian and perhaps suffer a fate similar to that of Marcellus, may have looked for a way to end his part in the campaign swiftly and without shame. However, by combining reciprocal Roman ill-will with what we know about Romano-Alamannic exploitation of the resources of the Rhineland,[100] and taking into account that, although Libanius implies that the 'barbarians' involved were hostile, he never explicitly says so, it is possible to advance a less dramatic but more plausible hypothesis.

This is that of an industrial accident, the impact of which was exaggerated to suit both Julian's and Barbatio's disinclination to proceed with the campaign as planned by Constantius. Barbatio brought boats to form the pontoons of his bridge, but he need not have brought the large timbers necessary to construct its superstructure. These he could have commissioned from the *pagi* of Gundomadus and Vadomarius. The wood would have been cut upstream, and floated down to the construction site. It would not have mattered if Alamannic working parties operated close by or at some distance. If close, they would have been accepted as friendly; if distant, they would have been able to transport the material to the best channels and to guide it down to where it was needed openly and without hindrance, probably with the trunks lashed together to form rafts. Any protective boom would have been raised on the news of an incoming consignment. All engineering work has its risks, and one may imagine a raft running out of control as it neared its goal and smashing into the unfinished bridge. The damage could have been repaired, but Julian and Barbatio welcomed it as a means of distancing themselves from each other. The bridge was

[100] Above 133–5, below 243.

abandoned with both sides blaming a handy scapegoat, the Alamanni, now cast as dangerous enemies not helpful allies. Barbatio then, ostensibly following Constantius' instructions not to endanger his forces unnecessarily[101] and to avoid provoking a full-scale war with the Alamanni, ordered withdrawal. Quite properly, before returning south he burned his surviving boats and the large amounts of supplies he had on the right bank of the river.[102] His departure must have convinced the Alamanni, who by now would have discovered what the Romans were planning, that they had won:[103] that Constantius had backed down and that they could keep their left-bank land. However, their relief was premature, for Julian had decided to break them.

Whoever was responsible for the abandonment of the bridge, this was an important turning point. Barbatio must have assumed that his departure would put an end to the whole campaign. When Julian showed signs of wanting to remain in the field by asking Barbatio for surviving boats and supplies, Barbatio refused.[104] He then began his own march back. It was towards the end of this march (and not, as Ammianus' text suggests, while he was still close to Julian) that his rearguard came under attack from supposed allied Alamanni, disturbed at what Julian was doing in his absence. This order of events is important, since it implies that Barbatio saw no point in killing Alamanni for its own sake. Julian, however, had already put a different interpretation on the situation—treating Alamannic removal of non-combatants to the Rhine islands not as pacific prudence but as a declaration of war, freeing the hands of those left behind. Once Barbatio was well on his way, and managing without boats, he launched an unprovoked attack on the islands, causing great slaughter of both sexes, 'without distinction of age, like so many sheep'.[105] Then he went to Strasbourg to plan his next move.[106]

From Strasbourg he supervised the rebuilding of the fort at Saverne, put in hand after the massacres on the islands.[107] This should not have been a problem to neighbouring Alamannic settlers

[101] Rosen (1970: 91); Lorenz, S. (1997: 42).
[102] Boats: 16.11.8; supplies: 16.11.12.
[103] So Lorenz, S. (1997: 44).
[104] AM 16.11.8, 12.
[105] AM 16.11.9: *sine aetatis ullo discrimine... ut pecudes.*
[106] AM 16.12.1.
[107] AM 16.11.11, 16.12.1. Geuenich (1997a: 46).

as obedient inhabitants of the Empire. However, their passions must have been roused by the murder of their dependants; and (on the excuse that nothing had been got from Barbatio) they now faced the large-scale requisitioning of supplies from their stores.[108] Even worse, these supplies were destined not only for the garrison of the fort, but also for the Gallic army as a whole, keeping it on campaign and so a likely threat to themselves. Julian was now treating the Alamanni like dirt, set on provoking them into what Constantius had sedulously avoided, pitched battle.[109]

It is, indeed, only after Julian's refortification of Saverne and his associated demands that Ammianus first mentions the alliance of seven Alamannic kings against him: Chnodomarius, Vestralpus, Urius, Ursicinus, Serapio, Suomarius and Hortarius.[110] They are depicted as arrogant and warlike. This may be explained as resulting from confidence generated by the departure of Barbatio.[111] On the other hand, it is odd that the Alamanni made their demand so late. If they were as bellicose and prepared as the sources would have us believe, why did they not try to deal as a group with Barbatio? The fact that they postponed this until they were left alone with Julian suggests that originally they had no plans for joint action and therefore none for wholesale resistance, and had been prepared to deal with Barbatio *rex* by *rex*. They were probably panicked into an alliance by Julian's unexpected aggression.

Likewise, the sources make much of Chnodomarius, the supposed ringleader, who took great heart from Barbatio's 'defeat'.[112] Ammianus goes out of his way to denigrate Chnodomarius as a troublemaker, referring to his defeat of Decentius and associating this with the recent wasting of Gaul and the routing of Barbatio.[113] It may be said that Ammianus makes Chnodomarius Vercingetorix to Julian's Julius

---

[108] AM 16.11.12: *ex barbaris messibus*; Libanius, *Orat.* 18.52.

[109] Rosen (1970: 106–7, 110); Barceló (1981: 35); Zotz (1998: 394–5). *Contra* Geuenich (1997a: 53), arguing for the unimportance of the battle of Strasbourg in absolute terms.

[110] AM 16.12.1–2. Barceló (1981: 35); Lorenz, S. (1997: 44); Zotz (1998: 394). Cf. Rosen (1970: 105–6), for the view that the alliance was forged even later than this, after Julian's rejection of the envoys.

[111] Zotz (1998: 394–5).

[112] AM 16.12.4: *princeps audendi periculosa*; cf. 16.12.24: *incentor.*

[113] AM 16.12.5–6, 61.

Caesar. But whereas Vercingetorix was a noble figure, Chnodomarius is a crude bully,[114] outfaced by the heroic Julian. All this suggests that we should see Chnodomarius as much as a literary construct as a historical figure. He is magnified through his conflict with Julian, who needed a redoubtable foe. It may be noted that Chnodomarius' defeat of Decentius is mentioned for the first time in this context, with no sign that Ammianus had touched on it before.[115] The 'defeat' of Decentius may therefore have been exaggerated, along with the force that Chnodomarius would have needed to face him 'on equal terms'.[116] The forces that opposed Julian after Barbatio's departure were probably nowhere near as menacing as the Julianic tradition relates. A hastily assembled alliance of disparate Alamannic *regna*, with no tradition of combined operations, would have been no match for a professional Roman army and a leader inexperienced but resolved and, above all, lucky, who was set on winning a great victory. Julian was certainly not interested in peace. He ignored likely documentary justification for Alamannic settlement; and his detention of the envoys amounted to a breach of international law.[117] It was a declaration of war, and led directly to the battle of Strasbourg.

The site of this battle has been identified as being near Oberhausbergen, *c.*3 km north-west of Strasbourg, on the road to Brumath. It was fought towards the end of August.[118] I will not go into the fighting, which has been the subject of numerous studies,[119] but will address three particular issues.

The first is that of Alamannic numbers. Ammianus says that the combined Alamannic army amounted to 35,000 men.[120] Some commentators sidestep the question of his reliability,[121] others simply accept his figure,[122] and still others dispute 35,000 as grossly

---

[114] Cf. Rosen (1970: 120–1).

[115] AM 16.12.5: *aequo Marte congressus.*

[116] Cf. below 337.

[117] Bowersock (1978: 71); Lorenz, S. (1997: 44).

[118] Lorenz, S. (1997: 47–8).

[119] See most recently Elton (1996a: 255–6), accepting Ammianus' figures of the number of combatants.

[120] AM 16.12.26: *armatorumque milia triginta et quinque, ex variis nationibus partim mercede, partim pacto vicissitudinis reddendae quaesita.*

[121] e.g. Zotz (1998: 395).

[122] e.g. Elton (1996a: 255); Geuenich (1997a: 44).

exaggerated, intended as usual to point up Julian's success.[123] Much ink has been spilled in attempting to resolve the issue.[124] I believe that 35,000 is too high, in line with Ammianus' emphasis on Alamannic populousness at this point, a concept rejected above.[125] What it should be reduced to is impossible to say with certainty, but an approximation may be made by taking into account the strategic and tactical context.

Ammianus says that Barbatio's army was 25,000 strong and Julian's 13,000, giving a total of 38,000.[126] These figures are comparable with Libanius' 30,000, 15,000 and 45,000 respectively,[127] and are likely to be more trustworthy than those for the Alamanni since the Roman commanders and commissariat will have needed to know them, and they will have been remembered by those concerned (and were perhaps even available on record) when Ammianus did his research for his 'History'. If Constantius' aim was to terrorize the Alamanni into a peaceful withdrawal, he would have taken care to give Barbatio and Julian overwhelming military superiority. Estimating this as an advantage in manpower of at least 3:1, the maximum envisaged Alamannic strength was *c.*13,000. Where were these men expected to come from? Presumably, in the first instance they would have been recruited from the *pagi* of the seven kings and from those of the upper and middle Neckar, leaned on by Constantius in 356: say nine *pagi* in all. A third-century raiding-band was about 600 strong.[128] Allowing that more settled conditions may have increased numbers and provided the opportunity to draw on veterans, this figure may be raised to around 1,000 fighting men per *pagus*. This produces a 'core' force of around 9,000. But a prudent commander-in-chief would also have feared recruitment further afield in Alamannia and the Elbgermanic triangle. Ammianus says that the army of 35,000 was raised 'from various nations, partly for pay and partly under agreement to return

[123] e.g. Stroheker (1975: 36): 'sicher übertrieben'. Cf. Lorenz, S. (1997: 45); Guzmán Armario (2002: 167), citing Dubois (1912).

[124] For useful reviews see Rosen (1970: 110–14); Lorenz, S. (1997: 45 and n.47).

[125] Cf. AM 16.12.6: *populosae gentes*; above 141–2.

[126] AM 16.11.2, 12.2.

[127] Libanius, *Orat.* 18.49, 54.

[128] Above 49.

the service'.[129] This does not suit the likely terms under which full *pagus* levies followed *optimates* and *reges*, but fits the wider engagement of individuals and smaller bands,[130] which gives the extra 4,000. Numbers at Strasbourg turned out to be larger. The core fighters were joined by those of Vadomarius and Gundomadus,[131] say another 2,000, bringing the army opposing Julian to *c.*15,000: indeed a larger force than his, but nowhere near three times its size.

The second issue is that of the Alamannic cavalry. The main body of Alamanni at Strasbourg comprised infantry. Indeed, these troops compelled Chnodomarius and other *regales* to dismount before the battle.[132] However, the Alamanni also deployed cavalry, which almost broke the Roman line.[133] The failure of his cavalry was a great embarrassment to Julian, and his rallying and then exemplary punishment of these troopers figures prominently in the sources.[134] This was probably the reason for Aurelius Victor's exculpatory reference to Alamannic populousness and ability as horse-soldiers.[135] Finally, Ammianus' report of Chnodomarius' capture makes mention of the large retinue that was taken with him—200 followers and three close friends.[136] This offers a glimpse into the working of Alamannic society.[137] (It is likely that Chnodomarius' colleague and nephew, Serapio, was also taken prisoner at this time.[138])

According to Ammianus, Strasbourg was a triumph of Roman discipline and Julian's inspired leadership over Germanic fury. It was followed by the ethnic cleansing of the left bank: all Alamanni were removed from 'our' territory.[139] Constantius II, as

---

[129] AM 16.12.26: *ex variis nationibus partim mercede, partim pacto vicissitudinis reddendae.*

[130] Above 163–6.

[131] Above 156.

[132] AM 16.12.34–5.

[133] AM 16.12.21, 37–8. Elton, S. (1996a: 255–6).

[134] AM 16.12.38–41; Zosimus 3.3.4–5; cf. Libanius, *Orat.* 18.56–9, 56. Rosen (1970: 126); Lorenz, S. (1997: 48–9).

[135] Above 141–2, 175–6.

[136] AM 16.12.60.

[137] Above 120.

[138] Libanius, *Orat.* 18.67. *PLRE* 1.824; Lorenz, S. (1997: 50 and n.170); cf. below 253. Whether the five other kings also fought themselves or only sent help is debated: Rosen (1970: 112); Lorenz, S. (1997: 45 and n.142); cf. Zotz (1998: 395).

[139] AM 17.11.2.

commander-in-chief, ultimately responsible for all military activities in the Empire, rightly took credit for his Caesar's success;[140] but he did not go out of his way to celebrate the event. There is no sign of his iteration of his earlier *Germanicus Maximus/Alamannicus* titles; and at Sirmium, Constantius' headquarters from 357 to 359, the imperial mint produced no victory issues.[141] This may indicate unease on Constantius' part: certainly at Julian's success, but perhaps also at Roman treatment of Alamanni who had helped him defeat Magnentius. The relatively lenient treatment of Chnodomarius as, later, that of Vadomarius, both clients of Constantius, is to be noticed.[142]

But Julian was not finished. His continuation of his campaign should not be eclipsed by Strasbourg. If he had been simply bent on pursuing the survivors of Strasbourg,[143] he should have crossed the Rhine into the immediately adjacent *pagi*, the territories of Chnodomarius, Serapio, Hortarius and Suomarius.[144] His march northwards, keeping to the left bank, will have convinced the Alamanni that he was leaving by the same route as he had taken the previous year. His sudden foray over the Mainz bridge into the Wetterau must have come as an enormous shock.

To judge from the chronology and pattern of their settlement in an important military area and from the pattern of local coin use,[145] it is likely that the Alamanni of this region were very close to Rome. The three kings who made peace with Julian had aided their neighbours to the south only after the battle of Strasbourg.[146] Libanius' reference to Julian's restoration of 'the two greatest cities' of the Rhineland must be to Cologne and Mainz.[147] Assuming that it was the former

[140] AM 16.12.68–70; cf. Aurelius Victor, *Caesares* 42.13.
[141] *RIC* 8.346, 382.
[142] Cf. below 251–2.
[143] So Geuenich (1997a: 48).
[144] Geuenich (1997a: 45): Chnodomarius and Serapio in the Ortenau, just across from Strasbourg; Lorenz, S. (1997: 38): between Karlsruhe and Strasbourg. Cf. below 243.
[145] Above 83, 88–9, 129–30.
[146] AM 17.1.13. I recognize that the orthodox interpretation of the phrase *qui misere victis apud Argentoratum auxilia* is that it describes those 'who had sent troops to Chnodomarius at Strasburg' (Elliott (1983: 82)). For *auxilia* as 'aid', not 'military support', see de Jonge (1977: 33).
[147] Libanius, *Orat.* 18.46.

that was 'in ruins as the result of a single recent attack',[148] we may envisage the latter as having 'been harried by countless inroads' and having 'become completely destitute', but not as having fallen under barbarian control, that is local Alamanni had left it alone.[149] Julian's attack threw them into total confusion, and exposed them to mindless raiding. This is the context of Roman destruction of 'Alamannic' villas, not far from the Mainz bridgehead, which may have been Roman property.[150]

That Julian was operating in a normally pacific area is also suggested by his restoration of the fort. We know that this was not far along his route (possibly the Friedberg road),[151] and it had recently been in use.[152] This, and Julian's regarrisoning of the place, suggests that it could not have been impossibly remote or vulnerable. Like Valentinian's fortified beaching areas over the Rhine, it may have been on a river—the Main or one of its tributaries—and therefore accessible to Roman warships.[153] We should note Julian's use of the Main as a highway in his pincer attack.[154] Lorenz's location of the structure in the vicinity of Frankfurt-am-Main is attractive.[155] As Matthews has pointed out, its 'Trajanic' dating could well be apocryphal.[156] What we may have is evidence for a regular Roman military presence in the Wetterau after the evacuation of the *limes*.[157]

The 'peace' that Julian secured was hardly wrenched from a mighty enemy. His aim in terrorizing innocent Alamanni must have been to demonstrate that he was now a power to be reckoned with. Even his agreement with the Wetterau-Alamanni may be seen as threatening. Ten months is an odd length of time; but it meant that the peace expired around 1 August 358, at the height of the next campaigning season: if the Alamanni did not abide by the agreement, Julian would

[148] Cf. above 208, 214–15.
[149] Above 84, 218–19.
[150] Above 85, 134–5.
[151] AM 17.1.8–9. Cf. above 129–30.
[152] AM 17.1.11.
[153] For Valentinian see below 295–302; for Julian's appreciation of naval power see Höckmann (1986: 414).
[154] de Jonge (1977: 11); Lorenz, S. (1997: 51 and n. 178).
[155] Lorenz, S. (1997: 52 and n.181).
[156] Matthews (1989: 310).
[157] Above 132.

be back in force.[158] An alternative explanation, equally aggressive, is that the Alamanni were put under orders not to interfere with the fort while it was empty in winter.[159] Again, we see Julian beginning a new phase in Romano-Alamannic dealings. He was not, as Lorenz would have it, simply continuing Constantius II's defensive strategy albeit 'with élan and verve', but rather, as Jankowski and others have said, going on the offensive,[160] as he did immediately against the Franks and would do so against both Franks and Alamanni in 358.

In 358, Constantius fought Sarmatians and Quadi. He was less violent than Julian was to be with Franks and Alamanni, controlling not crushing his enemies, and making peace.[161] In the same year, Iuthungi ravaged Raetia. These are probably the 'Suebi', whose attacks on Raetia were one of the reasons why Constantius left Rome in 357.[162] They were easily dealt with by Barbatio.[163]

In Gaul, Julian, wintering in Paris, was keen to come to grips with the Alamanni, who were 'not yet assembled into one body but were all venturesome and cruel to the point of madness after the battle of Strasbourg'.[164] Not waiting until the opening of the regular campaigning season, in July, Julian struck in late May or early June.[165] First, however, he directed himself against the Salian Franks, now settled in Toxiandria, whom he treated very roughly to obtain their absolute obedience. Chamavian Franks, attempting similarly to settle in the Empire, he expelled.[166] He then repaired three forts on the Marne, but ran into trouble with his own troops because of food shortages.[167]

Finally, he began his Alamannic campaign. He built a pontoon bridge and crossed the Rhine, but was hampered by a loss of nerve on

[158] Cf. Libanius, *Orat.* 18.47: after apparently conflating the three kings of Ammianus' account into one Alamannic leader, Libanius explains the short peace as 'rendering him better disposed through fear of what might follow'.

[159] Cf. below 301–2.

[160] Lorenz, S. (1997: 50–1 and n.174 (with wider references), 53).

[161] AM 17.12.

[162] AM 16.10.20. Above 48.

[163] AM 17.6.

[164] AM 17.8.1: *nondum in unum coactos*.

[165] AM 17.8.1–2.

[166] AM 17.8.3–5. Cf. above 200.

[167] AM 17.9.1–5.

the part of Severus.[168] Then Suomarius, an Alamannic king, turned up with his force and, despite his previous hostility at Strasbourg, made peace. He was allowed this on condition that he give up his Roman captives and supply Roman troops with food, as required, 'receiving security, just like an ordinary contractor'.[169] After this, Julian ferociously attacked the territory of Hortarius, another of Chnodomarius' helpers at the battle of Strasbourg, forcing him to sue for peace. Julian granted this on conditions, relating especially to the release of prisoners.[170] But Hortarius held some back. Therefore, when Hortarius was visiting him to receive gifts, Julian arrested four of his *comites*,[171] and in a personal confrontation, forced him to free the rest. He was also compelled to promise carts and timber from his own resources and those of his subjects. He could not supply grain because of the damage done to his country. At the end of a successful campaign, Julian went into winter quarters.[172]

The Alamannic phase of Julian's campaign appears to have taken place in late summer or early autumn 358.[173] He crossed the Rhine into Suomarius' territory, probably just south of Mainz. He then moved further south, up-river, into Hortarius' territory, possibly the Kraichgau, opposite Worms and Speyer. From the Rhine crossing this route would have taken him to Groß-Gerau and then along the old Roman highway by way of Ladenburg to beyond Heidelberg and the border of the territory of Serapio[174] (Fig. 20).

It appears that Julian was continuing to exploit the Alamanni to win a military reputation and political strength. As the difficulties over supplies revealed, despite his success at Strasbourg his troops were still reluctant to follow him without question. He had the excuse of needing to punish those who opposed him in 357, and was ready to use it. However, there was no real danger from the Alamanni, who proved easy targets. Julian's 'fear' of continuing Alamannic savagery

---

[168] AM 17.10.1–2.
[169] AM 17.10.3.
[170] AM 17.10.5–9.
[171] AM 17.10.8: *comites eius, quorum ope et fide maxime nitebatur.*
[172] AM 17.10.9–10.
[173] Lorenz, S. (1997: 54 and n.192).
[174] Lorenz, S. (1997: 54–5). On the location of the *pagi* of Suomarius and Hortarius see AM 18.2.8, 14 and below 249; for that of those of Serapio and Chnodomarius see above 240.

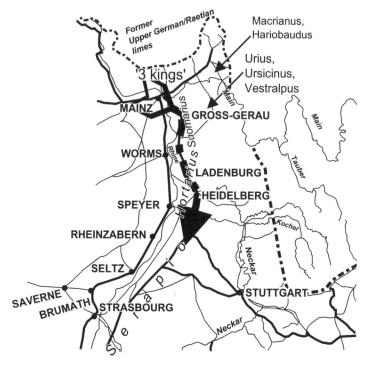

Fig. 20   The 358 campaign.

and a second attempt at joint action had no basis in reality, though by
stirring memories of the events of 357 (and possibly of those a
century earlier) he kept the bogeyman alive and justified whatever
he had in mind for the Alamanni. He operated double standards. The
Franks were subdued but not pursued, and some of them were
allowed to maintain their settlements within the Empire. The
Alamanni became again, as they had been under Constantine II,
the enemy of choice.

   Details of Julian's Alamannic campaign of 358 (as of that of 359)
invite consideration of Alamannic economy and society. Mention of
Hortarius' *comites* is significant, but more telling is Julian's constant
interest in what could be wrung from the Alamanni in material
terms. We see constant insistence on the return of prisoners and
the supply of foodstuffs and raw materials. The prisoners have been

dealt with.[175] Greed for *matériel* suggests an awareness of its availability (not just of grain and timber but also of stone and iron, and perhaps even salt),[176] and knowledge that it could be easily transported. Carts are mentioned, but we can assume that these served mainly to get bulky goods to waterways, for movement by boat or raft. We seem to be faced with an established process. Suomarius' and Hortarius' ready agreement to provide supplies (in the case of the former 'like a common contractor', carefully documenting his deliveries[177]) suggests that they had done so before, albeit under less punitive arrangements. The location of their territories puts them physically as close as they could be to the Empire. We thus return to the notion of a zone of influence, exploitation and cooperation, proposed earlier to explain the distribution of the coins.[178]

Within this context we may consider the outcome of Julian's dealings with Suomarius and Hortarius. These he had terrorized, but not killed or removed from power. On the contrary, Hortarius then expected to receive 'customary' gifts.[179] No doubt the same had already been given to Suomarius. Here, 'customary' cannot indicate a long-standing arrangement between the principal parties, since Julian had nothing to do with Hortarius down to 358. It signifies rather a general expectation: that Alamannic leaders took it for granted that any peace agreement with the Romans would be accompanied by gifts at its inception and on its renewal. Thus Hortarius' hoped-for gifts of 358 were to indicate the renewal of an earlier agreement, with Constantius II. Since Julian imposed harsh new terms on him, they marked a new treaty, with Julian in the name of Constantius II.

These gifts were personal 'presents', not any subsidies in cash or kind that may or may not have formed part of formal treaties. They would have consisted of precious objects—jewellery, dress, weaponry etc.—advertising the regard in which the recipient was held by the

---

[175] Cf. above 137–9.
[176] Above 133–5.
[177] Cf. de Jonge (1977: 252).
[178] Above 132.
[179] AM 17.10.8: *ex more.*

donor, with both parties being treated as social equals.[180] Though attention is usually directed to the use of such presents in foreign relations, they also occur in dealings between members of the imperial aristocracy.[181] This looks very much like Heather's 'client management'. The gifts would have added to the status of Rome's allies and, through their redistribution at the major hill-sites, have enabled them to strengthen their local political positions.[182] Julian would have been pleased to follow the tradition. What he did should not be regarded in any sense as buying peace from Hortarius. Having established his immediate security, Julian and his advisers needed to look further ahead. They will not have wished to have created anarchy beyond the Rhine by the time Julian wanted to leave. The support of friendly *pagus* leaders was essential, requiring them to be supported in their turn. But this was still exploitation of Alamanni: they did not pose a threat; stability in their lands could be created or destroyed according to Roman interests.[183]

Julian's Alamannic campaign of 359 is difficult to understand and rarely attracts the attention that it deserves. It occasioned Julian's deepest foray into Alamannic territory—the most extensive of any fourth-century emperor after Maximian—and offers much of interest concerning Rome's dealings with the Alamanni and their immediate neighbours.

By 359, Julian had a new *magister equitum*, Lupicinus. Julian decided on a surprise assault on the Alamanni because some *pagi* were liable to attack, and therefore needed to be suppressed like the rest.[184] The tribune, Hariobaudes, was employed to spy out the land. He went first to Hortarius, 'ostensibly as an envoy', and then further afield.[185] Before Julian set out, he restored seven cities on the Rhine below Mainz, using the Alamannic resources agreed in 358 (which included timbers over 50 feet—*c.*15 m—in length).[186]

---

[180] Cf. AM 17.5.15, 17.5.1: *munera* sent by Constantius II to the Persian emperor, and vice versa. Heather (2001: 26).

[181] See, e.g. Drinkwater (1987: 247) the case of T. Sennius Sollemnis.

[182] Heather (2001: 25–6).

[183] Below 263–5.

[184] AM 18.2.1.

[185] AM 18.2.2. On Hariobaudes, see above 149.

[186] AM 18.2.3–6.

To avoid disturbing territory pacified in 358, Julian did not cross the Rhine directly from Mainz, his rendezvous point, but moved south.[187] His crossing here was at first prevented by a mass incursion of Alamanni into the territories of Suomarius and Hortarius, forcing these, too, into hostility.[188] Julian moved still further south and then, while opposite the territory of Hortarius, managed to cross by a ruse. A party of 300 light infantry was sent by boat downstream, landed and panicked the enemy, causing them to withdraw and allowing the building of a bridge.[189] Julian passed peacefully through Hortarius' territory, and then ravaged the lands of 'hostile' and 'rebel' kings.[190] In this way, Julian reached the frontier with the Burgundians, marked by 'boundary stones', the *terminales lapides* discussed above.[191] Here he wished to receive Macrianus and Hariobaudus, 'full brothers and kings'.[192] On to the scene came Vadomarius, with a letter of recommendation from Constantius. He sought personal reconciliation and forgiveness for Urius, Ursicinus and Vestralpus (Chnodomarius' allies at Strasbourg and, apparently, the 'hostile' and 'rebel' kings).[193] Eventually, peace was granted to all—on the usual terms concerning the return of captives.[194]

The 359 campaign probably had two objectives: the punishment of the remaining principals of Strasbourg; and, more importantly, given that Julian and his advisers must have anticipated that it would not be long before they would have to leave Gaul,[195] the securing of the Main corridor. Crucial to understanding this campaign is the establishing of its route. I propose that Julian's march of 359 took him north-east.[196] He was concerned to deal with Macrianus and

[187] AM 18.2.7.
[188] AM 18.2.8, 13.
[189] AM 18.2.9–14; cf. Libanius, *Orat.* 18.88–9 for a slightly different version of events.
[190] AM 18.2.15: *infesti…rebelles.*
[191] AM 18.2.15. Above 110–12.
[192] AM 18.2.15: *germani fratres et reges.* I find this too strong, because it is too much at variance with the usual force of *suscipere* and its variants in Ammianus, Rolfe's translation (1963: 415) of *ut…susciperentur* as 'with the design of capturing'. Cf. de Jonge (1977: 228), (1980: 59).
[193] AM 18.2.16, 18.
[194] AM 18.2.18–19.
[195] Above 228.
[196] i.e. *contra* Lorenz, S. (1997: 59): south-east.

Hariobaudus. The former must be the Macrianus later confronted by
Valentinian I as king of the Bucinobantes.[197] At this time he was still
distant from Mainz and so still unaccustomed to Roman ways.[198]
Such an identification suits Ammianus' report that Julian moved
south from Mainz against the advice of his staff.[199] This suggests
that from the start the campaign was intended to settle matters with
communities up the Main valley. What Julian chose to embark upon
was a detour, which returned him eventually to the Main.

Ammianus says that hostile Alamanni advanced to the vicinity of
Mainz after Julian had arrived there, and that it was this that
confirmed his decision to go south.[200] However, Julian's sending of
Hariobaudes to Hortarius, his considered location of a Rhine bridge
into Hortarius' territory and his likely use of Hortarius in the failed
attempt to capture the Alamannic leaders[201] indicate that he had
decided much earlier to enter Alamannia south of the Rhine–Main
confluence. The demonstration of Alamannic hostility can hardly
have been unexpected. Once it had become clear that Julian was
marching to fight Alamanni, those leaders involved in Strasbourg
who had not already been defeated or pardoned must have guessed
that retribution was imminent and sought to protect themselves. But
how did they think they might achieve this? Ammianus, as usual,
refers to Alamannic bellicosity:[202] the unsophisticated response of a
warrior society. However, there was no random raiding; and the
leaders concerned, representing just the rump of Chnodomarius'
alliance (and without Macrianus and Hariobaudus in their number),
could not have hoped to defeat Julian. More likely, as happened with
Constantius II, is that they hoped that a show of power on both sides
could serve as a preliminary to negotiation. Julian, unlike Constantius,
was not prepared to oblige: before they were forgiven, the Alamanni
first had to be chastised.

---

[197] As *PLRE* 1.527 and, most recently, Gutmann (1991: 34); Heather (2001: 45).
Contra Lorenz, S. (1997: 62 and nn.236–7, 145), putting Julian's Macrianus on, or to
the east of, the upper Neckar. Cf. above 173–4; below 304–5.
    [198] AM 18.2.17.
    [199] AM 18.2.7.
    [200] AM 18.2.8–9.
    [201] Below 250.
    [202] AM 18.2.1, 9.

Ammianus describes the Romans at first teasing the Alamanni, as they moved southwards up the complex course of the old Rhine.[203] Although it seems that Julian knew precisely where he was heading,[204] he made a show of looking for a place to cross, goading the Alamanni to react. Presumably the Romans made for likely places, slowed down as if to use them, camped overnight and then moved on. This was clearly no forced march. Though both armies marched for several days,[205] they could have travelled at no great speed; indeed, Ammianus states specifically that the Alamanni marched slowly.[206] They are therefore unlikely to have covered a great distance. If they travelled at around 13 km per day, the speed of Julian's army in the final phase of his Persian campaign,[207] the Romans could have marched for around six days and then have crossed the Rhine between Worms and Speyer, south of the Neckar confluence. This accords with the likely location of Hortarius' *pagus*, into which they passed: straddling the Neckar[208] (Fig. 21). They could then have turned north, along the old Mainz road, and struck north-east from Gernsheim, which would have brought them to the old frontier, but not to the *limes* proper. Instead, they would have reached the former river frontier of the middle Main, between the old forts of Großkrotzenburg and Miltenberg. It was in this region that they found the territories of Urius, Ursicinus and Vestralpus, the Burgundian border and, just over the Main, the lands of Macrianus and Hariobaudus.[209] Julian's contact with the brothers had probably been arranged by Hariobaudes. He needed their cooperation to secure this strategically significant area.[210] They were ready to oblige: as Julian approached, they met him seeking peace.[211] Macrianus' alliance with Julian was the foundation of his Bucinobantian 'empire'.[212]

---

203 Cf. above 231.
204 AM 18.2.11.
205 Cf. Lorenz, S. (1997: 59 and n.225).
206 AM 18.2.10: *leniter*.
207 AM 25.1.10 (70 stades).
208 Lorenz, S. (1997: 55). Cf. above 243.
209 Above 224.
210 Cf. above 114, 190.
211 AM 18.2.15.
212 Above 247–8; cf. below 304–5.

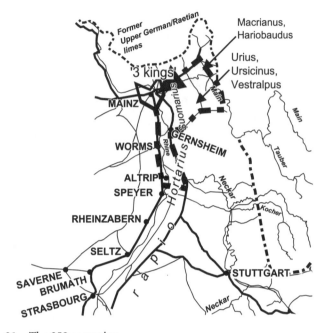

Fig. 21   The 359 campaign.

Three further aspects of the campaign of 359 merit attention.
The first is Hortarius' feast. On the night of the raid by Julian's
advance force over the Rhine, Hortarius had invited Alamannic
leaders to a banquet. His guests were attacked by these Roman troops
as they left in the early hours of the morning. The darkness and their
horses saved them, though not their menials.[213] Heather has drawn
attention to this incident as an indication of the importance of the
feast in Alamannic society, as a means of acquiring status and of
creating a network of clients. He relates such activity to the possible
evolution of an Alamannic Great King.[214] But the other passage that
Heather cites in this regard, concerning the capture of Vadomarius
while dining with imperial officials,[215] suggests that such junketing
could have been encouraged by Roman as much as by Germanic

[213] AM 18.2.13.
[214] Heather (2001: 412–43 and n.82); cf. above 119, 123, below 335–7.
[215] Below 255–6.

practices.[216] Indeed, Hortarius, who despite current circumstances was still plainly loyal to Rome, may have arranged the gathering at Julian's instigation. It is unlikely that it was discovered purely by accident by a small group of raiders in the dark. If the Alamannic settlement opposite Valentinianic Altrip was the lowland 'Herrschaftszentrum' of Hortarius and his successors,[217] it becomes the most likely venue for the feast: not far from the Rhine and in a place already well known to Romans. The Roman move south established the *bona fides* of Suomarius and Hortarius as Rome's 'enemies'. Therefore Hortarius' invitations were acceptable to his Alamannic 'allies'. However, despite Ammianus' half-denial,[218] the purpose of the feast was to bring about the detention of the Alamannic leaders. It was part of the usual late-Roman diplomatic repertoire of dirty tricks.[219]

Less speculative is the role of Vadomarius as an imperial politician: active and confident by virtue of the patronage of the senior emperor.[220] If Julian was operating in the north-east of Alamannia, he cannot have approached Vadomarius' territory opposite Kaiseraugst; and, therefore, Vadomarius cannot have felt directly threatened by his actions.[221] Thus, Vadomarius intervened as a third party on behalf of local kings. He did so no doubt with the knowledge, and perhaps even with the encouragement, of Constantius II. The Augustus will have been anxious for Roman military activity on the Rhine to be kept to a minimum. It seems, however, from Eunapius that Vadomarius also had a personal motive in coming to Julian, namely that the Caesar was still holding his son as hostage.[222] This helps explain Ammianus' remark that Vadomarius also came 'to secure his own safety'.[223] The boy had been taken, presumably, when Vadomarius made his peace with Julian after the battle of

---

[216] Note the grand birthday party that was used to launch the usurpation of Magnentius: Zosimus 2.42.3.
[217] Below 290–2.
[218] AM 18.2.13.
[219] Cf. Elton (1996a: 192).
[220] Cf. above 156.
[221] *Contra* Barceló (1981: 43).
[222] Eunapius, *Hist.* Fr. 19 (Blockley).
[223] AM 18.2.18: *qui suam locaturus securitatem in tuto.*

Strasbourg.[224] Though receiving Vadomarius courteously, Julian made his intense irritation at his (and so, by proxy, Constantius II's) interference clear. He ignored his appeal, granting peace to Urius, Ursicinus and Vestralpus only after they had pleaded their cases personally before him. And he only very reluctantly freed Vadomarius' son, claiming that Vadomarius still held Roman prisoners.[225]

Finally to be considered is Julian's overall relationship with Alamannia. Julian was soon proudly to proclaim himself conqueror of *Germani*, Franks and Alamanni.[226] All our sources imply that by 359 Julian had the whole of Alamannia at his feet. However, his ventures had been limited and precisely targeted. North to south, his Alamannic expeditions had taken him from Wiesbaden to just beyond the lower Neckar. West to east, he operated within a relatively narrow strip of territory. That the lands of the known Alamannic kings involved, Suomarius and Hortarius, were not wide is suggested by the fact that, in 359, Julian's troops cleared those of the latter quickly and with no trouble.[227] His most ambitious foray, to the Burgundian border, took him no more than *c*.50 km (30 statute miles) as the crow flies from the Rhine, and back to the Main valley where, if necessary, he could call on Roman naval power. He never left the zone of imperial influence indicated by the coins: far less extensive than the 'inner circle' of territory around the imperial frontier, at least 100 km deep, proposed as a general rule by Heather.[228] Most of Alamannia remained unvisited; and, as far as we know, Julian had not even bothered to punish the people of Chnodomarius and Serapio. Serapio, having given himself up,[229] may, indeed, have been given the lands of his uncle, in return for obedience: there is no sign of the area opposite Strasbourg being involved in the resistance of 359. Julian's restricted area of operations is consistent with habitual Roman

---

[224] Lorenz, S. (1997: 63 and n.242) suggests that the youth was handed over when Vadomarius dealt with Julian in 359, i.e. on the Burgundian border. However, this seems too late, especially in the light of Eunapius' reference to Roman captives supposedly still held by Vadomarius.

[225] Eunapius, *Hist.* Fr. 19 (Blockley). See Blockley (1983: 132–3 n. 37) and Lorenz, S. (1997: 62 n.241) for the association of this fragment with the campaign of 359.

[226] *Quellen* 6, Inscriptions no. 65 (=*ILS* 8945).

[227] AM 18.2.14.

[228] Heather (2001: 29–32).

[229] Above 239.

reluctance to campaign far to the east of the Rhine throughout the fourth century.[230] It appears that once he and his advisers felt that they were getting the west under control, they refused to be drawn into wider hostilities. As relations with Constantius II deteriorated, they needed to consolidate their position prior to an inevitable move eastwards.

The year 360 was one of high politics as Julian finally accepted the position of Augustus and as he and Constantius readied themselves for the struggle that must come. In 359 there had been serious trouble with the Persians in Mesopotamia, culminating, around the beginning of October, in the fall of Amida. Constantius was still on the Danube, but he wintered in Constantinople where he prepared to move to the eastern frontier in the following spring. It was his request to Julian for troops for the coming campaign that supposedly spurred the western army to a spontaneous proclamation of Julian as Augustus in Paris early in 360. However, as with much else in Julian's dealings with Constantius, the whole business appears very contrived.[231] It was what Julian and his circle had been aiming for. The Frankish and Alamannic campaigns had been a means to an end. Neither enemy had ever posed much of a threat; and Julian had by now beaten the spirit out of both of them.[232] The emphasis was now on imperial politics.

However, Julian and his advisers continued to exploit the 'barbarian threat'. Just before the usurpation, Lupicinus was despatched with an army to Britain to settle trouble there from Scots and Picts. Julian did not go himself, pleading that he did not want to leave Gaul without a ruler 'when the Alamanni were roused to rage and war'.[233] The truth seems rather to have been that it suited the conspirators to have Lupicinus, loyal to Constantius, well out of the way.[234] Current prejudicial perceptions of the Alamanni again proved useful when Julian, in his first major address to his troops after his usurpation, made much of their common experience against this foe.[235] It is in Ammianus'

[230] Cf. below 294.

[231] On the engineering of the usurpation (in which Julian was only indirectly involved), see Drinkwater (1983b: 370–83).

[232] On the absence of menace from the Alamanni by 360 see Lorenz, S. (1997: 64).

[233] AM 20.1.1: *Alamannis ad saevitiam etiam tunc incitatis et bella.*

[234] For the 'removal' of Lupicinus see Drinkwater (1983b: 378–9). *Contra* Matthews (1989: 95).

[235] AM 20.5.4–5.

account of events just before and just after Julian's proclamation that we learn that Julian had recruited men from 'beyond the Rhine', on condition that they would not serve 'beyond the Alps', according to him, a usual condition of service.[236] It is also here that we have the likely deliberate confusion of their unwillingness to leave Gaul with supposed fear on the part of regular troops that their departure would expose their families in Gaul to Alamannic attack.[237] Finally, it was in his early negotiations as Augustus with Constantius that Julian offered him laetic recruits.[238]

Once his position was secure, Julian crossed the Rhine and attacked the Atthuarian Franks. Though Ammianus claims that these Franks were 'lawlessly overrunning the frontiers of Gaul', commentators agree that, in fact, this attack was done without provocation, and was meant to maintain the fighting qualities of the Roman troops.[239] Significant here is that Julian did not extend this fighting to Alamanni: there were to be no campaigns against the remaining supporters of Chnodomarius and Serapio.[240] On the other hand, after his Frankish campaign, Julian journeyed up the Rhine to Kaiseraugst, 'carefully examining and strengthening the defences of the frontier'. At Kaiseraugst, 'having recovered the places that the savages had formerly taken and were holding as their own, he fortified them with special care and went by way of Besançon to Vienne to pass the winter'.[241]

Julian's inspection of the Upper Rhine is unexceptional, given what was to happen in the following year. However, what he did at Kaiseraugst is far from clear. The context suggests that the installations he recovered were on the left bank, but this can hardly be true.[242] The alternative is that they were bridgehead sites (or, allowing for exaggeration, one important site) on the right bank, previously

[236] AM 20.4.4. Cf. above 164.
[237] AM 20.4.10. Cf. above 165.
[238] Above 166.
[239] AM 20.10.2. See, e.g. Barceló (1981: 45); Lorenz, S. (1997: 66).
[240] Cf. above 238.
[241] AM 20.10.3.
[242] Jullian (1926: 225 and n.8), for example, suggests that Julian expelled Alamanni who were still occupying left-bank sites they had taken in 354–5, and that it was while doing this that he dealt with Vadomarius (cf. above 247). Szidat (1981: 48) pushes the date of occupation back to 352–3. However, it seems to me most unlikely that Julian would have tolerated Alamannic possession of Roman territory—still less of Roman military installations—for so long.

controlled by Vadomarius.[243] Again, this would fit the events of 361. Julian's tour of inspection was also useful in allowing an innocent-seeming removal of his headquarters from Paris to Vienne, more convenient for a move eastwards, that could be planned at leisure, 'now that Gaul was quieted'.[244]

The year 361 saw Julian's last Alamannic campaign and his departure from Gaul, never to return. Towards the end of winter, he learned that Alamanni from Vadomarius' territory had begun raiding widely by the Raetian border.[245] Stunned, Julian sent Count Libino, with the regiments of Celtae and Petulantes who were wintering with him, to sort out the situation.[246] Libino ran into hostile Alamanni near Sanctio. Disregarding or failing to notice their superior numbers, he attacked and was defeated. Though Libino lost his life early in the conflict, his men do not appear to have suffered heavy casualties.[247] Ammianus then reports the rumour that Vadomarius, as a long-standing ally of Constantius, had received written instructions from him to appear occasionally to break the peace by raiding into the Roman Empire, in order to detain Julian in Gaul.[248] Vadomarius, again according to rumour, obeyed with enthusiasm. He was found out only after a secretary (*notarius*), sent by him to Constantius, was discovered to be carrying a letter from Vadomarius, criticizing Julian as Caesar: a double betrayal, since this occurred at a time when Vadomarius was supposedly a loyal supporter of Julian Augustus.[249]

Julian set about arresting Vadomarius.[250] He was apprehended by Julian's secretary, Philagrius, at the close of a dinner with a Roman local military commander on the left bank of the Rhine.[251] The situation must have developed very quickly, since Vadomarius was informed of his secretary's arrest only after his own detention.[252]

---

[243] The most likely such site would have been a forerunner of Valentinian's bridgehead fort at Wyhlen, over the Rhine from Kaiseraugst: Fingerlin (1990: 130 and Fig. 34); cf. below 295.

[244] AM 21.1.6: *pacatis iam Galliis.*

[245] AM 21.3.1: *propinquante iam vere . . . vastare confinis Raetiis tractus.*

[246] AM 21.3.2.

[247] AM 21.3.3: *disiecti sunt nostri occisis paucis et vulneratis*; cf. 21.4.7.

[248] AM 21.3.4.

[249] AM 21.3.5.

[250] AM 21.4.1.

[251] AM 21.4.2–5.

[252] AM 21.4.6.

Vadomarius' *comites* were not seized.[253] He was taken to Julian's camp, confronted with the letter, and exiled to Spain. Ammianus says explicitly that this was to secure Gaul in case of Julian's departure.[254]

Julian led a successful sortie against those who had defeated Libino. He accepted the surrender of the survivors, accepting some as *dediticii* and promising peace to the rest.[255] He returned to Kaiseraugst where he announced to his troops his intention of marching against Constantius, and won their support.[256] He then quickly moved eastwards.[257] Dividing his army into three columns, he led one through the Black Forest to the Danube, where it embarked upon waiting vessels.[258]

The first Alamannic attacks probably took place in late February or early March.[259] Sanctio is now generally identified with Bad Säckingen, on the High Rhine, east of Kaiseraugst and *c.*72 km (43 statute miles) in direct line from the Raetian border.[260] Kaiseraugst was probably where Vadomarius was arrested, since Julian returned there following his campaign against Libino's killers.[261] Leaving Kaiseraugst, Julian's best route would have been due east, to Windisch, then north, crossing the Rhine at Zurzach. From here he could have taken the former imperial highway in the direction of Rottweil, forking eastwards once more at Hüfingen, along the road on the right bank of the Danube. This followed the river to the vicinity of modern Ulm, just beyond its confluence with the Iller, where it could certainly carry shipping, though a case has recently been made for embarkation further west[262] (Fig. 22).

---

253 AM 21.4.5. Cf. above 120.
254 AM 21.4.6.
255 AM 21.4.7–8. Cf. above 160, 166.
256 AM 21.5.1–10.
257 AM 21.8.1.
258 AM 21.8.2–9.2.
259 Szidat (1981: 91).
260 Szidat (1981: 88); den Boeft, den Hengst, and Teitler (1991: 35); Lorenz, S. (1997: 67 and n.263). Geuenich (1997a: 52 and n.21) prefers Besançon.
261 AM 21.8.1. Szidat (1981: 88); Matthews (1989: 315); Lorenz, S. (1997: 67) (Basel, Windisch, or Kaiseraugst).
262 den Boeft, den Hengst, and Teitler (1991: 109, 115). For an alternative land route (via Stein am Rhein): Szidat (1996: 77); for the debate over the location of Julian's embarkation: Szidat (1996: 72). For a possible relationship between Julian's Black Forest route and the information of the Peutinger Table see Benedetti-Martig (1993: 360–1) and cf. above 132.

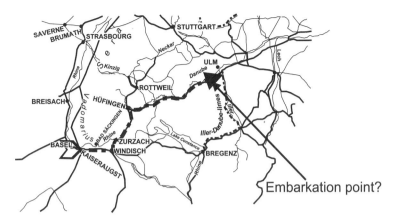

Fig. 22 The 361 campaign.

What happened in 361 can be understood only against the background of imperial politics. It was becoming clear that Constantius II and Julian would never reach a settlement. As the year progressed, there were ever stronger signs that the former was preparing to move west against his cousin.[263] However, for the moment, to keep control over as many as possible of the western provinces, Constantius had to work through loyal subordinates: internal—military and civil officials ensuring that forts and cities did not go over to Julian and preparing them against possible attack by him—and external—allies such as Vadomarius, who might spy on Julian and find ways to disrupt his plans. The question is, therefore, whether, as Ammianus' 'rumour' had it, Constantius went as far as to encourage Vadomarius to organize raids into Gaul, or whether Julian and his supporters chose to say that he did to discredit him and remove Vadomarius before he could do any actual harm.

Evidence in support of the rumour is to be found, apparently, in other texts. Only a short time after these events, still in 361, Julian himself, in his letter to the Athenians, declared that Constantius:

let loose against us the barbarians and among them proclaimed me his foe and paid them bribes so that the people of the Gauls might be laid waste . . . in fact the letters that he wrote I obtained from the barbarians who

---

[263] Browning (1975: 112–13).

brought them to me... [Constantius] had twice betrayed [the people of Gaul] to the enemy.[264]

On 1 January 362, in a panegyric to Julian, the Gallic orator Claudius Mamertinus talked of: 'the entire barbarian world raised to arms against the defender of Roman liberty... and of peoples recently conquered and stubbornly resisting the yoke newly placed on their necks incited by impious inducements to renewed fury'.[265] Libanius' great funeral oration on Julian, of 365, has Constantius resorting:

to the same trick of calling in the barbarians by letter as he had done before, and begging them as a favour to enslave Roman territory. One out of many he induced to break his word, and he began to ravage and also to make merry in the lands he had got as his reward, and he went to dine with the generals on our side as though he had done nothing wrong at all. This fellow, who had dared break the treaty, he arrested in his cups.... and, crossing over into his territory, [Julian] inflicted a well-deserved punishment for his treachery. Those who had bided loyally by their agreements gathered in alarm, greatly ashamed at such misconduct, and added oath upon oath, and he mounted a tribunal in the middle of barbarian country, gazed down upon their chieftains who stood as subjects with their hordes of followers, and after issuing threats and reminders took his leave.... The despatches sent by the cowardly, treacherous Constantius to the barbarians were of the greatest assistance to him, for as he sailed or marched along, he read these out to the cities and the garrisons.[266]

Against these charges is, as a number of commentators have argued, Vadomarius' apparent lack of concern in accepting the Roman offer of hospitality: unlikely if he had been guilty of major wrong-doing.[267] It is not impossible, of course, that this was an act of 'barbarian' bravado. However, although Ammianus clearly dislikes Vadomarius, calling him deceitful,[268] he never accuses him of being headstrong. In addition, the notion that Vadomarius should pretend to break the peace 'from time to time' (*subinde*) is meaningless. He could have shown himself an enemy only once, after which he would

[264] Julian, *Ep. ad Ath.* 286A–87B.

[265] *Pan. Lat.* 11(3).6.1 [trans. Nixon and Rodgers (1994)].

[266] Libanius, *Orat.* 18.107–8, 113; cf. also *Orat.* 12.62 of 1 Jan. 363.

[267] e.g. Barceló (1981: 46); Lorenz, S. (1997: 67–9). Cf. den Boeft, den Hengst, and Teitler (1991: 44); Nixon and Rodgers (1994: 402 n.38).

[268] AM 21.3.5.

have been condemned by all Roman authorities. This suggests that there was little hard evidence to link him to the troubles, and suits the surprisingly mild punishment meted out to him by Julian.[269] It should also be pointed out that Julian's proposed reoccupation of the Rhine bridgehead site or sites, in 360, was apparently unopposed by Vadomarius, and may itself have severely restricted his capacity to do harm.

Vadomarius was probably not the instigator of attacks on Gaul.[270] The accusations of Julian, Mamertinus and Libanius are not dispassionate reporting but court propaganda. The basic strategy of this propaganda was to accuse Constantius of doing in 361 what he had done against Magnentius from 351: of calling in the Alamanni. Its most powerful tactic was constant reference to Julian's discovery of letters sent by Constantius to 'the barbarians', that is, in the first instance, to several kings, including Vadomarius. This justified Julian's removal of Vadomarius and his embarking on civil war. But this was deception. Constantius had burned his fingers very badly in calling upon Alamannic help to deal with the earlier usurper; and Julian, a close relative and still the heir apparent, was no Magnentius. No Alamannic chief is likely to have been called on to repeat the experiment. When Ammianus came to look into the claim, he probably found little concrete evidence to substantiate it. The best he was able to come up with was mention of a letter from Vadomarius to Constantius that was highly disrespectful of Julian but not materially dangerous and hardly surprising in confidential correspondence between two allies.[271] Ammianus' 'rumour' is simply what was transmitted by the 'Julianic' sources. Libanius' declaration that Julian had Vadomarius flogged like a common criminal,[272] which is out of step with Ammianus' account of his immediate treatment and his subsequent career, should also be regarded as part of this deception. Libanius, needing to justify the shocking fact that it was Julian, not

---

[269] Cf. Geuenich (1997a: 52).
[270] Cf. Drinkwater (1996: 24 and n.22).
[271] Cf. den Boeft, den Hengst, and Teitler (1991: 37).
[272] Libanius, *Orat.* 13.35 [July 362]: 'And when many tribes had been summoned to oppose you by enormous payments, you captured their leader without difficulty and inflicted upon him the disgrace reserved for felons, teaching him, by the lash upon his ribs, not to make money in this way.'

Constantius, who took the Empire to the brink of civil war, was given to many flights of fancy in respect of Vadomarius and the Alamanni.[273] This undermines the historicity of the Alamannic 'durbar' which, according to Libanius, Julian held at the close of his expedition.

With Vadomarius out of the way, Julian was able to move eastwards. His short Alamannic campaign enabled him, legitimately, to concentrate his forces at Kaiseraugst in preparation for the coming war.[274] It also allowed him to give his troops one more Germanic victory before they faced a more redoubtable foe. The minor campaign, therefore, served a number of purposes, among which must have been Julian's assertion of his authority in the area after Vadomarius' deposition and, as part of this, his establishment of Vadomarius' son, Vithicabius, as king in his place: the position in which we find him in 368.[275]

However, what Julian and his circle subsequently made of Libino's disaster distances us from what actually happened earlier in 361. This was no minor incident. Celtae, Petulantes and *comes* together formed a first-rate fighting unit—a 'brigade' of the imperial field army— comprising paired infantry and cavalry regiments, in total about 1,200 strong, under a single commander.[276] The deployment of the brigade outside the normal campaigning season in an area that Julian had recently gone out of his way to secure suggests a response to a serious raid—made all the more serious by the defeat of the Roman force and the death of Libino. The action was a significant loss of face to the army and to Julian who, unused to failures of this kind and on the verge of the greatest military and political gamble of his career, needed to believe that the gods were still with him.[277] He could not, in the first instance, have welcomed it as an excuse to deal with Vadomarius. Certainly, there is no case for supposing that it was Julian who engineered the affair.[278] His last Alamannic campaign thus served also to avenge Libino and expunge the shame of his loss.

---

[273] Cf. den Boeft, den Hengst, and Teitler (1991: 47).
[274] Szidat (1981: 88).
[275] AM 27.10.3; 30.7.7. *PLRE* 1, 971. Below 281.
[276] Elton (1996a: 89, 91).
[277] Cf. Drinkwater (1983b: 370).
[278] Nixon and Rodgers (1994: 402 n.38).

The defeat would have been a major element in immediate Romano-Alamannic relations, whoever was to blame. Vadomarius' presence on Roman soil may therefore have been not entirely fortuitous. The tone of both Ammianus and Libanius implies that social intercourse between barbarians and Romans was not unusual. This hints at a fair degree of integration.[279] However, the dinner following which Vadomarius was taken may have been more than mere end-of-day entertainment, but the climax of a meeting (or series of meetings) intended to resolve a crisis. It may be significant that Julian sent Philagrius into the area clearly aware that he might well encounter Vadomarius within the Empire.[280] It is not impossible that among Philagrius' many other important duties (which may have included arrangements for Julian's coming move eastwards)[281] was liaison with local military commanders concerning the recent defeat. It may well have been in this sense—from his point of view, honest legitimate imperial business—that the senior officer involved in Vadomarius' fall invited him over on imperial orders.[282] This interpretation runs contrary to Ammianus' claim that Vadomarius crossed the Rhine fearing nothing, 'as was natural in time of profound peace, and pretending to know of no irregular doings',[283] but, given the calamity that had only just occurred, this rings untrue. One suspects that Vadomarius felt at ease because he knew he was not to blame.

But who was responsible for the attack? The raiders may have been a band of unruly warriors[284] from Vadomarius' territory simply out for mischief (stung, perhaps, by Julian's high-handed treatment of the previous year), and therefore out of their chief's control. Alternatively, the leader of a local war-band, knowing Vadomarius' attitude to Julian, might have wrongly believed that the king had given him some sort of permission to carry out an unofficial raid. Or Vadomarius himself, wrongly anticipating Constantius' instructions,

[279] Above 157.
[280] AM 21.4.2.
[281] AM 21.4.2. Szidat (1981: 89, 95).
[282] Cf. Browning (1975: 112); Lorenz, S. (1997: 68).
[283] AM 21.4.3: *ut nihil in profunda metuens pace nihilque secus gestorum simulans scire.*
[284] Cf. above 122, 222.

may indeed have encouraged such a sortie. Against the last of these is the case already presented and Vadomarius' knowledge of Constantius' method of working, and his need to cover his own back: he would never have initiated serious action without written instructions. Against the other two are the numbers and experience a war-party would have required to overcome Libino's brigade. This leaves a large war-band from the interior.

Although Ammianus says that the raiding Alamanni came from Vadomarius' territory, implying that the king was responsible for their misdeeds, he nowhere says that they were actually of it.[285] Population movement from the east was a constant feature of Alamannic development, dangerous to settled communities on the imperial frontier and to the Empire itself.[286] It is possible that more distant Alamannic communities were now being disturbed by Julian's preparations. When, in the spring of 361, Julian reached the navigable Danube he 'conveniently' found sufficient boats to hand.[287] The force of Ammianus' statement is debated, but it has been widely interpreted as indicating that Julian's administration prepared a fleet for him to use.[288] Such a fleet had to be fitted out or constructed on the Danube in Alamannic territory, upstream from Raetia.[289] Indeed, given the possibility that this river could have taken shipping upstream from Ulm, Julian may even have embarked his troops here. This was in an area which, to judge from the coin-finds, otherwise saw little Roman presence.[290] However, the operation was, presumably, founded on the combination of Roman expertise and Alamannic muscle and *matériel* that was commonplace on the Rhine.[291] A raiding-group, excited by Roman activity, might have moved into Vadomarius' territory before attacking the Empire over the Rhine. That it was an alien group that Julian dealt with later is

[285] den Boeft, den Hengst, and Teitler (1991: 48).

[286] Cf. above 106, 238–9.

[287] AM 21.9.2: *quos opportune fors dederat plurimos.* For the date see Barnes (1993: 228); Lorenz, S. (1997: 70).

[288] den Boeft, den Hengst, and Teitler (1991: 115); Szidat (1996: 71).

[289] Szidat (1996: 72).

[290] Above 129–30 and Fig. 16.

[291] Above 234.

hinted at in Ammianus' account of their fate—a somewhat detached story that suggests that Libino's killers (who, if they had been local, and especially after the removal of Vadomarius, would have scattered) were still operating as a single group.[292]

But there is another possibility. If, as Julian claimed,[293] Constantius had put Raetia on a war footing, and was collecting military supplies there, the province would have been a tempting target. Is it possible that Julian encouraged raiding on western Raetia, which then got out of hand? This would fit Ammianus' initial indistinct location of the troubles, on the Gallo-Raetian border, distant from Vadomarius' territory, which has occasioned debate.[294] It would also accommodate Szidat's suggestion that Libino was sent to negotiate a settlement with the raiders.[295] Overall, therefore, 361 began with a nasty surprise for Julian but, by demonizing Alamanni, he was able to turn this to his advantage.

Before moving to examine the conflict between Alamanni and Julian's successors, it is useful to review the relationship between Rome and the Alamanni as it had developed from around 260 to 361. Frequent reference has been made to the Roman need for the Rhine–Danube re-entrant to become an adjacent 'living-room' rather than an 'invasion-corridor'.[296] Rome constructed this room by encouraging the development of settled Alamannic chiefdoms along the border.[297] In the late third and early fourth centuries, any danger to the Empire came not from these 'kingdoms', which were small and divided, with weak economies and low populations,[298] but from

---

[292] AM 21.4.7. Cf. den Boeft, den Hengst, and Teitler (1991: 48).

[293] Julian, *Ep. ad Ath.* 286B: 'On the frontiers of Gaul in the cities near by he ordered to be got ready three million bushels of wheat which had been ground in Brigantia.' Against den Boeft, den Hengst, and Teitler (1991: 119) and Szidat (1996: 72), I follow Wright (1913: 287) in identifying 'Brigantia' as Bregenz/Brigantium, not Briançon/Brigantio. As Szidat says, Constantius' main fear was that Julian would seize Italy and, as we have seen (above 209), Bregenz was a major supply centre on the military highroad between the High Rhine and the Italian sub-capital at Milan. Benedetti-Martig (1993: 354) identifies the place as Szóny/Brigetio, which must surely be too distant.

[294] e.g. Szidat (1981: 91–2, 94); den Boeft, den Hengst, and Teitler (1991: 34–5); Lorenz, S. (1997: 67 and n.261).

[295] Szidat (1981: 92).

[296] e.g. above 80–1, 99, 163, 189.

[297] e.g. above 75, 81, 119, 122.

[298] Above 86, 91, 93, 105, 124, 143–4.

more distant Elbgermanic raiding-bands, which might suddenly appear and run riot in neighbouring provinces.[299] Rome wanted no repeat of the troubles of the 260s and 270s. This worked well. There was some raiding, in particular that leading to the battle of Langres,[300] but the Elbgermanic threat was generally met; and local Alamannic chiefs played a useful part in preventing Burgundian expansion down the Main.[301] Rome for the most part left the Alamanni alone, but they could be exploited by rulers needing a successful campaign.[302] Then, border stability was sacrificed for political gain, but any such sacrifice was localized and short-term. Roman superiority made victory inevitable and speedy, and followed by new agreements and renewed stability.

In the 350s came the usurpation of Magnentius and the Alamannic 'invasions'. These shook Roman confidence. Memories of the third century and general prejudice against barbarians obscured the fact that Alamannic aggression had been encouraged by close ties with the Empire, and that Alamannic communities remained weak. This allowed Julian to exploit the Alamanni as others had done before him, but on a much greater scale, making them figures of fear and hatred and picking fights with them for his own ends.[303] However, the decision to expel Alamanni recently settled within the Empire was taken by Constantius; and Julian, as others before him, was careful to restore stability once fighting was over. After the excitement of 357, Julian appears to have returned to Constantius' policy of cooperation with Alamanni, creating a buffer zone of imperial allies that would have been useful throughout his reign, had he lived.[304]

However, important in understanding what follows is, as in the case of the 'exclusion' of high-ranking Alamanni in the Roman army,[305] that this does not make Valentinian the villain of the

---

[299] Above 106, 189, 262.
[300] Above 187–9.
[301] Above 190.
[302] Above 200.
[303] Drinkwater (1997: 8); cf. the criticism of Martin (1998: 421).
[304] Barceló (1981: 47): from 360; Lorenz, S. (1997: 66): from 358.
[305] Above 159.

piece, arbitrarily renewing attacks on Alamanni simply to confirm his position as new emperor. Julian had set a precedent. Though he perished in the east, his reputation as the scourge of the Alamanni lived on. If Valentinian wanted to be emperor on the Rhine frontier, at some stage he had to show himself to be the equal, if not the superior, of the great Julian and wage war on Alamanni.[306]

[306] Cf. Raimondi (2001: 98–100); below 271.

8

Conflict 365–94

Julian left Gaul in spring 361 to face Constantius II. In the event he achieved sole control of the Empire without a fight as a result of his cousin's unexpected death in October or November of the same year.[1] Julian himself perished in June 363 during his invasion of Persia. There followed the short reign of Jovian and then the accession of Valentinian I and his brother, Valens, as joint Augusti. After dividing the military resources of the Empire between them, Valentinian and Valens parted company, the former moving west to Milan where he celebrated his first consulship on 1 January 365.[2]

Ammianus remains our main source down to 378, that is for the whole of Valentinian's reign and for the first few years of that of his western successor, Gratian. The absence of an extensive and coherent near-contemporary narrative for the 380s and 390s is regrettable and must, as in the case of the period 285–354, restrict our understanding of events. However, again like 285–354, there is enough evidence to be confident that what appear to be the main developments in the relationship between the Rhine-*Germani* and Rome are real historical phenomena and not artefacts of the source pattern.

For the first part of Valentinian's reign, Ammianus continues to describe imperial dealings with the Alamanni year by year, though in less detail.[3] There are problems in understanding the events of 364–6 because of Ammianus' inclusion of what is now generally regarded as no more than an introductory summary of all the foreign wars of the

---

[1] November: Barnes (1993: 224).
[2] Lorenz, S. (1997: 73).
[3] Elliott (1983: 159–60).

joint reign,[4] and, more confusing, because of the difficulties which, as he himself realized, he faced in dealing with simultaneous happenings in the western and eastern halves of the Empire.[5] As far as those in the west are concerned, Lorenz has recently assessed the current state of research and has proposed an ordering of events which I adopt here.[6]

According to Ammianus, the Alamanni raided Gaul fairly early in the reign of Valentinian. This was because representatives they had sent to Milan to receive the 'usual' gifts reported that what they had been offered had been of unacceptable quality and that they had then been treated very badly by the *magister officiorum*, Ursacius.[7] Raiding began around the same time as Procopius' usurpation against Valens. Valentinian was given news of both on the same day, around 1 November. He was in Gaul, journeying to Paris.[8]

Having arrived in Paris, he sent his *magister militum*, Dagalaifus, against the Alamanni. These, however, after devastating the frontier region, had already withdrawn.[9] In the meantime, agonizing as to whether he himself should march against Procopius, he finally decided to follow the advice he was being given and to stay in Gaul, and moved to Reims.[10] In January of the following year various formations of Alamanni attacked again.[11] The leading group was intercepted by Charietto (*comes per utramque Germaniam*) and Severianus, another military *comes* and commander of the garrison at Chalon-sur-Saône.[12] The Roman force was broken, with Severianus severely wounded, Charietto killed and a regimental standard almost lost.[13] Valentinian again sent Dagalaifus out from Paris against the Alamanni, but he failed to engage them, claiming that they

---

[4] AM 26.4.5–6. Tomlin (1979); Lorenz, S. (1997: 77 and n.32).

[5] AM 26.5.15.

[6] Lorenz, S. (1997: 84–91): basically, *contra* Seeck and Baynes, that Ammianus' Alamannic attack 'immediately after 1 January' (27.1.1) belongs where he puts it, in 366, and should not be seen as a doublet of events of 365.

[7] AM 26.5.7: *ex more*.

[8] AM 26.5.8.

[9] AM 26.5.9.

[10] AM 26.5.9–14.

[11] AM 27.1.1.

[12] Charietto: *PLRE* 1.200 (his office is otherwise unknown).

[13] AM 27.1.2–6.

were too scattered. He was then withdrawn, to share the consulship with Valentinian's young son, Gratian (born 18 April 359 and therefore only around seven years old).[14] Dagalaifus was succeeded in his command against the Alamanni by Jovinus, *magister equitum.* He surprised and massacred two Alamannic groups, at Scarponne and at an unnamed location by a river respectively.[15] Jovinus then tracked down and defeated a third group in a pitched battle near Châlons-sur-Marne. The Alamanni lost 6,000 dead and 4,000 wounded, the Romans 1,200 and 200.[16] The following day he pursued the survivors, but in vain. He was also distressed to discover that Roman troops had killed a captured Alamannic king and some of his followers.[17] Jovinus returned to Paris where he was welcomed by Valentinian and received the consulship for the coming year. 'At about the same time', Valentinian received the head of the vanquished Procopius.[18] Ammianus closes his account by noticing that: 'Besides these battles, many others less worthy of mention were fought in various parts of Gaul, which it would be superfluous to describe, both because their results led to nothing worthwhile, and because it is not fitting to spin out a history with insignificant details.'[19]

Ammianus regularly refers to the consuls of each year, to occurrences that are dateable from other sources, and to specific calendar dates. On this basis, the alienation of the Alamanni took place in summer 365 and their raiding began in October of that year, when Valentinian was already in Paris. This was also the date of Dagalaifus' first campaign against them.[20] They attacked again early in 366, when Dagalaifus went against them for the second time, only to be withdrawn and replaced by Jovinus.[21] The precise dating of Jovinus' victories is important. Ammianus puts them just before Valentinian's receipt of Procopius' head. Lorenz, allowing equal weight to the time it would have taken for this grisly trophy to reach the west following

[14] AM 27.2.1. Kienast (1996: 333).
[15] AM 27.2.1–3.
[16] AM 27.2.4–7.
[17] AM 27.2.8–9.
[18] AM 27.2.10: *eisdem diebus.*
[19] AM 27.2.11.
[20] Lorenz, S. (1997: 74).
[21] For the plausibility of Dagalaifus' taking the consulship with Gratian as late as March 366 see Lorenz, S. (1997: 79–80).

Procopius' execution on 27 May 366 and to Ammianus' indications of variable temperatures at the time, proposes that Jovinus crushed the Alamanni in the course of May 366.[22] However, given the imprecision of weather reporting, it is probably better to concentrate on what happened to Procopius' head. Taking into account that, as Ammianus explicitly tells us occurred at Philippopolis,[23] its transport would have been interrupted by public displays, its journey westwards would have taken significantly longer than a normal urgent despatch: at least six weeks and possibly more.[24] This dates its arrival in northern Gaul to early/mid-July, putting Jovinus' successes in mid/late June. It allows them to have been won after the receipt of news of Procopius' unexpected defeat on 27 May, racing in advance of his head and arriving in Gaul in early/mid-June.[25] It also allows the associated issuing of Valentinian's law on *postliminium* on 20 June 366, though with little time to spare.[26]

We know that Ammianus errs in reporting that Valentinian was still en route to Paris by late October/early November, since the *Codex Theodosianus* shows him resident in the city by mid-October; he remained there until January 366, when he moved to Reims.[27] It was probably in Reims, not Paris, that Jovinus was received by Valentinian following his defeat of the three Alamannic groups in mid-366.[28] The relative proximity of Jovinus' first and third victories suggests that the second must have been in the same area. The river

[22] Lorenz, S. (1997: 82–3).

[23] AM 26.10.6. Cf. Matthews (1989: 201) on this macabre 'tableau'; also now Lenski (2002: 81).

[24] It is *c*.2,150 km (1,290 statute miles) from Nakoleia in Asia Minor, where Procopius was defeated, to Reims. Increased by one-third, to take into account the physical vagaries of the route, this figure becomes 2,866 km (1,720 miles). On this basis, important news would have taken about 17 days to go from east to west; cf. Drinkwater (1994: 571). The four weeks or so that it took for the news of Procopius' revolt to reach Valentinian in late 365 cannot—as Lorenz, S. (1997: 83) does—be taken as a guide given uncertainty in Illyricum (AM 26.5.9) which had disappeared by early 366 (AM 27.10.4). I believe that the head itself travelled at no more than one-third this speed. Cf. Lorenz, S. (1997: 83).

[25] For the implications of this see below 277.

[26] Below 278.

[27] *CT* 11.1.13 [18 October 365]; *CT* 7.7.1 [28 January 366]. Seeck (1919: 226); Lorenz, S. (1997: 76 and n.24, 78–9, 83–4).

[28] Lorenz, S. (1997: 83), from Tomlin.

concerned could be the Moselle,[29] but given the direction in which the fighting was going it could just as easily be the Marne.

According to Ammianus, 365–6 saw a revival of the Alamannic menace.[30] All recent commentators have accepted the idea of a renascent 'Germanic threat' to explain Valentinian's decision, as senior emperor, to take the west as his sphere of responsibility and then refuse aid to Valens.[31] If one accepts that there was no such threat, another explanation is possible.

However one may interpret their later activities, Alamanni did not become a problem immediately after Julian's death.[32] It was not until mid-365, when Valentinian had been in Milan for several months, that we first hear of the Alamanni becoming hostile. Furthermore, their agitation was generated by the Roman decision to change the terms of a long-standing agreement. Thus, when Valentinian chose the west, he did not do so because he knew that it was currently enduring or would shortly face major trouble from over the Rhine. The reasons for his decision to leave the east must be sought elsewhere. Imperial politics were potentially fissile; and all emperors needed the loyalty of the western armies. This had been demonstrated recently in Jovian's moves to secure northern Italy and Gaul, in which Valentinian had played a leading role.[33] However, such considerations cannot wholly explain Valentinian's decision to become western emperor. He could, like Jovian, have dealt with the west through lieutenants or, if he felt he had to travel there in person, he could have returned to the east once the job had been done, putting Valens in charge.

The answer may be found in Raimondi's recent study of Valentinian's choice of the west. This is not her main proposal: that Valentinian chose the west because he felt that it was endangered by barbarians. The crucial point against this is the lateness of his arrival

[29] So Lorenz, S. (1997: 80).

[30] AM 27.1.1.

[31] Lorenz, S. (1997: 84 'Germanengefahr', cf. 78, 80, 177); Raimondi (2001: 91–3, 101, 129 'le regioni galliche minacciate dai barbari').

[32] Drinkwater (1997: 9); cf. Lorenz, S. (1997: 76–7). *Contra*, e.g. Jullian (1926: 234); Demougeot (1979: 105); Demandt (1989: 112). The idea of such trouble comes from an erroneous notice in Zosimus 4.3.4.

[33] AM 25.8.8, 9.8, 10.6. Raimondi (2001: 41–60).

in what would have been the most threatened areas. He did not hurry to the Rhine frontier, but moved to northern Italy, where he remained for around 10 months.[34] On the other hand, there is much in Raimondi's underlying idea that Valentinian acted as he did aware that the emperor against whom he was bound to be measured was Julian.[35] If Valentinian had made plain that his sphere of activity would be the east, he would have aroused expectations of imminent major campaigning in Mesopotamia. Julian had waged glorious if unsuccessful war against Persia. The treaty that Jovian had made with the Persians to extricate his army from their soil was regarded as shameful, and might be seen as having become void on his death. There would have been enormous pressure on Valentinian to show himself the worthy successor of Julian by recovering the territories ceded by Jovian. With the west under Valens, there would have been little chance of Valentinian's being able to claim that he was needed elsewhere; and, faced with the likelihood of attack, the Persians may anyway have launched their own invasion. All this was high risk and, as he was to show in Gaul, Valentinian was no great risk taker.[36] The easier course was to defy tradition, give the east to his junior colleague and prove himself in the west, where there was no great threat.

This helps explain Valentinian's revision of the Alamannic gifts. From the historic readiness of Alamannic leaders to deal directly with Roman emperors and officials, from their sensitivity to their supposed ill-treatment, and from the trouble they caused on their return, I take Ammianus' 'envoys' (*legati*) to have comprised at least some important *reges*. The description of the gifts they came to collect as 'customary' suggests that these were the same tokens of personal esteem that Hortarius had expected of Julian. Their composition was 'stipulated and fixed' (*certa et praestituta*) by long tradition, that is determined by no particular Roman ruler, and continued by those who wanted peace with bordering Alamannic communities.[37]

---

[34] Seeck (1919: 218–26).

[35] Raimondi (2001: 98–100). Cf. above 265.

[36] Seeck (1921: 5.12).

[37] Above 243; *contra* Lorenz, S. (1997: 74): they had been established by Julian. Cf. Gutmann (1991: 11).

The Alamannic expectation was probably related to the recent change of western emperor. Both sides appear to have accepted that gift-giving, though not strictly part of the process, accompanied the automatic renewal of treaties between Alamannic leaders and Rome. It was an important piece of imperial theatre. (The re-dating of these events, from New Year to summer 365, undermines the assumption that the giving of such presents was part of an annual routine, and that it therefore represented Rome's buying peace from the Alamanni.[38])

Valentinian had probably already concluded that the Alamanni would be his chief concern in the west, the core activity of his reign,[39] since this was now the only way in which he could emulate Julian. However, his attitude to the gifts should not be seen as marking a major shift in policy. Valentinian bent tradition, but did not break it. He reduced, but did not refuse, Roman gifts to the Alamanni. The wholesale alienation of border communities so soon after his accession and arrival in the west would have been needlessly risky.[40] What we see is Valentinian acting like Julian in both cowing and provoking the western enemy of choice. He made his presence felt by signalling that all previous agreements were subject to review—though not major revision or immediate cancellation, which would have been courting disaster.[41] (The lapse of treaties on the deaths of either of the contracting parties cut both ways.[42]) Most Alamannic communities would fall into line but, given the nature of their society, Roman action would inevitably goad some hotheads to fight. These could be picked off once Valentinian had reached the Rhine; but other events prevented this.

Valentinian did not expect serious trouble as a result of his actions and he did not get it. There was still no major Alamannic attack. This explains his late and apparently unhurried arrival in Gaul in the autumn of 365, perhaps in anticipation of Alamannic unrest but

---

[38] Routine: cf. Heather (2001: 25); 'Danegeld': Asche (1983: 98); Lorenz, S. (1997: 177).

[39] Lorenz, S. (1997: 75–6).

[40] Pabst (1989: 305 n.16).

[41] Cf. Gutmann (1991: 11–12).

[42] See Lorenz, S. (1997: 74 n.12).

more likely because it was time he visited the region anyway.[43] It also explains why he headed not for the Rhineland or even Reims (Trier was still being restored after the damage caused by Magnentius' rebellion[44]), but for Paris, Julian's old residence, on the margin of the region most likely to be affected by barbarian raids. His interest in the city may have been political: Valentinian wanted to appear as emperor at the site of Julian's proclamation of 360.[45] The situation changed in October 365 when Valentinian heard of the first Alamannic raids and his own advisers and representatives of the Gallic communities purportedly expressed worries about these so grave that the emperor felt obliged to deny help to his brother.

One might expect the new western emperor, who had already sought to establish his dominance over Alamanni and who needed to confirm his credentials as a soldier, to have taken immediate personal action. But Valentinian sent out Dagalaifus. Moreover, when Dagalaifus then, and again in 366, proved unable to bring the Alamanni to heel and was recalled, he did not suffer for his failure but, on the contrary, was given the immense honour of being appointed consul with no less a colleague than Valentinian's son and heir, Gratian.[46] After Dagalaifus, Valentinian again failed to go himself to fight the Alamanni but, in 366, sent another of Julian's old generals, Jovinus, who finally defeated them and was also honoured with a consulship. Jovinus' victories may be dated after the west had received news of Procopius' defeat. It is odd that Alamanni who were slippery and invincible during the rebellion were relatively easy to suppress afterwards.

The explanation for this strange run of events surely lies in its political context. Valentinian made much of Alamanni in announcing that he would not help Valens against Procopius. He is supposed to have been persuaded by his counsellors and deputations from the Gallic communities not to expose Gaul to barbarian attack by leaving the country, and to have reconciled himself to this difficult decision by appreciating that, while Procopius was merely the enemy of

---

[43] Cf. Lorenz, S. (1997: 76).
[44] Drinkwater (1997: 5–6).
[45] Raimondi (2001: 122–4).
[46] See Lorenz, S. (1997: 79 and n.42), for Valentinian's trust in Dagalaifus.

himself and his brother, the Alamanni were the enemies of the whole world.[47] This is very suspect.

Valentinian's prioritizing of the interests of the state over those of his family resembles the excuse given by Claudius II for not proceeding against the usurper Postumus in 268, and may be regarded as a convenient piece of moralizing.[48] Symmachus, in a speech delivered early in 369, seems defensive about Valentinian's early activities in Gaul, making him reach the Rhine quickly and (as Ammianus was to do in his turn) presenting the emperor's refusal to help Valens as the sacrificing of personal pride to the public good.[49] This suggests that the western court, realizing the sensitivity of the situation, took pains to put into circulation an old but reliable justification for Valentinian's refusal to accept the obligations traditionally due to a blood relative. Valentinian had no intention of returning east; and to avoid such a return he and his counsellors exaggerated a series of minor frontier skirmishes.[50] Again, this was made possible not because of what the Alamanni had recently done, or what they might do, but because of the image of them created in the 260s and 270s, and the 350s.[51] Contrary to what he claimed, it is likely that the emperor's mind was made up by his appreciation of the gravity of internal, not external, dangers.

Valentinian had to keep the western armies on his side. The revolt of Procopius will have shaken the new and untested dynasty. We need to visualize Procopius' rebellion as it may have appeared when it was enjoying its early successes: not, as Ammianus would have it, the last

---

[47] AM 26.5.12–13.

[48] Drinkwater (1987: 33).

[49] *Orat.* 1.14, 17–19, 23. Cf. below 289. *Contra* Raimondi (2001: 95), the date of this speech prevents its being used as direct evidence for the state of the Empire and for Valentinian's plans at the start of his reign.

[50] Crump (1975: 49) came close to this interpretation, but followed the current *communis opinio* in believing in the authenticity of the Germanic threat. Cf. Gutmann (1991: 12–13); Raimondi (2001: 121 and n.142). I find a striking resemblance between the basic sentiment, if not precise expression, of Ammianus' reports of Valentinian's apology at Paris (26.5.13: *hostem suum fratrisque solius esse Procopium, Alamannos vero totius orbis Romani*) and Dagalaifus' earlier advising him not to choose Valens as his colleague at Nicomedia (26.4.1: *si tuos amas . . . habes fratrem, si rem publicam, quaere quem vestias*). It may be that Ammianus followed the official line on the decision of 365, which showed Valentinian in a good light, and transposed this back to 363, when, as events were to prove, the new emperor ignored the public weal. Cf. Paschoud (1992: 74).

[51] Cf. above 264.

gamble of a pathetic and unworthy successor to Julian, but the promising debut of the true heir, through his relationship with Julian and his association with Constantius II's widow and daughter, to the throne of Constantine.[52] It is no wonder that, as soon as was decently possible after the suppression of Procopius, Valentinian had Gratian marry Constantius II's only child.[53] In November 365, he must have thought twice about taking troops to the east, to be directly reminded of their Flavian loyalties.

In addition, he cannot have felt completely confident about his own position in the west, where memories of Julian and his achievements will have been especially strong. The western establishment's ambivalence towards the new dynasty was to manifest itself in 367, when Valentinian's illness provoked intense speculation as to a successor and led to the unprecedented promotion of Gratian directly to the rank of Augustus.[54] In 365, precipitate departure from the west might compound the uncertainty caused by Procopius' rebellion by signifying Valentinian's lack of confidence in Valens' ability to deal with the usurper, and so create a political vacuum which others, acting for Procopius or themselves, might be eager to fill. There were also practical considerations. Events in the east were moving so quickly that Valentinian was unable to form a clear picture of what was happening: a reckless campaign might lead to his own defeat, or leave him the irreconcilable enemy of a renascent Flavian dynasty.[55] His best course was to stay put and hold firm: to take limited measures in Africa and Illyricum to prevent the revolt from spreading, but otherwise to trust in his brother.[56] On the other hand, despite what he said about the Alamannic threat, in such a state of flux it would have been unwise for him to lead a local campaign. Valentinian's eyes were on the east, and so he remained, aware of but apart from the military affairs of the west, in Paris.[57]

---

[52] Drinkwater (1997: 11); cf. Lenski (2002: 73–4, 82–4, 98–101).

[53] In 374, when Constantia was still only about 12 years old: AM 21.15.6; 29.6.7.

[54] AM 27.6.

[55] Matthews (1989: 198); Seeck (1921: 5.51).

[56] Africa: AM 26.5.14; Illyricum: AM 26.5.11, 7.11–12. On the not inconsiderable value to Valens of the securing of Illyricum see Gutmann (1991: 15–16).

[57] So already, though rather less positively, Seeck (1921: 5.23–4); and now Lenski (2002: 76): 'Ultimately, then, Valentinian did little more than secure his own position.'

But if Alamanni were no threat, why did the situation take a turn for the worse early in 366, with the defeat of Charietto and Severianus, and how was it put right? It must be understood that this defeat was not caused by a large-scale, concerted invasion—after 357, a second attempt to settle eastern Gaul and so destroy the work of Julian—or marked the onset of a developing crisis.[58] There was never any 'first' invasion. The Alamannic leaders of 357 thought that they had been invited into the Empire. Like them, those of 366 must have realized that settlement without imperial permission was pointless.[59] Major invasion is not suggested by Ammianus' account. His description of Jovinus' first two victories, over a 'great throng' and 'another mass' of Alamanni respectively,[60] does not suggest engagement with their main host. This happened at Châlons,[61] where he implies the presence of more than 10,000 Alamanni. Taking into account all three conflicts, a total of, say, even 20,000 is far less than the 35,000 he proposed for the barbarian army at Strasbourg. And, as with the latter, even this figure cannot be taken at face value. And if there was no invasion, there is no need to suppose a single leader, with a specific strategy.[62]

Events happened probably very much like those around the defeat of Libino in 361. Supposed Alamannic humiliation at the hands of Valentinian—a tale that grew in the telling[63]—provoked a run of raids by local hotheads and, perhaps, a band or bands from further afield. As those had implicated Vadomarius, these implicated Vithicabius.[64] Imperial disinclination to put an immediate stop to this predation would only have encouraged it. Then came something more serious, though still not invasion. One set of raiders, probably no more than a few thousand strong, broke through the regular

[58] *Contra* Lorenz, S. (1997: 84) and Gutmann (1991: 17). Cf. Gutmann's (1991: 20) subsequent qualification of the danger.

[59] Above 202, 215, 237.

[60] AM 27.2.1–2: *maiorem … plebem; alterius globi.*

[61] So Elliott (1983: 159).

[62] *Contra* Lorenz, S. (1997: 69, 80–1): that the Alamanni were probably under the overall command of a single *rex*, perhaps Vithicabius of the Brisigavi, and attempted an organized advance on Reims and Paris.

[63] AM 26.5.7.

[64] Cf. above 259, 262, below 287. Cf. Gutmann (1991: 16–17): that the raiding of 366 (and 365) was probably carried out by Alamanni from the Upper Rhine.

frontier troops and became the responsibility of the regional field army under Charietto and Severianus. These, like Libino, were *comites* commanding first-class units. However, their involvement was still a matter of routine, and the situation was not considered bad enough to call upon the main field army at Reims.[65] The disaster which followed again appears to have been caused by Roman over-confidence, which turned into panic following stiff Alamannic resistance and Severianus' accident. Our sources make much of military shame,[66] but very little of casualties, which suggests that Roman losses were not considerable—again very similar to what we know happened to Libino's force. Astonishing Alamannic success made the incursion more than an ordinary raid. It committed both parties to irrevocable action—the Romans to seek revenge[67] and the Alamanni to do the most damage they could before, as they knew they would, they faced Roman main strength.

Overall, however, the Alamanni had played into Valentinian's hands. Early in 366, the situation in the east was still very uncertain. It continued to be in Valentinian's interests to remain in Gaul, and Roman defeat allowed him to do so until news of the usurper's fall arrived in early/mid-June. Jovinus appears to have worked his way behind the Alamanni, bunching them up and cutting off their retreat. When the time was right he struck from the rear. Given the smaller numbers involved, and Jovinus' long experience as general, his victory at Châlons cannot be regarded as the equal of Julian's at Strasbourg,[68] but he did well, and there is more than a hint in Ammianus' account that his third encounter with them was no walkover. Roman casualty figures, which are likely to have been less distorted than barbarian ones,[69] especially the 1,200 dead, are unusually high. This may explain why after the battle the unnamed

[65] For the operation of the system see Elton (1996a: 179).

[66] As Lorenz, S. (1997: 88) proposes, Zosimus 4.9.2–4, reporting Valentinian's ceremonial humiliation of the Batavian regiment following their flight after a Roman defeat, must also refer to the events of early 366.

[67] Ammianus (27.2.1) states explicitly that Dagalaifus was sent out to 'make good' the defeat: *correcturus sequius*.

[68] *Contra* Lorenz, S. (1997: 82), following Rosen (1970: 128); Elliott (1983: 159).

[69] Cf. above 238.

(perhaps because, being from the interior, unknown[70]) Alamannic *rex* and his companions were killed out of hand.[71]

One piece of evidence adduced in support of the claim that the battle of Châlons-sur-Marne was as significant as Strasbourg is a law of Valentinian I, dated 20 (or 15) June 366 and issued in Reims, concerning *postliminium*: the rights of citizens detained against their will during barbarian invasion and now returned to the Empire.[72] Lorenz argues that its very existence is a direct measure of the importance of Jovinus' victory.[73] However, it is often difficult to relate a law in the *Codex Theodosianus* to a particular historical event. In this case, the situation that the rescript attempts to redress—the restitution of property (land and slaves) that, as a result of the prolonged absence of its rightful owners, had already passed to third parties—hardly suggests a very recent, or especially localized problem. And, even if the law does relate to Jovinus' liberating large numbers of Alamannic captives, Valentinian's interest in these people may be interpreted less positively. Since there is no mention of Jovinus pursuing the enemy back over the Rhine after Châlons, such captives would have been held and freed on Roman soil.[74] This implies that the Alamanni were allowed a great deal of free rein, which in turn suggests that the imperial policy of 'wait-and-see' was not in the best interests of the local population. Some of Ammianus' numerous 'trivial' wars of this period may have resulted from this: not further major campaigns,[75] but the suppression of civil disorder caused by general disruption, the precursor of the 'savage frenzy for brigandage in Gaul' which Ammianus records for 369.[76] (Another law, concerning the provision of services of the public post, addressed to Jovinus early in 367, indicates orderly and extensive

[70] *Contra* Gutmann (1991: 17).

[71] As Gutmann (1991: 19) observes, all involved would normally have been spared and recruited into the imperial army.

[72] *CT* 5.7.1. I take 20 June from Pharr (1952: 108); 15 June comes from Seeck (1919: 228), *XVII Kal. Iul.*, following Mommsen.

[73] Lorenz, S. (1997: 84).

[74] Cf. above 140.

[75] Cf. Demandt (1972: 85); Lorenz, S. (1997: 91); below 279.

[76] AM 28.2.10: *latrociniorum rabies saeva*. Cf. Drinkwater (1989: 194) on the possible link between this and the Bagaudae.

negotiations with barbarian leaders.[77] If these were Alamanni, the law suggests a speedy restoration of peaceful relations after a period of unrest.[78])

In 364–6, Valentinian simply consolidated his position. In summer 367 he faced the problem of his own serious illness (ominously, the second since his accession) and consequent political uncertainty at court, which forced him to appoint Gratian as fellow Augustus (24 August).[79] This happened at Amiens, which the court then left, heading for Trier. However, en route arrived news of trouble: the infamous 'Barbarian Conspiracy' of Picts, Attacotti and Scots in Britain, and Frankish and Saxon attacks along the northern coast of Gaul. Valentinian delegated these matters to his generals, and order was eventually restored by count Theodosius in 368.[80] This meant that by the end of 367 Valentinian, unlike Valens, still had personally to prove his military mettle. There are hints that in the latter months of both 366 and 367 there was successful fighting against the Franks, but this appears to have been restricted and did not involve Valentinian's personal participation.[81] The Alamanni remained the preferred game, and it is possible that Valentinian's move from Reims via Amiens to Trier in 367 was the next step in the preparation of a major campaign against them, interrupted by other concerns.[82] It comes as no surprise that the emperor renewed conflict with the Alamanni in 368.

Most of what we know about this and events down to Valentinian's death in 375 comes, as before, from Ammianus Marcellinus, but there is an important difference. As he did in the case of Constantius II and Julian, Ammianus appears to mention all Valentinian's

[77] *CT* 7.1.9.

[78] Cf. Gutmann (1991: 22).

[79] AM 26.4.4; 27.6.1–16. On this generally, see now Raimondi (2001: 131–69, esp. 163–4: the election of Gratian confirmed the western army's support of Valentinian).

[80] AM 27.8.1–10; 28.3.1–8. Demandt (1972: 84–91); Matthews (1989: 207); Drinkwater (1999a: 133–4).

[81] Demandt (1972: 82–4); Nixon and Rodgers (1994: 517–19); Lorenz, S. (1997: 83, 91). Gutmann (1991: 47 and n.26) relates this rather to count Theodosius' suppression of the Barbarian Conspiracy.

[82] Gutmann (1991: 23); Drinkwater (1999a: 133). Cf. Lorenz, S. (1997: 92), for possible preparations by Valentinian for a major Alamannic campaign while he was still resident in Reims.

military activities; however, contrary to what is often assumed, this should never be taken for granted.[83] There are three indications of omissions. First, Valentinian's campaign on the Rhine and Neckar in 369 is described in some detail by our second important source, the Roman senator Symmachus, but not by Ammianus. Second, we know from the writings of the high-ranking western courtier, Ausonius, that at some time during his sojourn on the Rhine Valentinian travelled to the source of the Danube. Much must have been made of this exploit. Symmachus lavishes praise on Valentinian's Alexander-like advance into 'unknown' territory beyond the Rhine and on the emperor's 'discovery' of the Neckar.[84] The reappearance of Roman arms at the Danube source must have been seen as a considerably more memorable event. It can be no accident that we find mention of it in Ausonius' *Mosella* and in two further poems by him, specifically commemorating the achievement.[85] If the Danube expedition caused official excitement in Trier, it is justifiable to assume that it was also celebrated in Rome, and was recorded and remembered there in close detail. However, when Ammianus, now researching and writing in the city,[86] came to construct his account of Valentinian's military exploits he ignored the incident.

From around 367 Ammianus gives us no more than a series of impressions of Valentinian's activities. His treatment has, indeed, been characterized as episodic and 'imprecise, eclectic and anecdotal'.[87] It probably suited him to pick up enough from imperial propaganda to intimate that Valentinian had much to do on the Rhine because Valentinian's barbarian enemies were those of Julian. Otherwise, however, Ammianus was not concerned to present a complete or balanced account of an emperor in whom he was interested only as the bane of the Roman élite, the employer of the 'good' count Theodosius, and the brother of Valens.[88] Finally, the Alamannic massacre of Roman troops at Mons Piri in 369 must have

---

[83] Thus *contra*, e.g. Sivan (1990: 384).

[84] Symmachus, *Orat.* 2.24, 30. Pabst (1989: 336).

[85] Ausonius, *Mosella* 424; *Epig.* 28, 31 [Peiper] (3, 4 [Green]).

[86] Matthews (1989: 20–1).

[87] Pabst (1989: 307): Ammianus' 'wenig präzise, eklektisch-anekdotische Erzählung'.

[88] On this see further Drinkwater (1999a: 131–2).

been followed by reprisals which went beyond the execution of hostages, but of these Ammianus makes no mention.[89] In short, we have to accept that it is now impossible to reconstruct anything like a full narrative of events on the Rhine and the upper Danube under Valentinian from 367.[90] I will therefore first summarize what Ammianus says of Valentinian's dealings with Alamanni down to the end of his reign, establish a basic chronology, and finally assess the significance of what occurred by year rather than by campaign.

Having reported trouble in the east, in Isauria, Ammianus continues that around this time, when Valentinian had already cautiously begun his campaign, an Alamannic prince (*regalis*), Rando, slipped into Mainz with a light raiding-party and took many captives and much booty. Rando was helped in his enterprise by his long preparation and by the fact that the city had been left unguarded and was celebrating a Christian holiday at the time.[91] Shortly afterwards there was better news. King Vithicabius, son and successor of Vadomarius, who had often fanned the flames of war against the Empire, was dead, slain by a personal attendant, suborned by Rome. This was the culmination of various Roman attempts to kill him, and led to some reduction in Alamannic raiding.[92]

After this, Valentinian launched a major campaign against the Alamanni, involving numerous troops assembled from all sides and carefully armed and provisioned. The reason for this was that the treacherous and irreducible nature of the foe posed a grave danger to public safety. At the beginning of the warm season, Valentinian, accompanied by Gratian, led his men over the Rhine.[93] Meeting no immediate resistance, the emperor advanced carefully and slowly, guided by scouts. After a few days, still having made no contact with the enemy, he ordered the burning of neighbouring fields and dwellings, and proceeded more slowly to Solicinium. Here he stopped, having been warned that the enemy was ahead. He was told that they, having decided to stand and fight, '... had stationed

---

[89] *Contra* Lorenz, S. (1997: 144), I cannot believe that Valentinian let this incident pass without retaliatory action.

[90] Cf. Raimondi (2001: 92).

[91] AM 27.10.1–2.

[92] AM 27.10.3–4; 30.7.7.

[93] AM 27.10.5–6. For Rhine rather than Main see below 287.

themselves on a lofty mountain, surrounded on all sides by rocky and precipitous heights and inaccessible except on the northern side where it has an easy and gentle slope'.[94] Valentinian hastily devised a battle plan. This involved stationing one of his generals, Sebastianus, on the northern slope, to attack the Alamanni as they fled. The rest of his army was to attack up the rocky heights, where scouts had found a path. Gratian was not to participate in the fighting. As this was being put into action, Valentinian dashed off with a small force to inspect the heights, believing that he could find a better way up.[95] However, he was ambushed and only just managed to escape alive. Battle was joined as originally planned, and Roman forces stormed the summit. There was heavy fighting. The Alamanni were surrounded and eventually fled. As planned, they were cut to pieces by Sebastianus.[96] Roman forces then went into winter quarters, with Valentinian and Gratian returning to Trier.[97]

Ammianus then tells us that Valentinian fortified the entire Rhine, from Raetia to the North Sea, in some places building on the river's right bank, in barbarian territory.[98] The emperor gave particular attention to a fort on the river Neckar, which he had had built, but which was in danger of being washed away. Valentinian came up with a plan to divert the current away from the structure which, under his direct supervision, was successfully executed.[99] Valentinian then decided to build another fortification over the Rhine, on Mons Piri. He entrusted the scheme to a *dux*, Arator, and, given the lateness of the season, ordered him to press ahead 'while deep silence reigned everywhere'. As work began, Arator and his successor, Hermogenes (who had, apparently, already been appointed), were approached by a delegation of leading men (*optimates*) of the Alamanni, claiming that what they were doing ran contrary to what had been agreed with them and begging them to stop. When the Romans refused they withdrew, sorrowing for sons of theirs who had been handed over to Rome as hostages under the terms of a treaty. A waiting war-party

---

[94] AM 27.10.6–9.
[95] AM 27.10.9–10.
[96] AM 27.10.12–15.
[97] AM 27.10.16.
[98] AM 28.2.1.
[99] AM 28.2.2–4.

then cut down the Roman troops engaged in building the fort, leaving only one survivor.[100] In the meantime, Gaul was afflicted by a 'savage frenzy for brigandage'. One of its victims was Constantianus, Valentinian's own brother-in-law and *tribunus stabuli*.[101]

Under the third consulship of Valentinian and Valens, Ammianus describes a Saxon attack on northern Gaul and its destruction by Roman forces.[102] After this, Valentinian concerned himself with 'how to break the arrogance of the Alamanni and their king Macrianus, who without limit or measure was confusing the Roman state by his restless disturbances'. He decided to use Burgundians as allies, and arranged with their leaders that while they attacked the Alamanni from one direction he would strike them from the other.[103] The Burgundians agreed, but arrived before Valentinian (still busy with his building) was ready for them. They reached the Rhine and 'caused the very greatest alarm to our people'.[104] When the emperor did not appear as arranged, the Burgundians sought his support to prevent their being attacked in the rear during their withdrawal. However, feeling that their demands were being ignored, their envoys left upset and angry. Their leaders were furious at their treatment, killed their prisoners and returned home.[105] In the meantime, count Theodosius, seeing that the Alamanni had been panicked by the Burgundian incursion, attacked them from Raetia, killed many and sent his prisoners to Italy, where they were settled on the Po.[106]

A little later, Ammianus returns to the story of Valentinian and Macrianus, leading into it from a discussion of the emperor's temper and cruelty and, yet, his work for the good of the state. He says that it was Valentinian's main concern to take the king alive, by whatever possible means, as Julian had taken Vadomarius. This was because Macrianus, 'amid the frequent changes in policy towards him, had

---

[100] AM 28.2.5–9: *dum undique altum esset silentium.*
[101] AM 28.2.10: *latrociniorum rabies saeva.*
[102] AM 28.5.1–7.
[103] AM 28.5.8–10.
[104] AM 28.5.11: *terrori nostris fuere vel maximo.* On the causes of Burgundian hostility to the Alamanni see above 109.
[105] AM 28.5.12–13.
[106] AM 28.5.15. Above 167.

increased in power and was now rising against our countrymen with full-grown strength'.[107] Having discovered from deserters where Macrianus was likely to be, and knowing that he expected no trouble, Valentinian threw a pontoon bridge over the Rhine and sent a small force, under his *magister peditum,* another Severus, to Wiesbaden. Severus at first advanced as ordered, then, worried by the small size of his force, halted. More troops arrived with Valentinian, also lightly equipped, and, as dawn approached, the Romans pressed forward, led by cavalry under count Theodosius.[108] There was, apparently (here there is a short lacuna in the text), a night raid on Macrianus' residence. The narrative continues with an account of Roman troops getting out of hand, and looting and burning. The noise woke Macrianus' attendants, who promptly moved him to a place of safety in the hills. Robbed of his prey, Valentinian laid waste enemy territory 'as far as the fiftieth milestone', then returned to Trier.[109] With Macrianus gone, he appointed Fraomarius king of the Bucinobantes. However, 'since a recent invasion had utterly devastated that canton', he soon transferred him to Britain with the rank of tribune. He also appointed the Alamannic chiefs Bitheridus and Hortarius to army commands, but later had Hortarius executed for having treasonably communicated with Macrianus and other barbarian leaders.[110]

Valentinian then fought a major war against the Quadi. In the following year, in the consulship of himself and Aequitius, having devastated several Alamannic *pagi,* he was building a fortification near Basel, 'which those living nearby called Robur', when he learned of further trouble on the Danube. Inclined to move there at once, he was, we are told, dissuaded by his counsellors on the grounds of the closeness of winter and the fact that he first needed to settle matters on the Rhine: 'They set before him the alleged savagery of the kings bordering on Gaul, and most of all of Macrianus, who was formidable and (as was well known) had been left unsubdued and would

[107] AM 29.4.1–2: *auctum inter mutationes crebras sententiarum iamque in nostros adultis viribus exsurgentem.*

[108] AM 29.4.2–5. Sabbah (1999: 27) has the Roman advance beginning with moonrise.

[109] AM 29.4.5–6: *ad usque quinquagesimum lapidem.*

[110] AM 29.4.7: *quoniam recens excursus eundem penitus vastaverat pagum.*

actually attack fortified cities.'[111] Valentinian immediately invited Macrianus to a meeting near Mainz. The king arrived on the bank of the Rhine 'while the clashing shields of his countrymen thundered all about him'. From the Roman side, Valentinian and his staff took to boats and drew near him. There were speeches on both sides, and an alliance was concluded with an oath. Valentinian then withdrew to Trier for the winter. Macrianus proved to be a steadfast ally, until his death while raiding into Frankish territory.[112] The following year, Valentinian moved to Illyricum to fight the Quadi. Here he died of apoplexy.[113]

The basic chronology of these events is fairly straightforward. The campaign which led to victory at Solicinium must have been in 368, the year after Gratian's proclamation as Augustus and the Barbarian Conspiracy. Valentinian's work on the Neckar and at Mons Piri must therefore have fallen in 369, as confirmed by Symmachus' second panegyric.[114] Ammianus' consular dating puts the Saxon attack and the alliance with Burgundians in 370.[115] Valentinian's attempt to capture Macrianus probably took place in 371, although some would put it in 372.[116] The year in which Valentinian built Robur and reached agreement with Macrianus preceded the year in which he died on campaign against the Quadi, and is anyway consular dated: it has to be 374. By this time Macrianus was clearly back in full command of the Bucinobantes. He must have driven out Fraomarius in 372 or 373.[117]

Valentinian was resident in Trier to the end of July 368, when he moved to the Rhine. He had returned to Trier and its region by

---

[111] AM 30.3.1–3: *quod appellant accolae Robur... vicinorum Galliis regum immanitatem, maxime omnium Macriani, ut formidati, tunc praetendentes, quem constabat impacatum relictum etiam ipsa urbium moenia temptaturum.*

[112] AM 30.3.4–7: *sonitu scutorum intonante gentilium.*

[113] AM 30.6.3.

[114] Below 289.

[115] Seeck (1919: 238–40): Valentinian was still in Trier on 1 June. By 31 July he could have been at Worms (though this is also attributable to 368—cf. below 287—or 373). He was back in Trier by 1 December.

[116] Seeck (1919: 242, 371); Demandt (1972: 92); Lorenz, S. (1997: 144, 152, 154 and nn.575–6).

[117] Seeck (1919: 244–6): Valentinian was in Trier to 20 June 374; he was at Robur on 10 July and appears to have been at Mainz on 7 September. He had returned to Trier by 3 December. Cf. below 309.

6 November at the latest (there is the possibility that he was back by the end of September).[118] His main campaign probably took place in August/September.[119] This was after Rando's raid and if, as generally accepted, the Christian festival that helped Rando in his enterprise was Easter, well after it.[120] However, the raid still fell too late to have occasioned Valentinian's large expedition. Indeed, Ammianus seems to say that it cut across preparations for war that were already well under way.[121]

Therefore what did Rando's raid amount to and what was its significance? Ammianus' account provides more questions than answers. Rando's light force is hardly likely to have captured Mainz, still one of the main military complexes of the Empire, consisting of the Kastel bridgehead, the city, and the legionary base.[122] What happened was probably not a major attack but a daring sortie by a princeling aware of a temporary dislocation in the garrisoning of the place (perhaps resulting from Valentinian's military build-up) and acting without the knowledge or, at least, the official permission of his king.[123] Rando may have come from a distance but, given his knowledge of Mainz and its inhabitants, it is more likely that he was from the territory around Wiesbaden.[124] Ammianus mentions no Roman reprisals for the action. This could well be another of his omissions, but it may signify that punishment was left to others: specifically, to king Macrianus or one of his dependants. If the regiment of 'Bucinobantes' was recruited in the period 365–8,[125] Macrianus must still have been regarded as friendly and dependable and capable of performing imperial police work. On the other hand, it may have been this incident that extended his sphere of influence

---

[118] Seeck (1919: 230–4); Demandt (1972: 83–4).

[119] Lorenz, S. (1997: 100): from early August.

[120] Seeck (1919: 232): in 368, Easter Sunday fell on 20 April. Lorenz, S. (1997: 98) prefers Whit Sunday, 8 June. Gutmann (1991: 24 n.105) puts Easter Sunday on 25 March.

[121] As Lorenz, S. (1997: 113–15).

[122] Höckmann (1986: 370); Lorenz, S. (1997: 97–8); Witschel (1999: 354); Carroll (2001: Fig. 16).

[123] Above 122.

[124] So Lorenz, S. (1997: 113).

[125] Above 170.

to the Rhine, and reminded Valentinian of the vulnerability of the Main valley and the Mainz bridgehead.[126]

Likewise, the assassination of Vithicabius is unlikely to have had a direct connection with Rando—too far to the north—or the 368 campaign. The most likely reason for Vithicabius' death is association with the raiding of 365/6.[127] Rome must have ensured that, as Vithicabius had replaced Vadomarius, he was replaced by another ruler, very likely from another family which was subsequently rewarded with the building of the Zähringer Burgberg. (Valentinian was in the immediate vicinity of this site in mid-June 369.[128]) Valentinian had gone out of his way to remove Vithicabius without military action. While the change of régime in his former kingdom was being managed, it would have made no sense to attack it.[129]

So where did Valentinian lead his troops? Modern historians have found it difficult to decide whether the Roman attack was north or south of the Main. However, proponents of both views have suggested that, wherever he was, Valentinian advanced relatively far: for example, if north of the Main, to Glauberg, in Oberhessen; if south, to Rottenburg-am-Neckar.[130] A crossing of the *Rhenum* (Rhine) is more easily read in the manuscript's *inhenum* than one of the *Moenum* (Main).[131] It also suits Valentinian's attitude towards Macrianus, whom he never faced head-on in his own territory and who was currently still well-regarded. From the distribution of hill-sites,[132] it seems likely that Valentinian crossed into or beyond the Odenwald. His justification is again likely to have been reprisals against communities involved in the raiding of 365/6. He may have crossed from Worms.[133] A long-distance strike hardly squares with

---

[126] Cf. above 115, 174, 190.

[127] Above 273–6. Cf. Lorenz, S. (1997: 114) on Vithicabius as a driving force in these attacks.

[128] Above 102, below 289.

[129] *Contra* Lorenz, S. (1997: 99, 111–12, 113–15).

[130] Glauberg: Demandt (1989: 112 and n.14). Rottenburg: Nagl (1948: 2173); Matthews (1989: 311); Gutmann (1991: 26–7). For discussion of these and other identifications, based for the most part on supposing a long-distance campaign, see Lorenz, S. (1997: 102, 108–10).

[131] Lorenz, S. (1997: 99, 182).

[132] Above 97.

[133] As Lorenz, S. (1997: 100 n.184), though arguing against such a route.

Ammianus' description of an unusually large army, accompanied by an important non-combatant (the boy-Augustus, Gratian, presumably with numerous attendants), marching cautiously for a few days, and then at an even gentler pace, before engaging the enemy at Solicinium. The latest estimate of the rate of march of a late-imperial army is *c.* 20 km (12 statute miles) per day;[134] but this is an average figure, and Ammianus' account provides grounds for assuming that Valentinian's force moved at a slower speed, perhaps only half this rate.[135] Rottenburg, *c.* 170 km (100 statute miles) from Mainz as the crow flies, is therefore out of the question as the location of Solicinium. Having crossed the Rhine, Valentinian probably struck north, as Julian had done in 359,[136] reaching Solicinium, like Ladenburg in the following year, not far from the river. There is nothing to substantiate the long-standing conjecture that identifies Solicinium with Heidelberg.[137]

In Solicinium, Ammianus could be describing a 'Höhensiedlung', large enough to accommodate a major battle.[138] The mass of rocks seized by the first wave of Roman troops in their attack might, therefore, have incorporated a drystone wall.[139] There is no reference to the conflict's being hampered by any internal buildings, which would suggest that, if the place was a hill-site, it functioned as an emergency redoubt rather than as a 'Herrschaftszentrum'.[140] However, if it was a refuge it is odd that there is no hint of any defence works protecting its open northern neck. As far as the fighting is concerned, it is significant that Gratian was removed from harm and that Valentinian early went out of his way to demonstrate his personal courage, in a no doubt much-bruited venture that Ammianus may have picked up from the official record, possibly even from paintings. Again, the emperor needed to project

[134] Elton (1996a: 245).

[135] The 25 km per day of Lorenz, S. (1997: 102 n.200) is certainly excessive. At 25.1.10, Ammianus appears to report that in the final stage of the Persian campaign Julian's army advanced only 70 stades (*c.*13 km) in a day. I doubt whether Valentinian's formation was able to maintain even this speed.

[136] Above 249.

[137] Lorenz, S. (1997: 108 and n.243).

[138] Above 96.

[139] AM 27.10.12.

[140] Above 95–6; cf. AM 27.10.9.

himself as an active soldier.[141] There is no need to judge the campaign a relative failure.[142]

Ammianus' treatment of the following year, 369, is uneven, consisting of a general notice of Valentinian's building activities, together with two examples of these. However, it can be better understood by taking into account Symmachus' oration in honour of Valentinian's third consulship, delivered at the beginning of 370.[143] Symmachus, a rising star of the Roman senate, had been on official business at the western court from the winter of 368/9.[144] An eye-witness,[145] he, like Ammianus, describes the commencement of Valentinian's great military building programme in 369 and gives examples.[146] However, he also recalls an expedition of the emperor over the Rhine in the same year, against a place called Alta Ripa—'High Bank'.[147] Though Symmachus' Alta Ripa lay on the right side of the Rhine, its name seems also to have been applied to a new Valentinianic fort sited on the left bank—identified as modern Altrip, south-east of Ludwigshafen (Fig. 23). Valentinian issued a law from Alta Ripa on 19 June 369, having remained in Trier until at least mid-May. He was still on the Rhine on 30 August, at Breisach (opposite the site of the Zähringer Burgberg), but had returned to Trier by 14 October. His 369 campaign must therefore have taken place in early summer, probably in June.[148] According to Symmachus, after careful preparation, a small force was sent over by boat (perhaps the type of large, shallow barge found in Xanten in 1993[149]). Once a landing had been made and the position secured, a pontoon bridge was built to bring over a larger force. Roman troops scaled the lofty bank that gave the place its name and then

[141] Cf. Mause (1994: 197) on the need for an emperor to be seen as an active soldier.

[142] *Contra* Lorenz, S. (1997: 116–17). Cf. Raimondi (2001: 168–9): the Solicinium campaign as the most important military expedition of Valentinian's reign, and the last great victorious military sortie of a Roman emperor over the Rhine.

[143] Symmachus, *Orat.* 2 (Pabst (1989: 66–91)). Later, of course, than *Orat.* 1: above n. 49.

[144] Matthews (1975: 32); *Quellen* 2, 28.

[145] Symmachus, *Orat.* 2.3, 22.

[146] Symmachus, *Orat.* 2.1, 28.

[147] Symmachus, *Orat.* 2.4.

[148] Seeck (1919: 236–8); Pabst (1989: 306).

[149] Bridger (2003: 24).

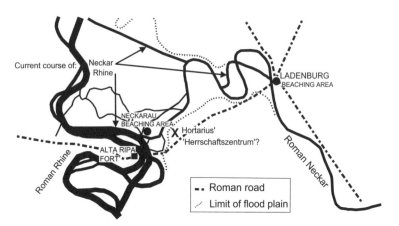

Fig. 23 Alta Ripa, Mannheim-Neckarau and Ladenburg [from Pabst (1989: 376 Fig. 2); © Frau Prof. Angela Pabst].

advanced on an Alamannic settlement. This they took, and forced its inhabitants to take flight.[150]

There is much of interest in Symmachus' account, beginning with the nature and location of the Alamannic settlement. To a Roman it will have seemed a very poor place, made up of thatched wooden huts.[151] However, it must have been large, to justify the size of the force directed against it; and it comprised women and children and men bearing arms. All this suggests that it was more than a 'village',[152] and that in Symmachus' description we have a lowland 'Herrschaftszentrum'.[153] The settlement also lay close to the Rhine, very possibly east-north-east of the fort at Alta Ripa, where raised ground (Symmachus' transrhenish 'high bank') afforded protection from the Rhine and the Neckar.[154] Such proximity implies that its inhabitants, like those of Mengen and the Zähringer Burgberg,[155] usually co-existed peacefully with the Empire. Its leader must have been a compliant king, from its location perhaps

---

150 Symmachus, *Orat.* 2.4–10, 26.
151 Symmachus, *Orat.* 2.10, 14.
152 Or, as Lorenz, S. (1997: 121), 'villages'.
153 Above 98.
154 Pabst (1989: 376 Fig. 2).
155 Above 89.

Hortarius or his successor.[156] The impression of cooperation is strengthened by what we are told about the Roman attack. If this settlement really was hostile, it is surprising that it was not earlier abandoned by its inhabitants in the face of what, despite Valentinian's alleged efforts at secrecy,[157] must have been an evident concentration of Roman forces over the Rhine. Equally odd is that the Alamanni did not keep a close watch on the river bank and that the Roman assault was apparently unopposed.[158] However, most astonishing is what happened when the Romans entered the settlement. Symmachus tells us that its occupants were not killed in their beds, nor driven from their huts by fire. They had already risen and had prepared themselves for the day, and they departed unmolested—according to the latest translation of the text—even being permitted to keep their weapons.[159] There is every reason to suspect that the whole thing was devised to impress visiting civilian dignitaries, and was not an authentic assault.[160] Again, a significant indicator of Valentinian's likely caution in all this is Gratian's presence in the imperial train.[161] The oddly secretive way in which Valentinian made his preparations was unlikely to have been a real precaution, generated by his fear of indiscretion, or worse, by Germanic officers,[162] but rather a reflection of Symmachus' ignorance of what was to happen, as the military establishment kept him and his fellows out of the 'information loop'. The subsequent building of the pontoon bridge looks very much like a peacetime exercise. It took only a day, and troops on both sides of the river competed cheerfully with each other in its construction. That it was covered with earth hints at some degree of overengineering, and further suggests that it was more for show than for use.[163]

What follows is more difficult to interpret, but it appears that the Roman force advanced to a former imperial town (as Symmachus

---

[156] Above 243, 249; cf. Lorenz, S. (1997: 121 and n.340).
[157] Symmachus, *Orat.* 2.5–6.
[158] Symmachus, *Orat.* 2.4, 6–9.
[159] Symmachus, *Orat.* 2.10; Pabst (1989: 75, 143 n.42). See Sogno (forthcoming) for Symmachus' treatment of their flight as circus spectacle.
[160] Matthews (1975: 32–3), with Drinkwater (1996: 28 and n.33).
[161] Symmachus, *Orat.* 2.31.
[162] *Contra* Pabst (1989: 309).
[163] Symmachus, *Orat.* 2.26. *Contra* Pabst (1989: 150 n.118).

puts it, a *colonia*, still with inscriptions and ruined buildings), and robbed it of materials in order to build a new fortification at the confluence of two rivers. Its construction was designed and supervised by Valentinian; and it turns out to have been one of this emperor's 'fortified beaching areas'.[164] Symmachus' subsequent emphasis on Valentinian's activity on the Neckar[165] indicates that this was the region where the 'campaign' took place: the two rivers are the Rhine and the Neckar, and the new fort is the one found at Mannheim-Neckarau.[166] Ammianus' reference to the Neckar in his first example of Valentinian's fort building tempts one to think that the structure concerned is also the one at Mannheim-Neckarau.[167] From a reference in Ausonius linking Neckar and Lopodunum,[168] the *colonia* is taken to be the former *civitas*-capital of Ladenburg—itself also later developed as a fortified beaching area.[169] Here, the most interesting aspect of this is that local Alamanni were recruited to enter Lopodunum and help strip it of building materials.[170] This suggests that the allied king of the peacefully evacuated 'Herrschaftszentrum' provided the labour and transport necessary for the operation as part of general Romano-Alamannic cooperation in the exploitation of the resources of the area, already discussed.[171] Part of his reward was probably continued permission to occupy his riverside settlement, albeit still obliged to give hostages.[172]

Cooperation takes us to Valentinian's military building at Mons Piri. What we see is clear Alamannic distress at Roman disregard of a peace agreement, perhaps made with Valentinian. If, as seems

---

[164] Symmachus, *Orat.* 2.15–16, 18–20. Below 295, 296–7.

[165] Symmachus, *Orat.* 2.24.

[166] Schönberger (1969: 185); Petrikovits (1971: 186); Pabst (1989: 145 n.67).

[167] So, firmly, Lorenz, S. (1997: 124–5, 130), though Matthews (1989: 285) has reservations.

[168] Below 293.

[169] Pabst (1989: 145–6 n.68); below 295. I see no reason to accept the assertion of Lorenz, S. (1997: 124–5 and n.358, 128) that Ladenburg was built before Mannheim-Neckarau.

[170] Symmachus, *Orat.* 2.15–16.

[171] Above 133–5; cf. Pabst (1989: 309).

[172] Asche (1983: 88); Lorenz, S. (1997: 121) from Symmachus, *Orat.* 2.23. See also below concerning Mons Piri. *Contra* Lorenz, S. (1997: 122), that Valentinian was engaged in creating an 'Alamanni-free' zone. This would surely have been too large and difficult to maintain.

likely, the work affected only a single *pagus*, Ammianus' '*optimates*' is a collective term for its chief and leading men.[173] Roman aggression now provoked unexpected reaction. Presumably the imperial authorities, assuming that the threat to the hostages was sufficient to keep these people submissive, had not bothered to consult them in advance about the fort. Again, as in 366, the Alamanni played into Valentinian's hands by confirming the Roman image of them as untrustworthy and dangerous foes who deserved firm treatment. The loss of Roman troops, though shaming, was no major defeat,[174] and must have been avenged.[175] However, the most important conclusion to be drawn from the incident is that communities living close to the frontier, in line with previous agreements, did not expect Roman harassment: the normal condition was peace. Mons Piri is generally located in the vicinity of Heidelberg, at no great distance from Mannheim-Neckarau and possibly in the same *pagus*.[176] This would explain the dismay of the *optimates*: having cooperated closely over the establishment of one fort in their territory, they were not expecting a second.[177] It may also be noted that, in the absence of the emperor, Alamanni were expected to deal with a senior army officer, as already proposed for the Iller-*limes*.[178]

A final question concerning 368 and 369 is whether Valentinian and Gratian travelled any distance beyond the Rhine. In his poem celebrating the Moselle, Ausonius declares that the river has seen the 'united triumphs of father and son' (that is Valentinian I and Gratian), which they have won by defeating enemies beyond the river Neckar and 'Lupodunum' (that is Lopodunum) and the source of the Danube.[179] Mention of the Neckar and Lopodunum fits what we know of Valentinian's activities for 368 and, especially, 369, but the Danube is more of a problem.

---

[173] Cf. above 118, 120.
[174] Lorenz, S. (1997: 142).
[175] Above 277.
[176] Cf. Gutmann (1991: 32); Lorenz, S. (1997: 142).
[177] Lorenz, S. (1997: 122, 124 and n.359, 141).
[178] Above 99, 157, 212.
[179] Ausonius, *Mosella* 422–4: *Nicrum super et Lupodunum/et fontem Latiis ignotum annalibus Histri.*

The imperial visit to its source appears to have been made much of in official circles.[180] It seems unlikely that, as commonly assumed, this had taken place by the end of 369, as a result of campaigning in 368 or 369.[181] We must not assume from the stray references in Ausonius and Symmachus that the years 368 and 369 were the only ones in which Valentinian and Gratian went into the field together. It is more probable that, like the sons of Constantine I, the boy was prepared for an imperial career by frequent association with the army.[182] Much will have been made of Gratian's first campaign as Augustus, and it is this that was picked up by Ammianus;[183] but there will have been later expeditions. However, as in 368 and 369, none of these will have been deep into Alamannic territory: Valentinian liked to stay close to home.[184] A likely date for the Danube visit is 370.[185] A sortie from, say, Windisch (only 60 km or so from the union of the headstreams of the Danube at Donaueschingen, along the old Roman road to Rottweil) would have been another grand but localized affair, polishing the image of Valentinian as the great explorer, introduced in 369 on his advance to the Neckar[186] (Fig. 4). Seeck's reconstruction of Valentinian's movements allows plenty of time for such an imperial expedition in the second half of 370.[187] The expedition need not have been aggressive in nature, but the attention given to it will have served to divert attention from Valentinian's failed attempt early in the year, probably in July and August,[188] to use the Burgundians against Macrianus.[189]

[180] Above 280.

[181] e.g. Evelyn-White (1919: xvi–xviii, 258); Nagl (1948: 2173–4); Piganiol (1972: 196 and n.7); Green (1978: 92); Heinen (1985: 245); Pabst (1989: 306–7); Sivan (1990: 383–4 and n.1); Green (1991: 379, 456, 507); Heinen (1995: 81–2); Lorenz, S. (1997: 102–8) with full bibliography and firmly for 368.

[182] Cf. above 197–8. Note AM 27.6.8: Valentinian, while presenting Gratian to the troops in 367, admits the need for him to be hardened in war. Cf. Lorenz, S. (1997: 101 and n.194).

[183] Cf. Nagl (1948: 2174).

[184] Cf. Seeck (1921: 5.24).

[185] Drinkwater (1999b: 449–50).

[186] Windisch: cf. Nagl (1948: 2173) citing Maurer, for 368.

[187] Seeck (1919: 238–40).

[188] Lorenz, S. (1997: 150).

[189] Below 305–6.

Ammianus famously praises Valentinian for his work in fortifying the length of the Rhine, 'from the beginning of Raetia as far as the strait of the Ocean'.[190] These words are confirmed by what he says elsewhere, by the earlier eyewitness account of Symmachus, and by archaeological discoveries. Valentinian built or restored forts and established lines of watchtowers (*burgi*) along the Rhine and the Danube. Along the Upper and High Rhine and the Danube–Iller–Rhine *limes* he was responsible for a number of major left-bank structures. Directly on the Upper Rhine, upstream from Mainz, we find forts at Speyer, Altrip, and Breisach. On the High Rhine, from Basel east to Lake Constance, and from Lake Constance up the Iller to the Danube, there is a line of *burgi*. Behind the actual line of the frontier, there were more forts and *burgi*. Near the Rhine, these are known at Alzey, Altinum, Horbourg, Kreuznach, Eisenburg, Irgenhausen, Schaan, Zurich, and along the Aare. Near the Danube are Wilten and Isny. All these structures were located on imperial territory, on the left bank of the Rhine and the right banks of the Iller and Danube. They were complemented by a number of constructions on the right bank of the Rhine. On the Upper and High Rhine there were bridgehead forts at Mainz, Jechtingen-Sponeck, Basel (possibly Ammianus' Robur) and Wyhlen.[191] In addition, on the right bank, there were specialized *burgi*, categorized by Schleiermacher as 'befestigte Schiffsländen'—'fortified beaching areas for ships'. Along the Upper Rhine, remains of these have been found at Wiesbaden-Biebrich, Mannheim-Neckarau and Ladenburg.[192] Valentinian's western building programme (which appears to have been mirrored by one directed by Valens, but ordered by Valentinian) was, to judge from literary, epigraphic and archaeological evidence, concentrated in the late 360s and early 370s.[193]

Why did Valentinian do what he did in the west, and how did his actions affect the Alamanni? Current opinion remains that Valentinian correctly perceived a renascent Germanic threat along

---

[190] AM 28.2.1: *a Raetiarum exordio ad usque fretalem Oceanum.*
[191] Maps: Schönberger (1969: Fig. 23); Petrikovits (1971: Fig. 32); Johnson (1983: Figs 51, 62).
[192] Höckmann (1986: 400); cf. above 292.
[193] Lenski (2002: 376); cf. Lorenz, S. (1997: 132–3).

the whole line of the western frontier and successfully countered it.[194] He must initially have believed in a 'threat': as both a product of Greco-Roman society and (as a soldier and emperor) a beneficiary of 'the politics of fear', he was bound to do so. However, his lack of haste in reaching the Rhine indicates that from the start he recognized there was no immediate danger; and his subsequent activities there suggest that he appreciated fairly quickly that neighbouring Alamannic communities were no major problem. He maintained the idea of a 'threat' because it enabled him to follow his own agenda: to avoid helping Valens; to confirm his position and that of his heir; to distance him, as a 'rough' provincial, from the sophisticated civilian society of Italy.[195] His new defence works may therefore be interpreted as defensive rather than aggressive, aimed at preventing sporadic raiding, not massive attack and, again following his own agenda, permitting him to indulge his passion for architecture and gadgetry.[196]

Valentinian's work was, in essence, not new. It followed an established pattern of linear defence which went back to Diocletian and even earlier, first and second-century, models. As Petrikovits says, on the Rhine and Danube the emperor 'found a defensive network already established; the need was to supplement it and make it more dense'.[197] (The idea that the Late Empire saw the development of an integrated strategy of 'defence-in-depth', popular after the publication of Luttwak's *Grand Strategy*, is now out of favour.[198]) What was original was Valentinian's building of right-bank 'Schiffsländen'.[199] These are also found on the left bank of the Danube, in Pannonia,[200] but here, in concentrating on the Alamanni, I restrict myself to the Rhine. Symmachus' description and archaeological

[194] Above 270. See also Alföldi (1946: 15). Schönberger (1969: 186); Matthews (1975: 33); Stroheker (1975: 38–9); Asche (1983: 42, 49, 53, 56, 98); Pabst (1989: 304); Lorenz, S. (1997: 183); Raimondi (2001: 94).

[195] AM 30.8.10. Nagl (1948: 2191).

[196] Symmachus, *Orat.* 2.18–20; AM 30.9.4; *Epitome* 45.6. Nagl (1948: 2203); Matthews (1975: 49); Wiedemann (1979: 143–5); Pabst (1989: 147–8, 329–38); Lorenz, S. (1997: 131).

[197] Petrikovits (1971: 184).

[198] Luttwak (1976: ch. 3). See, e.g. Brulet (1993: 135); Elton (1996a: 157); Mackensen (1999: 239): Raetia.

[199] Lorenz, S. (1997: 138 n.455).

[200] Lander (1984: 288).

excavation show them to be towers defended by close curtain walls, two of which are extended to run in parallel down into a nearby river[201] (Fig. 24). The enclosure thus created was used for the beaching of naval vessels (by this time the versatile light *lusoriae*, in service since the third century).[202] We cannot be sure if Valentinian invented the concept of the 'Schiffslände':[203] one may even have been deployed by Julian.[204] However, it certainly captured his interest. Symmachus records his close involvement, as an 'imperial builder', in the construction of such structures.[205] But it is the ships, not the buildings, that best indicate Valentinian's 'big idea' here: the use of naval power.

Regular Roman naval activity on the Rhine began in the reign of Augustus.[206] It was disrupted by internal troubles, and no more so than by those of the 350s. Barbatio had to bring his own boats in 357.[207] The situation was restored by Julian, but not completely: in 359, he had only 40 *lusoriae* available to him for his expedition over the Rhine.[208] To judge from his actions, Valentinian was aware of the deficiency, and sought to remedy it. He may have been alerted to the value of naval power when he served on the Rhine in 357. Though he was dismissed before the debacle of Barbatio's bridge and the full assembling of Alamannic forces before Strasbourg, both of which had lessons to teach about the controlling of rivers, he will have heard of these events. And he may earlier have witnessed Alamannic use of river craft—the crucial link between Alamannic settlements on opposite banks of the Rhine—and realized its dangers. He must also have been aware of the way in which Julian had used waterways.[209] More recently, Valentinian may have concluded that the Alamannic raids of 365 and 366 could have been prevented by naval power; and the initial assault of the expedition of 369 was launched by ship. Later,

---

[201] Symmachus, *Orat.* 2.20. Höckmann (1986: 399–400). Plans and reconstructions: Johnson (1983: Fig. 54); Höckmann (1986: Fig. 14); Pabst (1989: Figs 4–6).

[202] Höckmann (1986: 381, 392–3, 396–7 and Fig. 13).

[203] Lander (1984: 288).

[204] Above 241. Cf. Höckmann (1986: 414) on Julian's appreciation of naval power.

[205] Symmachus, *Orat.* 2.18–19: *artifex purpuratus.*

[206] Höckmann (1986: 379).

[207] AM 16.11.8. Above 233.

[208] AM 18.2.12. Höckmann (1986: 406); above 247.

[209] Höckmann (1986: 414).

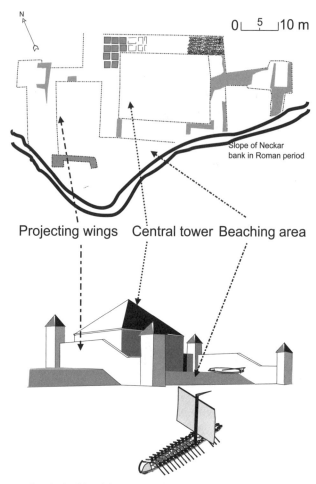

Projecting wings   Central tower   Beaching area

Fig. 24 The 'Schiffslände' at Mannheim-Neckarau. Upper: remains of foundations. Lower: reconstruction [from Pabst (1989: 379 Fig. 6); © Frau Prof. Angela Pabst], with *lusoriae* [© Prof. Dr. C. Schäfer].

he conducted his final dealings with Macrianus of the Bucino-bantes from a vessel.[210] Valentinian, therefore, has some claim to be regarded as Rome's first 'sailor emperor'. His naval concerns have

---

[210] Above 285, below 309.

been further argued by Höckmann, who proposes that the distribution of Valentinian's riverside left-bank forts indicates that these too had a primarily naval role. Each was home to a small (*c.*5–6 vessels) fleet of *lusoriae*, policing a short (*c.*33 km/20 statute mile-long) stretch of the Rhine and its major tributaries. The forts were a key element in a naval defence system in which the 'Schiffsländen' had only a subsidiary role.[211]

What was the purpose of this system? We must distinguish carefully between strategical and tactical considerations and, in respect of the former, between how Valentinian's strategy was presented and its likely practical aim. Valentinian never intended to conquer the Alamanni. He favoured short, focused campaigns, close to home. However, conquest was the traditional Roman way of dealing with an intractable enemy: the one which would have been expected of Valentinian and which, to a large degree, he would have expected of himself. He therefore pursued a defensive strategy, but presented it as conquest.[212] It was for this reason that Symmachus projected Valentinian's right-bank sorties and the building of 'Schiffsländen' as the extension of empire, which might (though not necessarily immediately) lead to the creation of a province of 'Alamannia'.[213] Symmachus treats *imperium* as other than the direct control of territory. Deploying an extended conceit, by which non-belligerent neighbours are peaceful neighbours and therefore subject neighbours, he claims that it is precisely by not subduing the Alamanni by force but by exercising *clementia* (and by practising diplomacy with the Burgundians), that the emperor could pacify, dominate and even Romanize them. *Imperium* no longer produced *pax*; rather *pax* was *imperium*. This allows Symmachus to maintain Roman claims of world rule and aspirations to world domination.[214] It also allows him to present the Alamannic 'wars' of his day, which were no more than expulsions of raiders and minor frontier skirmishes, as campaigns of

---

[211] Höckmann (1986: 397–9, 402–7).
[212] Asche (1983: 29, 50).
[213] Symmachus, *Orat.* 2.31.
[214] Asche (1983: 11–28, 31–2, 35–6, 42–5, 61, 73, 87, 90, 93, 96–108, 140–4). See Sogno (forthcoming) for Symmachus' stress on *clementia* as possible covert criticism of Valentinian.

conquest.[215] And, finally, it allows him to develop a further conceit: that Valentinian's 'Schiffsländen' were new 'cities' (*civitates, oppida, urbes*), cowing Alamanni and impressing Burgundians.[216] This version of events will have been highly gratifying to domestic audiences. The notion of a Roman presence on the right bank of the Rhine had been popular since the days of Julius Caesar. Most recently, it had been bruited by Julian.[217] Satisfaction at Valentinian's arrival on the Neckar and, later, at the Danube source must have been compounded by news of developments in Alamannia. Certainly, the idea of right-bank fortifications appears to have touched a chord with fourth-century writers who projected it back as an achievement of the 'good' emperors of the third-century Crisis.[218]

Some detect a core of substance in imperial propaganda. Lander and Pabst, interpreting the beaching areas as tactical bridgeheads, saw them as a means of expediting Roman amphibious expeditions, and therefore aggressive in purpose: 'Valentinian's frontier system included an offensive component.'[219] Pabst even proposes that Valentinian was bent on some real extension of Roman power/*imperium*, if not by conquest then through the cultivation of an extensive sphere of influence east of the Rhine, based on client kings.[220] Such thinking is undermined by Höckmann's analysis of the 'Länden'. He points out that the idea of a tactical role is not supported by the size and design of these buildings. Both beaching and accommodation areas are too small to have taken substantial attacking forces; and the latter appear unsuitable as permanent quarters for naval crews. And, anyway, there are no external gates from which troops might be deployed against an enemy. It appears that, rather than the towers defending the beaching areas, the beaching areas were there to secure the towers, that is to give shelter to ships supplying their small garrisons.[221] In short, the right-bank installations were just defended

[215] Asche (1983: 50–8, 64–5).
[216] Symmachus, *Orat.* 2.2, 12–13, 18–19.
[217] Julian, *Ep. ad Ath.* 280C; cf. Eutropius 10.14.2.
[218] *Historia Augusta, Tyranni Triginta* 5.4; *V. Probi* 13.7–8. Cf. above 160.
[219] Lander (1984: 284, quotation); Pabst (1989: 332).
[220] Pabst (1989: 306). For still more bullish interpretations see Lorenz, S. (1997: 134–5).
[221] Höckmann (1986: 400).

observation posts, maintained from outside. The system was based on naval control of the Rhine, but the naval bases proper were the left-bank forts.

So what was Valentinian's strategy? The creation of a new province of 'Alamannia' was, as a statement of fact or as an aspiration, fiction. Panegyrists and emperors were no fools. Both would have been aware that old-fashioned annexation was impossible, no matter how delicious were the lies that the former expressed and the latter graciously accepted. The practical alternative was the maintenance of cooperation with compliant border communities. The residual Roman presence over the Rhine may have been reduced by the unrest which followed the rebellion of Magnentius and Julian's campaigns of domination. On the other hand, Valentinian's visit to the Danube source, the continuing circulation of imperial bronze coins, and literary and archaeological evidence for Romano-Alamannic collaboration suggest that the Empire had no intention of turning its back on the Rhine–Danube re-entrant. In this respect, at least, Alamannia Romana was a reality. Therefore what was Valentinian about when he constructed a string of military sites over the Rhine? It appears that his plan was, while marking Rome's continued claim to territory over the river, to use naval power to seal the Rhine against local hotheads and long-distance intruders, Elbe-*Germani* and Burgundians alike: in short, internal security.[222] Roman forces would be alerted to danger by the transrhenish outposts and the river patrols. If the enemy attempted a crossing, the number and sophistication of Roman warships would make short work of the primitive vessels available to the barbarians (as was to happen to Goths on the Danube in 386).[223]

How effective were Valentinian's measures? Probably, not very. War fleets are notoriously difficult to maintain and crew. More particularly, Valentinian's naval bases and towers must have been vulnerable to the vagaries of the old Rhine: to being damaged by its floodwaters, or being left high and dry by the shifting of its main channel.[224] Prolonged periods of drought or freezing would also have

---

[222] Cf. Asche (1983: 88, 94–5, 99); Schönberger (1969: 185–6); Lorenz, S. (1997: 133–5), with Symmachus, *Orat.* 2.13.

[223] Zosimus 4.35.1, 38–9; Claudian, *De Quarto Cos. Hon.* 623–33, from Höckmann (1986: 389 and n.47, 395).

[224] Höckmann (1986: 369, 385–90); cf. above 282.

made them vulnerable: in the case of the beaching areas, inaccessible to *lusoriae* but accessible to anyone able to walk around their protecting wings. There was peace in the late fourth century, but this was probably because the Alamanni, generally tractable, were for the most part left undisturbed, and because there was a falling away in long-distance raiding.[225]

The Alamanni were there to be exploited as the emperor saw fit: as the recipients of imperial clemency or as the victims of imperial intolerance.[226] The occasional goading of neighbouring Alamannic communities into revolt was probably useful in maintaining the illusion that they constituted a major enemy, requiring the permanent presence of a large (and growing) army and a senior emperor and his court, and justifying the resources that were needed to support these. Valentinian may even have claimed that his system of defence saved the Empire men and *matériel*.[227] This brings us to the effect of Valentinian's right-bank forts on Alamanni.

The Alamanni must have resented the new restraints. They were a continuation of the exploitation by Julian, but on a greater scale: a painful sign of Alamannic subservience; a slight on the honour of precisely those communities which were, geographically and culturally, closest to Rome.[228] To add insult to injury, Symmachus' account of the building of the Mannheim-Neckarau base suggests that the construction, and perhaps the maintenance, of the 'Schiffsländen' may have been a routine charge on adjacent Alamannic communities. And to add further insult to injury, given the dangers of dealing with the old Rhine in winter, and Julian's odd 10-month-long agreement with Alamanni around the former *munimentum Traiani*, it may have been that riverside Roman bases were left unoccupied for part of the year, with local Alamanni under strict instructions not to interfere with them.[229] What is certain is that the erection of these structures caused the Romans to require local Alamanni to give

[225] Below 317.

[226] Clemency: Pabst (1989: 343–5); intolerance: AM 28.2.5–8.

[227] Expansion of the army etc.: Nagl. (1948.: 2192); Lorenz, S. (1997: 104). Justification: Drinkwater (1996: 26–8), (1999a: 133); Heather (2001: 54, 60).

[228] Cf. Asche (1983: 102).

[229] Above 242.

hostages for their good behaviour, a deeply unpopular and unsettling stipulation.[230]

On the other hand, though by nature choleric, Valentinian was no fool. He would not have thoughtlessly driven neighbouring Alamannic communities into hostility to Rome. There were break-downs in communication, causing serious incidents, as happened at Mons Piri,[231] but Valentinian's 'attack' on the Alamannic settlement suggests close cooperation with Alamannic rulers; and even the trouble at Mons Piri may have been due as much to Alamannic shock at a collapse in normally good relations as to Roman aggression. Under Valentinian, leading Alamanni continued to hold high positions in Roman service, albeit at not quite so exalted a level as previously.[232] The most dramatic evidence for a positive relationship between the Empire and local Alamannic chiefs is to be found in the massive hill-site of the Zähringer Burgberg.[233]

The picture that emerges from a study of Valentinian's campaign-ing and building is somewhat mixed. There was peace, though this was due more to traditional Alamannic compliance than to the emperor's military genius. The relationship between leading Alamanni and Rome was still positive, though less secure than under Constantius II. In this respect, the initial change had come about through Julian.[234] Valentinian followed in Julian's footsteps, and under him Romano-Alamannic relations became more calculat-ing.[235] This led to a number of misunderstandings, chief among which was Valentinian's vendetta against Macrianus.

Ammianus' account of events on the Rhine is now dominated by Valentinian's confrontation with Macrianus. He mentions two other conflicts with Alamanni, in Raetia and before the building of the fort at Robur; and Valentinian involved himself with matters not found in Ammianus' narrative, such as his visit to the Danube source. The question is therefore whether Macrianus really was Valentinian's

---

230 Above 282–3, 293.
231 Above 293.
232 Above 159.
233 Above 101–3.
234 Above 264–5.
235 Cf. Lorenz, S. (1997: 136).

major concern during this period. Ammianus' account of the later part of Valentinian's reign is selective. Though he praised the emperor's military building, he was not fond of him as a ruler.[236] He may have chosen to concentrate on Valentinian's dealings with Macrianus to show how anger can lead to errors of judgement. A case may, indeed, be made for the two other clashes with Alamanni being more significant than Ammianus suggests. Though count Theodosius' incursion into Alamannic Raetia may have been opportunistic, a turning to advantage of recent Burgundian penetration down the Main, this was an area that was to produce trouble under Gratian.[237] The same area, or, at least, its western portion, may have been the target of Valentinian's campaign before Robur, possibly launched from the High Rhine,[238] and, despite its cursory treatment by Ammianus, probably more than just a raid. Were the Lentienses proving difficult before 378, a circumstance which Ammianus chose to ignore in giving attention to Macrianus? Against this, justifying Ammianus' concentration on Macrianus, is the history of Romano-Alamannic relations since the later third century, the strategic significance of the Main corridor and the ambiguous position of the Burgundians as imperial allies. This is not just the story of a barbarian troublemaker and a choleric emperor. Macrianus emerges as a major historical figure: the greatest Alamannic leader we know.

From 359 Macrianus began to create a mini-empire down the Main, with the blessing of Julian and then, presumably, to begin with, Valentinian.[239] Crucial to the understanding of initial Roman tolerance and of later developments is that Macrianus was steadfast in his loyalty to Rome. He had supplied a regiment to Valentinian in the period 365–8; and he is unlikely to have been responsible for Rando's raid of 368.[240] There is no clear sign of his ever directly attacking the Empire. The complaints against him by Valentinian's counsellors in

---

[236] His list of Valentinian's vices is considerably longer than that of his virtues: 30.8–9.

[237] Below 310–11. Gutmann (1991: 35) makes Theodosius' campaign part of that against Macrianus, but the distance between the two areas concerned is surely too great for this.

[238] Lorenz, S. (1997: 158).

[239] Above 174, 250. Cf. Gutmann (1991: 34).

[240] Above 170, 286.

374[241] are suspiciously alarmist. Given Alamannic numbers and technology, regular attacks on fortified cities are implausible, more likely to reflect distorted and prejudiced recollection of what Mainz had suffered at the hands of Rando than any actions by Macrianus, guilty by association. Once his quarrel with Valentinian was patched up he stayed a loyal ally. How, therefore, can we explain the breakdown in the relationship between Valentinian and Macrianus? I propose that trouble began with Rando's raid, which exposed the vulnerability of Mainz and allowed Macrianus to extend his influence close to the Rhine in an area that was still very much Roman.[242] It was this, raising the spectre of barbarian 'threat', not any sort of direct incursions, that was seen as arrogant and that amounted to the 'restless disturbances' that 'confused the Roman state'.[243]

Valentinian's assessment of the 'danger' is discernible in the strength of his reaction to it. He was present in person at Wiesbaden early in June 369, prior to leading the manoeuvres at Alta Ripa.[244] (There is no reason to suppose that his visit to the right bank at this time was confined to Kastel.[245]) Here he probably ordered the construction of the 'Heidenmauer', a massive defence work, begun but never completed.[246] A date of 369 is likely for this enigmatic structure given the general pattern of Valentinian's military building.[247] It was, perhaps, in response to Rando's raid and its repercussions.[248] More dramatic, however, was Valentinian's calling on Burgundian support. The Burgundian alliance was not new.[249] Valentinian's links with these people must have been forged in 369 or earlier: Symmachus, in 'looking forward' to a Burgundian alliance early in 370, will have known that cooperation against Macrianus was already planned.[250]

---

[241] AM 30.3.3. Above 284–5.

[242] Above 286–7.

[243] AM 28.5.8: *Macriani regis ... fastus, sine fine vel modo rem Romanam irrequietis motibus confundentis.* Above 283.

[244] *CT* 10.19.6. Seeck (1919: 236): 4 June 369.

[245] i.e. *contra* Lorenz, S. (1997: 118).

[246] Schoppa (1974: 95–7); Schönberger (1969: 185).

[247] Above 295.

[248] *Contra* Lorenz, S. (1997: 141): after 371.

[249] Above 110, 190.

[250] Symmachus, *Orat.* 2.13. Lorenz, S. (1997: 146). Cf. Wood (1990: 58) on the possibility that by the time of Valentinian, Roman—including Catholic Christian—influence on Burgundians was greater than is usually thought.

What was new was the direct summoning of Burgundians to attack a Roman ally.

In 370 the Burgundians exceeded their instructions. Supposed to press Macrianus from the east while Valentinian struck from the west, they attacked prematurely and came straight down the Main, apparently meeting little resistance and causing enormous concern.[251] They gave an unwelcome demonstration of the vulnerability of Mainz and its region to people other than Macrianus and his Bucinobantes. Their request for Roman help could be interpreted as a request for aid to break the local Alamanni. Thus, instead of protecting the Main corridor, they now posed a threat to its security: one that Rome, still in a commanding position, could easily handle, but one that complicated frontier diplomacy. It comes as no surprise that Valentinian apparently ceased to involve himself with Burgundians. His sole desire was to re-establish the status quo, which returns us to Macrianus.

Valentinian's alternative strategy was not to break the Bucinobantes but, having arrested Macrianus, to put them under a less redoubtable ruler. This involved the customary Roman employment of deceit in dealings with barbarians—as demonstrated, as Ammianus says, by Julian, ever Valentinian's model, in his treatment of Vadomarius. Valentinian's device was the snatch raid, launched in 371. This is an illuminating episode. In order to understand it, we need to decide precisely what happened. Key issues here are the location of Valentinian's pontoon bridge and the destination of the Roman force.

As far as the bridge is concerned, one's immediate thought is that it must have been somewhere upstream from the permanent crossing at Mainz/Kastel, since anywhere downstream would have landed Valentinian's troops south of the Main confluence. A crossing into the region of modern Biebrich (with its 'Schiffslände'[252]) would have brought the army very close to Wiesbaden. But this raises questions as to why, since speed was so important, Valentinian did not use the

---

[251] Above 283; cf. Lorenz, S. (1997: 147). Among the prisoners executed by the Burgundians may well have been Roman citizens ordinarily resident on the right bank and not just, say, Rando's captives of 369. Cf. Lorenz, S. (1997: 148 n.532).

[252] Above 295.

Mainz bridge itself, and how, despite the Romans' best endeavours, a major military undertaking anywhere along the Upper Rhine could have been kept secret from Macrianus. I suggest that Mainz was not chosen because unusual activity here would indicate an imminent expedition. Forces concentrated opposite, say, Biebrich might, however, be passed off as participating in manoeuvres, of the sort practised at Alta Ripa in 369. In describing the progress of Severus' vanguard, Ammianus uses the phrase *contra Mattiacas Aquas*. Rolfe translates *contra* straightforwardly as 'against', but Ammianus uses this word in such a way only when describing conflicts against persons or people. When he employs it to specify a location—topographical, geographical or even astronomical—he always means 'over against', 'opposite' or 'facing', very often implying 'in full view of'.[253] Thus, Severus was to proceed through Wiesbaden, northwards into an area that looked towards the Taunus range, along the military highway that led from Mainz via Wiesbaden to the old *limes* fort at Zugmantel, the road along which Macrianus was able to flee to safety[254] (Fig. 4).

This must be where Severus encountered and killed, as a security risk, Ammianus' *scurrae*—probably Germanic mercenaries, taking war captives to market at Wiesbaden.[255] Macrianus' residence lay along this road, not in Wiesbaden itself. Macrianus' proximity to what was still a Roman settlement[256] will have resulted mainly from his move down the Main after the Rando incident. However, the fact that Macrianus' attendants had to get him away in a covered carriage suggests that he was indisposed, and so may have come close to Wiesbaden to use its healing springs. This could have been what Valentinian discovered from Alamannic deserters which persuaded him that Macrianus was expecting no trouble and would not resist

[253] AM 18.2.16; 22.8.4; 23.6.10, 53; 29.4.7; 30.3.5; 31.15.12. Cf. 19.5.6–6.6; 20.3.11, 11.26; 21.15.2; 22.8.20; 23.6.64.

[254] Lorenz, S. (1997: 153).

[255] AM 29.4.4. Above 135. *Scurra* is difficult to translate: see Sabbah (1999: 187 at n.107). In this context I interpret it as meaning Germanic warriors with some sort of affiliation to the Roman army, i.e. not 'hostiles', engaged in disposing of booty won through raiding other Germanic communities (perhaps Frankish).

[256] Above 305.

arrest.[257] Macrianus' possible illness hints that by 371/2 he was, through age, disease or inclination, no doughty warrior, on the model of Chnodomarius. The loyalty of his attendants, and his later return to prominence, speak volumes for his powers of leadership. The use of a carriage also says much about the passability of local roads. But this raises further questions. With Macrianus living close to Wiesbaden and frequently visiting the place, why did it take an expedition to seize him? Why not, as Julian had done in the case of Vadomarius, wait until he was on Roman territory and then simply detain him? Probably Macrianus was wise enough not to cross over to the left bank, and on the right bank he went nowhere without a significant entourage: much more than the handful of *comites* who had accompanied Vadomarius, perhaps even a small army. This would explain Severus' loss of nerve and the consequent prolongation of the enterprise. Given the short distance involved, Roman forces should easily have reached Macrianus in a day.[258] A night attack was not planned: Ammianus states that Roman troops had not been equipped to sleep in the open. It became necessary only after Severus had fallen back to wait for Valentinian, presumably in Wiesbaden.

Related to the difficulties the Romans faced in apprehending Macrianus, it is likely that Macrianus' residence was more than a house or mansion. Given the king's status and Ammianus' report that, when Roman forces found themselves close to him, they fell to looting, this residence is unlikely to have been a simple affair but rather, I would suggest, a lowland 'Herrschaftszentrum'.[259]

The raid failed. Valentinian always underestimated Macrianus' support. The more he pressed him, the more powerful he became.[260] However, for the moment, Macrianus had fled and Valentinian used the opportunity to terrorize his subjects. Ammianus' 'fifty miles' is probably a round number expressing the distance from Mainz up the

[257] AM 29.4.2. Schoppa (1974: 101 and 142 at n.143) while himself rejecting 'Macrianus' illness', discusses its historiography, attributing the original idea to Reuter, in an article published in 1871.

[258] Schoppa (1974: 101).

[259] Cf. above 98.

[260] AM 29.4.2.

Main valley to the old *limes* and the border with the Burgundians.[261] However, given the lack of preparation for the initial attack, this harrying must have been short-term and sketchy, and unlikely to inflict much lasting damage. It was not a major expedition, and was therefore probably delegated to Valentinian's subordinates. Valentinian's major Rhenish campaign remained that of 368. He then installed Fraomarius in place of Macrianus. This also failed. The speedy fall of Fraomarius reflects continuing support for Macrianus, even among high-ranking Alamanni in Roman service.[262] The 'recent invasion' that precipitated Fraomarius' removal can be interpreted as Macrianus and his supporters returning to claim power.[263] In the end, as Valentinian may have sensed (his decisive removal of Fraomarius from local politics is significant[264]), he had to deal with Macrianus; and the settlement of 374 is as illuminating as the snatch raid of 371.

Ammianus' dramatic details (with the imperial party afloat, Macrianus and his Alamanni on land, at the margin of the Rhine, presumably in the vicinity of Mainz) indicate negotiations between two powers.[265] Valentinian apparently gave up right-bank territory north of the Main (and any remaining Roman occupants) to Macrianus, with the exception, presumably, of riverine strongpoints such as Kastel and Wiesbaden-Biebrich.[266] This explains the non-completion of Wiesbaden's 'Heidenmauer'. Macrianus had every reason to be puffed up with pride, but the policy worked because of his basic loyalty. It is to be noted that when Valentinian really wanted to move, from Rhine to Danube, he was able to strike an effective deal with Macrianus. Overall, what we see again is previous Roman exaggeration of the Alamannic 'threat'.

Valentinian died suddenly in 375. He had fought barbarians because he was obliged to: like all Roman emperors, he must confirm his credentials as a military leader. Thanks to Julian, his enemy of

[261] From Mainz: Demandt (1972: 93).
[262] Cf. above 151.
[263] Gutmann (1991: 38); Sabbah (1999: 187–8 at n.109).
[264] Cf. Gutmann (1991: 38).
[265] Whittaker (1994: 241): 'a symbolic but artificial compromise between two powers with conflicting territorial claims'.
[266] Cf. Gutmann (1991: 248).

choice were Alamanni. However, by the end of his reign things had
settled. Valentinian had moved his centre of operations down the
Danube, and, despite occasional local difficulties, he appears to have
restored a positive working relationship with border Alamanni. His
fortifications on the Upper Rhine were designed for frontier policing,
not long-distance aggression. The case of Macrianus had demonstrated the danger of close reliance on border kings: it allowed them
to develop local power bases. On the other hand, it also showed that
the mightiest king could be checked by Rome and that, left to
themselves, Alamannic leaders were not inimical. Alamanni would
be attacked again by Gratian, but not because they posed a major
threat. Generally, by the end of the century they appear passive, and it
is not surprising that on the Rhine Roman animosity began again to
be directed towards Franks.

Valentinian's death caused great political uncertainty on the
Danube. To secure the situation the leaders of the imperial court
there proclaimed his younger son, and half-brother of Gratian, Valentinian II (born 371), Augustus in his place. This, done without the
permission or even the knowledge of Gratian or Valens, was, strictly
speaking, usurpation. However, the two senior emperors accepted the
expedient and continued in their roles as rulers of the west and east
respectively. Valentinian II was controlled by Gratian.[267] Then, in 376,
the east was destabilized by the arrival of large numbers of Goths over
the Danube. The immigration had been sanctioned by Valens, but
Roman mismanagement provoked Gothic resistance and then
outright rebellion in Thrace. During 377, the situation became so
serious that Valens decided to confront the Goths in person, and
asked Gratian to come in support with western troops.

It is at this point that Ammianus refers again to Alamanni as
causing trouble. The Lentienses broke a long-standing treaty
and raided into the Empire.[268] They had been encouraged by the
loose talk of one of their countrymen, an imperial guardsman, who
while home on leave revealed that Gratian would soon be leaving
the west to help Valens.[269] They formed raiding-parties which, in

---

[267] Lenski (2002: 357–61).
[268] AM 31.10.1–2.
[269] AM 31.10.3.

February, attempted to cross the frozen Rhine, but were thrown back.[270] Undaunted, and still mindful that Roman attention was being diverted eastwards, they concentrated their forces, amounting to some 40,000 men (or 70,000: Ammianus gives both figures but prefers the former), and entered Roman territory.[271] Gratian recalled the units he had already sent ahead into Pannonia, combined these with forces he had held back in Gaul, put the army under the generals Nannienus and Mallobaudes and sent it against the enemy.[272] Battle was joined at Argentaria. It was hard fought, but eventually the Romans won. No more than 5,000 Alamanni escaped and among the dead was king Priarius, 'the inciter of the deadly battles'.[273]

Gratian, already moving eastwards, heard of the victory and 'secretly' swung northwards over the Rhine aiming to repay the Lentienses for their perfidy by destroying them.[274] Stunned and unable to resist, they fled to the hills where, 'taking their place round about on the sheer rocks', they sought to save themselves, their property and their families.[275] The Romans set up a crack squad to overcome 'obstacles like those of city walls'. These men, spurred on by the emperor's presence, tried to storm the heights; but the fighting lasted into the night, with heavy losses on both sides.[276] Gratian then resolved to starve out the enemy. The Lentienses, however, broke out and made for other heights, with Gratian in hot pursuit. Recognizing that the emperor would not give up, they surrendered. Under the terms of an agreement, they gave young men for distribution through the Roman army; the rest were allowed to depart unmolested.[277] Ammianus' comment on these events runs: 'Incredibly great energy and conspicuous rapidity were shown by Gratian, while he was hastening in another direction, when through the favour of the eternal deity he won this victory, which was at once seasonable and profitable, since it

---

[270] AM 31.10.4.
[271] AM 31.10.5.
[272] AM 31.10.6.
[273] AM 31.10.8–10: *exitialium concitator pugnarum.*
[274] AM 31.10.11: *latenter.*
[275] AM 31.10.12: *abruptisque per ambitum rupibus insistentes.*
[276] AM 31.10.13–14: *velut murorum obicibus.*
[277] AM 31.10.15–17.

tamed the western nations.'[278] Having set matters right in Gaul,
and having punished the treacherous guardsman who started the
trouble, he set off east, making for Sirmium on the Danube.[279] He
was too late to be of any use to Valens who was defeated and killed
by the Goths at the great battle of Adrianople, on 9 August 378.

All these conflicts occurred in 378. Gratian's crossing of the Rhine
must have occurred between 20 April, when he was still in Trier, and
mid-August, when he is reckoned to have been in residence in
Sirmium.[280] Ammianus' 'Argentaria' is generally held to be the
Argentovaria of Ptolemy, the Peutinger Table and the Antonine
Itinerary, traditionally identified as Horbourg, near Colmar on the
Upper Rhine.[281] On the other hand, a strong claim has recently been
made for Biesheim-Kunheim, also near Colmar but to the east of
Horbourg—in fact, just west of Breisach[282] (Fig. 17).

However, the first part of the story is difficult to make sense of. The
Lentienses, of whom nothing has been heard since Constantius II's
clash with them in 355 when they offered little real resistance,[283] are
now suddenly able to deploy an enormous army and make massive
trouble for the Roman Empire. It took a pitched battle to destroy their
main force which had managed to travel from its home territory and
penetrate Roman defences on the Upper Rhine, an area of particular
imperial interest at a time of intense military activity. There is too much
vagueness. On the other hand, with regard to the loose talk of Gratian's
guardsman, and to his fate, the tale is suspiciously detailed and glib. In a
section that is almost pure panegyric of Gratian,[284] the whole thing
crackles with the electricity of political 'spin', but, apart from remark-
ing that Ammianus' numbers are probably exaggerated,[285] most have
been content to accept his account more or less as it stands.

---

[278] AM 31.10.18: *Hanc victoriam, opportunam et fructuosam, quae gentes hebetavit
occiduas, sempiterni numinis nutu, Gratianus incredibile dictu est, quo quantoque
vigore exserta celeritate aliorsum properans expedivit.*

[279] AM 31.10.20, 11.6.

[280] Seeck (1919: 250); Lorenz, S. (1997: 172–3).

[281] Moreau (1983: 129).

[282] Talbert (2000: Map 11 Gazetteer), from Petit and Mangin (1994: 160).

[283] Above 211.

[284] Sabbah (1999: 272 n.486).

[285] e.g. Sabbah (1999: 272 n.479). Zotz (1998: 399) enthusiastically accepts
Ammianus' figures, and so the impressive size of the venture.

The simplest solution would be to break the link between Argentaria and Argentovaria, putting Argentaria closer to Lake Constance, and having the Lentienses cross the High Rhine.[286] However, this is made impossible by a small but significant group of sources, probably derived from Jerome and possibly related to Ammianus, which locate Argentaria in Gaul and so support the identification Argentaria/Argentovaria.[287] Progress may be made by putting this problem to one side and considering what Gratian made of the incident. Why did he turn aside to wage war on the Lentienses? Ammianus presents Gratian's Lentiensian campaign as a major factor in Valens' defeat, to the detriment of the senior emperor. Gratian did what a good emperor was supposed to do, destroy barbarians.[288] Valens, brimming with envy at his nephew's success, refused to wait for his arrival, forced battle against the Goths, and lost.[289] But it is possible to see events the other way round. Gratian, unwilling to travel as far as Thrace and expecting that Valens would be victorious against the Goths, required an activity that would detain him in the west and give him a military reputation to match that of his uncle.[290] (Gratian's despatch to Valens announced his latest victory, his personal achievement, not the earlier one won by Nannienus and Mallobaudes.[291]) But against whom might he gain this, and where?

This returns us to the question of Argentaria. I propose that there was trouble with Elbgermanic/Alamannic raiders that resulted in fighting near Colmar, but that this may be attributed to other than a major Lentiensian push. Alamannia and neighbouring imperial territories are likely to have been subject to long-distance raiding,[292] and in the late 370s such raiding may have been encouraged by contemporary problems with the Goths. It was dealt with by the

---

[286] Cf. Lorenz, S. (1997: 170).

[287] Jerome (Eusebius), *Chron.* 248, 14–16; Orosius, *Hist.* 33.8; *Epitome* 47.2; Jordanes, *Rom.* 312. See Festy (1999: 221–2 n.2, 224 n.2).

[288] Cf. Sabbah (1999: 272 n.483).

[289] AM 31.12.1, 4–7.

[290] Cf. Lenski (2002: 357–8, 361–2, 366–7) on the generally poor relations between nephew and uncle.

[291] AM 31.11.6. Cf. the fuss made of Gratian's recent victory by Ausonius (*Grat. Act.* 2.8–9): Sivan (1993: 122).

[292] Above 261–2, 276.

system.[293] If the war-bands crossed the Rhine at Breisach,[294] they did not get far. Their numbers were probably fairly small. However, and the more so given the possibility of recent unrest in the area,[295] they may have been joined by some Lentienses, including king Priarius. In other words, Priarius was not the main instigator but a local ruler swept up by the tide. His death on Roman soil, however, provided Gratian with the opportunity to exploit the situation. Making the most of this and Lentiensian 'treachery' (the tale of the garrulous guardsman), he picked a fight with Lentienses. The venture, now regularly bruited as the last great imperial campaign over the Rhine[296] and clearly made much of at the time (note Ammianus' suggestion that the emperor and his guard were in the thick of the fighting[297]), was ill-timed, unnecessary and basically unsuccessful in that Gratian won no great victory in the field. And in the long term it seriously damaged the Empire by contributing to defeat at Adrianople.[298]

These events also reveal two aspects of Alamannic society, already touched upon. The first, from the case of the gossiping guardsman (where what might be believed of him is more important than what—if he ever existed—he actually did), is the routine nature of Alamannic service in the Roman army and continuing contact with home.[299] The second, from the means by which the Lentiensians evaded full defeat, is Alamannic use of defensive hill-sites—not just one, but a chain.[300] The most likely locations of this chain are north of Lake Constance, along the Danube or even along the Swabian Alp.[301] Gratian therefore probably crossed the Rhine at Zurzach, and struck into the modern Linzgau.[302] 'His' Lentienses were thus not

[293] Cf. above 277.

[294] Damage to Breisach's 'bridgehead fort' at Jechtingen-Sponeck has been attributed to the 378 troubles: Fingerlin (1997a: 105), though this may be a garbling of Fingerlin (1990: 101), referring to those of 383.

[295] Above 304.

[296] Cf. Lorenz, S. (1997: 174–5).

[297] AM 31.10.13–14.

[298] Cf. Seeck (1921: 5.112); Lenski (2002: 365–6).

[299] Above 155, 176.

[300] Above 311.

[301] Above 97.

[302] Lorenz, S. (1997: 172); Sabbah (1999: 272–3 n.484).

those of Constantius II, encountered more to the east: a further indication that the name should be interpreted as a loose label attached by Roman authorities to a regional grouping of *pagi*, not as a 'people'.[303]

Ammianus terminated his 'History' with Adrianople and its immediate consequences. References to Alamanni in our sources now become scattered, thin, and varied in nature and quality.[304] I shall summarize what these say, and then consider the significance of what happened down to Theodosius' taking over the west in 394.

Gratian never moved beyond Sirmium, but he eventually solved the Gothic crisis by appointing Theodosius, son of count Theodosius, as eastern emperor (19 January 379). Then, according to Socrates and Sozomen, he left to deal with Alamannic raids on Gaul.[305] In 383 the general Magnus Maximus revolted in Britain and crossed the Channel. Gratian attempted to confront him in Gaul, but fled and was captured and killed at Lyon (25 August 383). Again according to Socrates and Sozomen, at the time of Magnus Maximus' departure from Britain, Gratian was heavily engaged in fighting Alamanni.[306]

At first Magnus Maximus ruled the west from Trier. Italy was governed by Valentinian II and his advisers. Ambrose tells us that following the murder of Gratian, Iuthungi raided into Raetia but were repulsed by Valentinian II's general, Bauto, using Huns and Alans as allies. These were so successful that they threatened Gaul and, at Magnus Maximus' request, Valentinian paid them to leave.[307] In 387, Maximus moved into Italy, forcing Valentinian to flee to Theodosius. In 388, Theodosius came west, defeated and killed Maximus and restored Valentinian.

Valentinian was sent into Gaul under the direction of the Frankish general, Arbogast. Relations between the two deteriorated, and Valentinian was found dead in mysterious circumstances at Vienne (15 May 392). Arbogast then set up his own emperor, Eugenius (22 August), and early in the following year the two left Gaul for

[303] Above 123, 172.
[304] See the handy compilations of Stroheker (1975: 40–2); Kuhoff (1984: 110–13); Runde (1998: 672–4).
[305] Socrates 5.6.2; Sozomen 7.2.1, 4.1–2.
[306] Socrates 5.11.2; Sozomen 7.13.1.
[307] Ambrose, *Ep.* 18.21, 24.8.

Italy. Before leaving they renewed old treaties with the kings of the
Alamanni and Franks.[308] They confronted Theodosius at the great
battle of the Frigidus, on 5–6 September 394, and were defeated.

Events down to the 380s may be interpreted as following the
standard pattern of Romano-Alamannic relations, that is Roman
superiority and exploitation, unchanged by what had happened at
Adrianople. Thus, it is likely that in 379 Gratian made much of the
'Alamannic threat' for his own ends. He was not back in Gaul until,
at the earliest, high summer, which suggests that he was kept busy
elsewhere. Indeed, Ausonius had to deliver his speech of thanks for
his consulship in Gratian's absence.[309] However, in an earlier poem,
written late in 378 on the eve of his inauguration as consul,
Ausonius was already looking forward to Gratian's imminent
reappearance;[310] and in the final section of the speech of thanks,
where he describes Gratian's return to Gaul, he makes no mention
of what the emperor had been engaged in for most of 379 nor gives
any hint of trouble with Alamanni or any other *Germani*.[311] This
last is particularly remarkable since, if there had been fighting,
Ausonius would have used it to praise Gratian's martial skills.
(Even though, in the speech of thanks, Ausonius undertakes to
deal with Gratian's military achievements in a separate work,[312]
he expresses himself weakly and never fulfilled his promise.[313])
We can conclude that Gratian dawdled back to Gaul in 378/9,
uninvolved in any major warfare. This is confirmed by an itinerary
that took him directly from Sirmium to Milan.[314] If he fought
Alamanni in 379, this could only have been while en route for Trier,
and so not part of any specific campaign. Overall, Gratian was
not catapulted into going west by a military emergency involving
Alamanni. The Alamannic 'threat' was, as ever, a means of distancing
himself from a difficult situation—military and political—on the
Danube. (A mention in the Theodosian Code, of late 379, concerning

[308] Gregory of Tours, *Dec. Lib. Hist.* 2.9.55.
[309] Green (1991: 537).
[310] Ausonius, 20 (*Precationes*).2 [Green], 34; Green (1991: 537).
[311] Ausonius, *Grat. Act.* 18.82.
[312] Ausonius, *Grat. Act.* 2.9.
[313] Sivan (1993: 122).
[314] Seeck (1919: 250–2).

disruption of judicial procedure by enemy action, need not necessarily refer to Gaul.[315])

Four years later Gratian was in great need of military glory because of Theodosius' success and his own growing reputation for idleness and declining popularity among his troops.[316] His 383 campaign against Alamanni gave him a means of acquiring such a reputation, and so could have been contrived. It should not be seen as necessarily reflecting Alamannic aggression. Indeed, the fact that Gratian's campaign fell just before Magnus Maximus' usurpation perhaps indicates just how bad his political situation had become: sensing political danger he decided to show his military mettle, but too late. The trouble just after his death is therefore explicable as the aftermath of this venture. Gratian's unnecessary and abortive expedition may have stirred up unrest among Alamanni/Iuthungi which needed to be quieted.[317] And again, such trouble could have been exaggerated for political ends: Bauto may have made more of the war than was necessary to undermine Magnus Maximus.[318]

Then there is quiet. That this is not just an artefact of the poor sources is demonstrated by reports of more trouble with Franks.[319] The usual explanation for this is that the 'terrifying' Alamanni were finally broken.[320] Better is that this happened because, as in the days before Julian and Valentinian I, the Alamanni were left in peace; and this occurred because Adrianople had changed the imperial situation. Straws in the wind had been Valentinian's sharing of the Empire with Valens in 364, and the failure of Valentinian and Gratian to come to Valens' help in 365 and 378. However, it is only after 378 that we can clearly see the Roman Empire, still nominally a single entity, evolving into two states, usually allied but increasingly inclined to pursue their own interests. This forced the rulers of each to keep a closer watch on each other; and in the west it resulted in a diversion of interest and, eventually, the transfer of the imperial

---

[315] *CT* 11.31.7.
[316] *Epitome* 47.4–6.
[317] For the confusion of the name see above 62.
[318] Cf. Matthews (1975: 177); Lotter, Bratož, and Castritius (2003: 83).
[319] Below 318.
[320] e.g. Lorenz, S. (1997: 174–5); Pohl (2002a: 170).

presence from the Rhine to Italy. The process began in 382 with
Gratian's move from Trier to Milan, continued in 387 with Magnus
Maximus' personal intervention in Italy, and culminated in 402 with
Honorius' retreat to Ravenna. Overall, therefore, the Alamanni of the
380s and 390s were hardly the bogeymen presented by Ammianus as
he published his 'History'. A feature of the period is not trouble from
them but from Rome's earlier bugbear, the Franks.

Around 380, Macrianus of the Bucinobantes was killed by the
Frank Mallobaudes.[321] In 388, Franks attacked into Germania II.
According to Gregory, citing Sulpicius Alexander, these were led by
Genobaudes, Marcomeres and Sunno, and did great damage. Some
of them were defeated but the rest, who had already crossed back over
the Rhine, inflicted a heavy defeat on a pursuing Roman force.[322] In
389, Arbogast, acting according to the wishes of Valentinian II,
though himself in favour of a much more retributive policy, made
an agreement with Marcomeres and Sunno.[323] Arbogast got his way
some years later when, having reduced Valentinian II to a cipher, he
attacked Sunno and Marcomeres in the middle of winter, crossing
the Rhine and devastating Frankish territory, but failing to make
decisive contact with the enemy.[324] According to Gregory, Eugenius
went to the Rhine border and renewed the old traditional treaties
with the kings of the Alamanni and Franks in order to show off his
massive army.[325] Marcomeres and Sunno were finally destroyed by
Stilicho. (Marcomeres was sent into exile in Italy; Sunno, champion-
ing Marcomeres, was killed by his own people.[326])

One has to be careful in assessing this apparent resurgence in
Frankish activity because our principal informant, Gregory of
Tours, was interested solely in searching out what he could about
the early history of the Franks of his day. However, the likelihood that
an increase in Frankish raiding is a real historical phenomenon is
strengthened by the fact that Sunno and Marcomeres receive mention in Claudian, a contemporary. The main cause of this was

---

[321] AM 30.3.7. Above 174, 285.
[322] Gregory of Tours, *Dec. Lib. Hist.* 2.9.52–4.
[323] Gregory of Tours, *Dec. Lib. Hist.* 2.9.55.
[324] Ibid.
[325] Ibid.
[326] Claudian, *De Cos. Stil.* 1.241–5.

probably the diverting of imperial attention by civil war. However, it seems to have been exacerbated by personal hostility between Arbogast and the Frankish chiefs. The trouble was settled once control of affairs had passed into the hands of the capable Stilicho.

At one level, therefore, it appears that despite the change that affected the Roman world after Adrianople the relationship between the Empire and Alamanni and Franks remained much as before, indeed that it reverted to that of the earlier period. However, this is not the whole of the story. There is also a hint that the change which affected the Roman world also influenced what went on between Romans and *Germani*. Because this change provoked greater internal conflict, there was an increased demand for troops among rival parties. Thus, although according to Gregory of Tours, Eugenius went to the Rhine in 392 to cow the kings of the Franks and Alamanni into submission prior to his moving elsewhere, it is likely that he and Arbogast raised troops from them.[327] A line in Orosius implies that Frankish contingents fought for Eugenius and Arbogast at the battle of the Frigidus.[328] If these were raised at the same time as Eugenius' appearance on the Rhine then Alamannic contingents are also a possibility, although this is not stated explicitly (and Eugenius' recruitment may have involved only Franks, newly active and with some, at least, having tribal links to Arbogast). Whatever, after 383 there is no further record of significant Roman conflict with Alamanni.[329]

---

[327] i.e. along the lines of Models I and II above (163).
[328] Orosius, *Hist.* 7.35.11–12.
[329] Stroheker (1975: 40–1).

9

The Fifth Century

Theodosius died in Milan on 17 January 395, leaving the Empire to be governed by his two sons, the east by Arcadius and the west by Honorius. Like Valentinian II, however, both were thought incapable of ruling alone, and so were subordinated to 'regents'. In the west was Stilicho, Theodosius' nephew by marriage. Not long after Theodosius' death, probably in 396,[1] Stilicho visited the Rhine. According to Claudian, Stilicho went to calm this river's fierce nations and to bring peace to the region. He travelled swiftly, with no escort, receiving the submission of *reges* from source to mouth, and granting them peace without needing to fight them. He was away for only a few weeks at most. The Rhine-*Germani* offered military aid, but this he courteously refused.[2]

In the western section of the *Notitia Dignitatum*, where one expects to find reference to the frontier commander (*dux*) of Germania I, there is instead reference to two local commands: a frontier commander at Mainz (*dux Mogontiacensis*) and, even more oddly, the commander of a field army based in Strasbourg (*comes Argentoratensis*).[3] There has been great debate about the date and circumstances of the creation of these posts, with suggestions ranging from 369, and Valentinian I's work on the frontier, to 413, and the reforms of Constantius III in Gaul following his defeat of the usurper Constantine III.[4] The issue here is whether they resulted from imperial considerations or were mainly in response to external factors, that

---

[1] Gutmann (1991: 111).
[2] Claudian, *De Quarto Cos. Hon.* 439–59; *De Cos. Stil.* 1.188–245. Cf. above 171.
[3] *Not. Dig.* Occ. 41; 27.
[4] Demougeot (1975: 1123/59); Stroheker (1975: 41 n.45); cf. below 324.

is to some sort of shift in the nature of the 'threat' from neighbouring Alamanni. Demougeot, developing an established line of thinking, favours the former, seeing the new posts as the work of Stilicho in the period 396–400. Stilicho created them with a view to internal security, following other changes he made to the army and administration in Gaul.[5] I therefore exclude the offices of *dux Mogontiacensis* and *comes Argentoratensis* from discussion here. However, since there is a case for dating the former somewhat later, to the period following the overthrow of Constantine III, I will return to them below.[6]

Stilicho kept himself busy. In particular, he involved himself closely in the affairs of the east, attempting to gain dominance over Arcadius. This drew him into alternating conflict and alliance with Alaric, leader of a Gothic army, who exploited tensions between the two halves of the Empire in the hope of gaining a high imperial position. In 402, for example, Stilicho had to expel Alaric from Italy, but in 408 sought his aid in actions planned against the administration of Arcadius and the western usurper, Constantine III. Between rejection and recruitment of Alaric, in 405 Stilicho had to face invasion of Italy from the Danube region by another barbarian general, Radagaisus. And then came the incursion by Vandals, Alans and Suebi which began on 31 December 406 (or 405[7]) and which eventually affected much of Gaul and Spain.[8] Jerome (by mentioning Vandals, Alans and Alamanni, but not Suebi) hints that the Suebi were in fact Alamanni; and Gregory of Tours, describing their crossing into Spain with the Vandals, directly equates Suebi and Alamanni.[9]

These events exacerbated trouble in Britain which led, in 407, to the emergence of the last of the traditional western usurpers, Constantine III. He, like all his predecessors, crossed to Gaul, where he renewed old treaties of alliance and aid and agreed new ones with Franks, Alamanni and Burgundians.[10] These and other

---

[5] Demougeot (1975: 1124–6); cf. Bury (1923: 1.118 n.3).

[6] Scharf (1990); below 328.

[7] Kulikowski (2000a).

[8] Prosper, *Chron.* ad ann. 406; Orosius, *Hist.* 7.38.3; Hydatius, *Chron.* ad ann. 409 (34 [Burgess 42]).

[9] Jerome, *Ep.* 123.16; Gregory of Tours, *Dec. Lib. Hist.* 2.2: *Suebi, id est Alamanni.*

[10] Drinkwater (1998a: 282).

disasters led to the fall and execution of Stilicho (22 August 408), and for a while Constantine seemed to be about to control or even displace Honorius. However, fortune began to run against him. In 411, under attack in southern Gaul from the Spanish kingmaker, Gerontius, he sent his Frankish general, Edobichus, north to raise an army from Franks and Alamanni.[11] Gerontius besieged Constantine in Arles, but withdrew before an imperial army under Honorius' generals Constantius and Ulphilas. Constantine held on, waiting for Edobichus, but when Edobichus arrived he was defeated.

What light do these events shed on the relationship between the Alamanni and Rome? First, why did Stilicho journey along the Rhine? His refusal of military aid is odd: given his tense relationship with the east, Stilicho must have sought to build up his military strength even before Alaric's first invasion of Italy. Therefore, despite Claudian, it is usually assumed that Stilicho recruited Germanic allies.[12] Claudian's remark may be taken as defensive: to protect the half-Vandal, 'semi-barbarian' Stilicho from the (truthful) charge of hiring barbarians. Embarrassment would have been justified. Because barbarian leaders were able to satisfy such demand, they, as allies rather than enemies, began to gain the initiative in dealing with the Empire, a circumstance of which the imperial political nation began to be increasingly aware. On the other hand, the case for such recruitment remains speculative. In particular, Stilicho's formation of regiments of Brisigavi can no longer be taken as disproving Claudian's claim:[13] there is a case for such regiments being imperial in nature.[14] If he did recruit, Stilicho, like Eugenius, may have directed most of his attention towards Franks.

Stilicho is frequently blamed for cannibalizing the western garrison for his eastern adventures and to defend Italy.[15] There seems little doubt that he removed troops.[16] However, whether he recklessly

[11] Sozomen 9.13.2.

[12] So Bury (1923: 1.119), tentatively; Demandt (1989: 141), with assurance. Cf. above 171.

[13] *Contra* Stroheker (1975: 41 n. 44).

[14] Above 170–1.

[15] e.g. Bury (1923: 1.169); Demougeot (1975: 1127–8); Stroheker (1975: 41 and n.43); Demandt (1989: 142).

[16] Claudian, *Bell. Get.* 416–18 (Alaric). Bayard (1993: 227).

ran down the western defences is debatable, at least in respect of the Rhine region.[17] There had never been a major Germanic 'threat'. The Empire experienced some trouble in dealing with its neighbours, but it could handle this through police action. The large garrison in Gaul had resulted from historical, political reasons, not local need. It was unnecessary and, in encouraging usurpation, dangerous.[18] The Rhine garrison could, and probably should, be reduced. The problem for Stilicho was that Gaul was invaded not by established neighbours, but by warriors from the blue.

This brings us to the Vandals, Alans and Suebi. Given the nature of their society, it is very likely that some bands of Alamannic warriors joined the newcomers and were swept with them over the Rhine. There is, indeed, a case for Gregory of Tours' king Respendial being an Alamannic leader operating in southern Gaul and Spain in 410, rather than an Alanic chief on the Rhine in 407.[19] However, given their customary behaviour, it is equally unlikely that a substantial number of Alamanni allied themselves with Vandals and Alans and, as the Suebi of our sources, raided across Spain and into Gaul. Further, if Alamanni moved en masse against Rome, how may we explain the loyalty of the Franks, who appear to have resisted them, and even the relative docility of the Burgundians?[20] Jerome's catalogue of invaders must be regarded as fanciful;[21] and Gregory of Tours' gloss should likewise be seen as speculation on the nature of the mysterious Suebi.

The origin and identity of all three groups remains a mystery.[22] The surprise they caused suggests speed and military skill. This was

---

[17] For what follows see Drinkwater (1996: 29–30).

[18] Below 362.

[19] Wynn (1997: 81–5).

[20] Franks: Orosius, *Hist.* 7.40.3; Gregory of Tours, *Dec. Lib. Hist.* 2.9 (though see Wynn (1997) on the chronological and textual problems involved in the customary reading of this passage). Zöllner (1970: 25). Anton (1981: 238–40), following Jerome and Orosius, has elements of Burgundians caught up with the Vandals, Alans and Suebi, but clearly demonstrates that further Burgundian movement was then only by Roman invitation.

[21] Freeman (1904: 21).

[22] See Kulikowski (2000a: 341–2).

no 'Völkerwanderung'.[23] We should suppose a group of war-bands. Perhaps the best explanation for the arrival of mixed forces of Vandals, Alans and Suebi on the Rhine around 406/7 is that of Edward Gibbon: they were survivors of Radagaisus' force, defeated in northern Italy by Stilicho early in 406.[24] As one group may have moved directly westwards, and reached Gaul over the Cottian Alps, another could have escaped over the Julian Alps, first north towards the Danube and then west to cross the Rhine at Mainz.[25] The Suebi were Danubian Suebi.[26] The real nature of the Alamannic 'threat' is demonstrated in what happened next: Franks resisted the invaders; Alamanni did nothing. Apart from Vandals, Alans and Suebi, the people of the moment were the Burgundians. The events of the early fifth century suggest that by 406 they had come down the Main, reaching the Rhine and displacing local Alamanni.[27] They were now able to cross the river and become a force in Gaul: Jovinus, Constantine III's successor, was raised to power by Burgundians and Alans.

Constantine III used Franks and Alamanni as Eugenius and Stilicho had: not fighting them but recruiting them for his army, the last time through Edobichus. Gregory of Tours reports that Constantine surrendered having been told that Jovinus had declared against him in the north and was heading south with a large force,

[23] Thus *contra* Demougeot (1979: 432). The conventional view that the 406/7 invaders comprised a massive folk movement (e.g. Bury (1923: 1.185): 'vast companies of Vandals, Suevians and Alans'; Thompson (1977: 303): accompanied by 'their womenfolk, their children and their old people') appears to derive from the rhetoric of Jerome (*Ep.* 123.16: *innumerabiles et ferocissimae gentes*) and Orosius (*Hist.* 7.40.3). Among its most recent proponents is Burns, who (1994: 205–7, 223) likewise supposes a mixed composition and large numbers, but rejects the idea of planned 'invasion' in favour of 'mismanaged *receptio*' as the starving Vandal nation sought refuge within the Empire and then overwhelmed Roman resources: in effect, a repeat of the Gothic immigration over the Danube under Valens.

[24] Gibbon (1901: 268); *contra*: Freeman (1904: 22) and, for example, Petrikovits (1980: 272–3: an independent movement of peoples previously settled by the Romans on the upper Danube). For the likely relatively modest size of Radagaisus' army, despite ancient exaggeration of its strength, see Burns (1994: 198, cf. 189 for similar remarks concerning Alaric's forces).

[25] Paschoud (1989: 22–4, 28–9).

[26] Above 48, 168. Cf. Castritius (2005: 202–3): these Danubian Suebi were the descendants of Quadi.

[27] Martin (1997b: 163–4) also citing archaeological evidence.

including Alamanni. This, however, is a doublet of the tale of Edobichus' relief force. Alamanni did not march south twice in 411.[28] The old order appeared to continue, but change was on the way.

The fifth-century history of the Roman west may be said to have begun with the elevation of Jovinus, probably in Mainz, in 411. The west had produced many usurpers, but Jovinus was the first to depend on the support of local barbarian leaders, in his case Goar of the Alans and Guntiarius of the Burgundians. This brings to mind the machinations of future Germanic kingmakers inside and outside the Empire, in particular of king Theoderic II of the Visigoths (who created the emperor Avitus) and of the Suevo-Visigothic *magister militum* Ricimer (who destroyed him and his successors).[29] However, one has to be careful. Once in power, Jovinus was no creature of his backers, who should therefore be regarded as simply powerful helpers.[30] On the other hand, it is clear that the balance of power in the west was shifting in favour of *Germani*.

Jovinus proved unsuccessful, destroyed by Honorius' Gothic ally, Athaulf. Peace and order of a sort were re-established in the west. The Theodosian dynasty endured and preserved stability in Gaul and on the Rhine for over a generation. This achievement was rooted in two long reigns—of Honorius (395–423) and of Valentinian III (425–55)—and the abilities of two Roman western commanders-in-chief—Flavius Constantius (died 421) and Flavius Aëtius (murdered 454).[31] It was Aëtius who inflicted a major defeat on the Iuthungi in 430–1, after which we hear no more of them.[32] However, this stability was only relative. The Roman west was changing out of recognition. The acceptance of autonomous communities of barbarians within the Empire created internal political and military boundaries. In Gaul, an early precedent had been set by Franks in Toxiandria.[33] In 413 and 418 these were joined by Burgundians on the Rhine (and later in Savoy) and by Visigoths in Aquitania, respectively. At a

[28] Gregory of Tours, *Dec. Lib. Hist.* 2.9.56; see Drinkwater (1998a: 289 n. 136).
[29] See most recently MacGeorge (2002: 178–214).
[30] Drinkwater (1998a: 288).
[31] On these, see now Lütkenhaus (1998) and Stickler (2002).
[32] Hydatius, *Chron.* 93 [Burgess 83]; Sidonius Apollinaris, *Carm.* 7.234; Stickler (2002: 189–90). Above 62–3.
[33] Above 200.

slightly later date there was settlement by scattered groups of Alans.[34] In addition, the north-western region of Aremorica appears, like Britain, to have gone its own way; and, again as Bagaudae, disaffected Roman citizens were quite capable of disrupting nominal imperial territory.[35] In addition, western emperors and generals had to find time to manage the difficult relationship with Constantinople. And dominating everything was the problem of North Africa. Geiseric of the Vandals had invaded the area from Spain in 429 and had quickly taken it under his control. Its loss was a crippling blow in terms of morale, rents and taxes. Roman attention was much given to the questions of how, at best, to reconquer it or, at least, to prevent Geiseric from using his fleet against the Italian archipelago and the peninsula itself.[36]

The impression given by our scanty sources is of Constantius, and, particularly, Aëtius, struggling to maintain the situation in Gaul, not to improve it. An adventurous policy, aimed at, say, the recovery of Britain, or even Aremorica, would have endangered the army and the renown that kept Aëtius in power and were the west's only shield against the eastern Empire and the Vandal kingdom. It is best to envisage Roman authority in Gaul, especially in northern Gaul and along the Rhine, in the first half of the fifth century as one force striving to be the leader among many.[37] In this, military police work against, say, Burgundians and Visigoths is not surprising: these were new and potentially very dangerous presences in Gaul. More significant is the relative frequency of reports concerning Frankish aggression, including the multiple sacking of Trier.[38] This is in line with renewed Frankish activity in the later part of the fourth century,[39] and, of course, with the success of Clovis at the end of the fifth.[40]

---

[34] Burgundians: above 108; Visigoths: Heather (1991: 221); Alans: Thompson (1982: 25) and, imaginatively, Kovalevskaja (1993: 210).

[35] Thompson (1982: 31–7); Drinkwater (1992: 215–16), (1998a: 285–6).

[36] See, e.g. Bury (1923: 1.256).

[37] Wood (1987: 260); cf. Elton (1992: 170).

[38] At least four times before the middle of the century, though the precise dates are disputed: e.g. Anton (1984: 9–12): 410, 413, 419 or 420, 428 or 435; Runde (1998: 675–6): 411, 413, c.420, c.428.

[39] Above 318. Though Stickler (2002: 175–9) assumes that agreements must have been struck between Romans and Franks in the 430s and 440s, in order to explain the relative peace of the 450s.

[40] Below 344.

West of the Rhine, therefore, the situation was stable, but such stability was bound to be only temporary.

What was the place of the Alamanni in all this? Surprising, given their reputation, but to be expected, given the history of their relationship with the Empire, is their general passivity. This is not to say that there was no trouble. The Alamanni still comprised a warrior society, and despite the absence of any mention of them in the sources we should envisage raiding-bands attacking out of Alamannia as the opportunity presented itself. One result of such activity may have been the destruction of the second fort at Alzey, north-west of Worms, at some date after 425.[41] However, beyond the middle of the fifth century there appears to have been no significant Alamannic movement over the Rhine.[42] The conventional explanation is that the Alamanni were blocked by the Burgundians.[43] However, given what Alamanni had shown themselves capable of in the past when imperial attention had been diverted, this is unsatisfactory. If they had wanted to make real trouble they could have done so. A major discovery of recent years is indeed that, on the contrary, some of them, in company with other *Germani*, helped to defend the Empire.

The first indications of this came from excavation of burials at the fort of Krefeld-Gellep, south of Xanten on the Lower Rhine. Finds indicated the recruitment of right-bank *Germani* from the late third into the early fourth century and from the late fourth to the mid-fifth century, when they formed the bulk of a regular garrison.[44] Other sites, for example Jülich, Alzey and Neuss, subsequently yielded very similar results.[45] The clearest signs of Alamannic involvement were

[41] Oldenstein (1993: 126).

[42] Stroheker (1975: 43); Keller (1993: 101–2); Koch (1997a: 196); Stickler (2002: 186–7, 203). *Contra* Fingerlin (1990: 110), that there was movement into Alsace from the time of Stilicho's withdrawal of the frontier garrisons.

[43] e.g. Thompson (1982: 29, though cf. 32–3 and 36–7, where he shows the weaknesses of this analysis in respect of Savoy); Stroheker (1975: 46); Runde (1998: 676 n. 105, 677); Stickler (2002: 186) though again with doubts over Savoy (203). Cf. Pohl (2002a: 173).

[44] Pirling (1993); Reichmann (2003: 43–5).

[45] Oldenstein (1993: 25–6); Böhme (1998: 51–3); Kaiser (1998: 35). For further likely fifth-century Roman military sites on the Rhine see: Bayard (1993: 226–7); Bridger (2003: 25–6); van Enckevort and Thijssen (2003: 94–7).

found at Wyhl, some 8 km (5 statute miles) north-east of the bridge-head fort at Jechtingen-Sponeck and 17 km (10 statute miles) north-east of Breisach. Here it appears that for several decades after *c.*400, to beyond the middle of the fifth century, a crossing over the Rhine was guarded on its right bank by an Alamannic warrior-band under 'princely' leaders. Such a presence is comparable to that at Wyhlen (*sic*), over the Rhine from Kaiseraugst. On the left bank a process more in line with that at Krefeld-Gellep may be visible at Jechtingen-Sponeck where, from the later fourth century, burials in the military cemetery are indistinguishable from those in the neighbouring region. It is tempting to suppose that this indicates local service, in other words that, even before 400, local Alamannic males were being recruited to serve in the Roman fort, and were accompanied by their dependants.[46] Generally, it now appears that there was some sort of imperial military presence along the length of the Rhine until around 455, after which the forts concerned fell under independent local Germanic leaders.[47]

This raises three issues. First, though the overall direction of these strongpoints will have borne very little resemblance to that of the fourth century, some sort of organization must have existed.[48] If there was a Rhine command, or commands, there must have been a commander, or commanders. In other words, these discoveries add weight to the idea that the local generals mentioned in the *Notitia Dignitatum* may have been in post after 406/7.[49] Oldenstein suggests that Alzey was under the command of the *dux Mogontiacensis*.[50]

Second, what was the strategic purpose of such installations? They no longer offered the sophisticated, naval-based defence of Valentinian I, which disappeared in the troubles following 406/7.[51] And in any case, with barbarian and dissident imperial communities far to the west of the Rhine and with imperial attention being drawn increasingly to Constantinople and Africa, the Rhine-line could

---

[46] Fingerlin (1990: 110, 123–31), (1993: 75–9), (1997a: 108); Quast (1997: 172); Bücker (1999: 218–19). Qualified above 175.

[47] Brulet (1993: 136–7).

[48] Böhme (1998: 52–4); Kaiser (1998: 39–40).

[49] Above 321.

[50] Oldenstein (1993: 125–7).

[51] Above 297; Höckmann (1986: 403, 415).

hardly have been much to do with external defence: it probably looked inwards. The suggestion has been made that its function was to check neighbouring left-bank barbarians, in particular Burgundians.[52] However, it may have had a wider role. Its existence cannot have been planned. It was there because it had always been there: a 400-year-old system of pay and provisioning (latterly, presumably, from levies on local communities[53]) was impossible to destroy overnight. This gave the Late Empire a valuable resource, an anomalous projection of Roman military strength from northern Italy to the North Sea. It could be used to police local barbarians; but it could also serve as a reservoir of men and supplies for Aëtius' field army: vital not just for Gaul but for the whole of the area administered or claimed by Ravenna.[54] If so, Roman Gaul may be seen as having resumed something of its ancient role as a military holding base.[55]

Finally, it may be held that the development of left-bank Alamannic garrisons, probably under their own Romanized leaders,[56] and with their dependants, represented Alamannic expansion of a sort. Thus, in satisfying the demands of the most ambitious bands, it may help explain the lack of more aggressive Alamannic movement in this period.[57] It should be noted that the eastern Raetian frontier, along the Iller and upper Danube, appears to have been held until around 430 though there is as yet no evidence for Alamannic garrisons.[58]

There are hints of a weakening in the imperial grasp on the Rhine frontier from the 440s,[59] but real decline began in the 450s. The relative stability of the first half of the fifth century was destroyed by the Hunnic invasion of Gaul in 451, the murder of Aëtius by Valentinian III in 454, and Valentinian's assassination in 455. There followed a period of intense political flux and military defeat (Rome

---

[52] Bayard (1993: 226); cf. Kaiser (1998: 39).

[53] For the fiscal importance of the *civitates*, see Drinkwater (1998a: 295–6), less positive than here. On the continuity of military dependence on taxation into the Merovingian period, see Martin (1993: 461, from Durliat).

[54] Cf. Elton (1992: 170).

[55] Drinkwater (1983a: 120); cf. above 14.

[56] Cf. Böhme (1998: 54–5), on similar developments among the Franks.

[57] See further below 358.

[58] See Mackensen (1999: 239).

[59] Brulet (1993: 228), from study of Argonne ware.

was sacked by Geiseric in 455) and, within 20 years, the end of the western Empire. Attila led a large, mixed force west from Pannonia. We do not know his exact route, but since he broke into Gaul on the middle Rhine it is likely that he went through Alamannia, perhaps down the Main.[60] Aëtius and his Gallo-Germanic allies repulsed Attila near Troyes in midsummer 451. We do not know how the Hunnic incursion and withdrawal affected the Alamanni, or to what extent Alamannic communities resisted Attila. Almost certainly, like Burgundians and Franks, Alamanni were to be found on both sides.[61] Beyond this we may guess that the Huns had a significant impact on Alamannic society, but what this was we cannot say exactly.[62] One result, visible in the archaeology of the period, was the appearance of skull deformation effected in infancy, a Central Asiatic custom. However, in Alamannia this appears to have been a restricted and temporary phenomenon, found among individual adult (mainly non-Mongolian) immigrants, not throughout Alamannic society as a whole.[63]

In political and military terms, the best indication of change among the Alamanni in the troubles that followed the Hunnic invasion and withdrawal are the first clear signs of their expansion.[64] In this they were not unique. All barbarian communities in Gaul— Visigoths, Burgundians and Franks—exploited Roman weakness to increase their power. Around 457 Franks took Cologne, and at around the same time Childeric, father of Clovis, began to lay the foundations of Merovingian greatness.[65] What is unusual is that, for the first time since Jovinus, Alamannic warriors find mention in the literary sources.

[60] Maenchen-Helfen (1973: 129), though on the grounds that, since the Alamanni are not explicitly named among Attila's allies, he must have taken a route around their territory; Geuenich (1997a: 68). Sidonius Apollinaris' reference to Attila's Frankish allies as living by the Neckar (*Carm.* 7.325) is not helpful here (*contra* Anton (1984: 16–18)).

[61] Geuenich (1997a: 68); cf. Sidonius Apollinaris, *Carm.* 7.320–5.

[62] Martin (1997b: 166).

[63] Quast (1997: 178); Wahl, Wittwer-Backofen, and Kunter (1997: 341–2). For an alternative, but equally commonplace, explanation see Steuer (1998: 309–11): skull deformation not as the result of invasion, but as the diffusion of a female fashion.

[64] Martin (1997b: 166).

[65] Runde (1998: 677). Following Springer (1998: esp. 305), I avoid identifying these specifically as 'Ripuarian' or 'Rhineland' Franks.

Our best evidence for expansion comes from Sidonius Apollinaris, an imperial politician and subsequently bishop of Clermont in the Auvergne. His father-in-law, and fellow Gaul, Eparchius Avitus, was the short-lived (9 July 455–17 October 456) successor of Petronius Maximus, who had engineered the assassination of Valentinian III. In his panegyric to Avitus, delivered on 1 January 456, Sidonius describes how Saxons and Franks had exploited the recent troubles to raid Gaul, and admonishes 'the bold Alaman' for 'drinking the Rhine from the Roman bank, and proudly lording it over both sides, a citizen or a conqueror'.[66] At a slightly later date, in a second pan-egyric that, awkwardly, Sidonius had to address to Avitus' successor, Majorian (28 December 457–2 August 461), he recounts Majorian's activities as *magister militum*, in the interval between the fall of Avitus and his succession. Amongst these was his destruction of an Alamannic war-band. This band, 900-strong, attacked over the Raetian Alps into the Campi Canini,[67] but was defeated by Majorian's subordinate, Burco, with a small force.[68]

As good a source as Sidonius is the sixth-century hagiographer, Eugippius, who in his 'Life' of St Severinus records an Alamannic king, Gibuldus, active on the border of Raetia and Noricum in the period 470/6. Though Gibuldus and his Alamanni subjected the town of Passau to regular attack, he greatly respected Severinus and eventually yielded to the saint's demands that he end his raids and free his Roman captives.[69] Eugippius later mentions other serious Alamannic raiding against Passau and against Künzing (to its west) and, further east, into northern and southern Noricum.[70] This brought Alamanni into contact with Rugi, pushing westwards.[71] Eugippius elsewhere mentions that Passau was subject to attack by one Hunumundus and his men. Hunumundus is generally identified as the daring 'Suavian' (that is Suebian) king Hunimundus, described by Jordanes, in his sixth-century 'History of the Goths', who,

[66] Sidonius Apollinaris, *Carm.* 7.369–75: *Rhenumque, ferox Alamanne, bibebas Romani ripis et utroque superbus in agro.*

[67] For the location of this area see above 209.

[68] Sidonius Apollinaris, *Carm.* 5.373–80.

[69] Eugippius, *V. Severini* 19 (=*Quellen* 2, 73–4). Date: Runde (1998: 678).

[70] Eugippius, *V. Severini* 27.1–2; 25; 31.4 (=*Quellen* 2, 74–6).

[71] Eugippius, *V. Severini* 31, 1–5 (=*Quellen* 2, 75–6).

together with his Alamannic allies, had been thrashed by the Ostrogothic king, Theodemer, in a battle fought over the Danube around 470.[72] The anonymous author of the 'Life' of bishop Lupus of Troyes, also writing in the late fifth/early sixth century, records that at about the same time an Alamannic king called Gebavultus yielded to Lupus' plea to free war captives in his diocese.[73] Finally, Gregory of Tours relates how, in the 15th year of his reign, Clovis went to war against the Alamanni. Hard-pressed in battle, Clovis vowed to Christ that if he were successful he would abandon his own gods and become a Christian. Thereupon the enemy turned tail, their king was killed and the Alamanni yielded unconditionally to Clovis.[74] Gregory's narrative is traditionally supplemented by a further reference in his text. This is his remark that Sigibert the Lame, king of the Franks on the Rhine, received the crippling wound that gave him his name in a battle against Alamanni at Zülpich.[75] These two elements are usually combined to reconstruct a major Alamannic advance northwards, down the Rhine, towards Cologne, in the late 490s. To counter the threat, king Sigibert had to call upon his allies, including Clovis, and the combined Frankish army fought a decisive battle at Zülpich, near Euskirchen just south of Cologne, in 496 or 497.[76]

Mapping of these events appears to produce a zone of Alamannic expansion and control at its greatest extent *c.*750 km (420 statute miles) long, east to west, and *c.*650 km (390 statute miles) wide, north-west to south-east: Geuenich's 'Aktionsradius'[77] (Fig. 25). The existence of such an area is questionable. Sidonius' Rhineland Alaman is impudent, and on its left bank gulps down the river following some military success. On the other hand, he is a much less mobile and dangerous a figure than Sidonius' Saxon pirate or his Frankish bane of the provinces of Germania I and Belgica II. Sidonius' complaint may concern no more than Alamannic military

[72] Eugippius, *V. Severini* 22; Jordanes, *Get.* 277–80; *PLRE* 2.57, 1069. Castritius (2005: 199): probably 469.

[73] *V. Lupi* 10 (=*Quellen* 4, 13).

[74] Gregory of Tours, *Dec. Lib. Hist.* 2.30.

[75] Gregory of Tours, *Dec. Lib. Hist.* 2.37.

[76] e.g. Koch (1997a: 191).

[77] Geuenich (1997a: 70–1). I follow Geuenich here in eschewing the difficult and suspect evidence of the 'Ravenna Cosmography' (=*Quellen* 4, 9–12); cf. Runde (1998: 679 n.118) concerning Alamannic expansion.

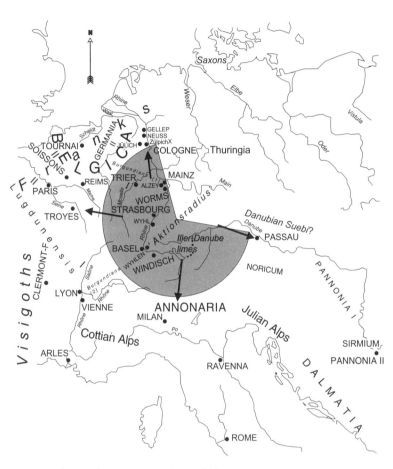

Fig. 25 The north-western provinces, fifth century.

leaders on the left bank claiming as their own territory over which they had long since exercised de facto control under nominal imperial suzerainty:[78] there was no massive Alamannic 'invasion' of Alsace.[79] Indeed, further afield in Germania I any Alamannic interlopers would have been in competition with Sidonius' expanding Franks.[80]

Sidonius' account of the success of Burco makes plain that he encountered no more than a war-party. At 900-strong, this is in size little different from those proposed for the third century,[81] and calls to mind the war-bands that figure in Eugippius' 'Life' of Severinus. The young bloods of Alamannic warrior society were, as ever, exploiting imperial weakness to show their mettle. Significant in this respect is the difference between them and Feletheus, king of the Rugi, who realized that if he was to control an area and its people he had to do so through its towns.[82] 'King' Gibuldus, in contrast, was no more than a war-leader, who had no desire to take or hold land.[83] 'King' Gebavultus appears to have been another war-leader—if what we are told about him can be trusted.[84]

An enigmatic and controverted statement by Gregory of Tours— to the effect that in the late 460s one 'Odovacrius' (clearly the Odovacer who deposed the last western emperor in 476) allied with Childeric against Alamanni who had penetrated Italy[85]—could be further evidence for such raiding. Current debate, in which some have amended 'Odovacrius' to 'Adovacrius' (a Saxon leader in Gaul) and 'Alamanni' to (Gallic-based) 'Alani', concerns not whether

---

[78] For the image of barbarians drinking from particular rivers as a poetic means of indicating their geographical location cf. Nemesianus, *Cynegetica* 67–8 (=*Quellen* 2, 118). Cf. Goetz and Welwei (1995: 1.272 n.57) for Veleda as being honoured by *Rhenopotai.*

[79] See Martin (1997b: 167) and Wieczorek (1997: 241–2), for the lack of archaeological evidence for Alamannic settlement in Alsace. Cf. Siegmund (2000: 287–92), for a likely partition of the area between Franks and Alamanni, but not until the period 530–670.

[80] Martin (1997b: 168); Wieczorek (1997: 242, 246–7).

[81] Above 49, 61.

[82] Eugippius, *V. Severini* 31.1, 4 (=*Quellen* 2, 75–6).

[83] On the weakness of Gibuldus see Pohl (1998a: 642).

[84] Below 336.

[85] Gregory of Tours, *Dec. Lib. Hist.* 2.19.

Alamanni were capable of such attacks, but whether an early Merovingian king possessed such international contacts.[86]

Finally, assessment of the battle of Zülpich is not straightforward. It is impossible to establish whether Clovis' great Alamannic victory and Sigibert's wounding relate to the same event. And, anyway, it is now realized that for Gregory the victory itself was less important than the Catholic conversion and baptism that it is supposed to have accelerated, and that this conversion may have influenced Gregory to exaggerate Clovis' military success. There was probably no huge Alamannic force, and no conclusive victory. Other sources suggest that the process by which Clovis absorbed the Alamanni lasted several years, and involved the defeat of a number of local leaders. All this weakens the likelihood of a massive Alamannic push north to Cologne.[87]

Overall, therefore, instead of an area of concerted Alamannic expansion we should envisage one of marginal settlement and heavy raiding.[88] Where the latter occurred it led to terrorization of civilian populations, not permanent and regular control.[89] Short-term expansion by Danubian Suebi into Noricum, checked by Theodemer and ending in the flight of Hunimundus and his followers, was probably the occasion of their absorption by Alamanni already touched upon.[90]

We return to the question of the Great King.[91] In his account of Clovis' victory, Gregory of Tours appears to pitch the Frankish king against a single, supreme Alamannic ruler, leading his army into a mighty battle which he seems well able to win. His initial success forces Clovis to extreme measures; and his death precipitates the surrender of his people. He is a powerful figure. Some who believe in his existence have sought support for the idea that by the end of the

---

[86] *PLRE* 2.791–2; James (1988: 69); Wood (1994: 39); MacGeorge (2002: 102 n. 88).

[87] On 'Zulpich' see Geuenich (1997a: 78–82, 85–6), (1998); with Wood (1994: 45–6); Runde (1998: 680 n.122); Pohl (2000: 32); and below 344–6.

[88] See Martin (1997b: 167–9 and Figs 170a–b), for archaeological evidence to suggest the movement of high-status Alamannic families down the Middle Rhine and into the Cologne Bight. However, as Martin remarks, these were clearly few in number and may well have been political refugees.

[89] Thus *contra* Keller (1993: 101–2). Cf. Pohl (2000: 31).

[90] Above 48, 168; Keller (1993: 92–3); Geuenich (1997a: 14), (1997c: 145); Pohl (2000: 103–4); Lotter, Bratož, and Castritius (2003: 111); Castritius (2005: 196–9): these Danubian Suebi were descended from Marcomanni.

[91] Above 123.

fifth century the Alamanni were capable of producing paramount kings in the identification of Gibuldus of Passau and Gebavultus of Troyes as one and the same person. As Childeric was consolidating Frankish power in northern Gaul, the writ of an Alamannic ruler ran from Bavaria to Champagne. As Clovis outdid Childeric, so might another Alamannic leader have outperformed Gibuldus/Gebavultus in fighting in 396/7 or, as part of a subsequent campaign of resistance to the Franks, *c*.500. The current *communis opinio* is, however, with Geuenich, against the notion of an Alamannic Great King. The case for a common identity for Gibuldus and Gebavultus is weakened by the strong possibility that the exploits of the second may be no more than a doublet of those of the first.[92] And the more that Gregory's account of Clovis' defeat of the Alamanni in 496/7 is seen to relate to religious affairs the less important becomes the battle itself and the Alamannic leader who figured in it. He becomes one of many such leaders in the long process of Alamannic defeat and decline.[93] From beginning to end, independent Alamannia was politically fragmented.

However, the idea of some sort of consolidation of Alamannic power structures should not be dismissed entirely out of hand. The Alamanni of the fifth century were not the same as those of the fourth. Since 406/7 and, especially, 455, much had happened (including the emergence of a Thuringian kingdom[94]), and we should allow that Alamannic society and politics may have changed in response.[95] As Geuenich says, unlike those of other Germanic peoples of the Roman west, we know nothing of the pedigrees and marriage alliances of fifth-century Alamannic royal families; and we have uncovered no great Alamannic royal palace or graves.[96] However, this last is suspect as an *argumentum ex silentio*. The sumptuous burial of Childeric, found at Tournai in 1653, is unique and was uncovered only by accident.[97] To be airbrushed out of history is the

[92] *Quellen* 4, 13 n.1; Geuenich (1997a: 74).

[93] For the debate see Geuenich (1997a: 72–5, 83–5), (1997c: 144–8), (1998: 423–30). *Contra*: Martin (1997b: 167); Lotter, Bratož, and Castritius (2003: 119–21).

[94] See Pohl (2000: 40–1).

[95] Keller (1998: 585–91); below 343.

[96] Geuenich (1997a: 85–6), (1997c: 148), (1998: 431).

[97] James (1988: 58–64); Brulet (1997: 164–70); Müller-Wille (1997: 206–11); Périn and Kazanski (1997).

frequent fate of the loser. Clovis' success was unexpected: without it there would have been no great Merovingian kingdom, and Gregory of Tours would never have had occasion to seek out details of Clovis' ancestors. More substantive is that if we accept a protracted process of Frankish conquest of Alamannia in the later fifth and early sixth centuries we must accept that the various Alamannic leaders with whom Clovis contended were no mean figures. They held out against one of the ablest generals of the age for a considerable period of time, and must therefore have been able to draw on significant resources. This indicates a fair degree of political sophistication. Indeed, the authority eventually exercised over the Alamanni by Clovis, and elsewhere by the Ostrogothic king, Theoderic, suggests the availability of a significant level of local control.[98] The Alamanni had produced major leaders in the shape of Chnodomarius and, especially, Macrianus. These had been broken by Rome, but after the middle of the fifth century Roman control had vanished.[99] As Wolfram says, again noting the case of Franks under Clovis, with the right talents and in the right circumstances, in this period a Great King could emerge out of nowhere;[100] so why not from the Alamanni? I propose that in this period the Alamanni may have had not one Great King but several 'greater kings',[101] some possibly from a new centre of power on the Neckar.[102]

Given the nature of the literary sources, likely major economic and social developments are accessible only through archaeology. Though, as ever, difficult, this yields intriguing signs of continuity and change.

The late fourth and fifth centuries were the great age of the 'Höhensiedlungen'. These continued and flourished in their role as regional centres down to the middle of the fifth century.[103] Their existence may have operated against the emergence of super-regional power bases, that is against the emergence of a Great, or even greater kings, down to around 455.[104]

[98] Hummer (1998: 16); for Theoderic see below 344.
[99] Above 330–1.
[100] Wolfram (1998: 614–15).
[101] Cf. Keller (1998: 591).
[102] Below 343.
[103] Steuer (1990: 196, 202); Pohl (2002a: 174).
[104] Cf. above 124; below 344.

Change is reflected in pollen evidence from Hornstaad and Moosrasen, already referred to as an indicator of a decrease in population in Alamannia from the third century.[105] This shows that the reforestation that was a feature of the fourth century, and resulted from agricultural neglect, was reversed at the beginning of the fifth century. Deforestation lasted for about 50 years, after which reforestation again set in, and intensified from *c.*500.[106] Deforestation suggests a rise in farming activity and therefore an increase in population from *c.*400. The reversal of this process, from *c.*450, was perhaps initiated by the Hunnic incursion and continued by the longer-term political and military disruption that preceded and followed the Frankish takeover *c.*500.

A significant factor in the early-fifth-century rise in population appears to have been new Elbgermanic immigration from the east, especially from the area of modern Bohemia. It may have been these people who were responsible for Alamannic reoccupation of former Burgundian territory east of the Rhine after the Burgundian defeat of 436. As well as on the lower Main and in the foothills of the Taunus, burials and settlement sites yielding 'Bohemian'-style artefacts have been discovered on the middle and lower Neckar. Since Bohemian archaeology reveals no sign of depopulation, such migrants must, like those of earlier periods, have moved in small bands.[107] Population increase and deforestation may have been the cause of a new pattern of farming. From around 400 Alamannic settlement shifted closer to water sources, that is away from the Roman pattern.[108] That Alamannic farming was now pressured to explore new methods of production is also suggested by the Osterburken hoard of iron tools.[109] These, found just north of Jagsthausen, on the line of the old *limes*, have been interpreted as the working inventory of a large estate, which was busy developing animal husbandry.[110] Though broadly dated to the period 400–500, they suit the conditions of

[105] Above 91 n.57.

[106] Rösch (1997: 324, 327–9 and Figs 357–8).

[107] Major sites at Eschborn (Frankfurt, near the Ebel-bei-Praunheim villa: cf. above 85) and Ladenburg, Pleidelsheim and Renningen: Martin (1997b: 164–6); Quast (1997: 174–7); Wamers (1997). Cf. above 48.

[108] Weidemann (1972: 114–23, 154); Keller (1993: 99–100).

[109] Above 90.

[110] Henning (1985: 592–3).

the first 50 years of the century. An oddity is that Alamannic burials continue to favour native hand-thrown pots over Roman wheel-thrown ceramics and glasswares. Alamannic grave deposits thus appear 'poorer' than, say, Frankish; and it has been suggested that Alamanni may have been more dependent on cheaper wooden vessels.[111] As ever, the problem is whether funerary offerings reflect contemporary economic conditions or fossilized custom, or something between.

Though all Alamanni, 'old' and 'new', were bound to have been dependent upon farming for their basic needs, the primary attraction for immigrants (or, rather, their controlling males) was probably Roman military service, in line with the archaeological evidence for such service already noted.[112] The Basel area appears to have been especially attractive. The presence of Alamannic troops at Wyhlen, across the Rhine from Kaiseraugst, has been mentioned.[113] Artefacts suggesting the early to mid-fifth-century stationing of Germanic (Alamannic, Elbgermanic immigrants and others) fighters to defend the Basel bridgehead have also been found in cemeteries at Herten and Basel-Gotterbarmweg. Though these burial grounds were fairly large, their corresponding settlements appear to have been relatively small, prompting the suggestion that the settlements were originally those of family groups, that buried their dead in particular sections of general cemeteries. The nature of the artefacts found— high quality, with large quantities of Roman imports—suggests the leadership of local 'chiefs', living off imperial pay, not agriculture.[114] In other words, traditional upper-class Alamannic dependence on Rome continued into the fifth century, raising the question as to what happened to this society when the Empire withdrew from the Rhine. But, before this, another problem that Roman service created for Alamanni in the fifth century may have been that many eastern migrants passed through their territory en route for the Empire or, after service, returning home. If the distribution of artefacts reflects the movement of people, such a phenomenon is suggested by finds of eastern Germanic and even Asiatic material on Gallic sites, and of

---

[111] Siegmund (2000: 130–1, 145–50, 303–5).
[112] Quast (1997: 172); above 327–8.
[113] Ibid.
[114] Giesler (1997: 209–11), noting the presence of Thuringian artefacts.

Roman-style military brooches as far as the Elbe.[115] The Alamannic 'room' may again have become a 'corridor', with all the dislocation that this was likely to cause.[116]

Cemetery evidence in general appears to show continuity yielding to major change during the second half of the fifth century. Funerary archaeology remains difficult with, for example, male preference for Roman military dress making it hard to identify burials as 'Germanic', let alone 'Alamannic' or 'Frankish' etc.[117] However, it can be seen that important developments occurred in burial practices during this period. These included changes in the nature of grave-goods, most dramatically in the introduction of horse burials, with the animals interred, harnessed and saddled, alongside their masters. The custom may have been introduced by outsiders, as immigrant Bohemian Elbe-*Germani* or Thuringians, or as invaders, Attila's Huns.[118] It is important to note, however, that it extended into Gaul, as recently confirmed by the discovery of horse burials closely associated with the grave of Childeric.[119] It has also been pointed out that horse burials are concentrated in south-east Alamannia, on the Danube.[120] The historical significance of the practice therefore lies not in showing, say, that the Alamanni were particularly keen horsemen,[121] but that in the shifting conditions of the later fifth century they were becoming part of a wider Westgermanic world.

There was also change in the composition and size of Alamannic burial sites. Down to the middle of the fifth century Alamanni did not really have true 'cemeteries'. Burial places were family affairs, comprising the graves of individuals or small groups (up to about half-a-dozen) of people. Then, in the period *c.*440/50–80, there was a rapid shift to larger collections of burials.[122] These new cemeteries resemble, though were never as huge or as tightly regimented as, the Merovingian 'Reihengräber' of the sixth century. Nor were they, in

---

[115] Kazanski (1993); Vallet (1993), with the criticisms of Martin (1993: 460); Schach-Dörges (1997: 82); Böhme (1998: 51 and Fig. 16).

[116] Cf. below 343–4.

[117] Above 4; Steuer (1998: 313) from Böhme.

[118] Quast (1997: 175, 179, Figs 179–80); Stork (1997: 295).

[119] Above n. 65; and Beck (1998: 481).

[120] Müller-Wille (1997: 209–10 and Fig. 146); Siegmund (2000: 124–5 and Fig. 28).

[121] Cf. above 175–6.

[122] Quast (1997: 171–2).

terms of construction and grave-goods, as economically and socially homogeneous, since some still accommodated substantial, rich, 'old-fashioned' burials of individuals and distinct groups. The tradition of dispersed single and group burials also continued.[123] This is not settlement archaeology. We are dealing with more people being buried together, not living together. Alamannic communities remained small.[124] Furthermore, change was not confined to Alamanni. 'Proto-Reihengräber' appear from the later fourth century in northern Gaul, in what some have seen as a Germanic (specifically Frankish) and others a decidedly Roman context.[125] We are in the presence of a widespread change in burial custom, the roots of which have been sought both in the Roman Empire and in Elbgermanic Bohemia.[126] However, Alamannic and Frankish custom and usage may have altered in response to changes in local conditions, such as leaders seeking other means of controlling their communities as imperial support disappeared.[127]

Such an idea fits well with another Franco-Alamannic innovation in funerary habits from the mid-fifth century: burying males with swords. The weapons vary in type and quality, but include a number of magnificent gold-hilted double-edged longswords: *spathae*.[128] The evolution of this custom is debated, with emphasis placed on its likely Roman or Romano-Germanic origin in northern Gaul, beginning no later than the late fourth century. Many swords, indeed, appear to have been made within the Empire, perhaps in imperial arms workshops. The appearance of sword burials coincides with that of 'proto'-'Reihengräber' in the same area.[129] It is argued that the practice spread to wider Germanic communities, including the Alamanni, during the fifth century as a result of barbarian service in the Roman army. Again, wherever it came from, its adoption surely betokens socio-political change in Frankish and Alamannic society.

---

[123] Quast (1997: 171–2, 187–8); Siegmund (2000: 97–8).
[124] Quast (1997: 171–2).
[125] Halsall (1992); Böhme (1998: 41–4); Siegmund (2000: 125).
[126] Quast (1997: 171–2, 174–6, 188).
[127] So Keller (1998: 589–90, 599); cf. Pohl (2000: 31).
[128] Quast (1997: 186).
[129] Quast (1997: 187); Böhme (1997: 95–6), (1998: 34–5, 38, 40–4); Siegmund (2000: 320–7). For the overall distribution of such swords see Hedeager (1993: 125 Fig. 1).

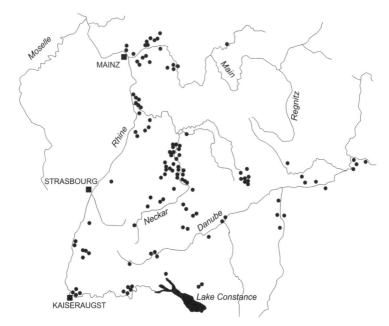

Fig. 26   Distribution of burials, late fifth to early sixth century [from Quast (1997: 172 Fig. 173); © Archäologisches Landesmuseum Baden-Württemberg].

And again, such overt display of wealth and military power may be explained by reference to growing aristocratic control.[130]

Gold-hilted *spatha* burials occur among both Alamanni and Franks and include the grave of Childeric. Thus, they are a general, 'hyper-ethnic', upper-class custom,[131] which tells us little about Alamanni. However, Alamanni seem to have had a greater preference for sword burials than Franks did;[132] and a number of these are concentrated on the middle Neckar, where there is also a clustering of the new, larger cemeteries[133] (Fig. 26). A key site here is

[130] Cf. Keller (1998: 600). Kleeman (1997) suggests similar developments in contemporary Lower Saxony, where the introduction of weapon burials (especially, of *spathae*) reflected a battle for status under conditions of social change.

[131] Siegmund (1998: 574); 'hyper-ethnic' is my translation of his 'überethnisch' (2000: 320, 326–7).

[132] Siegmund (2000: 79, 177, 179–82).

[133] Steuer (1997a: 160, Fig. 160, swords); Quast (1997: 171 Fig. 172, 172 Fig. 173, cemeteries).

Pleidelsheim (Fig. 4), where cemetery burials from the mid-fifth century indicate the presence of three family groups. Burials of Family 1 (my categorization) suggest modest wealth, though by its third generation this family could afford to deposit a *spatha* and rich female jewellery. A male grave of Family 2 contained rich goods, including a gold-hilted *spatha*. The even greater standing of Family 3 is indicated by a pair of horse burials and what appear to be associated graves of dependent horsemen.[134] In the high-Roman period the fertility of the Neckar valley had supported a fair number of urban and rural sites.[135] It figures little in what we know of the third and fourth centuries, but now it may have regained importance. After *c.*455, as imperial interest in the Rhine evaporated and as the Roman-based subsidy culture of the 'Höhensiedlungen' declined, Alamannic leaders would have been forced back on their own, agricultural, resources.[136] This may have led to the rise of rural power centres, with the hill-sites now serving to defend the more important lowland settlements.[137] The Neckar valley could have emerged as a new, broader, power base, allowing the emergence of a 'greater' king.[138]

This takes us to evidence for a second wave of fifth-century settlement, after 450. The period 460–80 appears to have produced an increase in middle-Danubian influences on burials in Alamannic cemeteries. This has been explained as resulting from people brought westwards by the Huns in the early 450s. However, this is not sufficient explanation for the mass and distribution of the finds, which more likely reflect a second phase of fifth-century immigration, mainly (though not entirely) restricted to Alamannia, in small family groups.[139] The likeliest, though very speculative, explanation

---

[134] Koch (1997b: 219–23).

[135] Sommer (1999: 179 Fig. 67, 188).

[136] Cf. Steuer (1998: 30) concerning the falling away of Roman-style military belts in sites on the Elbe from the middle and late fifth century, surely a direct indication of the ending of service in the Roman army and hence of the income derived from it in places other than Alamannia.

[137] Steuer (1997a: 153, 159). Cf. Steuer (1997a: 159) and Pohl (2000: 31) on swords as symbolizing the rise of 'eine selbstbewußte Kriegerschicht'.

[138] Above 337. Cf. Steuer (1997a: 159–60), that the (regularly spaced) rural sites may have been royal gifts to warrior elites.

[139] Quast (1997: 179–82). For eastern settlers in northern Gaul in the later fifth century see Pilet, Buchet, and Pilet-Lerrière (1993: 160).

is Danubian Suebi moving westwards following military defeat and fusing with Alamanni.[140] The newcomers appear to have settled in areas which were already occupied, that is they did not open up new land. As seen, this suggests a decline in Alamannic population after *c*.450, and explains the ending of deforestation. More than this, however, it also suggests control: that, since it would not have been in the interests of Alamannic leaders to allow them to form islands of population, they were made to integrate.[141] It is interesting that, despite mongrel beginnings, a history of dispersed settlement and significant losses and gains in population, Alamannic burial customs appear to reflect a general cultural homogeneity.[142] If true, this would also help promote social integration and so political unity. Again we encounter the likelihood that, just before its end, the leaders of independent Alamannic society were becoming more sophisticated in their political practices and aspirations, acquiring the potential to produce greater or even Great Kings.

But Clovis defeated the Alamanni at Zülpich, and with 'Zülpich'— the 'process', if not the battle—we reach the end of the story of the Alamanni and Rome. Independent Alamannic history was at its end, as was that of the western Empire. In 497, the eastern emperor, Anastasius, recognized Theoderic, king of the Ostrogoths and conqueror of Odovacer, as ruler of Italy;[143] and in 508, following Clovis' victory over the Visigoths, Anastasius honoured the Frankish king with 'some sort of consular office', allowing him and his successors to play the Roman ruler in Gaul.[144]

However, to complete the story of the Alamannic 'fall', Alamannia was under full Frankish control by 506/7, to the extent that Clovis could contemplate an incursion into Raetia, within northern Ostrogothic territory. This emerges from a letter written by Theoderic to Clovis, now his brother-in-law, in 507, and preserved by Cassiodorus. Theoderic, declaring himself proud to be associated with Clovis, congratulates him (in a somewhat double-edged fashion) on his

[140] Quast (1997: 183–6); Hummer (1998: 17); Castritius (2005: 199); above 168, 335.

[141] Quast (1997: 186).

[142] Siegmund (2000: 301).

[143] *PLRE* 2.1077–84, at 1083.

[144] Gregory of Tours, *Dec. Lib. Hist.* 2.38; quotation: Wood (1994: 165). Cf. James (1988: 87–8); Wood (1994: 48–9, 179), (1997: 360).

success in recent conflict with Alamanni: in fact, on having subdued the Alamanni, weakened by the loss in battle of their leading men (*fortiores*). However, Theoderic continues, though Clovis is right to pursue the ringleaders, he should not hold everyone to account. He advises Clovis to temper his actions against the 'shattered remnants' (*fessae reliquiae*) who have fled to his (Theoderic's) protection (either into Raetia south of the Danube or into former Alamannic Raetia, over which Theoderic now claimed control[145]): these deserve to be left in peace. Clovis should be content with what he has achieved so far, which includes the fall of 'that king' (*ille rex*) and 'the pride of the race' (*gentis...superbia*). He ends by asking Clovis to respect his request, and no longer concern himself with an area that he recognizes as being under Theoderic's control.[146] The size of the Alamannic column of refugees is reflected in another letter of Theoderic concerning the movement of Alamanni south through Noricum, from which it is clear that they had significant numbers of draught animals (*boves*: 'oxen').[147] Large-scale Alamannic flight into Ostrogothic territory following the loss of a king is confirmed by Ennodius, in his panegyric on Theoderic. He praises Theoderic for having successfully settled Alamanni on good land, transforming traditional raiders of Italy into its guardians.[148] Alamannic collapse around 506 is also suggested by Fredegarius.[149]

These documents demonstrate that whatever happened in 496/7 was not conclusive, being followed either by continued Alamannic resistance and Frankish campaigning or partial Alamannic surrender then fierce rebellion.[150] They may also tell us a little more about independent Alamannic society at the very end of its development. First, it is clear that Clovis' war of *c.*505/6 brought about, and possibly culminated in, the death of a major Alamannic king. Theoderic knew about this king, referred to him specifically (*ille*), and therefore

---

[145] Lotter, Bratož, and Castritius (2003: 129).

[146] Cassiodorus, *Var.* 2.41.1–3 (=*Quellen* 2, 102); Barnish (1992: 43–4 and n.33), with Fridh, against Mommsen, reading *causis* (not *caesis*) *fortioribus*—'have yielded to a stronger power'—but expressing uncertainty.

[147] Cassiodorus, *Var.* 3.60.1–3 (=*Quellen* 2, 103).

[148] Ennodius, *Paneg. dictus Theoderico* 15 (72–3) (=*Quellen* 2, 72).

[149] Fredegarius, *Chron.* 3.21 (=*Quellen* 2, 14).

[150] Resistance: James (1988: 84–5); Geuenich (1997a: 85–6), (1997c: 148). Revolt: Koch, R. and U. (1997: 270); Babucke (1997: 250).

must have been aware of his name. However, in his letter to Clovis he leaves him ingloriously anonymous. This, the common fate of the vanquished, shows that the absence of Alamannic royal names in this period is no good evidence for the non-existence of Great or greater kings.[151]

Second, Theoderic's emphasis on the plight of those who have taken refuge in his territory is unusual. It may be no more than a ploy, aimed at, say, avoiding the awkward international incident that would result if Clovis crossed into his territory without authorization. On the other hand, Theoderic's concern may have been real if the refugees included Alamannic aristocrats: able to call on Ostrogothic royal protection.[152] Clovis' anxiety to apprehend them might therefore reveal a major element in his strategy of dealing with a subject Alamannia (consistent with his treatment of Frankish rivals[153]): to eliminate all traces of the indigenous ruling elite.

This fits archaeological evidence for the decline and abandonment of the hill-sites, the existence of which was no doubt judged a potential challenge to Frankish authority.[154] Interesting here is the fate of the Runder Berg (1) which was suddenly evacuated around 500, with many valuables being hidden and never recovered.[155] Archaeological finds also appear to confirm the flight of the wealthy from the Middle Rhine, whatever form we envisage for Alamannic expansion in this area, and northern Alamannia (the Main region, the middle Neckar and the Swabian Alp) into Raetia by way of Noricum from around 500. As always, this is based on the assumption that the distribution of the artefacts resulted from the movement of people rather than from trade or, in this period, the looting of Alamannic sites by outsiders.[156] Similar finds suggest that some Alamanni went even further eastwards, seeking refuge among Lombards, while others found safety in the west, with Burgundians.[157] A few, settled as refugees or prisoners of war, may even be detected on Merovingian territory.[158]

---

[151] Above 336–7.
[152] For the rich as likely refugees, see Koch (1997a: 192).
[153] Below 354.
[154] Werner (1965: 90); Steuer (1997a: 154, 160); Dierkens (1998: 456).
[155] Koch (1997a: 192–4).
[156] Koch (1997a: 194, 196–7 and Fig. 206, 199), cf. (1997b: 237).
[157] Koch (1997a: 197–9).
[158] Koch (1997a: 199–200).

It is reasonably assumed that Franks soon occupied the lands vacated by Alamanni, forcing the 'slippage' of medieval Alamannia by comparison with its Roman predecessor.[159] However, further south, Franks appear to have moved in slowly. At Pleidelsheim, though the elimination of the leaders of independent Alamannic society is hinted at in the early-sixth-century disappearance of Families 2 and 3, the more modest Family 1 survived, and its artefacts indicate its production of a local chief. Close Frankish interest in what remained of Alamannia began only in the second quarter of the sixth century. It was then, again as at Pleidelsheim, that there was significant Frankish settlement, reflected in the appearance of true 'Reihengräber'.[160] Under the Franks, Alamannia was for the first time organized as a single administrative unit: 536 or 537 may have seen the beginnings of the Merovingian dukedom. However, this was not fully organized or integrated with the Merovingian kingdom until the seventh century, a process closely related to its Christianization. Medieval 'Alamannia', coterminous with the diocese of Constance, did not emerge until the Carolingians.[161] (It was only under the Franks, in the sixth and, especially, the seventh century, that Alamanni gradually moved into Switzerland.[162])

As Wood says, in the fourth century no one could have imagined the Franks emerging as one of the mightiest Germanic peoples of Europe.[163] Their success raises a number of questions. The most obvious is how the Franks were able to overcome the Alamanni; but there are others. How did the Franks thereby achieve a conquest that had apparently eluded Rome? How did it happen that the Franks, in crossing the Rhine into Alamannia and Thuringia, managed to reverse the direction of Germanic conquest, from east-to-west to west-to-east? I deal with the first of these immediately below; the rest I will return to at the end.

Frankish success is usually explained in terms of Frankish strength. This is founded on the belief that Franks were significantly more

---

[159] So Geuenich (1997a: 87–8); Koch, R. and U. (1997: 273); Wamers (1997: 266–7). Cf. above 125.

[160] Koch, R. and U. (1997: 274–5, 277–81); Koch (1997a: 192), (1997b: 224–6).

[161] Geuenich (1997a: 93–7, 100–3), (1997d: 204–6).

[162] Giesler (1997: 211, 214–15, 217); cf. Windler (1997: 261–4, 266–7).

[163] Wood (1997: 358).

Romanized than their neighbours. The Lower Rhine tribes that formed the Franks had long had intimate contacts with Rome; and these were intensified by the early acquisition by some Frankish communities of rights of settlement within the Empire. The experience of living within the imperial structure of provinces and 'cities' (urban centres and surrounding territory: *civitates*) stimulated the political and military development of these, giving them unity and strength and, when they established their own kingdoms on imperial soil, allowing them to work easily with their Gallo-Roman subjects. The Franks' inheritance of the legacy of Rome is seen as causing them to appreciate what remained of the imperial structure in Gaul: above all, the *civitates*, during the fifth century increasingly run by their bishops. One of the two icons of Frankish Romanization is the letter of Remigius, bishop of Reims, welcoming the still-pagan Clovis as the successor of Childeric in the province of Belgica II and advising him as to how he should rule.[164] Clovis' conversion to Catholic Christianity, in an age when other Germanic monarchs in Gaul were Arians, confirmed the bond between Merovingian monarchy and Christian episcopate which was to find its greatest expression in Gregory of Tours' great 'History'.[165]

All of this comes from literary sources, but funerary archaeology has been called upon to strengthen the model of Frankish sophistication and strength. Siegmund, for example, has drawn attention to the high (relative to the Alamanni) level of Roman artefacts in Frankish graves, and interpreted the phenomenon as a significant example of technology transfer.[166] Most significant, however, in this respect has been Böhme's concept of the 'composite culture'.[167]

Böhme argued, from small, scattered groups of rich inhumation burials, that increasing Roman recruitment of Germanic soldiers led to a change of culture in northern Gaul. Warriors, settled within the Empire for significant periods, accepted it and fitted into its ways:

---

[164] Remigius, *Ep. Austrasiacae* 2. The second icon is Fredegarius' account of a myth tracing Frankish descent, like that of the Romans of old, from Trojans: Fredegarius, *Chron.* 3.2.

[165] On this see generally Wood (1994: 33–5, 40–1), (1997: 358–62); Heinzelmann (1997); Lewis (2000).

[166] Siegmund (2000: 130–1, 302, 306–7, 348–50).

[167] Principally Böhme (1974), but cited below from his convenient condensed and revised treatments of 1997 and 1998.

they became 'native'.[168] This process had begun by the late third or early fourth centuries, and reached its peak a hundred years later. It resulted in something new: a composite Gallo-Germanic culture, a 'Mischzivilisation'. The Merovingians continued and benefited from the tradition. Childeric and Clovis collided with Rome, and finally destroyed her power in Gaul, but they had worked for the Empire and in pursuing their independent ambitions were happy to use imperial institutions, that is the *civitates* and the Church, in 'the continuing organic development of the Romano-Frankish relationship in northern Gaul and the Rhineland'.[169] In Pohl's words, what was decisive in Frankish success was not so much the Frankization of Gaul as the long-term Gallicization of Franks west and east of the Rhine.[170] The Frankish takeover was therefore not that of brute barbarians, but of senior soldiers trained by the Empire they were replacing: not conquest but 'regime change', with, for example, an army still supported by *civitas* taxation.[171] Frankish domination of Romans, Alamanni and others was natural, evolutionary, inevitable.

Böhme's thinking has been very influential, for example, helping Whittaker to develop the notion of the evolution of a distinct frontier zone, applicable far beyond north-east Gaul.[172] It also forms part of current research by Barlow who, initially approaching the topic from a different direction, is taking the concept of a northern Gallic 'Mischzivilisation' still further. Barlow dates the birth of future 'Romano-Frankish' culture as early as Julius Caesar, and locates its first major historical impact in the Batavian revolt of AD 69.[173] In his view, it was northern Gauls and *Germani*, operating with their own agendas within the imperial structure (and therefore usually appearing in the sources as 'Romans'), who created a tradition of separatism that 'border' Franks were able to exploit in the fifth century.[174]

As Franks were fated to succeed, so Alamanni, their mirror image, were fated to fail. Living on the margin of imperial life, they were

---

[168] Böhme (1997: 101), 'heimisch'.
[169] Stickler (2002: 223), 'die organische Weiterentwicklung des römisch-fränkischen Verhältnisses im Nordgallien und im Rheinland'.
[170] Pohl (1998a: 643), 'Frankisierung ... Gallisierung'.
[171] Böhme (1998: 56), 'Machtwechsel'. Böhme (1998: 40 (citing Durliat), cf. 55).
[172] Whittaker (1994: 237). Cf. above 40.
[173] Above 22.
[174] See, e.g. Barlow (1993, 1996, forthcoming).

significantly less Romanized. They had not been in contact with Rome for centuries; and when contact came it was in areas which had been Roman for only a couple of hundred years.[175] The Alamanni therefore never became part of a 'Mischzivilisation'; and their leaders never grew used to working with provincial *civitates* or the Church.[176] Their kings, unlike those of the Franks, never served at the same time as leaders of Germanic communities and Roman officers on Roman soil. And excluded from Roman high office from the later fourth century, their leaders, unlike Childeric and Clovis, had no experience of working within the internal imperial structure. They were never fully attached to the Roman world.[177] Martin has gone so far as to propose that integration of the Alamanni foundered in the mid-fourth century because of basic Alamannic rejection of classical *mores*: there were fundamental 'differences in outlook' between (provincial) Romans and Alamanni.[178] Alongside such 'systemic' failings, it has been argued that during the fifth century Alamannic society was disturbed and potential Romanization impeded by continuing Germanic immigration from the east—and, presumably, by the likely movement of easterners through Alamannia, intent on or returning from Roman military service over the Rhine.[179] Some, indeed, have interpreted this period, which saw the disappearance of the Iuthungi and the arrival of the Danubian Suebi, as one of the initiation of new 'ethnogenetic' processes among the Alamanni.[180] Lacking a clear focus or strong leadership, the Alamanni remained politically and militarily fragmented.[181] When, from around 455, they were presented with the opportunity to occupy Roman soil, they failed because disunity led to a diffusion of effort.[182]

Examination of Frankish 'strength' and Alamannic 'weakness' reveals that neither is as straightforward as it might seem. The

---

[175] Martin (1998: 407); Pohl (1998a: 643); Pohl (2000: 31–2).

[176] Martin (1997b: 169).

[177] Steuer (1997a: 149–50). Cf. Pohl (1998a: 642–4), (2000: 31): lack of imperial recognition.

[178] Martin (1998: 409–11), 'Mentalitätsunterschieden'. Cf. Stroheker (1975: 33) and above 106, 157–8.

[179] Pohl (1998a: 646); above 338, 343.

[180] Stickler (2002: 187); Castritius (2005: 200).

[181] Stroheker (1975: 48).

[182] Pohl (2000: 31).

concept of 'Mischzivilisation', closely tied to the debate concerning the origins of the 'Reihengräber' and of weapon burials, is not without difficulties.[183] There is no hard evidence for extensive Germanic integration west of the Rhine. The literary sources are inconclusive, and there has been dispute as to the extent to which the archaeological material indicates Germanic, as opposed to Gallo-Roman, burials, since the deceased were buried with Roman or Roman-style grave-goods, such as ceramics and weapons.[184] There is now wide accept-ance of Böhme's argument that the non-Roman origins of some of the dead are visible in the female jewellery, which indicates the women's conservative attachment to Germanic dress.[185] On the other hand, there is no unanimity. A growing tendency appears to be to accept some sort of Germanic presence, while suggesting that the totality of the deceased were from a wide range of backgrounds, Gallo-Roman and Germanic, and that the new burial rites reflected social—asser-tions of local power—rather than ethnic change.[186]

Even if the occupants of the northern Gallic inhumation graves are accepted as *Germani*, there remain problems. We cannot say how many people were involved or how their numbers related to those of the indigenous population. With respect to 'Mischzivilisation', we have equally little idea as to how the indigenous population may have been Germanized, and what their reaction was to the newcomers: welcoming, neutral or hostile. There is controversy concerning the newcomers' precise status. Werner, in a pioneering study of the proto-'Reihengräber', had proposed that they were *laeti*. This was criticized on the grounds that the burials are too grand; and Böhner, followed by Böhme, categorized them as 'federate' troops. Following criticism that this term implied too great a degree of autonomy for the warriors concerned, Böhme now sees the graves as those of troops ('Verbände') of Germanic warriors, under their own leaders but subject to Roman military authority, that is serving in irregular

---

[183] Cf. also above 39–41.

[184] Halsall (1992), (2000).

[185] Böhme (1997: 93–4), (1998: 43, 47). Acceptance: e.g. James (1988: 44–51); Pohl (1998a: 644); MacGeorge (2002: 140–1).

[186] Whittaker (1994: 232–5); Halsall (2000: 177–9). Cf. Kleeman (1997) for a similar interpretation of fifth-century burials in Lower Saxony—new rituals were variously adopted as people chose different ways of advertising social status.

units within the imperial army.[187] In terms of a Frankish 'Mischzivilisation', however, this generates its own complications. Böhme's
recent research has led him to propose that 'Verbände' were drawn
from different peoples: not just Franks but also Alamanni and Saxons
and even, though in smaller numbers, Thuringians, Scandinavians,
Anglo-Saxons and various East-*Germani*. Some may have been poly-
ethnic.[188] Böhme has also distinguished different distribution
patterns of artefacts within northern Gaul, in particular pointing
out that types of female dress-pins found in the provinces of Belgica
II and Lugdunensis II differ from those found in Belgica I and
Germania I and II. He suggests that the difference may be a very
early sign of the separate evolution of Salian and Rhineland Franks,
but admits that this is very speculative;[189] and the distinction is
anyway questionable.[190] Assuming that the burials are 'Germanic',
all that can safely be said is that the brooches may indicate differences
between military *Germani* on the lower Rhine and those nearer the
Channel coast.[191] This leads to the conclusion that the fifth-century
Germanic population of northern Gaul was very mixed. Böhme
guesses that 'the proportion of Frankish contingents must have been
extraordinarily high', but elsewhere admits that it is impossible to be
precise about the numbers and ethnicity of those involved.[192] If there
was a 'Mischzivilisation', Franks were not its sole creators, nor did they
have exclusive rights to its benefits. 'Mischzivilisation', if it existed,
was not a time bomb, ticking down to ignition, but an inert explosive
in need of a powerful detonator, which brings us to leadership.

Böhme allows that some of his 'Verbände' may have been poly-
ethnic, but stresses that others must have been the retinues/
'Gefolgschaften' of particular princes or kings.[193] Belief in the presence of high-status leaders is clearly very important to him, probably
because it allows him to see Childeric and Clovis as the culmination

[187] Böhme (1997: 100–1), (1998: 36, cf. 38); Halsall (2000: 168). For *laeti* see
above 166–9.
[188] Böhme (1997: 97 and Fig. 73), (1998: 37, 50–1).
[189] Böhme (1997: 94–5), (1998: 47 and Fig. 12).
[190] Above 330 n.65.
[191] So Böhme (1997: 95).
[192] Böhme (1997: 94 ('doch muß der Anteil fränkischer Kontingente
außerordentlich hoch gewesen sein'), 97), (1998: 42).
[193] Böhme (1997: 101).

of a long tradition of royal *Germani* in the service of Rome: established leaders who cooperated with, learned from and could eventually supplant the Empire. His models are the Alamannic Fraomarius and the Frankish Mallobaudes, but these are awkward. Fraomarius' career was hardly typical. The failed successor of Macrianus of the Bucinobantes, he was the creature of imperial politics, and entered Roman service as a political refugee, not an ambitious military leader. There is no reason to assume, with Böhme, that his British command comprised his 'Gefolgschaft': it was probably a regular regiment, raised well before Fraomarius was shipped to Britain.[194] Mallobaudes, Ammianus' 'warlike king' who killed Macrianus in Francia around 380,[195] is commonly identified with the '*comes domesticorum* and Frankish king' who helped Rome to victory at the battle of Argentovaria.[196] But Mallobaudes' case is, again, hardly typical. It is unlikely that during the fourth century Rome routinely recruited established Germanic 'kings'.[197] And it is also unlikely that Mallobaudes could have functioned as such during his time in the Roman army.[198] He looks more like a Frankish prince who, having made his name in the Empire, returned to his homeland—perhaps, as Barlow suggests, to protect it from the depredations of Macrianus[199]—and then became a king there. Ammianus' description of him as *rex* in 378 suits what he became, not what he then was. His decision to return home and his success in destroying Macrianus may well have increased his fame in the Empire. Germanic military leaders entered Roman service to better themselves. Those who succeeded must have become highly Romanized.[200] Some will have retained links with their communities of origin;[201] but the number of those who then fully re-immersed themselves in

[194] Böhme (1998: 39); above 151, 170, 309.
[195] Above 285, 318.
[196] AM 31.10.6. *PLRE* 1.539; Waas (1971: 92); Böhme (1998: 39); above 311.
[197] Above 154.
[198] Waas (1971: 92). One very early possible example of a Roman army officer of Germanic origin retaining royal rank is provided by Vindolanda tablet 93.1544, on which the Batavian Flavius Cerialis is addressed as 'my king' by one of his men. But the editors interpret 'king' as 'patron': Bowman and Thomas (1996: 323–4). I owe this reference to Dr F. López Sánchez.
[199] Barlow (1996: 231).
[200] Above 153, 156.
[201] Above 155, 176, 203.

Germanic society must have been minimal and have attracted attention, and the more so if this resulted in the death of a famous *Germanus*. In terms of the creation of a 'Mischzivilisation', such a choice runs contrary to the concept of 'Mischung': it was impossible to become part of *civitas* life east of the Rhine.

There was no established tradition of Frankish, or any other, Germanic kings operating within the Roman Empire as major links between the imperial population and barbarians. The process of Germanic military recruitment did not put major Germanic figures on the ground in northern Gaul. The chiefs who arrived were relatively minor and subject to the Roman army. They were probably leaders of war-bands, accompanied by their warriors and, as a special privilege, by their families. The rich but rare graves of their women and children very much resemble those of the earlier period. Lesser fighters may, as before, have paired with local girls.[202] Those who bettered themselves went off to pursue a full career within the Roman military. There was no Frankish proto-state waiting to explode upon the political scene. If there had been, it would have shown itself much earlier. The run of senior Frankish imperial figures, succeeding the Alamannic, was over by the end of the fourth century.[203] The long interval cannot be filled by reference to the eminence of Allobichus and Ebdobichus under Honorius and Constantine III. This pair did not reach the heights of their predecessors and after them there is still a gap of a generation or more.[204] Childeric and Clovis did not continue an old tradition. They created a new one, in new times. They were the detonators who released whatever explosive force there was in Gallic 'Mischzivilisation'.

But to do this they had to use enormous violence and cunning. The new 'ethnogenetic' processes proposed as having disturbed Alamanni in the fifth century can hardly have been more disruptive than the ways in which Clovis brought his fellow Franks under control.[205] And, as far as the Gallo-Roman population is concerned, the looting of churches in Soissons and elsewhere under Clovis does not say much for the level of Frankish integration with Roman

---

[202] Böhme (1997: 96–8), (1998: 40, 47–8); above 49, 127.
[203] Above 159.
[204] *Contra* Stickler (2002: 172).
[205] Cf. Pohl (1998a: 645–6).

society.[206] Merovingian success required the energy and genius of Childeric and Clovis: '... it was the historical accident of exceptional leadership rather than political and military power that acted as the stimulus to [Frankish] expansion.'[207]

In different circumstances, others might have done the same. For the first half of the fifth century the most likely Germanic heirs of Rome in Gaul were the Visigoths, ably led by Theoderic I (418–51), Theoderic II (453–66) and Euric (466–84).[208] Sidonius Apollinaris waxes lyrical over Theoderic II's grasp of Roman culture;[209] and, had he lived, Euric might well have been a match for Clovis. By the mid-fifth century, Burgundians were coming to the fore, with one of their kings, Gundioc, being appointed Gallic *magister militum*, probably in the 460s.[210] Visigothic and Burgundian monarchs may nominally have been hindered by their Arian Christianity, which isolated them from their Catholic subjects. But, as the Burgundian experience shows, court Christianity was complex and changeable;[211] and it would surely not have been beyond the imagination of an ambitious monarch to throw over Arianism in pursuit of a valuable secular prize: like Henry IV of France, to declare that 'Paris is well worth a Mass'. Even among the pagan Franks, those of the Rhineland appear to have been in a much better position than the Salians to have exploited any 'Mischzivilisation', taking Cologne around 456.[212]

Merovingian dominance of the west was not fated. Things might well have turned out very differently if the Visigoths had won at 'Vouillé'[213] or even the Alamanni at 'Zülpich'. In the swirling history of the fifth century, an age that could produce the astonishing success of an individual such as Odovacer, it would not have been impossible for the Alamanni—now a little more politically sophisticated[214]—to produce a Great King to take them to victory in battle. One can imagine historians in an alternative universe explaining Frankish

[206] MacGeorge (2002: 128).
[207] MacGeorge (2002: 163), citing an unpublished conference paper of mine.
[208] *PLRE* 2.427–8, 1070–3.
[209] Sidonius Apollinaris, *Carm.* 7.495–9. Stevens (1933: 23, 74).
[210] *PLRE* 2.523–4; Elton (1992: 172).
[211] Wood (1994: 45).
[212] James (1988: 72).
[213] For the location of this battle at Voulon, near Poitiers, see Wood (1994: 46).
[214] Above 344.

'failure' on the grounds of their long and 'natural' hostility to Rome, and Alamannic 'success' on the grounds that, having been allowed to settle close to central Gaul and northern Italy, they had become perfectly attuned to classical *mores*. For it is clear that Alamanni were not 'naturally' opposed to classical ways.[215] Throughout the fourth century, their leaders showed themselves as willing as any to work with and, if possible, to live peaceably within the Empire. They were not marginal. The Alamanni found themselves in a region which, though broken up geographically, had areas of good agricultural land with rich reserves of timber and minerals, and which had earlier been opened up to settlement by Roman ideas and technology. For 150 years—five generations (260–410)—they nestled close to the heart of a powerful western Empire. Furthermore, Romans might well have continued to live and settle alongside them, forming a bridge between the two communities.[216] The Franks, meanwhile, initially found themselves on the margin of imperial life in a second-rate area, threatened by the sea.[217]

In the early to mid-fourth century, therefore, with their nobles doing well in Roman service, the Alamanni must have seemed by far the more likely to adopt Mediterranean ways. Alamannic communities did not develop in Gaul not because Alamanni did not want them, but because Rome turned against them. Likewise, Alamannic 'exclusion', though it would have eventually occurred anyway, was probably accelerated by imperial political concerns.[218] Yet Alamannic failure to settle in the Empire did not ruin Romano-Alamannic relations. A closeness of sorts was reinstated under Valentinian I. The greatest known example of technology transfer in the fourth century is not between Romans and Franks, but between Romans and Alamanni, in the building of the Zähringer Burgberg.[219] This must have involved Roman expertise directing skilled native labour. Alamannic capacity to develop technical skills (mirroring that of the

---

[215] Above 350.

[216] Above 133–5.

[217] Cf. Witschel (1999: 220). For initial Frankish settlement on the Lower Rhine see above 200; and for Gallo-Roman disdain for the area of the Lower Rhine see *Pan. Lat.* 4(8).8.1–3.

[218] Above 228, 264.

[219] Above 101–2, 303.

third-century Goths in their Black Sea boat-building[220]) was earlier reflected in the work they did for Julian and, contemporary with the remodelling of the Zähringer Burgberg, for Valentinian I.[221] If there was a developing 'Mischzivilisation' anywhere in the west, it was in fourth-century Alamannia, focused on the 'Herrschaftszentren'.[222]

However, the Alamanni did not challenge the Empire by throwing up leaders like Theoderic I and II, Euric, Gundioc, Childeric and Clovis. Further, one suspects that, even if they had, by the mid-fifth century such a man would have been out of his depth in dealing with the complexities of Germano-Roman politics in Gaul and the Mediterranean. Everything was up for grabs. The Franks were not destined to succeed; and the Alamanni were not hopelessly weak. An extraordinarily able leader might still have led them to victory over Clovis. But success would probably have been temporary, and the long-term beneficiaries of Frankish defeat would have been Visigoths or Burgundians. Something other than 'differences in outlook' seems to have held the Alamanni back from fully exploiting the impressive lead that they had gained in their early contact with the Empire.

What was this impediment? An important opportunity for Alamanni to participate directly in imperial affairs had been lost in 357, through Roman refusal to tolerate their settling on the left bank of the Rhine. A permanent Alamannic community in Gaul would have served the Empire well during the fourth century and might have acted as the kernel of a powerful Germanic successor kingdom in the fifth. However, the absence of such settlement cannot wholly explain the lack of Alamannic political dynamism in the fifth century. Extensive prior experience in provincial affairs was not as important for the Franks as has been thought; and Visigoths and Burgundians managed very well without it. Furthermore, the disruption which followed the Alamannic expulsion from west of the Rhine was relatively short-lived, and there was a restoration of traditional relationships. There were occasional local misunderstandings and sometimes disruptive long-distance raids; and Roman leaders remained ready to launch Alamannic campaigns for political ends.

---

[220] Zosimus 1.34.1, 42, see also 1.35.2, 43.1, for their use of wagons and even siege engines.

[221] Above 245, 292.

[222] Cf. above 40.

However, Franks again became the enemy of choice; and the prevailing state of affairs between border Alamanni and Romans was one of peace, with the former willing to accept the superiority of the latter. It was this last, the persistence of what may be called the 'imperial habit', that best explains the lack of Alamannic movement around 410, and the way in which Alamanni, unable to envisage a world without the Empire, fell behind other western *Germani*.

This attitude helps explain what may at first sight appear a contradictory feature of Alamannic development. Though close to the heart of the western Empire, Alamannic *regna* and *pagi* show no signs of significant spontaneous Romanization. Small and primitive, they remained incapable of producing sophisticated administrative structures or even Roman-style building projects.[223] In part this was due to imperial policy. Rome favoured the continuation of the status quo. Overmighty chieftains threatened her mastery so, as in the case of Macrianus, she clipped their wings.[224] On the other hand, it is unlikely that, even if expansion in size and infrastructure had been achievable, Alamannic leaders would have indulged in the game of upper-class competition (*aemulatio*) that had driven the Romanization of the west under the High Empire.[225] The promotion of monumental urbanization was now outmoded. In the Late Empire in the west, extensive street-grids and grand secular buildings were only for imperial cities. Impressive building was still possible in the case of churches, but the Alamanni showed no interest in converting of their own accord and imperial Christians none in evangelizing them. And, anyway, what would have been the point of such activity? In the late Iron Age and early Roman periods the reward for *aemulatio* had been consolidation of upper-class power and advancement in the Roman world. Throughout the fourth century, leading Alamanni received this anyway, through Roman subsidies and Roman service. There was now no need for *aemulatio*[226] and this

[223] Cf. above 105.

[224] Also above 124.

[225] Drinkwater (1983a: 142, 157).

[226] The provenance of the Hariulfus inscription (above 116) is significant here: such Roman-style self-advertisement was practised only within the confines of the Empire. As in the case of the Alamanni, *aemulatio* was, apparently, not possible on barbarian territory: see Schmitz (2003: 406), on the adoption of the 'epigraphic habit' by Romanized *Germani*.

probably suited those in charge of Alamannic society. Kings and *optimates*, like the war-band leaders from whom they were descended, treated Alamannia as a convenient base of operations, a jumping-off point, not a homeland. Their aim was not to develop the region but to optimize their own strategic positions within it.[227] Like Tacitus' *Germani*, their main concern was probably the control of men and animals rather than land.[228] The stronger they were the more they could obtain from the Empire; and if this did not run to settlement they were happy to accept subsidies and service. Like the Romans, they too favoured the continuation of the status quo.

Alamanni never formed a major successor kingdom. They were always the dependants of a stronger power, Roman or Frankish. Unlike the Franks, they have no claim to be called the 'pioneers of modern Europe'.[229] Their chief role in history is that they offer a unique insight into the nature of the Romano-barbarian relationship.

The most important aspect of this relationship was symbiosis. Such symbiosis was more than the purely economic ties often examined by modern historians.[230] Rather, as in the case of the Early Empire, we should recognize an important political interdependency between Empire and barbarians. Alamannic leaders' dependence on Rome has been dealt with. The idea of Roman political dependence on Alamanni has been touched upon above, but now needs to be stated explicitly.[231] In recent years a number of historians, for example, Goffart, Whittaker and Miller, have attempted to correct ancient and modern misconceptions of barbarian aggression under the Late Empire.[232] However, they have enjoyed remarkably little success. Like the ancients, we still seem to need the Germanic bogeyman.[233] Those who have attempted to reassess the *Germani* have

---

[227] Cf. above 104.

[228] A. Kreuz, *pers. comm.*

[229] 'Wegbereiter', hence the title of *Franken* (1997).

[230] e.g. Whittaker (1994: 113–21); Witschel (1999: 215); Burns (2003: 40).

[231] Cf. above 177. The following is drawn mainly from Drinkwater (1996, 1997, 1999a).

[232] Goffart (1980: esp. ch. 1); Whittaker (1994); Miller (1996). Cf. Steuer (1998: 280–1).

[233] Cf. above 179. I have borrowed and adapted 'bogeyman' from Nixon and Rodgers (1994: 137).

interpreted their relationship with the Roman world in various ways. What I propose here is that, as far as the late Roman west is concerned, the 'Germanic threat' was an imperial artefact—an indispensable means of justifying the imperial presence and imperial policies, and of maintaining provincial loyalty to the Empire.

Alamanni and Franks became dangerous only when the Empire was distracted by civil war. Then they were encouraged to raid by Roman weakness and, sometimes, Roman invitation. In such circumstances, careless generalship might result in tactical Roman defeats. Even in nominally quiet times, the difficulties of policing a grossly asymmetrical power relationship (in particular, the need for the greater power to deploy massively disproportionate force to control its partners because these are too elusive to be dealt with more economically) might, as in the case of Macrianus, lead to unnecessary and fruitless violence and, in the end, a diplomatic settlement favourable to the Germanic side. However, none of this made the western barbarians a strategic threat. Rome retained the upper hand; and the prevailing condition was peace and cooperation. Yet Rome itself could be an awkward neighbour and, when it suited its purpose, a savage aggressor. Most of the time Alamanni and Franks were victims rather than oppressors, exploited by later Roman emperors as their predecessors had been exploited by earlier rulers for the needs of internal politics.

Most instances of such exploitation can again be categorized as promoting three main objectives (none mutually exclusive): 1) to acquire or enhance a military reputation; 2) to steady Roman armies in uncertain political or military situations, often readying them for service elsewhere within the Empire; and 3) to provide western emperors with a good excuse to go to, or remain in or on, northern Gaul and the Rhine frontier when, for political reasons, it suited them to be there.[234] However, more depended on imperial exploitation of the frontier than even this analysis suggests.

First, the office of Roman emperor evolved from the activities of the late Republican warlord. To survive, an emperor had to have a reputation as a general. Emperors therefore needed to maintain

---

[234] Above 41–2. For examples of such behaviour, see above 198 (Constantine II), 260 (Julian), 313 (Gratian).

strong armies and to lead them to victory over foreign enemies. In the Late Empire, western rulers therefore projected Alamanni and Franks as numerous and ferocious, and the more so when eastern colleagues were enjoying success over Persians.[235]

Next, inflation of the Germanic danger explained the concentration of forces in Gaul and along the Rhine, and so justified the maintenance of the whole imperial system in the west. The system comprised the soldiers and officers whose careers depended on the continued existence of a strong western army. We are so used to the institution of the Roman army that we cannot imagine the Empire without it. But it was a late feature of Roman history, and was resented and criticized by some contemporaries who looked forward to a day when it could be disbanded or, at least, substantially reduced.[236] It also included the civil administration necessary to collect the taxes that supported the army and itself, and which provided the civilian well-to-do with prestigious and lucrative imperial offices. And it, too, was headed by the western emperor, who drew his power from his control of both military and civil structures. The leaders of the civil population, educated to believe in the German menace along the Rhine, impressed by imperial 'busy-ness', and open to imperial persuasion through their desire for imperial generosity and imperial office, were happy to give this structure their support. The 'Germanic threat' thus allowed western emperors, generals, administrators and local aristocrats to validate their high position in society, by allowing them to be diligent: diligently spending the taxpayers' money, to their own economic and social advantage.[237]

Finally, neither Romans nor *Germani* posed a real threat to each other. Barbarians were unable to do any significant damage to the

---

[235] Cf. above 182.

[236] Drinkwater (1999a: 133).

[237] Matthews (1975: 32–3) came very close to this interpretation by hinting that Symmachus participated in stage-managed fighting against 'helpless (and one suspects, harmless) Alamanni', and that Valentinian successfully exploited this leading senator's fact-finding tour to convince him—and through him, his peers—'that the taxes which he had brought were well spent'. However, Matthews then accepted that the Rhine frontier was at this time facing a real military threat. Similarly, in a later work (1989: 280), Matthews virtually characterized the late Empire as a tax-collecting machine designed to support the military establishment: 'One might define the state, without exaggeration, as a system for the financing of war.'

Empire; and western rulers, convinced by their own propaganda concerning the invincibility of the *Germani* and content with matters as they stood, were unwilling to go out of their way to conquer them. The 'Guard on the Rhine', which the imperial establishment sold so successfully to contemporaries and to later historians, was an artefact.[238] If these ideas of the frontier as 'stage-show', and of the stage-show as both justification and support of the imperial order are acceptable,[239] they raise other issues. For example, it is usually understood that, from the third century, imperial power was divided because the Empire, under pressure, needed armies led by emperors on most of its frontiers. An alternative interpretation is that, even from the third century, imperial collegiality became the norm because effective control of the totality of the frontier armies upon which imperial political power rested had become a rare skill. Lieutenant Caesares and Augusti were despatched to the main political power centres to maintain the loyalty of the troops, where necessary by leading them to victory against neighbouring peoples. However, on the Rhine an underworked army was still a dangerous army, which may explain the relative frequency of usurpations in the west in the fourth century.[240]

This returns us to the two questions posed earlier in this chapter: how did the Franks, in conquering the Alamanni, succeed where Rome had failed; and how did they reverse the flow of conquest from east-to-west to west-to-east? The answer is that Clovis and his successors, as relative latecomers, not the children of 'Mischzivilisation', were not subject to established imperial preconceptions. Free from traditional Roman fears of Brennus, the Cimbri and Arminius,

---

[238] Here I come very close to Goffart's view that the imperial frontier was generally the cause of imperial insecurity, and that the frontier therefore justified the imperial regime by pointing up or creating something which the inhabitants of the Empire could be told they needed to be defended against (1980: 30; 1989: 6). On the other hand, unlike Goffart (1989: 7), I doubt very much whether, in the west at least, there was ever a threat big enough to justify the size of garrison that was kept on the frontier.

[239] They appear to be gaining some currency: see Pohl (2000: 35): 'Für die am Rhein konzentrierten römische Truppen waren die Barbarenkrieger jenseits des Rheins nicht nur Rekrutierungreserve, sondern rechtfertigten auch die eigene Bedeutung und Existenz'; *Heather (2001: 51); Burns (2003: 13 n.3).*

[240] Cf. Drinkwater (1998c) and above 323.

they were immune to 'the power of nightmares, the politics of fear'. *Germani* themselves, they could see the continuity of conditions and society west and east of the Rhine and knew that they had to control both sides of the river. And *Germani* themselves, they were not frightened of fellow *Germani*: fully aware of their enemies' (including other Franks') weakness in numbers, organization and military strength, they knew they could defeat them. Finally, as Germanic chiefs, not Roman emperors, they did not need their opponents as a permanent threat to justify their political position: not only could they defeat, they were prepared to do so. So the Franks conquered the Alamanni; and so ended Alamannic independence, less than a generation after the fall of the last western Roman emperor.

APPENDIX

The Lyon Medallion

The much-discussed Lyon 'medallion' is, in fact, a trial-strike, *c*.8 cms in diameter, in lead of the reverse die of a large denomination gold coin, with the legend *Saeculi Felicitas*, 'The Happiness of Our Time'. Its two registers show a pair of Roman rulers receiving men, women and children. These are clearly depicted as crossing into the Empire over the defended bridge at Mainz-Kastel (Fig. 27). The *communis opinio* is that it commemorates the settlement of Germanic war-captives in Gaul by Maximian Augustus and Constantius I Caesar in the later 290s.[1] But there are problems. A coin of this quality must reflect a major imperial victory that could be presented as bringing undeniable benefit to the Empire.[2] M. Alföldi identifies this victory as that won by Constantius I against Franks on the Scheldt. She places it in 296, in line with A. Alföldi's location—on stylistic grounds—of the *terminus post quem* for the production of the medallion in this year.[3] However, Constantius' Scheldt campaign took place before his British victories in 296. There is a hint of a second Frankish campaign following Constantius' defeat of Allectus, but if fighting occurred it is unlikely to have been serious.[4] More telling is the medallion's location of the events it depicts at Mainz.[5] Mainz was the base for Roman operations into Alamannia, not Francia: why defeat Franks on the Lower Rhine and then move them miles upstream? Finally, the demeanour of most of the 'settlers' on the medallion hardly matches that of the broken Frankish captives described in a panegyric of 297 which, according to M. Alföldi, provides a snapshot of the events which inspired the scene on the medallion.[6]

The two imperial figures dominate the upper register. The pair, nimbate and magnified, are plainly superior to their supplicants. This part of the composition conforms to Brilliant's rules for the depiction of submission: 'a

---

[1] Alföldi (1953: esp. 66–8). Brilliant (1963: 193); *Gallien* (1980: 27–8, no.2); Nixon and Rodgers (1994: 121 n.28); Burns (2003: 303).

[2] Alföldi (1953: 67 nn.19–20).

[3] Alföldi (1926: 168–70); Alföldi (1953: 68).

[4] Above 187.

[5] Cf. Alföldi (1953: 66–7 and n.18).

[6] *Pan. Lat.* 4(8).9.1.

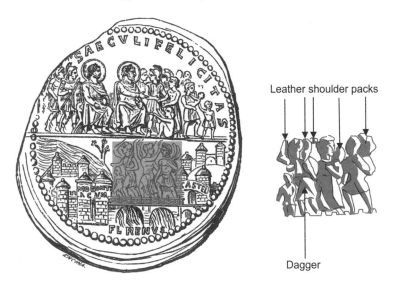

Fig. 27   The Lyon 'medallion'. Main drawing from the first publication of the piece in *Revue Numismatique* 1862 [after Alföldi (1953: Fig. 2)]. Shaded area re-traced from a photograph [Bastien (1989: pl. 2)].

triangular form with the head of the great personage at the apex of the triangle.'[7] However, some sense of independence on the part of the inferior is given by the three figures on the extreme right—two adults carrying infants and a small child (the taller adult is depicted incorrectly on the 1862 drawing, but is visible in photographs), who look away towards their fellows still crossing the bridge. These, shown in the lower register, are even more strongly presented. There is no triangle: all the adults are much the same size, striding confidently across. Slung around their necks or hung over their shoulders are large double-packs. The first on the left is armed with a dagger.[8] All look ahead, except for the striking central figure of a woman who, in looking back as if to encourage those behind her, takes on something of the authority of the rulers shown above. She presents a very powerful figure, with no air of the captive. Early commentators saw her as a Victory (mistaking her pack for wings).[9] Many previous commentators, including

---

[7] Brilliant (1963: 189).
[8] Bastien (1989: 7).
[9] Alföldi (1953: 65); Bastien (1989: 17).

A. Alföldi, put a positive interpretation upon the scene, for example seeing it as a *largitio*, a distribution of largesse.[10]

Two other explanations are possible. The first conflates an earlier interpretation, that the events depicted were the result of Maximian's expedition of 287,[11] with Unverzagt's (1919) view, that it records the happy return of Roman troops from barbarian captivity.[12] The two rulers are, therefore, Maximian and Diocletian, and the barbarian captors were Alamanni. Such an interpretation has recently been proposed by Turcan (1987) and confirmed, at least in part (concerning the identity of the emperors), by Bastien.[13] Bastien dates the trial-strike to 297,[14] but this is no hindrance to relating the events it shows to 287. In the First Tetrarchy, rulers' reputations had to be carefully balanced.[15] In 297, Maximian needed something to counter Constantius I's brilliant success in Britain. Why not recall a major result of his most daring foreign war on the Rhine? The returning captives are not prisoners of war, but civilians taken during raids into the Empire. Bastien objects that no such exploit is mentioned in the panegyric of 289;[16] but it was not needed then. However, in 297 Maximian needed an act of 'restoration' that matched that of Constantius.

The second is to suppose that the suppliants are immigrant *Germani*, but that these are not to be associated with Constantius I's Frankish victory (M. Alföldi) or with general Germanic resettlement by Maximian while holding the Rhine for Constantius during the latter's British campaign (Bastien).[17] Rather, the medallion picks up another theme of imperial propaganda by showing Diocletian and Maximian not as conquerors but as civilizers of barbarians.[18] This is a role in which the panegyrist of 297 famously cast Constantius I;[19] and, albeit subject to variation (with the transformation of wild warriors taking place east of the Rhine), it was also emphasized by Symmachus in respect of Valentinian I.[20] It found its greatest exponent in the east, in Themistius.[21] However, the medallion's reference to

---

[10] Alföldi (1926: 169), 'keine Unterwerfungsakt'; Alföldi (1953: 65–6). Cf. Bastien (1989: 18).

[11] Cf. Alföldi (1926: 169 and n.1); Alföldi (1953: 65).

[12] Cited from Bastien (1989: 8 n.1).

[13] Turcan: cited by Bastien (1989: 1); Bastien (1989: 7, 9–12).

[14] Bastien (1989: 24–5).

[15] Cf. Rees (2002: 25).

[16] Bastien (1989: 21).

[17] Bastien (1989: 24).

[18] I owe this important point to Professor Ralph Mathisen.

[19] *Pan. Lat.* 4(8).9.3–4.

[20] Above 299.

[21] Guzmán Armario (2002: 276–7).

Mainz signifies that the people involved were not Franks or *Germani* in general but Alamanni. And it shows these not as broken and dejected but confident and pleased. It suggests that in the late 280s Maximian settled a significant number of Alamanni by agreement west of the Rhine. The Alamannic settlers of the 350s might therefore have been able to cite precedent in support of their request for residence in the Empire.[22]

[22] Above 218.

References

Abegg-Wigg, A., Walter, D., and Biegert, S. (2000), 'Forschungen in germanischen Siedlungen des mittleren Lahntales', in Haffner and Schnurbein (ed.): 55–65.

Alamannen (1997), *Die Alamannen*, Stuttgart.

Alföldi, A. (1926), 'Die Donaubrücke Konstantins des Großen und verwandte historische Darstellungen auf spätrömischen Münzen', *Zeitschrift für Numismatik* 36: 161–74.

—— (1939), 'The invasions of peoples from the Rhine to the Black Sea', in *Cambridge Ancient History* XII, Cambridge: 138–64.

—— (1946), 'Valentinien Ier, le dernier des grands pannoniens', *Etudes d'Histoire Comparée* n.s. 3: 1–24.

Alföldi, M. (1953), 'Zum Lyoner Bleimedaillon', *Schweizerische Münzblätter* 8: 63–8.

Amory, P. (1997), *People and Identity in Ostrogothic Italy, 489–555*, Cambridge.

Amrein, H., and Binder, E. (1997), 'Mit Hammer und Zange an Esse und Amboss', in *Alamannen*: 359–70.

Anton, H. H. (1981), 'Burgunden. II. Historisches', in *Reallexikon der Germanischen Altertumskunde* (2nd edn) Berlin/New York: 4.235–48.

—— (1984), 'Trier im Übergang von der römischen zur fränkischen Herrschaft', *Francia* 12: 1–52.

Asche, U. (1983), *Roms Weltherrschaftsidee und Außenpolitik in der Spätantike im Spiegel der Panegyrici Latini*, Bonn.

Baatz, D. (1975), *Der Römische Limes. Archäologische Ausflüge zwischen Rhein und Donau* (2nd edn), Berlin.

Babucke, V. (1997), 'Nach Osten bis an den Lech', in *Alamannen*: 249–60.

Bakker, L. (1993), 'Raetien unter Postumus—Das Siegesdenkmal einer Juthungenschlacht im Jahre 260 n. Chr. aus Augsburg', *Germania* 71: 369–86.

Barceló, P. A. (1981), *Roms auswärtige Beziehungen unter der Constantinischen Dynastie (306–363)* (Eichstätter Beiträge 3), Regensburg.

Barlow, J. (1993), 'The success of the Franks. Regional continuity in northern Gaul in late Antiquity', Ph.D. thesis (Sydney).

—— (1996), 'Kinship, identity and fourth-century Franks', *Historia* 45: 223–39.

—— (forthcoming), 'The morality of the Franks', in J. F. Drinkwater and R. W. B. Salway (ed.), *Wolf Liebeschuetz Reflected*, London.

Barnes, T. D. (1982), *The New Empire of Diocletian and Constantine*, Cambridge MA/London.

—— (1993), *Athanasius and Constantius. Theology and Politics in the Constantinian Empire*, Cambridge MA/London.

—— (1998), *Ammianus and the Representation of Historical Reality*, Ithaca NY/London.

Barnish, S. J. B. (ed. and trans.) (1992), *Cassiodorus: Variae* (Translated Texts for Historians 12), Liverpool.

Barrett, A. A. (1989), *Caligula. The Corruption of Power*, London.

Bastien, P. (1989), *Le médaillon de plomb de Lyon* (Numismatique romain. Essais, recherches et documents 18), Wetteren.

Bayard, D. (1993), 'Le fin de la domination romaine dans le nord de la Gaule: l'apport de la sigillée d'Argonne', in Vallet and Kazanski (ed.): 223–40.

Bechert, T. (2003), '*Asciburgium* und *Dispargum*. Das Ruhrmündungsgebiet zwischen Spätantike und Frühmittelalter', in Grünewald and Seibel (ed.): 1–11.

Beck, H. (1998), 'Probleme einer Völkerwanderungszeitlichen Religionsgeschichte', in Geuenich (ed.): 475–88.

Benecke, N. (2000), 'Archäozoologische Befunde zur Nahrungswirtschaft und Praxis der Tierhaltung in eisen- und kaiserzeitlichen Siedlungen der rechtsrheinischen Mittelgebirgszone', in Haffner and Schnurbein (ed.): 243–55.

Benedetti-Martig, I. (1993), 'I Romani ed il territorio degli agri decumati nella tarda antica', *Historia* 42: 352–61.

Bidez, J. (1930), *La vie de l'empereur Julien*, Paris.

Bird, H. W. (1994), *Aurelius Victor: De Caesaribus* (Translated Texts for Historians 17), Liverpool.

Birley, A. R. (1987), *Marcus Aurelius. A Biography*, London.

Bleckmann, B. (1999), 'Decentius, Bruder oder Cousin des Magnentius?', *Göttinger Forum für Altertumswissenschaft* 2: 85–7.

—— (2002), 'Die Alamannen im 3. Jahrhundert: althistorische Bemerkungen zur Ersterwähnung und zur Ethnogenese', *Museum Helveticum* 59: 145–71.

Blockley, R. C. (1980), 'Constantius II and his generals', in C. Deroux (ed.), *Studies in Latin Literature and Roman History II* (Collection Latomus 168), Brussels: 467–86.

—— (1983), *The Fragmentary Classicising Historians of the Later Roman Empire, vol. II. Eunapius, Olympiodorus, Priscus and Malchus*, Liverpool.

Böhme, H. W. (1974), *Germanische Grabfunde des 4. bis 5. Jahrhunderts zwischen unterer Elbe und Loire. Studien zur Chronologie und Bevölkerungsgeschichte* (Münchener Beiträge zur Vor- und Frühgeschichte 19, 2 vols), Munich.

—— (1997), 'Söldner und Siedler im spätantiken Nordgallien', in *Franken*: 1.91–101.

—— (1998), 'Franken und Romanen im Spiegel spätrömischer Grabfunde im nördlichen Gallien', in Geuenich (ed.): 31–58.

Böhme-Schönberger, A. (1997), 'Germanisch-römische Trachtbeziehungen im 1. und 2. Jahrhundert?', in Bridger and Carnap-Bornheim (ed.): 7–11.

Bowersock, G. W. (1978), *Julian the Apostate*, London.

Bowersock, G. W., Brown, P., and Grabar, O. (ed.) (1999), *Late Antiquity. A Guide to the Postclassical World*, Cambridge MA/London.

Bowlus, C. R. (2002), 'Ethnogenesis: the tyranny of a construct', in Gillett (ed.): 241–56.

Bowman, A. K., and Thomas, J. D. (1996), 'New writing-tablets from Vindolanda', *Britannia* 27: 299–328.

Brather, S. (2002), 'Ethnic identities as constructions of archaeology: the case of the *Alamanni*', in Gillett (ed.): 149–75.

Bratož, R. (ed.) (1996), *Westillyricum und Nordostitalien in der spätrömischen Zeit*, Ljubljana.

Bridger, C. (2003), 'Das spätantike Xanten—eine Bestandaufnahme', in Grünewald and Seibel (ed.): 12–36.

Bridger, C., and Carnap-Bornheim, C. von (ed.) (1997), *Römer und Germanen—Nachbarn über Jahrhunderte* (BAR International Series 678), Oxford.

Bridger, C., and Gilles, K.-J. (ed.) (1998), *Spätrömische Befestigungsanlagen in den Rhein- und Donauprovinzen* (BAR International Series 704), Oxford.

Brilliant, R. (1963), *Gesture and Rank in Roman Art. The Use of Gestures to Denote Status in Roman Sculpture and Coinage* (Memoirs of the Connecticut Academy of Arts and Sciences 14), New Haven CT.

Browning, R. (1975), *The Emperor Julian*, London.

Brulet, R. (1993), 'Les dispositifs militaires du Bas-Empire en Gaule septentrionale', in Vallet and Kazanski (ed.): 135–48.

—— (1997), 'Tournai und der Bestattungsplatz um Saint-Brice', in *Franken*: 1.163–70.

Bücker, C. (1997), 'Reibschalen, Gläser und Militärgürtel. Römischer Lebensstil im freien Germanien', in *Alamannen*: 135–41.

—— (1999), *Frühe Alamannen im Breisgau* (Archäologie und Geschichte. Freiburger Forschungen zum ersten Jahrtausend in Südwestdeutschland, Bd 9).

Bücker, C., Hoeper, M., Höneisen, M., and Schmaedecke, M. (1997), 'Hof, Weiler, Dorf', in *Alamannen*: 311–22.

Burns, T. S. (1994), *Barbarians Within the Gates of Rome*, Bloomington/ Indianapolis IN.

—— (2003), *Rome and the Barbarians, 100 BC–AD 400*, Baltimore MD.

Bury, J. B. (1923), *History of the Later Roman Empire from the Death of Theodosius I to the Death of Justinian (AD 395 to AD 565)* (2 vols), London.

Cameron, A. (1968), 'Agathias on the early Merovingians', *Annali della Scuola Normale Superiore di Pisa* n.s. 37: 95–140.

Carroll, M. (2001), *Romans, Celts and Germans. The German Provinces of Rome*, Stroud.

Castritius, H. (1998), 'Semnonen-Juthungen-Alemannen. Neues (und Altes) zur Herkunft und Ethnogenese der Alamannen', in Geuenich (ed.): 349–66.

—— (2000), 'Jungmannschaften', in *Reallexikon der Germanischen Altertumskunde* (2nd edn) Berlin/New York: 16.123–5.

Castritius, H. (2005), 'Sweben', in *Reallexikon der Germanischen Altertumskunde* (2nd edn), Berlin/New York NY: 30.193–212.

Cornell, T., and Matthews, J. F. (1982), *Atlas of the Roman World*, London.

Creighton, J. D., and Wilson, R. J. A. (ed.) (1999), *Roman Germany. Studies in Cultural Interaction* (*Journal of Roman Archaeology* Supplementary Series 32), Portsmouth RI.

Crump, G. A. (1975), *Ammianus as a Military Historian* (Historia Einzelschriften 27), Stuttgart.

Cüppers, H. (ed.) (1990), *Die Römer in Rheinland-Pfalz*, Darmstadt.

Curta, F. (2002a), 'From Kossinna to Bromley: ethnogenesis in Slavic archaeology', in Gillett (ed.): 201–18.

—— (2002b), review of Heather (2001), in *The Medieval Review*: 02.03.14.

De Koning, J. (2003), 'Why did they leave? Why did they stay? On continuity versus discontinuity from Roman times to the Early Middle Ages in the western coastal area of the Netherlands', in Grünewald and Seibel (ed.): 53–82.

Demandt, A. (1972), 'Die Feldzüge der älteren Theodosius', *Hermes* 100: 81–113.

—— (1989), *Die Spätantike. Römische Geschichte von Diocletian bis Justinian 284–565 n. Chr.*, Munich.

Demougeot, E. (1975), 'La *Notitia dignitatum* et l'histoire de l'Empire d'Occident au début du Vᵉ siècle', *Latomus* 34: 1079–34 (repr. in E. Demougeot (1988), *L'empire romain et les barbares d'Occident (IVᵉ–VIIᵉ siècles)*, Paris: 115–70).

—— (1979), *La formation de l'Europe et les invasions barbares* (tome 2.2), Paris.

den Boeft, J., den Hengst, J., Teitler, H. C. (1987), *Philological and Historical Commentary on Ammianus Marcellinus XX*, Groningen.

den Boeft, J., den Hengst, J., Teitler, H. C. (1991), *Philological and Historical Commentary on Ammianus Marcellinus XXI*, Groningen.

Derks, T., and Roymans, N. (2003), 'Siegelkapseln und die Verbreitung der lateinischen Schriftskultur im Rheindelta', in Grünewald and Seibel (ed.): 242–65.

de Ste Croix, G. E. M. (1981), *The Class Struggle in the Ancient Greek World*, London.

Dierkens, A. (1998), 'Christianisme et "paganisme" dans la Gaule septentrionale aux Ve et VIe siècle', in Geuenich (ed.): 451–74.

Drinkwater, J. F. (1978), 'The rise and fall of the Gallic Iulii: aspects of the development of the aristocracy of the Three Gauls under the Early Empire', *Latomus* 37: 817–50.

—— (1983a), *Roman Gaul. The Three Provinces. 58 BC–AD 260*, London.

—— (1983b), 'The "Pagan Underground", Constantius II's "Secret Service" and the usurpation and survival of Julian the Apostate', in C. Deroux (ed.), *Studies in Latin Literature and Roman History III* (Collection Latomus 180), Brussels: 348–87.

—— (1984), 'Peasants and Bagaudae in Roman Gaul', *Classical Views* 28, n.s. 3: 349–71.

—— (1987), *The Gallic Empire. Separatism and Continuity in the North-Western Provinces of the Roman Empire AD 260–274* (Historia Einzelschriften 52), Stuttgart.

—— (1989), 'Patronage in Roman Gaul and the problem of the Bagaudae', in A. Wallace-Hadrill (ed.), *Patronage in Ancient Society*, London: 189–203.

—— (1992), 'The Bacaudae of fifth-century Gaul', in Drinkwater and Elton (ed.): 208–17.

—— (1994), 'Silvanus, Ursicinus and Ammianus: fact or fiction?', in C. Deroux (ed.), *Studies in Latin Literature and Roman History VII* (Collection Latomus 227), Brussels: 568–76.

—— (1996), 'The "Germanic threat on the Rhine frontier": a Romano-Gallic artefact?', in Mathisen and Sivan (ed.): 20–30.

—— (1997), 'Julian and the Franks and Valentinian I and the Alamanni: Ammianus on Romano-German relations', *Francia* 24: 1–15.

—— (1998a), 'The usurpers Constantine III (407–411) and Jovinus (411–413)', *Britannia* 29: 269–98.

—— (1998b), 'England not *Anglia*, *Francia* not Frankreich', *Nottingham Medieval Studies* 42: 231–6.

—— (1998c), review of Paschoud and Szidat (ed.) 1997, in *Francia* 25: 304–6.

—— (1999a), 'Ammianus, Valentinian and the Rhine Germans', in J. W. Drijvers and D. Hunt (ed.), *The Late Roman World and its Historian: Interpreting Ammianus Marcellinus*, London: 127–37.

—— (1999b), 'Re-dating Ausonius' war-poetry', *American Journal of Philology* 120: 443–52.

—— (2000), 'The revolt and ethnic origin of the usurper Magnentius (350–353), and the rebellion of Vetranio (350)', *Chiron* 30: 131–59.

—— (2001), review of Siegmund (2000), in *Göttinger Forum für Altertumswissenschaft* 4: 1045–50.

—— (2004), review of Burns 2003, in *American Journal of Philology* 125: 618–22.

—— (2005), 'Maximinus to Diocletian and the "crisis"', in *Cambridge Ancient History XII* (2nd edn), A. Bowman, Averil Cameron and P. Garnsey (ed.), Cambridge: 28–66.

Drinkwater, J. F. (forthcoming), 'Crocus, king of the Alamanni', in G. Halsall (ed.) (Proceedings of the York conference, 17–20 July 2006).

Drinkwater, J. F., and Elton, H. (ed.) (1992), *Fifth-Century Gaul. A Crisis of Identity?*, Cambridge.

Dufraigne, P. (1975), *Aurelius Victor. Livre des Césars*, Paris.

Elbe, J. von (1977), *Roman Germany. A Guide to Sites and Museums*, Mainz.

Elliott, T. G. (1983), *Ammianus Marcellinus and Fourth Century History*, Sarasota FL.

Ellis, L. (1998), ' "Terra deserta": population, politics and the [de]colonization of Dacia', *Population and Demography* 30: 220–37.

Ellmers, D. (1997), 'Zeugnisse für römische Küsten- und Binnenschiffahrt ins freie Germanien', in Bridger and Carnap-Bornheim (ed.): 1–6.

Elton, H. (1992), 'Defence in fifth-century Gaul', in Drinkwater and Elton (ed.): 167–76.

—— (1993), 'Borders, bandits and barbarians: comparative responses of the Romans in fourth-century Gaul and the British in nineteenth-century India', unpublished paper delivered at the 12th Oklahoma Conference for Comparative Frontier Studies, March.

—— (1996a), *Warfare in Roman Europe AD 350–425*, Oxford.

—— (1996b), *Frontiers of the Roman Empire*, London.

Erdrich, M. (2000a), 'Germanen. Fremde und Freunde. Römische Germanienpolitik im 1. Jahrhundert', in Wamser (ed.): 193–6.

—— (2000b), 'Römische Germanienpolitik in der mittleren Kaiserzeit', in Wamser (ed.): 227–30.

—— (2001), *Rom und die Barbaren. Das Verhältnis zwischen dem Imperium Romanum und den germanischen Stämmen vor seiner Nordwestgrenze von der späten römischen Republik bis zum Gallischen Sonderreich* (Römisch-Germanische Forschungen Bd 58), Mainz.

Evelyn-White, H. G. (1919), *Ausonius I* (Loeb), London/Cambridge MA.

Favrod, J. (1997), *Histoire politique du royaume burgonde (443–534)* (Bibliothèque historique vaudoise no. 113), Lausanne.

Fehr, H. (2002), '*Volkstum* as paradigm: Germanic peoples and Gallo-Romans in early medieval archaeology since the 1930s', in Gillett (ed.): 177–200.

Festy, M. (1999), *Pseudo-Aurélius Victor. Abrégé des Césars*, Paris.

Fewster, D. (2002), 'Visions of national greatness: medieval images, ethnicity, and nationalism in Finland, 1905–1945', in Gillett (ed.): 123–46.

Fingerlin, G. (1990), 'Frühe Alamannen im Breisgau. Zur Geschichte und Archäologie des 3.–5. Jahrhunderts zwischen Basler Rheinknie und Kaiserstuhl', in Nuber et al., 1990: 97–137.

—— (1993), 'Die alamannische Landnahme im Breisgau', in Müller-Wille and Schneider (ed.): 1.59–82.

—— (1997a), 'Grenzland in der Völkerwanderungszeit. Frühe Alamannen im Breisgau', in *Alamannen*: 103–10.

—— (1997b), 'Siedlungen und Siedlungstypen. Südwestdeutschland in frühalamannischer Zeit', in *Alamannen*: 125–34.

Frank, K. (1997), 'Vorboten an Main und Tauber. Germanen in Taubergebiet vor und nach der Aufgabe des Limes', in *Alamannen*: 69–72.

Franken (1997), *Die Franken. Wegbereiter Europas* (2 vols), Mannheim.

Freeman, E. A. (1904), *Western Europe in the Fifth Century*, London.

Frézouls, E. (1962), 'La mission du "magister equitum" Ursicin en Gaule (355–57)', in M. Renard (ed.), *Hommages à Albert Grenier* (Collection Latomus 58), Brussels: 673–88.

Gallien (1980), *Gallien in der Spätantike*, Mainz.

Garbsch, J. (1970), *Das spätrömische Donau–Iller–Rhein Limes*, Aalen.

Garzetti, A. (1974), *From Tiberius to the Antonines. A History of the Roman Empire* AD *14–192*, J. R. Foster (trans.), London.

Geary, P. J. (1988), *Before France and Germany. The Creation and Transformation of the Merovingian World*, Oxford/New York NY.

—— (1999), 'Barbarians and ethnicity', in Bowersock et al. (ed.): 107–29.

Gechter, M. (1997), 'Zur Wechselwirkung zwischen römischer und germanischer Bewaffnung und Kampferweise an Rhein und Donau während der Prinzipatszeit', in Bridger and Carnap-Bornheim (ed.): 13–17.

—— (2003), 'Die Militärgeschichte am Niederrhein von Caesar bis Tiberius-eine Skizze', in Grünewald and Seibel (ed.): 145–61.

Germanen (1986), *Die Germanen. Ein Handbuch, Bd 2*, Berlin.

Geuenich, D. (1997a), *Geschichte der Alemannen*, Stuttgart.

—— (1997b), 'Ein junges Volk macht Geschichte. Herkunft und "Landnahme" der Alamannen', in *Alamannen*: 73–8.

—— (1997c), 'Widersacher der Franken. Expansion und Konfrontation', in *Alamannen*: 144–8.

—— (1997d), 'Zwischen Loyalität und Rebellion. Die Alamannen unter frankischer Herrschaft', in *Alamannen*: 204–8.

—— (1998), 'Chlodwigs Alemannenschlacht(en) und Taufe', in Geuenich (ed.): 423–37.

—— (2000), 'Juthungen. Historisches', *Reallexikon der Germanischen Altertumskunde* (2nd edn) Berlin/New York NY: 16.14–44.

Geuenich, D. (ed.) (1998), *Die Franken und die Alamannen bis zur 'Schlacht bei Zülpich' (496/97)*, Berlin/New York NY.

Gibbon, E. (1901), *History of the Decline and Fall of the Roman Empire*, vol. 3, J. B. Bury (ed.), London.

Giesler, U. (1997), 'Völker am Hochrhein. Das Basler Land im frühen Mittelalter', in *Alamannen*: 209–18.

Gillett, A. (ed.) (2002a), *On Barbarian Identity. Critical Approaches to Ethnicity in the Early Middle Ages*, Turnhout.

—— (2002b), 'Was ethnicity political in the earliest medieval kingdoms?', in Gillett (ed.): 85–121.

Goetz, H.-W., Jarnut, J., and Pohl, W. (ed.) (2003), *Regna and Gentes. The Relationship between Late Antique and Early Medieval Peoples and Kingdoms in the Transformation of the Roman World* (The Transformation of the Roman World, vol. 13), Leiden.

Goetz, H.-W., and Welwei, K.-W. (ed.) (1995), *Altes Germanien. Auszüge aus den antiken Quellen über die Germanen und ihre Beziehungen zum römischen Reich. Quellen der Alten Geschichte bis zum Jahre 238 n. Chr.*, Parts 1 and 2, Darmstadt.

Goffart, W. (1980), *Barbarians and Romans, AD 418–514*, Princeton NJ.

—— (1989), *Rome's Fall and After*, London.

—— (2002), 'Does the distant past impinge on the invasion age Germans?', in Gillett (ed.): 21–37.

Graves-Brown, P., Jones, S., and Gamble, C. (ed.) (1996), *Cultural Identity and Archaeology. The Construction of European Communities*, London/New York NY.

Green, R. P. H. (1978), 'The *éminence grise* of Ausonius' *Moselle*', *Respublica Litterarum* 1: 89–94.

—— (1991), *The Works of Ausonius*, Oxford.

Groenman-van Waateringe, W. (1979), 'Urbanisation and the north-west frontier of the Roman Empire', in W. S. Hanson and L. J. F. Keppie (ed.), *Roman Frontier Studies* (BAR International Series 71): 1037–44.

Grünewald, T. (1989), 'Ein epigraphisches Zeugnis zur Germanenpolitik Konstantins des Grossen', in H. E. Herzig and R. Frei-Stolba (ed.), *Labor omnibus unus. Gerold Walser zum 70. Geburtstag* (Historia Einzelschriften 60), Stuttgart: 171–85.

Grünewald, T. (2004), *Bandits in the Roman Empire. Myth and Reality*, J. F. Drinkwater (trans.), London/New York NY.

Grünewald, T., and Seibel, S. (ed.) (2003), *Kontinuität und Diskontinuität. Germania Inferior am Beginn und am Ende der römischen Herrschaft* (Ergänzungsbände zum Reallexikon der Germanischen Altertumskunde 35), Berlin/New York NY.

Gutmann, B. (1991), *Studien zur römischen Außenpolitik in der Spätantike (364–395 n. Chr.)*, Bonn.

Guzmán Armario, F. J. (2002), *Los bárbaros en Amiano Marcelino*, Madrid.

Haberstroh, J. (2000a), *Germanische Funde der Kaiser- und Völkerwanderungszeit aus Oberfranken* (Materialhefte zur Bayerischen Vorgeschichte. Reihe A., Bd 82), Kallmünz.

—— (2000b), 'Verzierungen auf handgeformter Keramik des 3.–6. Jahrhunderts im Main-Regnitz-Gebiet', in S. Biegert, S. von Schnurbein, B. Steidl and D. Walter (ed.), *Beiträge zur germanischen Keramik zwischen Donau und Teutoburger Wald* (Kolloquien zur Vor- und Frühgeschichte Bd 4), Bonn: 227–64.

Haffner, A., and Schnurbein, S. von (ed.) (2000), *Kelten, Germanen, Römer im Mittelgebirgsraum zwischen Luxemburg und Thüringen*, Bonn.

Halsall, G. (1992), 'The origins of the *Reihengräberzivilisation*: forty years on', in Drinkwater and Elton (ed.): 196–207.

—— (2000), 'Archaeology and the late Roman frontier in Northern Gaul: the so-called "Föderatengräber" reconsidered', in W. Pohl and H. Reimitz (ed.), *Grenze und Differenz im frühen Mittelalter* (Österreichische Akademie der Wissenschaften, Philosophisch–Historische Klasse Denkschriften, Bd 287), Vienna: 167–80.

Heather, P. J. (1991), *Goths and Romans 332–489*, Oxford.

—— (1998), 'Disappearing and reappearing tribes', in W. Pohl and H. Reimitz (ed.), *Strategies of Distinction. The Construction of Ethnic Communities, 300–800*, Leiden: 95–111.

—— (2001), 'The late Roman art of client management: imperial defence in the fourth century west', in W. Pohl, I. Wood, and H. Reimitz (eds.), *The Transformation of Frontiers from Late Antiquity to the Carolingians*, Leiden/Boston MA/Cologne: 15–68.

—— (2005), *The Fall of the Roman Empire. A New History*, London.

Hedeager, L. (1993), 'The creation of Germanic identity. A European origin-myth', in P. Brun, S. van der Leeuw, and C. R. Whittaker (ed.), *Frontières d'empire. Nature et signification des frontières romaines* (Mémoires du Musée de Préhistoire d'Ile-de-France 5), Paris: 121–31.

Heiligmann, J. (1997), 'Mit anderen Augen gesehen. Rom und seine germanischen Nachbarn', in *Alamannen*: 54–8.

Heinen, H. (1985), *Trier und das Trevererland in römischer Zeit* (2000 Jahre Trier, Bd 1), Trier.

—— (1995), 'Die "Bissula" des Ausonius', in M. Weinmann-Walser (ed.), *Historische Interpretationen: Gerold Walser zum 75. Geburtstag* (Historia Einzelschriften 100), Stuttgart: 81–96.

Heinrichs, J. (2003), 'Ubier, Chatten, Bataver. Mittel und Niederrhein ca. 70–71 v. Chr. anhand germanischer Münzen', in Grünewald and Seibel (ed.): 266–344.

Heinzelmann, M. (1982), 'Gallische Prosopographie 260–527', *Francia* 10: 531–718.

—— (1997), 'Gregor von Tours: Die ideologische Grundlegung fränkischer Königsherrschaft', in *Franken*: 1.381–8.

Henck, N. (1998), 'Images of Constantius II: *ho philanthrōpos basileus* and imperial propaganda in the mid-fourth century AD', D.Phil. thesis (Oxford).

Henige, D. (1998), 'He came, he saw, we counted: the historiography and demography of Caesar's Gallic numbers', *Annales de démographie historique*: 215–42.

Henning, J. (1985), 'Zur Datierung von Werkzeug-und Agrargerätfunden im germanischen Landnahmegebiet zwischen Rhein und oberer Donau— Der Hortfund von Osterburken', *Jahrbuch des Römisch-Germanischen Zentralmuseums* 32: 570–94.

Hind, J. G. F. (1984), 'Whatever happened to the *Agri Decumates*?', *Britannia* 15: 187–92.

Höckmann, O. (1986), 'Römische Schiffsverbände auf dem Ober- und Mittelrhein und die Verteidigung der Rheingrenze in der Spätantike', *Jahrbuch des Römisch-Germanischen Zentralmuseums* 33: 369–416.

Hoeper, M. (1998), 'Die Höhensiedlungen der Alemannen und ihre Deutungsmöglichkeiten zwischen Fürstensitz, Heerlager, Rückzugsraum und Kultplatz', in Geuenich (ed.) 1998: 325–48.

Hoffmann, D. (1969), *Das spätrömische Bewegungsheer und die Notitia Dignitatum* (Epigraphische Studien Bd 7, 2 vols), Düsseldorf.

—— (1978), 'Wadomar, Bacurius und Hariulf. Zur Laufbahn adliger und fürstlicher Barbaren im spätrömischen Heere des 4. Jahrhundert', *Museum Helveticum* 35: 307–18.

Homo, L. (1904), *Essai sur le règne de l'empereur Aurélien (270–275)*, Paris.

Hummer, H. J. (1998), 'Franks and Alamanni. A discontinuous ethnogenesis', in Wood (ed.): 9–32.

Isaac, B. (1992), *The Limits of Empire. The Roman Army in the East* (rev. edn), Oxford.

James, E. (1988), *The Franks*, Oxford.

Jehne, M. (1996), 'Überlegungen zur Chronologie der Jahre 259 bis 261 n. Chr. im Lichte der neuen Postumus-Inschrift aus Ausburg', *Bayerische Vorgeschichtsblätter* 61: 185–206.

Johnson, S. (1983), *Late Roman Fortifications*, London.

Jones, A. H. M. (1964), *The Later Roman Empire 284–602* (3 vols), Oxford.

—— (1966), *The Decline of the Ancient World*, London.

Jones, B. W. (1992), *The Emperor Domitian*, London.

Jonge, P. de (1939), *Sprachlicher und historischer Kommentar zu Ammianus Marcellinus XIV, 2. Hälfte (c.7–11)*, Groningen.

—— (1977), *Philological and Historical Commentary on Ammianus Marcellinus XVII*, Groningen.

—— (1980), *Philological and Historical Commentary on Ammianus Marcellinus XVIII*, Groningen.

Jullian, C. (1926), *Histoire de la Gaule* (vol. 7), Paris.

Kaiser, M. (1998), 'Ein spätrömisches Militärlager in Neuss-Norf und Überlegungen zur Verteidigung der Rheingrenze im 5. Jahrhundert', in Bridger and Gilles (ed.): 35–40.

Kazanski, M. (1993), 'Les barbares orientaux et la défense de la Gaule aux IVe–Ve siècles', in Vallet and Kazanski (ed.): 175–86.

Keller, H. (1993), 'Probleme der frühen Geschichte der Alamannen ("alamannische Landnnahme") aus historischer Sicht', in Müller-Wille and Schneider (ed.): 1.83–102.

—— (1998), 'Strukturveränderungen in der westgermanischen Welt am Vorabend der fränkischen Großreichsbildung. Fragen, Suchbilder, Hypothesen', in Geuenich (ed.): 581–607.

Kienast, D. (1996), *Römische Kaisertabelle. Grundzüge einer römischen Kaiserchronologie* (2nd edn), Darmstadt.

Kleeman, J. (1997), 'Bemerkungen zur Waffenbeigabe in Föderatengräbern Niedersachsens', in Bridger and Carnap-Bornheim (ed.): 43–8.

Koch, R. and U. (1997), 'Die fränkische Expansion ins Main- und Neckargebiet', in *Franken*: 1.270–84.

Koch, U. (1997a), 'Besiegt, beraubt, vertrieben', in *Alamannen*: 191–201.

—— (1997b), 'Ethnische Vielfalt im Südwesten', in *Alamannen*: 219–32.

Kokabi, M. (1997), 'Fleisch für Lebende und Tote', in *Alamannen*: 331–6.

Kolb, F. (1987), *Diocletian und die Erste Tetrarchie. Improvisation oder Experiment in der Organisation monarchischer Herrschaft?*, Darmstadt.

—— (1997), 'Die Gestalt des spätantiken Kaisertums unter besonderer Berücksichtigung der Tetrarchie', in Paschoud and Szidat (ed.): 35–45.

König, I. (1997), 'Die Postumus-Inschrift aus Augsburg', *Historia* 46: 341–54.

Kovalevskaja, V. B. (1993), 'La présence alano-sarmate en Gaule: confrontation des données archéologiques, paléoanthropologiques, historiques et toponymiques', in Vallet and Kazanski (ed.): 209–22.

Kreuz, A. (1999), 'Becoming a Roman farmer: preliminary report on the environmental evidence from the Romanization project', in Creighton and Wilson (ed.): 71–98.

—— (2000), ' "*tristem cultu aspectuque?*" Archäobotanische Ergebnisse zur frühen germanischen Landwirtschaft in Hessen und Mainfranken', in Haffner and Schnurbein (ed.): 221–41.

Kuhoff, W. (1984), 'Zeittafel von 213 bis etwa 530', in *Quellen*: 6.101–13.

Kulikowski, M. (2000a), 'Barbarians in Gaul, usurpers in Britain', *Britannia* 31: 325–45.

—— (2000b), 'The *Notitia Dignitatum* as a historical source', *Historia* 49: 358–77.

—— (2002), 'Nation versus army: a necessary contrast?', in Gillett (ed.): 69–84.

Kuntić-Makvić, B. (1996), '*Illyricianus*: l'histoire de mot et l'histoire de l'Illyrique', in Bratož (ed.): 185–92.

Küster, H. (1998), 'Die Landschaft der Spätantike in Mitteleuropa aus vegetationsgeschichtlicher Sicht', in Bridger and Gilles (ed.): 77–82.

Lander, J. (1984), *Roman Stone Fortifications. Variation and Change from the First Century* AD *to the Fourth* (British Archaeological Reports, International Series 206), Oxford.

Lendon, J. E. (1997), *Empire of Honour. The Art of Government in the Roman World*, Oxford.

Lenski, N. (2002), *Failure of Empire. Valens and the Roman State in the Fourth Century* AD, Berkeley CA.

Lewis, C. M. (2000), 'Gallic identity and the Gallic *civitas* from Caesar to Gregory of Tours', in S. Mitchell and G. Greatrex (ed.), *Ethnicity and Culture in Late Antiquity*, London/Cardiff: 69–81.

Lindenthal, J., and Rupp, V. (2000), 'Forschungen in germanischen und römischen Siedlungen der nörlichen Wetterau', in Haffner and Schnurbein (ed.): 67–75.

Lippold, A. (1981), 'Constantius Caesar, Sieger über die Germanen, Nachfahre des Claudius Gothicus?', *Chiron* 11: 347–69.

Lorenz, S. (1997), *Imperii fines erunt intacti. Rom und die Alamannen 350–378* (Europäische Hochschulschriften, series 3, vol. 722), Frankfurt/ Berlin.

Lorenz, Sönke (1997), 'Missionierung, Krisen und Reformen. Die Christianisierung von der Spätantike bis in karolingische Zeit', in *Alamannen*: 441–6.

Lotter, F. (with Bratož, J., and Castritius, H.) (2003), *Völkerschiebungen im Ostalpen-Mitteldonau-Raum zwischen Antike und Mittelalter (375–600)* (Ergänzungsbände zum Reallexikon der Germanischen Altertumskunde 39), Berlin/New York NY.

Lütkenhaus, W. (1998), *Constantius III. Studien zu seiner Tätigkeit und Stellung im Westreich 411–421*, Bonn.

Luttwak, E. N. (1976), *The Grand Strategy of the Roman Empire. From the First Century* AD *to the Third*, Baltimore MD/London.

MacGeorge, P. (2002), *Late Roman Warlords*, Oxford.

Mackensen, M. (1999), 'Late Roman fortifications and building programmes in the province of *Raetia*: the evidence of recent excavations and some new reflections', in Creighton and Wilson (ed.): 199–244.

MacMullen, R. (1963), *Soldier and Civilian in the Later Roman Empire*, Cambridge MA.

Maenchen-Helfen, O. J. (1973), *The World of the Huns. Studies in their History and Culture*, Berkeley CA/Los Angeles CA/London.

Martin, M. (1993), 'Zusammenfassende Betrachtungen für das westliche Imperium Romanum', in Vallet and Kazanski (ed.): 459–64.

—— (1997a), 'Zwischen den Fronten. Alamannen im römischen Heer', in *Alamannen*: 119–24.

—— (1997b), 'Historische Schlagzeilen, archäologische Trümmer. Wandlungen der alamannischen Siedlungs- und Herrschaftsgeschichte zwischen 436 und 506 nach Christus', in *Alamannen*: 163–70.

—— (1998), 'Alemannen im römischen Heer-eine verpaßte Integration und ihre Folgen', in Geuenich (ed.): 407–22.

Martin-Kilcher, S. (1993), 'A propos de la tombe d'un officier de Cologne (Severinstor) et de quelques tombes à armes vers 300', in Vallet and Kazanski (ed.): 299–304.

Mathisen, R. W., and Sivan, H. S. (ed.) (1996), *Shifting Frontiers in Late Antiquity*, Aldershot.

Matthews, J. F. (1975), *Western Aristocracies and Imperial Court* AD *364–425*, Oxford.

—— (1989), *The Roman Empire of Ammianus*, London.

Mause, M. (1994), *Die Darstellung des Kaisers in der lateinischen Panegyrik* (Palingensia 50), Stuttgart.

Miller, D. H. (1996), 'Frontier societies and the transition between late Antiquity and the early Middle Ages', in Mathisen and Sivan (ed.): 158–71.

Moreau, J. (1983), *Supplément au dictionnaire de géographie historique de la Gaule et de la France*, Paris.

Müller, C. (1928), *Fragmenta Historicorum Graecorum*, Paris.

Müller, W. (ed.) (1975), *Zur Geschichte der Alemannen* (Wege zur Forschung, Bd 100), Darmstadt.

Müller-Wille, M. (1993), 'Zwischenstand', in Müller-Wille and Schneider (ed.): 339–54.

—— (1997), 'Königtum und Adel im Spiegel der Grabfunde', in *Franken* 1.206–21.

—— (1999), *Opferkulte der Germanen und Slawen*, Darmstadt.

Müller-Wille, M., and Schneider, R. (ed.) (1993), *Ausgewählte Probleme europäischer Landnnahmen des Früh- und Hochmittelalters* (Vorträge und Forschungen 41), Sigmaringen.

Murray, A. C. (2002), 'Reinhard Wenskus on "Ethnogenesis", ethnicity, and the origin of the Franks', in Gillett (ed.): 39–68.

Nagl, A. (1948), 'Valentinianus I', *RE* VIIA.2, 2158–2204.

Neumann, G. (1981), 'Bucinobantes', in *Reallexikon der Germanischen Altertumskunde* (2nd edn) Berlin/New York: 4.89.

—— (2000), 'Juthungen. Der Name', in *Reallexikon der Germanischen Altertumskunde* (2nd edn) Berlin/New York: 16.141–2.

Nicolay, J. (2003), 'The use and significance of military equipment and horse gear from non-military contexts in the Batavian area: continuity from the Late Iron Age into the Early Roman period', in Grünewald and Seibel (ed.): 345–73.

Nixon, C. E. V., and Rodgers, B. S. (1994), *In Praise of Later Roman Emperors. The Panegyrici Latini*, Berkeley CA/Los Angeles CA/Oxford.

Nuber, H. U. (1990), 'Das Ende des Obergermanisch–Raetischen Limes-eine Forschungsaufgabe', in Nuber et al: 51–68.

—— (1993), 'Der Verlust der obergermanischen–raetischen Limesgebiete und die Grenzsicherung bis zum Ende des 3. Jahrhunderts', in Vallet and Kazanski (ed.): 101–8.

—— (1997), 'Zeitwende rechts des Rheins. Rom und die Alamannen', in *Alamannen*: 59–68.

—— (1998), 'Zur Entstehung des Stammes der *Alamanni* aus römischer Sicht', in Geuenich (ed.): 367–83.

Nuber, H. U., Schmid, K., Steuer, H., and Zotz, T. (ed.) (1990), *Archäologie und Geschichte des ersten Jahrtausends in Südwestdeutschland* (Archäologie und Geschichte. Freiburger Forschungen zum ersten Jahrtausend in Südwestdeutschland, Bd 1), Stuttgart.

Okamura, L. (1984), *Alamannia Devicta: Roman–German Conflicts from Caracalla to the First Tetrarchy (AD 213–305)*, Ann Arbor MI.

—— (1996), 'Roman withdrawals from three transfluvial frontiers', in Mathisen and Sivan (ed.): 11–19.

382 References

Oldenstein, J. (1993), 'La fortification d'Alzey et la défense de la frontière romaine le long du Rhin au IVe et au Ve siècle', in Vallet and Kazanski (ed.): 125–33.

Pabst, A. (ed., trans. and comment.) (1989), *Quintus Aurelius Symmachus. Reden*, Darmstadt.

Paschoud, F. (1971), *Zosime. Histoire nouvelle, tome I. Livres I–II*, Paris.

—— (1979), *Zosime. Histoire nouvelle, tomes II^{1–2}. Livres III–IV*, Paris.

—— (1986), *Zosime. Histoire nouvelle, tome III^1. Livre V*, Paris.

—— (1989), *Zosime. Histoire nouvelle, tome III^2. Livre VI et index*, Paris.

—— (1992), 'Valentinien travesti, ou: la malignité d'Ammien', in J. den Baeft, D. den Hengst, and H. C. Teitler (ed.), *Cognitio Gestarum. The Historiographic Art of Ammianus Marcellinus*, Amsterdam: 67–84.

Paschoud, F., and Szidat, J. (ed.) (1997), *Usurpationen in der Spätantike* (Historia Einzelschriften 111), Stuttgart.

Périn, P. (1998), 'La progression des Francs en Gaule du Nord au Ve siècle', in Geuenich (ed.): 59–81.

Périn, P., and Kazanski, M. (1997), 'Das Grab Childerics I.', in *Franken*: 1.173–82.

Petit, P., and Mangin, M. (ed.) (1994), *Atlas des agglomérations secondaires de la Gaule Belgique et des Germanies*, Paris.

Petrikovits, H. von (1971), 'Fortifications in the north-western Roman Empire from the third to the fifth centuries AD', *Journal of Roman Studies* 61: 178–218.

—— (1980), *Die Rheinlande in römischer Zeit*, Cologne.

Pharr, C. (1952), *The Theodosian Code and Novels*, Princeton NJ.

Piganiol, A. (1972), *L'empire chrétien* (2nd edn), Paris.

Pilet, C., Buchet, L., and Pilet-Lerrière, J. (1993), 'L'apport de l'archéologie funéraire à l'étude de la présence militaire sur le *limes* saxon, le long des côtes de l'actuelle Basse-Normandie', in Vallet and Kazanski (ed.): 157–74.

Pirling, R. (1993), 'Römische Gräber mit barbarischem Einschlag auf den Gräberfeldern von Krefeld-Gellep', in Vallet and Kazanski (ed.): 109–23.

Planck, D. (1990), 'Die Wiederbesiedlung der Schwäbischen Alb und des Neckarlands durch die Alamannen', in Nuber et al. (ed.): 69–96.

Pohl, W. (1998a), 'Alemannen und Franken. Schlußbetrachtungen aus historischer Sicht', in Geuenich (ed.): 636–51.

—— (1998b), 'Introduction: strategies of distinction', in W. Pohl and H. Reimitz (ed.), *Strategies of Distinction. The Construction of Ethnic Communities, 300–800*, Leiden: 1–15.

—— (2000), *Die Germanen* (Enzyklopädie Deutscher Geschichte, Bd 57), Munich.

—— (2002a), *Die Völkerwanderung. Eroberung und Integration*, Stuttgart.

—— (2002b), 'Ethnicity, theory and tradition: a response', in Gillett (ed.): 221–39.

Quast, D. (1997), 'Vom Einzelgrab zum Friedhof. Beginn der Reihengräbersitte im 5. Jahrhundert', in *Alamannen*: 171–90.

Quellen, Quellen zur Geschichte der Alamannen, C. Dirlmeier, G. Gottlieb, U. Koch, W. Kuhoff, K. Sprigade (ed. and trans.), vols 1–7 (1976–87), Simaringen.

Raimondi, M. (2001), *Valentiniano I e la scelta dell'Occidente*, Alessandria.

Rees, R. (2002), *Layers of Loyalty in Latin Panegyric. AD 289–307*, Oxford.

Reichmann, C. (2003), 'Das Kastell von Gelduba (Krefeld-Gellep) im 4. und 5. Jahrhundert', in Grünewald and Seibel (ed.): 37–52.

Reuter, M. (1997), 'Aspekte zur frühen germanischen Landnahme im ehemaligen Limesgebiet: Münzen des Gallischen Teilreiches in germanischem Fundkontext am Beispiel der villa rustica von Wurmlingen', in Bridger and Carnap-Bornheim (ed.): 73–8.

Riese, A. (1892), *Das rheinische Germanien in der antiken Litteratur*, Leipzig.

Roeren, R. (1960), 'Zur Archäologie und Geschichte Südwestdeutschlands im 3. bis 5. Jahrhundert n. Chr.', *Jahrbuch des Römisch-Germanischen Zentralmuseums* 7: 214–94.

Rolfe, J. C. (1963), *Ammianus Marcellinus I* (Loeb, revised edn), London/Cambridge MA.

Rösch, M. (1997), 'Ackerbau und Ernährung. Pfanzenreste aus alamannischen Siedlungen', in *Alamannen*: 323–30.

Rollinger, R. (1998), 'Zum Alamannenfeldzug Constantius' II. an Bodensee und Rhein im Jahre 355 n. Chr. und Julians erstem Auftenthalt in Italien. Überlegungen zu Ammianus Marcellinus 15, 4', *Klio* 80: 163–94.

—— (2001), 'Ammianus Marcellinus' Exkurs zu Alpenrhein und Bodensee. Eine Studie zu Amm. 15,4.2–6', *Chiron* 31: 129–52.

Rosen, K. (1970), *Studien zur Darstellungskunst und Glaubwürdigkeit des Ammianus Marcellinus*, Bonn.

Roth, H. (1998), 'Bemerkungen und Notizen zur "Ethnogenese" von "Franken" und "Alemannen"', in Geuenich (ed.): 628–35.

Rübekeil, L. (1992), *Suebica. Völkernamen und Ethnos* (Innsbrucker Beiträge zur Sprachwissenschaft, Bd 68), Innsbruck.

Runde, I. (1998), 'Die Franken und Alemannen vor 500. Ein chronologischer Überblick', in Geuenich (ed.): 656–90.

Sabbah, G. (1978), *La méthode d'Ammien Marcellin*, Paris.

—— (1999), *Ammien Marcellin. Histoires, tome vi, livres xxxix–xxxi*, Paris.

Salzman, M. R. (1990), *On Roman Time. The Codex Calendar of 354 and the Rhythms of Urban Life in Late Antiquity* (Transformation of the Classical Heritage 17), Berkeley CA/Los Angeles CA.

Saunders, R. T. (1992), 'Aurelian's *two* Iuthungian wars', *Historia* 41: 311–27.

Schach-Dörges, H. (1997), '"Zusammengespülte und vermengte Menschen". Suebische Kriegerbände werden sesshaft', in *Alamannen*: 79–102.

Schallmayer, E. (1995), *Der Augsburger Siegesaltar. Zeugnis einer unruhigen Zeit* (Saalburg-Schriften 2), Bad Homburg.

Scharf, R. (1990), 'Die Kanzleireform des Stilicho und das römische Britannien', *Historia* 39: 461–74.

Schmauder, M. (2002), 'Verzögerte Landnahmen? Die Dacia Traiana und die sogenannten *Decumates Agri*', in W. Pohl and M. Diesenberger (ed.), *Integration und Herrschaft. Ethnische Identitäten und soziale Organisation im Frühmittelalter* (Österreichische Akademie der Wissenschaften, Philosophisch–Historische Klasse, Denkschriften, Bd 301. Forschungen zur Geschichte des Mittelalters, Bd 3), Vienna: 185–215.

—— (2003), 'The relationship between Frankish *gens* and *regnum*: a proposal based on the archaeological evidence', in Goetz et al. (ed.): 271–306.

Schmid, K. (1990), 'Begründung und Zielsetzung des Forschungsvorhabens', in Nuber et al. (ed.): 9–27.

Schmitz, W. (2003), '*Quiescit in pace*. Die Abkehr des Toten von der Welt der Lebenden. Epigraphische Zeugnisse der Spätantike als Quellen der historischen Familienforschung', in Grünewald and Seibel (ed.): 374–413.

Schnurbein, S. von (2000), 'Zum vorrömisch-keltischen, gallorömischen und germanischen Siedlungswesen. Rechtrheinisches Arbeitsgebiet— Zentrale Fragestellung', in Haffner and Schnurbein (ed.): 51–3.

—— (2003), 'Augustus in *Germania* and his new "town" at Waldgirmes east of the Rhine', *Journal of Roman Archaeology* 16: 93–107.

Scholz, M. (1997), 'Namen von Kelten, "Römern" und "Germanen"? Die Bevölkerung von Nida-Heddernheim im Spiegel von Namensgraffiti', in Bridger and Carnap-Bornheim (ed.): 49–57.

Schönberger, H. (1969), 'The Roman frontier in Germany: an archaeological survey', *Journal of Roman Studies* 59: 144–97.

Schoppa, H. (1974), *Aquae Mattiacae. Wiesbadens römische und alamannisch-merovingische Vergangenheit*, Wiesbaden.

Schröter, P. (2000), 'Mensch und Umwelt. Anthropologie der Römerzeit', in Wamser (ed.): 177–81.

Schulze-Dörlamm, M. (1985), 'Germanische Kriegergräber mit Schwertbeigabe in Mitteleuropa aus dem späten 3. Jahrhundert und der ersten Hälfte des 4. Jahrhunderts n. Chr. Zur Entstehung der Waffenbeigabensitte in Gallien', *Jahrbuch des Römisch-Germanischen Zentralmuseums* 32: 509–69.

Schwarz, P.-A. (1998), 'Die spätrömischen Befestigungsanlagen in Augusta Raurica-ein Überblick', in Bridger and Gilles (ed.): 105–11.

Seeck, O. (1919), *Regesten der Kaiser und Päpste für die Jahre 311 bis 476 n. Chr.*, Stuttgart.

—— (1921), *Geschichte des Untergangs der Antiken Welt* (4th edn, 6 vols), Stuttgart.

Shaw, B. D. (1999), 'War and violence', in Bowersock et al.: 130–69.

Siegmund, F. (1998), 'Alemannen und Franken. Archäologische Überlegungen zu ethnischen Strukturen in der zweiten Hälfte des 5. Jahrhunderts', in Geuenich (ed.): 558–80.

—— (2000), *Alemannen und Franken* (Ergänzungsbände zum Reallexikon der Germanischen Altertumskunde, Bd 23), Berlin/New York NY.

Sivan, H. (1990), 'Redating Ausonius' *Mosella*', *American Journal of Philology* 111: 383–94.

—— (1993), *Ausonius of Bordeaux. Genesis of a Gallic Aristocracy*, London/New York NY.

Sogno, C. (forthcoming), 'Barbarians as spectacle: the account of an ancient "embedded reporter" (Symm. *Or.* 2.10–12)'.

Sommer, C. S. (1999), 'From conquered territory to Roman province: recent discoveries and debate on the Roman occupation of SW Germany', in Creighton and Wilson (ed.): 161–98.

Springer, M. (1998), '*Riparii*-Ribuarier-Rheinfranken nebst einigen Bemerkungen zum Geographen von Ravenna', in Geuenich (ed.): 200–69.

Staehelin, F. (1948), *Die Schweiz in römischer Zeit* (3rd edn), Basel.

Steidl, B. (1997), 'Die germanische Siedlung von Gaukönigshofen (Lkr. Würzburg) vor dem Hintergrund der kaiserzeitliche Besiedlung Mainfrankens—erste Ergebnisse der Ausgrabungen 1994–1996', in Bridger and Carnap-Bornheim (ed.): 73–8.

—— (2000), 'Die Siedlungen von Gerolzhofen und Gaukönigshofen und die germanische Besiedlung am mittleren Main vom 1. Jahrhundert v. Chr. Bis zum 4. Jahrhundert n. Chr.', in Haffner and Schnurbein (ed.): 95–113.

—— (2002), 'Lokale Drehscheibenkeramik römischer Formgebung aus dem germanischen Mainfranken. Zeugnis für die Verschleppung römischer Reichsbewohner nach Germanien?', *Bayerische Vorgeschichtsblätter* 67: 87–115.

Steuer, H. (1990), 'Höhensiedlungen des 4. und 5. Jahrhunderts in Südwestdeutschland. Einordnung des Zähringer Burgberges Gemeinde Gundelfingen, Kreis Breisgau-Hochschwarzwald', in Nuber et al.: 139–205.

—— (1997a), 'Herrschaft von der Höhe. Vom mobilen Soldatentrupp zur Residenz auf repräsentativen Bergkuppen', in *Alamannen*: 149–62.

—— (1997b), 'Krieger und Bauern—Bauernkrieger', in *Alamannen*: 275–87.

—— (1998), 'Theorien zur Herkunft und Enstehung der Alemannen. Archäologische Forschungsansätze', in Geuenich (ed.): 270–324.

Stevens, C. E. (1933), *Sidonius Apollinaris and his Age*, Oxford.

Stickler, T. (2002), *Aëtius. Gestaltungsspielräume eines Heermeisters im ausgehenden Weströmischen Reich* (Vestigia 54), Munich.

Stobbe, A. (2000), 'Die Vegetationsentwicklung in der Wetterau und im Lahntal in den Jahrhunderten um Christi Geburt. Ein Vergleich der palynologischen Ergebnisse', in Haffner and Schnurbein (ed.): 201–19.

Stork, I. (1997), 'Friedhof und Dorf, Herrenhof und Adelsgrab. Der einmalige Befund Lauchheim', in *Alamannen*: 290–310.

Stribrny, K. (1989), 'Römer rechts des Rheins nach 260 n. Chr. Kartierung, Strukturanalyse und Synopse spätrömischer Münzreihen zwischen Koblenz und Regensburg', *Bericht der Römisch-Germanischen Kommission* 70: 351–505.

Strobel, K. (1996), *Die Galater*, Berlin.

—— (1998), '*Raetia amissa*? Raetien unter Gallienus: Provinz und Heer im Licht der neuen Augsburger Siegesinschrift', in Bridger and Gilles (ed.): 83–93.

—— (1999), 'Pseudophänomene der römischen Militär- und Provinzgeschichte', in N. Gudea (ed.), *Roman Frontier Studies. Proceedings of the XVIIth International Congress of Roman Frontier Studies*, Zaläu: 9–33.

Stroheker, K. F. (1961), 'Alamannen im römischen Reichsdienst', in *Eranion. Festschrift für Hildebrecht Hommel*, Tübingen: 127–48 (repr. in K. F. Stroheker (1965), *Germanentum und Spätantike*, Zürich/Stuttgart: 30–53).

—— (1975), 'Die Alamannen und das Spätrömische Reich', in Müller (ed.) 1975: 20–48.

Stupperich, R. (1997), 'Export oder Technologietransfer? Beobachtung zu römischen Metallarbeiten in Germanien', in Bridger and Carnap-Bornheim (ed.): 19–24.

Südwestfunk (1997), 'Die Barbaren ziehen im Land umher', Programme 1 of the series *Die Alamannen* (videotape).

Syme, R. (1958), *Tacitus* (2 vols), Oxford.

—— (1999), *The Provincial at Rome*, A. R. Birley (ed.), Exeter.

Szidat, J. (1981), *Historischer Kommentar zu Ammianus Marcellinus Buch XX–XXI. Teil III. Die Konfrontation* (Historia Einzelschriften 38), Stuttgart.

—— (1996), *Historischer Kommentar zu Ammianus Marcellinus Buch XX–XXI. Teil II. Die Verhandlungsphase* (Historia Einzelschrift 89), Wiesbaden.

Talbert, R. J. A. (ed.) (2000), *Barrington Atlas of the Greek and Roman World*, Princeton NJ.

Teichner, F. (2000), 'Eine Siedlung der römischen Kaiserzeit im thüringischen Sülzdorf, Kr. Hildburghausen', in Haffner and Schnurbein (ed.): 77–93.

Thompson, E. A. (1947), *The Historical Work of Ammianus Marcellinus*, Cambridge.

—— (1977), 'Britain, AD 406–410', *Britannia* 8: 303–18.

—— (1982), 'The settlement of barbarians in southern Gaul', in E. A. Thompson, *Romans and Barbarians. The Decline of the Western Empire*, Madison WI: 23–37 (*Journal of Roman Studies* (1956) 46: 65–75).

Todd, M. (1992), *The Early Germans*, Oxford.

Tomlin, R. S. O. (1979), 'Ammianus Marcellinus 26.4.6–6', *Classical Quarterly* 29: 470–8.

—— (1987), 'The army of the Late Empire', in J. S. Wacher (ed.), *The Roman World*, London: 107–33.

Trumm, J. (2002), *Die römerzeitliche Besiedlung am östlichen Hochrhein* (Materialhefte zur Archäologie in Baden-Württemberg, Heft 63), Stuttgart.

Urban, R. (1985), *Der 'Bataveraufstand' und die Erhebung des Iulius Classicus* (Trierer Historischer Forschungen, Bd 8), Trier.

Vallet, F. (1993), 'Une implantation *militaire* aux portes de Dijon au Ve siècle', in Vallet and Kazanski (ed.): 249–58.

Vallet, F., and Kazanski, M. (ed.) (1993), *L'armée romaine et les barbares du IIIe au VIIe siècle*, Paris.

van Driel-Murray, C. (2003), 'Ethnic soldiers: the experience of the Lower Rhine tribes', in Grünewald and Seibel (ed.): 200–17.

van Enckevort, H., and Thijssen, J. (2003), 'Nijmegen und seine Umgebung im Umbruch zwischen Römerzeit und Mittelalter', in Grünewald and Seibel (ed.): 83–118.

van Ossel, P. (1992), *Etablissements ruraux de l'antiquité tardive dans le nord de la Gaule* (Gallia Suppl. 51), Paris.

Waas, M. (1971), *Germanen im römischen Dienst (im 4. Jh. n. Chr.)*, Bonn.

Wahl, J., Wittwer-Backofen, U., and Kunter, M. (1997), 'Zwischen Masse und Klasse', in *Alamannen*: 337–48.

Wamers, E. (1997), 'Alamannisch-fränkische Kontinuität im Untermaingebiet', in *Franken*: 1.266–9.

Wamser, L. (ed.) (2000), *Die Römer zwischen Alpen und Nordmeer*, Mainz.

Watson, A. (1999), *Aurelian and the Third Century*, London.

Weidemann, K. (1972), 'Untersuchungen zur Siedlungsgeschichte des Landes zwischen Limes und Rhein vom Ende der Römerherrschaft bis zum Frühmittelalter', *Jahrbuch des Römisch-Germanischen Zentralmuseums* 19: 99–155.

Wells, C. M. (1972), *The German Policy of Augustus. An Examination of the Archaeological Evidence*, Oxford.

Wenskus, R. (1961), *Stammesbildung und Verfassung. Das Werden frühmittelalterlichen gentes*, Cologne/Graz ((1977) 2nd unrevised edn, Cologne/Vienna).

Werner, J. (1965), 'Zu den alamannischen Burgen des 4. und 5. Jahrhunderts', in *Speculum Historiale. Festschrift für Johannes Spörl*, Freiburg/Munich: 439–53 (reprinted in Müller (ed.) (1975): 67–89).

—— (1973), 'Bemerkungen zur mitteldeutschen Skelettgräbergruppe Hassleben-Leuna: zur Herkunft der *ingentia auxilia Germanorum* des gallischen Sonderreiches in den Jahren 259–274 n. Christus', *Festschrift für Walter Schlesinger* (Mitteldeutsche Forschungen 74/1), Cologne/Vienna: 1–30.

Whittaker, C. R. (1994), *Frontiers of the Roman Empire. A Social and Economic Study*, Baltimore MD.

Wieczorek, A. (1997), 'Die Ausbreitung der fränkischen Herrschaft in den Rheinlanden vor und seit Chlodwig I', in *Franken*: 1.241–60.

Wiedemann, T. E. J. (1979), 'Petitioning a fourth-century emperor: the *De Rebus Bellicis*', *Florilegium* 1: 140–7.

Wigg, A. (1997), 'Germanen und Römer im Gießener Lahntal von augustischer Zeit bis zum 3. Jahrhundert', in Bridger and Carnap-Bornheim (ed.): 59–65.

—— (1999), 'Confrontation and interaction: Celts, Germans and Romans in the Central German Highlands', in Creighton and Wilson (ed.): 35–53.

Wigg, D. G. (1991), *Münzumlauf in Nordgallien um die Mitte des 4. Jahrhunderts n. Chr.* (Studien zu Fundmünzen der Antike 8), Berlin.

—— (2003), 'Die Stimme der Gegenseite? Keltische Münzen und die augusteische Germanienpolitik', in Grünewald and Seibel (ed.): 218–41.

Windler, R. (1997), 'Franken und Alamannen in einem romanischen Land', in *Alamannen*: 261–8.

Witschel, C. (1999), *Krise-Rezession-Stagnation? Der Westen des römischen Reiches im 3. Jahrhundert n. Chr.*, Frankfurt/Main.

Wolfram, H. (1979), *Geschichte der Goten*, Munich (*History of the Goths* (1988), T. J. Dunlap (trans.) Berkeley LA).

—— (1990), *Das Reich und die Germanen. Zwischen Antike und Mittelalter*, Berlin.

—— (1998), 'Typen der Ethnogenese. Ein Versuch', in Geuenich (ed.): 608–27.

Wood, I. N. (1987), 'The fall of the Western Empire and the end of Roman Britain', *Britannia* 18: 251–62.

—— (1990), 'Ethnicity and the ethnogenesis of the Burgundians', in H. Wolfram and W. Pohl (ed.), *Typen der Ethnogenese unter besonderer Berücksichtigung der Bayern*, vol. 1, Vienna: 53–69.

—— (1994), *The Merovingian Kingdoms, 450–751*, London.

—— (1997), 'Die Franken und ihr Erbe-"Translatio Imperii"', in *Franken*: 1.358–64.

—— (2003), '*Gentes*, kings and kingdoms—the emergence of states: the kingdom of the Gibichungs', in Goetz et al. (ed.): 243–69.

Wood, I. N. (ed.) (1998), *Franks and Alamanni in the Merovingian Period. An Ethnographic Perspective* (Studies in Historical Archaeoethnology, vol. 3), San Marino.

Woods, D. (2000), 'Ammianus Marcellinus and the *rex Alamannorum* Vadomarius', *Mnemosyne* 53: 690–710.

Wright, W. C. (1913), *The Works of the Emperor Julian II* (Loeb), London/ Cambridge MA.

Wynn, P. (1997), 'Frigeridus, the British tyrants, and the early fifth century barbarian invasions of Gaul and Spain', *Athenaeum* 85: 69–117.

Zöllner, E. (1970), *Geschichte der Franken*, Munich.

Zotz, T. (1998), 'Die Alemannen in der Mitte des 4. Jahrhunderts nach dem Zeugnis des Ammianus Marcellinus', in Geuenich (ed.): 384–406.

Index

Aare 295

Adrianople, battle of 312, 314, 317, 319

aemulatio 358 and n. 226

Aequitius 284

Aëtius 57, 62, 108, 325, 326, 329

Africa 142, 199, 275, 326, 328

Agathias 58, 63, 64, 117

Agenarichus 155

Agilo 146, 147, 149, 151, 153, 157, 176, 204, 207

Agri Decumates 33, 40, 51, 126

agriculture 80, 81, 82, 83, 90, 91, 93, 104, 134, 137, 139, 169, 227, 236, 243, 338, 343, 344

Agrippa 15

Ahenobarbus 18

Alamanni
  and Aurelian 72, 77
  cavalry 176, 239, 340
  and cities 218
  'exclusion' of, 4th c. 158–9
  expansion, 5th c. 327, 332, 335, 350
  and Iuthungi 61, 62, 77
  later 3c. 79
  laws 121
  name 4, 6, 7, 44, 45, 46, 48, 51, 58, 63–70, 122
  origins 32, 43, 45, 48, 43–79
  service 82, 145–76
  settlement 39, 48, 49, 80–106, 163, 189, 206, 213, 214, 215, 217, 218, 219, 224, 228, 231, 233, 240, 262, 263, 276, 290,
    293, 335, 341, 343, 367; *see also* hill-sites
  society 96, 103, 104, 117–44, 245, 245–6, 261, 314, 341, 344, 345; *see also* kings, nobles, *pagus, plebs, populus, regnum*
  'sub-tribes' 82, 122–3, 124, 125, 170, 172–4
  violence 121

Alamannia 4, 44, 46, 48, 68, 69, 81, 82, 86, 99, 106, 107, 110, 115, 117, 122, 123, 124, 125, 126, 127, 128, 131, 132, 133, 135, 136, 138, 139, 140, 143, 154, 158, 172, 176, 179, 181, 189, 190, 191, 195, 196, 197, 198, 199, 203, 221, 224, 227, 228, 238, 248, 251, 252, 299, 301, 313, 327, 330, 336, 337, 338, 340, 343, 344, 346, 347, 350, 357, 359, 364

Alamannia devicta 196, 198

Alamannicus 69, 198 and n. 137, 199 n. 142, 205, 240

Alambannoi 43

Alans 48, 315, 321, 323, 324, 325, 326

Alaric 29, 321, 322

Albannoi 43

Alemania 1, 125

Allectus 187, 188, 189, 364

Allemagne 1, 125, 179

Alp, Swabian 33, 83, 88, 97, 99, 126, 143, 160, 314, 346; *see also* Suebia